PROPERTY OF
MARGARET BARNETT WILLIAMS

4 Personality of Jesus as a cause of system of Christianity Does not stand

84 Acts give no biographical facts of Jesus,
   Peter's speeches — not true

85 Gospels give no basis for the expression going about and doing good

111 Mark XIV 51-52 Young man with a blanket

125 Ethics of Sermon on the Mount traced to prior sources, Greek etc

148 - Cor. 1. 2 - to end a juggle — (nonsense)

168 The matchless Jesus characters a modern invention —

169 The alleged vivid human portraiture is not really present in the new Testament,

170 Topographical argument great
   Read No reminiscence of Jesus in Galilee where of all places there should be

186 Contradictions inconsistencies — motives etc

ECCE DEUS
STUDIES OF PRIMITIVE
CHRISTIANITY

ECCE DEUS

STUDIES OF PRIMITIVE CHRISTIANITY

BY

WILLIAM BENJAMIN SMITH

O YE WHOE'ER HAVE UNDERSTANDINGS SOBER
PONDER THE DOCTRINE DEEP THAT LIETH HIDDEN
UNDER THE VEIL OF VERSES ENIGMATIC.—*DANTE*

[ISSUED FOR THE RATIONALIST PRESS ASSOCIATION, LIMITED]

UNITY SCHOOL LIBRARY
Unity Village
Lee's Summit, Missouri 64063

THE OPEN COURT PUBLISHING COMPANY,
623-633 S. WABASH AVE., CHICAGO

CONTENTS

	PAGE
PREFACE	ix

PART I.
THE PROTO-CHRISTIAN PROPAGANDA

ORIENTATION	1
THE DILEMMA	4
ARGUMENT FROM PERSONALITY	9
METHOD OF THE FOURTH GOSPEL	25
THE PRIMITIVE MISUNDERSTANDING	31
"ESOTERISM" IN THE GOSPEL	34
CONTENT OF THE GOSPEL	45
THE SECRET OF PRIMITIVE CHRISTIANITY	60
THE ACTIVE PRINCIPLE OF CHRISTIANITY	67

PART II.
TESTIMONY OF THE NEW TESTAMENT

PRELIMINARY	77
WITNESS OF ACTS	84
WITNESS OF REVELATION AND HEBREWS	89
WITNESS OF THE GOSPELS	95
JEW AND GENTILE	101
SYMBOLIC INTERPRETATION NECESSARY	108

CONTENTS

	PAGE
EXAMPLES OF SYMBOLISM	110
THE DIDACTIC ELEMENT	125
THE PAULINE QUADRILATERAL	132
ADDENDA: I. JESUS THE LORD	135
II. DIFFUSED LIGHT OF SYMBOLISM	140
III. THE SO-CALLED PAULINE TESTIMONY	146
IV. THE EKTROMA	157
V. THE GOSPEL PORTRAIT	160

PART III.

THE PILLARS OF SCHMIEDEL

THE BULWARKS OF HISTORICISM	177
EMINUS	182
COMINUS	189
CONCLUSION	205
ADDENDA: I.	208
II. CASTING OUT DEMONS	210
III.	226

PART IV.

THE SILENCE OF JOSEPHUS AND TACITUS

THE SILENCE OF JOSEPHUS	230
THE SILENCE OF TACITUS	238
OTHER PAGANS: FINAL REMARKS	251
ADDENDA: I.	257
II.	260

CONTENTS

PART V.

THE KINGDOM AND THE CALL TO REPENTANCE

Statistics	267
Nature of the Kingdom	270
Preaching of the Kingdom	275
Repentance in the Old Testament	277
Repentance in the New Testament	281
Conclusion	288

PART VI.

"A CITY CALLED NAZARET"

Preliminary	291
New Testament Use of "Called"	292
Conclusion	299

PART VII.

(I)SCARIOT(H) = SURRENDERER

Form and Meaning of the Word	303
Judas = Judæus	309
Addenda: I.	317
II.	321

Postscript	327
Index of Passages	345
Index of Names	350

CORRIGENDA

P. 1, line 3, *for* " deuvicinia " *read* " de vicinia "
P. 4, line 7, *for* " interdependent " *read* " independent "
P. 17, line 22, *for* " *Jusus* " *read* " *Jesus* "
P. 26, line 16, *for* " tuberculosic " *read* " tuberculotic "
P. 49, last line, *for* " *gnechische* " *read* " *griechische* "
P. 60, line 15, *for* " cult of " *read* " cult, of "
P. 63, line 18, *for* "learning, and " *read* " learning and "
P. 64, line 3 from below, *for* " *Soloman* " *read* " *Solomon* "
P. 81, line 20, *for* " *nascitur* " *read* " *nascetur* "
P. 86, line 18, *for* " wind " *read* " wing "
P. 94, line 28, *for* " μαρτίρομαι " *read* " μαρτύρομαι "
P. ,, line 36, *for* " Vanens " *read* " Vannens "
P. 103, line 25, *for* " reasons " *read* " reason "
P. 105, footnote, *for* " ania," " ani " *read* 'ania', 'ani'
P. 107, last line, *for* " 2 × 2 = 4 " *read* " 2 × 2 = 4ii "
P. 111, line 2, footnote, *for* " certain man " *read* " certain young man "
P. ,, line 3, ,, omit " *him* "
P. 117, line 29, *for* " doubly " *read* " double "
P. 127, last line, *for* " mud " *read* " mid "
P. 142, line 15, *for* " ξ " *read* " ζ "
P. 145, line 27, *for* " Maschal " *read* " Mashal "
P. ,, last line, *for* " 115 " *read* " 116 "
P. 150, line 12, *for* " *capable* " *read* " *capables* "
P. 159, line 1, *for* " ideas " *read* " idea "
P. 171, line 2, *for* " there the " *read* " there were the "
P. 172, line 6 from below, *for* " eschatologie " *read* " eschatologic "
P. 191, line 19, *for* " ἐξέστα ταιάντούς " *read* " ἐξέστατai αὐτούς "
P. 225, line 9, *for* " web " *read* " deck "
P. 236, line 20, *for* " human " *read* " divine "
P. 237, line 16, *for* " Hence " *read* " For "
P. 242, line 25, *for* " ot " *read* " to "
P. 252, line 4 from below, *for* " *Arché*," *read* " *Arché* "
P. 304, line 12, *for* " א, and " *read* " א and "
P. 319, line 2 from below, *for* " montaine " *read* " montane."

PREFACE

THE reader of these inquiries into the source and sense of primitive Christianity will not fail to remark that certain matters come up repeatedly for discussion. The lines of thought pursued are numerous and in general mutually quite independent—wherein lies, in fact, in great measure the logical worth of the book, if any such it have—and it is not strange that here and there they should touch or indeed intersect each other. Naturally such points of coincidence are often highly important, and fully deserve the emphasis of repetition. Inasmuch as the path of approach has much significance in argumentation, and as it seemed well to direct the reader's attention again and again to such nodal and cardinal points, no attempt has been made, in the interest of artistic unity, to reduce these different treatments to a single presentation. It would be unwise to secure an esthetic gain by a logical loss.

The author has been at no pains to produce the impression of originality; on the contrary, he has made open acknowledgment when conscious of any important indebtedness to others. But he feels quite sure that the life of the soul is by no means exhausted in consciousness, and that he may owe unwittingly to others, especially to Volkmar, more than might at first appear. The *Marcus* of this intrepid truthseeker came to the author's hand nearly a generation ago, some twenty years before he began to approach his present point of view, when he was sunk in Pauline and apocryphal studies, while the ground assumptions of liberal criticism were still accepted by him as entirely unassailable. It was not strange, then, that Volkmar's discourse about *Lehr-* and *Sinnbilder* passed by without making much impression, without exciting secret doubts or questionings. Nearly a quarter-century afterwards, when the author's present standpoint had long since been fully attained, and in fact along the paths laid out in *Der vorchristliche Jesus*, as he was busied with renewed study of the Gospels, he was surprised to recognise suddenly that his new interpretations were breathing as it were the breath of Volkmar, though he has never consulted *Marcus* to ascertain how close in detail the resemblance may be. While, then, what he consciously owes to the indefatigable Züricher is very small, he takes this opportunity to avow that his unconscious indebtedness may be much larger.

But a greater than Volkmar, the noblest and most illustrious of the Church Fathers, following not servilely in the footsteps of spirits and thinkers perhaps still greater, nearly 1,700 years ago affirmed emphatically and repeatedly the imperative necessity of a thoroughgoing symbolic exposition of the Gospels. Herewith is by no means meant that he rejected their recitals as unhistoric—far from it!—but that a thoroughgoing symbolism cannot be denied, that the sources do not contain pure history, that acceptance of the accounts at face-value is impossible—on all of this it is that Origen insists so earnestly and convincedly. Now, however, if the symbolic sense is the main thing, as this Father so clearly perceived, then the immediate and manifest corollary must deprive the narratives of their seemingly historical content. To depict the progress of the Jesus-cult, to represent in narrative form the revelation to men of the knowledge of God, as a series of highly coloured and dramatically grouped historical incidents—that would be picturesque, beautiful, impressive, yea, vividly instructive and wholly unexceptionable; under certain (actual) conditions such a procedure was to be recommended unconditionally, as alone proper and effective. But to suppose that such events, thus full of spiritual significance, did prosaically happen would be worse than puerile and ludicrous. For reflection can fix itself and dwell on the spiritual content *only when* the historical investiture is recognised as feigned and unreal; so long as this latter is accepted as real and thinkable, so long must it reign o'er sense and thought, especially when it is marvellous, and so long must the deeper sense be neglected. As a pure symbolism the miracle of the loaves and fishes might enforce a profound and beautiful doctrine; as a literal occurrence it could not teach any such truth at all, for it would divert and fasten the attention of all upon the astounding material prodigy. Hence it is clear that Jesus could not have portrayed his teaching in such pictures, that in every single case the recognition of a symbolic aim entails the surrender of the historical content. It is very hard to believe that Origen did not himself admit this obvious consequence, though he did not openly proclaim it.

But while calling attention to this Father's broad recognition of symbolism in the Gospels, we need by no means approve of his allegorical method as applied to the Old Testament, nor adopt his over-refined interpretations of evangelic narratives. Indeed, it seems strange at first that he saw in general so distinctly and in particular so dimly—a puzzling chiaroscuro. But we must remember that he was sundered by at least two centuries from the origin of the Gospel stories, and by a far wider chasm from the spirit that shaped them. His was an Hellenic intelligence, prone to abstractions, set to interpret the product of a mind at least half-Semitic, that busied itself almost exclusively with the concrete. Somewhat wanting in historic sense, he could hardly envisage the conditions of a distant past, and fell an easy victim to the super-subtlety of his age and his race.

But it would be a grievous error to attribute his perception of the symbolic element itself to any such lack of historic feeling. For this element is too patent and prominent to escape even the half-opened eye, and is acknowledged in some measure even in the materialising patristic and in conservative modern theology. Among liberals, Schmiedel and Loisy have perceived and emphasised its frequent presence. In his compendious work, *Les Évangiles Synoptiques*, epitomising and supplanting whole libraries, the latter displays an unmistakable partiality for the adjective "symbolique"; and in countless places we read, "le miracle figure" or "présage," not only in Luke (the great allegorist, according to Loisy), but even in the (reputedly) clumsy, awkward, and simple-minded Mark.

That from the earliest times and in the most uncorrupt Gospel narratives, not merely in the miraculous but also in other portions, there has always been an extensive and important symbolic element cannot, indeed, be doubted. So much at least seems certain. Hence arises the unavoidable question: Where shall we draw the boundary-line? How and according to what principles shall we delimit the symbolic from the non-symbolic and authentic? To answer this query seems to be the inevitable obligation of the liberal critic. Schmiedel has, indeed, met it openly and bravely—with what success the reader may judge after reading this volume. But, in general, the critics appear to have edged cautiously round—at least, not to have given any clear, unambiguous answer. Loisy assures us repeatedly that this or that is undoubtedly authentic, Harnack also likewise, and Wellhausen less often. But one seeks in vain for the grounds of their confident pronouncements. Never does their judgment appear determined by objective facts, but uniformly by subjective caprice. The critic seems to have thought out or formed some "Jesus-shape" for himself—how, no man can say—but in every case under the guidance of his own temperament and predisposition. His "Jesus-shape" is merely what it seems to him under all the circumstances a Jesus should have been. With this "Jesus-shape" every single feature of the Gospel-Jesus is then carefully compared: if it seems consistent with the imagined "shape," it is accepted as probable; if it seems essential, it is declared certain; if inconsistent, it is rejected as improbable, or even impossible.

But when we ask for the justification of the Shape itself, then, alas! none is given, none has been, none will be, even unto years of many generations. Without further ado the critic announces Jesus was this, and not that! But the same can never be proved, can never be made probable. The domain of possible individuality cannot be defined so narrowly, nor so sharply. No one can say whether a mystical dreamer or a strenuous reformer, whether a far-seeing theorist or a stout-hearted man of action, was the more probable. The most various traits of character may be ascribed with equal right to Jesus, compatible and incompatible—yea, even though directly contradictory; nor can we ever prove that some were antecedently probable, others improbable, or in truth impossible. Even if any one particular type should seem to be more likely than any *one* other, it would still be unlikely in comparison with *all* others possible. It is, in fact, a problem in the theory of combinations: In how many ways can you select n things out of r things? The number of possible solutions is so

PREFACE

great that the probability of any *one*, even the most probable, is only vanishingly small; that is, we must give up the problem as practically insoluble, unless the solution be sought along a path widely divergent from that hitherto trod. To show such a path, and to follow it some distance, is precisely the goal and aim of this volume.

However, it is only the general idea, the method of exegesis, upon which the writer would lay stress. It may well be that in many particulars he has gone astray, while none the less some such exposition is imperatively required. This latter fact shines even through the valiant strivings of Schmiedel and Loisy to prove at least some, however quite insignificant, traits of the evangelic paintings to be purely historic. The important question is not where and in how many details the present writer has erred, but where and in what measure he is right, and what are the legitimate deductions therefrom. Almost every one of his contentions draws with it a long train of results, so that unless they be all repelled the consequences may be very serious.

Furthermore, how is it possible to blink this other notable fact, that the historical picture which Harnack, Wellhausen, Loisy, Burkitt, would retain or restore is extremely dim and colourless. With such vague and dull outlines they fail utterly to arouse our admiration, to charm our fancy, to win our love, much more to explain the great religious movement in whose focus it is placed solely for the sake of the long-desiderated explanation—nay, rather it is a Personality scarcely in any respect attractive or impressive, but almost repellent, that these critics in their need have conjured up as the Founder of Christianity. Harnack cannot point to a single incident in the life of Jesus that marks him as an especially eminent or lovable man. See chapter iv of his *Mission and Expansion of Christianity*. After a brilliant prologue he comes to "Jesus Christ and the World-Mission." But what has he to say of the share of Jesus in this world-mission? In fact, nothing at all. We read some high-sounding sentences about the preaching of Jesus, how he directed his Gospel exclusively to the Jews—which Harnack is at great pains to prove. But all remains hopelessly dark and nebulous. Harnack mentions no new or weighty definite conception that Jesus introduced, no new principle of conduct that he proposed or proved, no new motive, no new inspiration that he breathed into human life—for it had all been there already; nay, more, what is still more significant, no expressions of human affection, no words of cheer, of comfort, of encouragement in the battle of life, not one single deed of human kindness, tenderness, magnanimity, or self-sacrifice. Even though there be something in the words or deeds of Jesus that might have the appearance at first of modifying these statements, yet, on closer scrutiny, it will be found to demand altogether another interpretation, to have a bearing dogmatic and not biographic, or to be the fiction of a later dramatising fancy. As an example, take the genuinely human and supremely noble prayer on the cross (Luke xxiii, 34) : " Father, forgive them ; for they know not what they do." Here is really a sentiment whereof not only Christendom but humanity may boast, the like of which we find rarely even in the New Testament, before which even the rebel soul of Rousseau might tremble and bow. Nevertheless, it is a "Western interpolation," as admitted by Westcott and Hort—"we cannot doubt that it comes from an extraneous source "; bracketed in ℵ, wanting in B, D, in the Sinaitic-Syriac, and in some old Latin witnesses ; "beyond all doubt," says Wellhausen, "it is interpolated." Now, if this, the very best of all in the New Testament, be an insertion, at once the conclusion leaps into our sight : the authors of the Holy Scriptures were well able to invent a Personality still greater than that ascribed to Jesus ; and the only reason why the figure of Jesus does not tower up more glorious still must be one of two—either the historic Jesus was not cast in the noblest of moulds, or else the evangelists were not concerned particularly to sketch a model human character, but rather to depict the progress of a "new doctrine," to represent symbolically the triumphant march of the cult of the Jesus. Alas ! Harnack and the critical school do not seem to hesitate before this alternative, but nerve themselves to accept a Jesus that does not measure up to the stature of Socrates, nor even of Aristotle. For there is no human action of the Harnackian Jesus that seems to be so beautiful or so noble as that related of the Stagirite. (See p. 127.)

In fact, the Saviour of the Berlin professor never lifts himself up to the notion of man as man. From beginning to end he remains a stiff-necked Jew, a Hebrew of the Hebrews. He was not even a liberal Jew of that day. Essentially he was a severe critic of the Pharisees, and only after the apparent failure of his message had embittered him did he begin to predict the impending judgment on the children of the Kingdom, the rejection of his people, the destruction of the temple, and the admission of strangers to the table of the Father. Nowadays we should call such a preacher an ill-natured, disgruntled dyspeptic. Harnack will not hear of it, that Jesus cherished any idea of a world-mission. This magnanimous thought, he maintains, never arose in the heart of the genuine Jewish prophet, never dwelt in his bosom, never formed any part of the primitive tradition. Still, it was in the world before Christ and after Christ, only not in the cramped horizon of the Saviour! Naturally, then, Harnack finds it quite impossible to insert either the influence or the personality of Jesus in his own historical picture. In fact, so far from explaining the course of events, the purely human, narrow-hearted Jewish preacher makes everything inexplicable and unintelligible. He is only a disturbing parenthesis, an isolated eddy in the stream of history.

Splendidly may Harnack sketch the preconditions of the world-preaching (chapters i–iii), masterfully delineate its progress through the Roman Empire; but what has the purely human Jesus to do therewithal? We still wait for an answer. Yea, indeed, Jesus was certainly the content of that preaching—by no means, however, as a man, *but solely as a God*. Not only does the human Personality play no *rôle* in this proclamation, but according to Harnack it could merely hinder or annul the world-mission, since such preaching was neither commanded nor intended by the Saviour. Indeed, Harnack bears witness of the Jew-Christians, who remained true to the precepts and the example of Jesus, that "crushed by the letter of Jesus they died a lingering death."

Strong and brave words are these, but not too brave nor strong. In Harnack's view the Apostles were distinctly superior to the purely human Jesus. The disciples were greater than the master, the servants than the lord. Nor is this the whole of the matter. At one point, at least, Loisy, in harmony with Harnack, represents Jesus as beyond measure visionary, as in fact insane.

He thinks that the Saviour undoubtedly spoke the words, "I will destroy this temple, and in three days build it again" (i, 99), which, as Loisy fancies, were borrowed from the real trial and (of course) transferred to the purely fictitious trial—by night, before Caiaphas (i, 102 ; ii, 599 : "ce procès nocturne, qui sans doute n'a pas eu lieu"). Moreover, agreeing with Wellhausen, he ascribes to the Saviour a caution that savours unpleasantly of cowardice : "As he travelled through Galilee and did not wish any one to know it" (Wellhausen). Loisy explains "this incognito" by "the anxiety not to attract the attention of Herod" (i, 93). In general, in estimating the monumental work of Loisy, one may recall his judgment of the net result of the illuminating labour of his colleague in Göttingen, "which, if it clears up many a detail, certainly does not tend to render more intelligible either the life or the death of Jesus." Yes, we may go still further. Not only do the works of this trio of representative critics contribute naught to our understanding, whether of the life or of the death of Jesus, but their marked effect is to void both the one and the other of all significance for the well-attested Proto-Christian movement, and, what is still worse, to rob the personality of the Saviour of all that might inspire love or reverence or even admiration. We may smile at the romantic and brilliantly coloured painting of Renan, but it is in many ways preferable to the dim and scanty pencil-sketching of the later masters.

Wellhausen has, to be sure, clearly perceived that his historical Jesus is only a shadow, and destitute of any religious value, and for that very reason almost instantly blurred by the primitive community. Very weighty are the words on the last page of his "Introduction" : "For what is lost with the Gospel, the historical Jesus, as the basis of religion, is only a very doubtful and unsatisfactory compensation. But for his death he would never have been historical at all. The impression left by his career is due to the fact that it was not completed, but was abruptly broken off when it had scarcely begun." Similarly Harnack opens the important fifth chapter (*op. cit.*) with the words : "Christ's death was mightier than his life.......it could not shatter the belief in him as a messenger sent from God, and thence arose the conviction of his Resurrection."

Such is the very best that Liberalism has to offer in explanation of the origin of the Proto-Christian preaching. Was there ever anywhere an all-important phenomenon so insufficiently explained? Not only is the explanation manifestly inadequate, but it is even self-contradictory. Hundreds of noble and impressive persons have suffered sudden, premature, and tragic death, but which of them has been instantly preached abroad over the world as arisen from the grave, ascended to heaven, and clothed with all the might, majesty, and dominion of the Most High? Which of them has been forthwith enthroned as Lord and God, as Alpha and Omega, as Ruler of the universe and co-equal with deity supreme? Nay, the death explains nothing at all. Never could it have been "mightier than the life," had not the life been unexampled, without any parallel, and beyond all imitation.

The assumed wonderful effect of the death presumes a still more wonderful—yea, even miraculous—life; naught else could have crazed and enchanted the disciples in such astounding and unheard-of fashion. The people believed on John also as sent from God; apparently the impression of his personality in life was quite as deep as that made by Jesus; his career also was interrupted just as abruptly; neither was the belief in him thereby shattered. Nevertheless, his most faithful followers never dreamed that he was re-risen and ascended to heaven, there to be worshipped, seated at the right hand of God.

Next to the instantaneous proclamation of Jesus Divine after his supposed death on the malefactor's cross, the most urgent riddle of early Christianity is the practically immediate mission to the heathen, directly against the supposed precept and precedent of Jesus, and without any intelligible origination—a mission that became at once world-wide in its extension and its success. As is set forth in *Der vorchristliche Jesus*, the preaching of Paul can throw no light on this mystery, for it cannot explain Ananias of Damascus, nor Apollos of Alexandria, nor the Twelve at Ephesus, nor Aquila and Priscilla at Rome. The fact of the primitive worship of Jesus and the fact of the primitive mission to all the Gentiles are the two cardinal facts of Proto-Christianity, both of which must be explained by any acceptable theory of Christian origins, both of which are explained fully by interpreting Proto-Christianity as from the start a more or less concerted movement to enlighten the Gentiles, to introduce everywhere the monotheistic Jesus-cult, and neither of which has ever been explained in any feature by the utmost ingenuity in the manipulation of the liberal notion of the purely human Jesus.

If any one still doubts this, let him read the recent works of Wrede and J. Weiss, and the eloquent championship of the latter's "eschatological" theory by Schweitzer, whose great work, *Von Reimarus zu Wrede* ("The Quest of the Historical Jesus"), is a cemetery of departed hypotheses, including the "eschatological" itself. This is not the place to controvert this latter in detail, nor is it needed, for Schweitzer has to chide Weiss for shrinking back in his later work from his own doctrine, which, in fact, sees in the Jesus merely a Messianic agitator whose enthusiasm, as in Loisy's representation, verged closely on lunacy. Of all the "Jesus-shapes," this seems the least lovely and the most inadequate. It explains neither of the two cardinal facts; on the contrary, it makes each tenfold harder to understand than before. The eschatological theory is, indeed, the *reductio ad absurdum* of the liberal purely human hypothesis; while its logical successor, the psychopathic theory of Binet-Sanglé and his peers, is the *reductio ad nauseam*.

It would seem, then, that the doctrine of the purely human Jesus is but shifting sand; that it affords no firm footing for liberal critics, no matter how strongly they may emphasise this or that detail as certain or undoubted or even indispensable. All such averments have only rhetorical meaning. How empty they are logically may be concluded from this circumstance: Their sole foundation is the fact that the detail in question agrees with a preconceived conception concerning Jesus. Meanwhile not one step is taken to justify this conception, to prove it necessary, or to show that the incident in question ever really happened. As an example, consider the following: Harnack discusses the thanksgiving (Matthew xi, 25-30)—manifestly a hymn, an outpouring of the Christian consciousness in view of the widespread triumph of the Jesus-cult among the Gentiles; but he holds it is imaginable that his imagined Jesus could have actually said something of the kind, and therefore expresses himself thus: "The saying thus contains nothing that can be objected to, and may therefore be used as one of the most important sources of our knowledge of the personality of our Lord" (*The Sayings of Jesus*, p. 220). Mark well the word "therefore," and the implied major premise: All (relevant) Gospel matter containing naught objectionable may be used as a source of our knowledge of the personality of Jesus; that is, no Evangelist could and would invent a wholly unobjectionable "saying" of Jesus! Why not? Is that really true? What could be less objectionable than the prayer on the cross? And yet it "is beyond all doubt interpolated." The incaution of this major is plainly evident, and yet precisely this dark thread of hasty assumption stretches itself through the whole Harnack-Loisy-Wellhausen web of argument. Assuredly such a fallacy cannot always escape the keen eye of Liberalism; and no wonder that Bousset, in a recent address in Berlin, seemed to be concerned to prepare the temper of his hearers for a complete and final abandonment, at no distant date, of all forms of historicism.

In the admirable and priceless book just quoted Harnack calls attention in a noteworthy footnote to the fact, which some doubt-monger might perchance be tempted to exploit, that this most primitive source (Q) breaks off before the Passion-week! It may be some satisfaction to the historian of dogma to learn that exactly at this point his foreboding was true and inspired; yea, that even before it was uttered it had already gone into fulfilment. During more than twenty years it had always seemed to the present writer that the "Sayings" presented the oldest extant literary form in which the Jesus-cult clothed itself, as it gradually took shape among the less orthodox Jewish sectaries in the inner religious circles of the Dispersion. Even the Marcan symbolism seemed to him to be a somewhat later thought, and much of the apparently historical looked like a transparent invention, to visualise or dramatise "Sayings" already current. To be sure, the counter-proof of Wellhausen looks very strong, and his philologic reasoning is always instructive, and sometimes confounding; but it can hardly avail to overcome the other total impression permanently. However, this interesting question of relative priority seems to entail with its answer no especial consequences; perhaps it may not even be categorically answerable. Inasmuch as both the "Sayings" and the Proto-Marcan source originated gradually—none can say in how many years—it may well be, as Jülicher has conjectured, that they are in some measure contemporary, each the older, each the younger. In any case, it must strike the careful reader that the whole Judæan ministry does not seem to go with the Galilean together as one piece, but rather looks like an afterthought, an appendix. This feeling has often come over the present writer, and years before he had the happiness to read Harnack's book it was greatly strengthened by the observation of the fact to which Harnack calls attention, that the Logoi-source knows naught of the Passion. For a while the importance thereof was not perceived; but later, even at the risk of being dubbed absurd and impertinent, the writer was forced to regard the fact as highly significant, since it distinctively suggests, even though it may not prove, that the personal historical form in which the Jesus-cult is clothed in the Gospels has undergone a gradual development. In the first rank would seem to have stood the great idea of the Redeemer, the Saviour-God. The redemption, the salvation, referred to *ignorance of God*, false worship, idolatry in its myriad forms. It was only the *Gnosis*, the true knowledge of God, that could work the cure. And the knowledge could be introduced, communicated, spread abroad by a doctrine only. Hence Jesus was at first presented as the healing God (in Mark and the Gospel according to Hebrews), and perhaps still earlier as the Teacher (in the Logoi-source Q). Moreover, the circuit of this healing, teaching activity (two equivalent aspects of the same cult) was strictly Galilean—*i.e.*, Galilee of the Gentiles was fittingly chosen as the symbolic region, where out of the midnight of the shadow of death the glorious light of the all-saving cult arose. In time the stately doctrine, "the teaching concerning the Jesus," spread itself out, budding and putting forth shoots like a noble tree, on which many wild-olive branches were engrafted—many related, many unrelated propositions were incorporated in the growing doctrinal body, and were more or less perfectly assimilated. Among these was the old-world notion of a "Dying God," which was fused together with the Platonic thought of the crucified Just and the Isaianic idea of the vicariously suffering Servant of Jehovah. Meantime the growing estrangement of the Jews suggested that Jerusalem, and Jerusalem alone, was the place where the pathetic fifth act of this drama of "stateliest and most regal argument" should be unrolled. Hence arose the Passion-week as the awful though not originally intended climax, and naturally the Resurrection as necessary epilogue. Accordingly, that Q finds no place for this sublime *finale* need bewilder no one, and accords perfectly with the view herein set forth of Proto-Christianity, though hardly, if at all, reconcilable with the hitherto prevailing conception.

In his valuable edition of the Odes of Solomon the unwearied Berliner, although properly complaining that an "unauthorised dilettante" has "disquieted Christendom," yet rejoices in the fact that the Odes were not earlier published, else the disquieter had certainly perverted them to his own unholy uses. Visibly a case of special providence. This is not the place to discuss these Odes, or the question of Christian interpolation ; but it may be allowable to call attention to a syllogism whereby they are forcibly coerced into rank among the witnesses for the liberal "Jesusbild."

Harnack concedes and underscores that these Odes discover for us a possible source both of the thought and temper, and also of the form of expression, met with in the Johannine Scriptures. The great importance of Harris's find is in this respect clear ; in fact, in reading the Odes, one seems to be moving in the atmosphere of the Fourth Gospel. "Even in details," says Harnack, "the 'Johannine' seems to be prepared beforehand in these Odes." However, he does not find therein the "Jesus as he presents himself to us in the purified sources of the Scriptures—*i.e.*, the historical Jesus." Granted. And what does Harnack conclude therefrom? "The historicity and the originality of Jesus appear confirmed anew." A remarkable piece of reasoning. Suddenly there comes to light a long-vanished psalm-book, which attests clearly the existence of a form hitherto unsuspected of intense religious individualism in early Christian or pre-Christian times (50 B.C. to A.D. 67) in a remote branch of Judaism. On one (the Johannine) circle of ideas and conceptions of Jesus this unexpected discovery shows an almost blinding light ; on another (the Synoptic) it sheds scarcely a single ray ; hence it is inferred that no new light can be thrown on this latter ! "The historicity and originality of

Jesus appear confirmed anew." Consider the syllogism that guarantees this conclusion :—

What is attested in the newly-published manuscript (as the thought and feeling of the Johannine Scriptures) cannot be accounted as historical or original with the evangelists ;

The purified Synoptic " Jesus-shape " is not so attested in the manuscript ;

Therefore this shape may be accounted historical and original (its "historicity and originality are confirmed anew ").

From two negative premises a positive conclusion is drawn. It is not so written in approved texts on logic. Why, to-morrow another psalm-book of some other sect may be unearthed, which may illumine the Synoptics quite as brilliantly as these Odes have illumined the Johannines.

This leads to the consideration of Dr. Schechter's very recent publication, *Fragments of a Zadokite Work*. In spite of the great learning and ingenuity that he has expended upon this mysterious book, its seals do not yet seem to be fully loosed. The discoverer himself leaves ample room for differences of opinion. However, of one thing we may be sure, that Margoliouth's premature expositions, which sought so eagerly to find in the venerable document some confirmation of prevalent prejudices in favour of the historicity of Jesus, have hopelessly miscarried. Indeed, it is not so easy to take them at all seriously. To identify these Zadokites with primitive Christians, even the genuine Jewish, to discover Jesus himself in the "Teacher of righteousness" (*i.e.*, of exact observance of the Law), this indeed calls for courageous criticism. Even the Haggadic, much more the Halachic, parts of this fragment rebel on almost every page against such exegesis. This congregation, in fact, far surpasses even the Pharisees in the strictness of its nomism—*e.g.*, it is declared (against the Rabbinic rule) : " If it (a beast) falls into a pit or a ditch, he shall not raise it on the Sabbath......And if any person falls into a gathering of water or into a place of......he shall not bring him up by a ladder or a cord or instrument." Truly this is a righteousness that " exceeds the righteousness of the scribes and Pharisees," and possibly Matthew v, 20 may squint towards something of the kind ; but that it proceeded from an historical Jesus or made itself felt in Proto-Christianity is entirely unthinkable. Margoliouth's whole interpretation is so evidently biassed and made to order that one need dwell on it no longer. With Rabbi Margolis we may rest confident that the date of the origin of the document is definitely pre-Christian (*Jewish Comment*, xxxiii, 18, 1). We may also accept the judgment of Schechter (p. xxix): "Naturally all this class of *pseudepigrapha* is of supreme importance for the history of Christianity, which undoubtedly was the consummation of all sectarian endeavour preceding it, and must have absorbed all the hostile elements arrayed against official Judaism."

This interesting discovery reveals to us a phase of Jewish sectarianism almost the polar opposite of that revealed in the Odes of Solomon. Now, do these two poles form the whole sphere of non-official Judaism? Or shall we rather believe that a rich and rank growth flourished in the mid-region? Certainly this intermediate realm was ample, and it would go against all precedent and all sound human understanding not to assume the presence therein of intermediate forms. Unless the falcon eye and ruthless hand of the old Catholic Church have done their work only too well, we may expect future researches to throw light on the Synoptics. In any case, even the worst, the lack of such testimonies can militate against the existence of such Proto-Christian sects and ideas only in the same sense and degree in which the well-known "missing links" disprove the general doctrine of descent with modification.

The author will very gladly learn from any opponent who will call his attention to any mistakes in statement of fact or process of reasoning in this volume; for he cannot doubt that such lapses are to be found therein, especially in view of the circumstances attendant upon both the composition and the publication of his critical works. But not even many such could really weaken the general structure of thought, just as a wall may still remain firm and unshaken in spite of the removal of divers crumbling stones. It is the collective judgment that must finally prevail, and it is to the formation and justification of the same that the thoughtful reader will give his special attention.

It seems hardly necessary to add that the sharpest polemic against the views of distinguished critics by no means implies any depreciation of their abilities or their achievements. Precisely as the most perfect flower of liberal criticism have they been chosen as special objects of attack, since they allow the *a fortiori* argument : If they do these things in the green tree, what shall be done in the dry? If unexcelled learning and acumen must yet leave unsolved nearly all that demands solution, what is there to hope from any other efforts along the same lines? Surely the fault lies not in the men, but in the methods, in the postulates, with which the problem has been approached. Such is the author's deepest conviction, and it is exactly the perception of this necessity of a new hypothesis that has emboldened him to enter the arena against specialists far more erudite than he. For it grows daily more manifest that no conceivable keenness or scholarship can ever avail to derive the Proto-Christian propaganda from a single personal purely human focus, even as neither patience nor knowledge nor mathematical adroitness can ever suffice to trisect an angle or to square a circle. The present is a case where the battle is not to the strong, where the weak may confound the mighty.

A well-disposed reviewer of *Der vorchristliche Jesus* has expressed the opinion that the book contains the most and the main arguments at the command of the author. This volume should reveal and correct that error. Let no one suppose, however, that the author's quiver is herewith emptied. On the contrary, the evidences not yet produced seem to him to be both abundant and convincing.

" Her strongest-wingèd shaft the muse is nursing still."

W. B. S.

New Orleans, April 15, 1912.

PART I.
THE PROTO-CHRISTIAN PROPAGANDA

Longe deuvicinia veritatis erratis qui putatis Deum credi aut meruisse noxium aut potuisse terrenum.—OCTAVIUS.

ORIENTATION

1. WHEN in 1906 *Der vorchristliche Jesus* was laid before the critical public, it was the aim of the author thereby to invite the attention of scholars to a body of obscure phenomena that seemed thitherto to have been undeservedly overlooked, and to bear very weighty witness touching the most important and the most fascinating as well as the most perplexing of all historical problems—the problem of the origin of Primitive Christianity. The material therein published was in fact only a small fraction of the mass already then assembled, and in manuscript, but still not quite ready for the press. The difficulty in securing this readiness was rather of an artistic than of a critical or scientific character. The variety of matter was so great, it had been gathered from so many mutually alien and widely separated fields of research, that only by constant and extreme coercion could it be reduced to anything like organic unity. In fact, the author well-nigh despaired of attaining any such unity, and had planned and brought far towards completion five volumes dealing each with some distinct aspect of the matter. Of these the first was "The Pre-Christian Jesus" (a kind of reconnaissance in force); the second (about half written) was to bear some such title as "Gnostic Elements in the New Testament"; the third (also about half written) the title "Behind the New Testament"; the fourth (nearly complete) would deal with the "Pauline Epistles," especially Romans; the fifth (hardly then begun) was to consummate the investigation by a treatment of the "Witness of the Gospels."

2. Transferred by request in 1906 to a chair of philosophy, the writer found little time, under the pressure of professional duties, to give to the actual further preparation of these incomplete volumes. Appointed as Delegate of the United States to the Pan-American Scientific Congress held at Santiago, Chile, in 1908, he was compelled for many months to lay aside critical studies. These were resumed in 1909, and it is in some measure the results of such later studies that are now submitted to the judgment of specialists. These results form a first part of the fifth volume already mentioned, which it was not the original purpose to print until the other volumes had been published. The change in the order of publication has been induced by a number of circumstances.

3. In the first place, a careful consideration of all the reviews of *Der vorchristliche Jesus* that came to hand, as well as of many private communications, showed clearly that the prevailing criticism relied for its support mainly on the Gospels, on the "Jesusbild," the personality supposed to be delineated there in such bold, vivid, impressive, and withal original features as to settle once for all the question of its historicity, and to dull the edge of all counter-argument that might be drawn from collateral considerations. It seemed, indeed, that it would almost be love's labour lost to carry, however successfully, all the outposts of the "liberal" position so long as this central citadel remained unattempted. In fact, it might easily be and almost certainly would be construed as a sign of conscious weakness, of felt inability to meet opponents in their full strength, if the writer should any longer delay to join battle on their own chosen ground, where, to be sure, the final test of argument must in any case be made.

4. To this view of the matter the writer was particularly inclined by the remark of a discreet reviewer, Windisch, in the *Theologische Rundschau*, xii, 4, 149: "The author might be in the right, if we knew concerning Jesus only the little that he has touched in his sketches." Here the author's reasonings seem to be definitely rejected, *not on their own merits*, but in view of supposed more extensive and accurate knowledge touching Jesus, and such is to be found, if at

all, only in the New Testament, particularly in the Gospels. On reading this deliverance, the writer determined to abandon the scheme of publication long fixed in his mind, though it still appeared to be scientifically preferable, and to proceed at once with what might be called the Evangelic argument. The book herewith offered to the public is a partial fulfilment of that determination.

5. The plan then adopted consisted in a minute study, verse by verse, of the Gospels, especially the Synoptics, and first of all the Gospel of Mark. This study had been carried through Mark and half through Matthew, when it was interrupted and partially suspended by the urgency of professional duties. Nevertheless, it was still kept up until the echoes of the recent polemic in Germany began to invade the writer's ears. Then it seemed wise once more to reform plans, not to await the final completion of a verse-by-verse exposition of the Gospels, but to gather up some of the more important results already reached, and to submit them to the judgment of the competent. This course seemed the more to be recommended as these results appeared in themselves sufficient to justify very definite and far-reaching conclusions, and unlikely to be seriously modified in general outline by still further inquisition, though, of course, leaving very many details to be filled in and many interesting and important questions to be put and answered.

6. Such, then, is the genesis of the book that now lies before the reader, a book not at all such as lay and still lies in the mind of the author, but such as the circumstances of the case have moulded it in a measure against his will. Herewith is implied no apology for the content of the work, but only an historical explanation of its form, so different from the cherished conception.

7. It has already been remarked that the inherent diversity of the material under consideration has firmly defied reduction to perfect organic unity. Indeed, the author's own research in this region has not been like unto a straight-trunked towering pine of the North, nor even to some single-stemmed though wide-branched evergreen oak of the South; but rather to some banyan tree of India, that sends down shoot after shoot and strikes them into the earth wherever

the soil permits, and so spreads its many-footed growth over the whole region round about. Such seems to be the literal state of the case, and it is one that critics might do well to observe carefully. For it is absolutely essential to any proper logical evaluation of the considerations presented in this volume and in its predecessor to note that these considerations are mutually interdependent though mutually confirmatory items of evidence. They must be refuted singly, it is true, but that is by no means enough. They must also be refuted collectively. The rods must be broken one by one, and they must also be broken in the compact bundle of all. It must be shown that the whole system of facts presented, and the whole mode of their conjunction, whereby they acquire coherence and interdependence, whereby they present themselves to our understanding as a thinkable organic unity—that all this internal harmony and mutual illumination is unreal and illusory, and that it is only when viewed from the opposite pole of opinion, from the hypothesis of the mere humanity of Jesus, that this whole complexus of facts acquires consistency and transparency, and satisfies the reason, whose supreme function it is to reduce the facts of the universe to logical order.

8. Now, it is precisely this duty of appreciation as a whole, of striking a collective judgment, that seems so imperative, and at the same time so disagreeable, to the prevalent criticism. Yet it cannot be postponed nor avoided indefinitely. The mind must accept, sooner or later, one or the other of two opposite conceptions; must accept it as a whole, not in this or that detail, and must reject the other as a whole, and not merely in this or that particular.

THE DILEMMA

9. For there is a certain sufficiently well-ascertained body of literary-historical Proto-Christian facts, and these must be reduced to unity. Chief and supreme among them is the fact of *the worship, the cult, of the Jesus*. This fact is all-dominant in the New Testament; it seems impossible to exaggerate its hegemony. The concept of the Jesus, if we estimate it merely statistically, far outweighs any other. Its

only rival, the Christ, is left much overbalanced, and in the Gospels is not comparable, appearing almost only as a late intruder. *The worship of this Being is the very essence of the New Religion.* Strike out this essence, and there is left very little—indeed, hardly anything—that is worth fighting about. Eliminate the doctrine of the Jesus, and what would become even of the Epistle to the Romans? It would be reduced to a more or less disconnected series of moral, philosophical, theological essays, such as two or more Greek-Roman-Judaic Stoics might have composed. The golden thread that holds them together in unity is a Doctrine of the Jesus. It seems needless to enlarge upon what no one, perhaps, would deny— the regulative moment of the Jesus and the worship of the Jesus for the whole of the New Testament and the whole of Proto-Christianity.

10. That this Being, this Jesus, is presented in the New Testament, and accepted in all following Christian history, as a God is evident beyond argument. It is made clear on almost every page of the New Testament with all the clearness that can belong to human speech. There is no debating with anyone that denies it. But it is equally clear that He is also presented as a man, as conceived, born, reared, hungering, thirsting, speaking, acting, suffering, dying, and buried— and then raised again. How, then, are we to conceive this Being? The answer of the present Church, of Orthodoxy, is unequivocal. We must conceive him precisely as he is represented, both as God and also as Man. But suppose this be impossible, in spite of all learned subtleties about the essential divinity of Humanity (which, of course, in a certain sense, may and must be accepted)? Again the answer of Orthodoxy is unequivocal: though we cannot think it, nor understand it, yet we must *believe* it none the less; and this, it is said, is the victory of faith. With this position, so highly respectable and venerable, and in a certain measure so logical and self-consistent, we have at present nothing to do. Right or wrong, for good or for ill, the human spirit has gone definitely and finally beyond it, and it is hopeless to suppose it will ever retrace its steps. Indeed, it could not if it would. The reason of this and the next centuries can no more believe in the God-man (in the orthodox sense) than

it can believe in the geocentric theory of Ptolemy or the special creations of Linnæus. For reason, constituted as it now is, the God-man is a contradiction in terms, an incongruity with which it can have no peace, with which it can never be reconciled. The ultramontane is right—to accept this fundamental notion is to abjure reason. Some minds seem able to do this—minds in which there is a rift running all through, a fundamental duality, minds built like ocean liners, on the compartmental plan, with no intercommunication between compartments. Such minds obey the laws of universal reason in all matters but the most important. When they unlock their oratory they lock up their laboratory.[1] With intellects so constituted we have no controversy in these pages.

11. It is only with normally acting intelligence that we are here concerned. Such intelligence must resolve the antinomy God-man into its constituents; it must affirm the one and therewith deny the other. In view, then, of all the undisputed and indisputable facts, it must affirm one of two opposite theses: Jesus was a deified man, or The Jesus was a humanised God. There is no *tertium quid*. One of these alternatives is necessary, the other impossible; one is true, the other is false. Hitherto criticism has with practical unanimity assumed the first alternative, and has lavished its splendid resources of learning and acumen in the century-old attempt to understand the New Testament and primitive Christianity from the standpoint of this assumption. It is not the writer's intention to review, or to refute, or in any way to criticise in detail, any of these elaborate and ingenious essays. The notable fact is that, in spite of all the knowledge and the constructive talent called into play, none of these endeavours has been crowned with success, not one has

---

[1] A letter from one of the brightest ornaments of present British philosophy would indicate that the foregoing is stated too strongly. This scholar regards the destruction of the liberal *Jesusbild* as complete, saying: "On the negative side I am entirely at one with you......But I feel through all your polemic the presence of a 'neglected alternative.'" This latter is the formula of Chalcedon —"very man *and* very God." Against such a view we shall neither strive nor cry, nor let any voice be heard in this book. In another volume it may be otherwise. According to B. Russell, learning "to believe that the law of contradiction is false" is "a feat which is by no means as difficult as it is often supposed to be."

commanded any general assent, not one has established itself for longer than a short time or in more than a narrow circle. In this connection the writer may be allowed to quote from his own article on New Testament criticism, written in 1904, and published in *The Americana* (Encyclopædia), 1905:—

When so many wingèd hounds of Zeus thus find that their quarry forever eludes them, the suggestion is inevitable that there is something radically wrong in their method of pursuit, that in some way their finest sense has betrayed them. We hold that the nature of their error is now at length an open secret. They have sought to explain Christianity as an emanation from a single individual human focus, as the reaction upon history and environment of a single human personality; they have sought "to understand Jesus as the originating source of Christianity." They have failed, and they must forever fail; for no such explanation is possible, because no such origination was real. Over against all such attempts we oppose the fact that every day comes to clearer and clearer light, that now flashes continually into evidence around the whole horizon of investigation; the fact that was perceived nearly a decade ago, but whose effective proclamation called for the publication of a series of preparatory investigations; the fact that the genesis of Christianity must be sought in the collective consciousness of the first Christian and immediately pre-Christian centuries; that in the Syncretism of that epoch of the amalgamation of faiths, when all the currents of philosophic and theosophic thought dashed together their waters in the vast basin of the Roman circum-Mediterranean empire, was to be sought and found the possibility and the actuality of a new faith of Universal Humanity that should contain something appealing to the head and the heart of all men, from slave to emperor, a faith in which there should be no longer male and female, Jew and Greek, bond and free, but all should be one by virtue of a common Humanity, of the ageless, timeless, spaceless Son of Man. It is as the outcome of this Syncretism, as the final efflorescence of the Judæo-Græco-Roman spirit, of the Asiatic-European soul, that Christianity is wholly intelligible and infinitely significant; the notion that it is an individual Palestinian product is the *Carthago delenda* of New Testament criticism.

12. Under such conditions, in view of the notorious failure of the thoroughly tested hypothesis of a merely human Jesus, of a deified man, it becomes the unavoidable duty of criticism to test with equal care and thoroughness the single and exclusive alternative, the counter hypothesis of a divine Jesus, of a humanised God. Nor should there be brought to this trial any religious feeling or dogmatic prejudice; neither, above all, should it be tainted by any *odium theologicum*.

The inquiry should be pursued calmly, dispassionately, with scientific caution and accuracy, with no appeal to passion, with no resort to rhetoric, according to the rules of the syllogism and the formulæ for Inverse Probability, with firm resolution to accept whatever conclusions may eventually be recommended, and with absolute confidence not only that the truth will ultimately prevail, but that it is also for the highest and holiest interests of humanity that it should prevail, whatever it may be. We must, in fact, remember the noble words of Milton :—

> And now the time in special is, by privilege to write and speak what may help to the further discussing of matters in agitation. The temple of Janus, with his two controversial faces, might now not unsignificantly be set open. And though all the winds of doctrine were let loose to play upon the earth, so truth be in the field, we do injuriously......to misdoubt her strength. Let her and falsehood grapple; who ever knew truth put to the worse, in a free and open encounter?

It is, of course, superfluous to argue such self-evident propositions; and it would, indeed, seem almost equally superfluous even to state them, had not the recent example of the attacks on Professor Drews, and in less measure upon the present writer, made clear that there is really great need to stress such sentiments with peculiar emphasis. On this point one need not dwell. The animus of the polemic pamphlets in question is plain enough to such as have read them, and to others it were, perhaps, better not revealed.

13. With the substance of these booklets the present writer is in no great measure immediately concerned. The main bulk of the refutation goes against the theories of such as Robertson, Kalthoff, and Jensen, with whom the writer has never united forces, from whom he has persistently held his own thought independent and distinct. Not that he might not learn much from such scholars and thinkers, but that he has preferred not to poach on their preserves; rather to follow his own paths at his own gait and in his own manner. *Spartam tuam exorna* has been his motto. Why the critics in question have so preferred to deal with other works rather than with *Der vorchristliche Jesus* is a question not without interest, but which he presumes not to answer. There is, however, a certain amount of common ground which

nearly every participant in this controversy must traverse. It is hard to avoid speaking of the Personality revealed in the Gospels, of the supposed witness of the Pauline Epistles, and of the testimonies of profane writers. To these should be added the acute argument of Schmiedel touching the Nine Pillars, which many years ago, on its first appearance in the *Encyclopædia Biblica*, appeared to the writer, as it still appears, to be incomparably the most plausible plea ever made for the liberal contention. It seems to have figured far too little in the present controversy, and accordingly no small part of this volume is surrendered to its consideration.

ARGUMENT FROM PERSONALITY

14. Overshadowing significance attaches in the minds of most to the argument from the Evangelical Personality. It is this that Von Soden has accented so forcefully. It is this to which Harnack makes his appeal. Closely allied therewith is the thought that great events of history presuppose and imply great historical personalities; hence it seems to be inferred that the origin of Christianity as the greatest of historical events implies the greatest of personalities. A strange paralogism! Even if we granted the conclusion, the question would still remain, But who was that personality? Was it Paul, or Peter, or John, or Mark, or some Great Unknown, like the Fourth Evangelist? Or was it, perhaps, all of these notable personalities working in more or less perfect accord, and producing a total result of which no one, nor two, nor three might have been capable? There seems to be not the slightest reason for doubting that the Proto-Christian period was rich in personality, and in personalities of a very marked variety. But there has not yet been presented one iota of proof that the Jesus was one of these persons. In fact, he does not stand at all in line with any of them. Between Jesus and Paul or Peter or John even the most distant parallel is absolutely unwarranted. One might just as well align Jupiter Stator with Fabius Cunctator. Whoever dreamed of worshipping James or John, of praying to Peter as Lord, of casting out demons in the name of Luke the beloved physician, of preaching that Paul had died for

men, or that Stephen had risen from the dead, or that Apollos had ascended into glory? It seems superfluously manifest that all of these distinguished personalities, the brightness of whose distinction we at this distance may only dimly perceive, stand entirely out of line with Jesus, with whom to compare them would be like comparing a planet with the Newtonian law of gravitation.

15. Such men, be it repeated, were in all probability very able and exceptional characters. If we judge them by the work they accomplished, we must surely admit they were most remarkable. This notability is generally conceded willingly enough to Paul, but rather grudgingly to Peter and James and John[1] and the rest—yet without any good reason. The notion that these latter were only ignorant Galilean fishermen, who merely misunderstood the teachings of Jesus and very inadequately reproduced them—this notion is itself the gravest misunderstanding, for which there is not the faintest shadow of justification. The epistle that goes under the name of James is a well-written—indeed, almost learned—disquisition. It contains allusions to matters astronomical and others (as in i. 17, iii. 6—*wheel of birth*—and elsewhere) that reveal clearly a cultured intelligence. The letter to the Hebrews is plainly the work of a highly-trained intellect not guiltless of the graces of literary expression. The Johannines proceed manifestly from a circle accustomed to deep musings on philosophic and theosophic themes. The Petrines are not ignorant of Stoical doctrine. Of the Evangelists, Luke has received even exaggerated recognition at the hands of eminent critics; but as a fervid and impassioned declaimer and rhetorician he is still notably inferior to Matthew, while Mark surpasses all in the rugged strength of his thought and the still depth of his symbolism. The fact is that the New Testament is a wonderful body of literature, and attests unequivocally a high level of mental power and artistic sense in its authors. That the Greek is far from classic signifies nothing, save that the *milieu* of its composition was half-Jew,

---

[1] Of course, we attach no weight to these or to any other mere names. It is enough that among the Proto-Christians there were many men who thought great thoughts, wrote great writings, and did great deeds—call them what you will.

half-Greek; that much of it was at least thought, if not originally written, in Aramaic; and that the forms of speech were often loaded with ideas beyond what they were able to bear.

16. When, now, we pass beyond the apostolic circle, we still find men that must have possessed impressive personalities. Consider Simon Magus. It is a stupendous blunder to regard him as a mere charlatan. Harnack speaks (*D. G.*, I. 233, *n.* 1) appreciatively of his "attempt to create a universal religion of the Most High God." That he *belonged to the primal Christian* influences seems certain. It is characteristic of the desperation of the ablest liberal criticism that Harnack feels compelled to recognise an influence of Jesus (and Paul) on Simon Magus: "He is really a counterpart to Jesus, whose activity can no more have been unknown to him than was that of Paul." "We know that out-and-out new religious organisations were attempted in the apostolic age in Samaria, in the production of which, in all likelihood, the tradition and proclamation of Jesus had already exerted influence" (p. 233). A strange example of prolepsis. According to Acts viii. 5-13, Simon was one of the very first converts outside of Jerusalem, in the first year after the resurrection, and had already, for a "long time" previous, held sway in Samaria. He was also reputed to be the father of heresy; and, since it was the habit and the interest of the Christians never to antedate, but rather to postdate, all heresies, we may be sure that the date given in Acts is at least not too early, and that Simon's teaching was considerably pre-Christian. Notice now that he is represented as converted at the first preaching of Philip in Samaria, and as attaching himself devotedly to Philip. The story of his simony is, on its face, a mere invention, like other stories of the heresiographers. The fragments preserved from the *Apophasis* that went under his name indicate a deep thinker, a kind of pre-Hegelian Hegel, and lead us to believe that we behold in them the ruins of a daring and high-aiming religious cosmogony. Likewise the sentiments attributed to the most ancient Naassenes testify indubitably to bold and comprehensive theosophic speculation. If the systems of these primitive Gnostics had reached us in their entirety, and not

merely in detached bits transmitted and perhaps often disfigured by hostile hands, it seems in the last degree probable that we should be compelled to yield them a large tribute of respect as earnest religionists and no mean thinkers.

17. When, now, we descend to the first half of the second century, we are confronted by three names of veritable heroes of philosophic-religious speculation—Basilides, Valentinus, Marcion. It signifies nothing that they were all heretics. Such, too, were Bruno and Huss and Luther and Melanchthon and Zwingli and Calvin and Knox, and who knows how many others? Such, too, at least in a measure, was the oceanic Origen. Of the pre-eminence of these three, not to mention many others of whom we know, there can be no question. With regard to the second, it is enough to read the testimony of the Fathers and the judicious appreciation by Harnack. The overshadowing pre-eminence of Marcion is even more incontestable. On the whole, he seems to have been the greatest religious figure of that era. Apparently, however, both he and Valentinus were excelled in profundity of thought by Basilides, of whom we hear hardly so much, most likely because the depths of his thinking were less accessible to the search of the heresy-hunters, and because he made less appeal to the general intelligence. But it seems impossible to read carefully the few fragments that remain of his numerous works without feeling oneself in the presence of something very like philosophic-religious genius. It is a well-known merit of Harnack's *Dogmengeschichte* that it recognises unequivocally the intellectual superiority of the Gnostics and their decisive significance for scientific theology: "It is beyond doubt that theologic literature had its origin among the Gnostics" (*o.c.* p. 230, *n.* 1). The general result, then, is that, in spite of the deplorably fragmentary state of the surviving evidence, and in spite of the painful misrepresentation that meets us at every turn, it is impossible not to recognise the two centuries 50 A.C.–150 P.C. as extraordinarily prolific in commanding religious personalities. There seems, indeed, to have been almost a plethora of theosophic genius. Nor is there any compelling reason why we should set the year 50 A.C. as an upper limit. We might very well throw this limit back one hundred years or more, into Maccabean

times. Information is, indeed, wanting; but there is no improbability in such dating. Moreover, there is no reason for supposing that those early thinkers—the Proto-Naassenes, for example—were in any way inferior to their successors and expounders, such as Paul, Peter and John, Simon, Menander, Basilides, Valentinus, Marcion, and the rest. In fact, the analogies of history might lead us to believe they surpassed all their followers, if not in elaboration of detail, yet at least in elemental strength and in boldness of outline. There may very well have been some such succession as that of Æschylus, Sophocles, Euripides, or of Socrates, Plato, Aristotle. To the writer's mind, the Old-Christian literature, in particular the New Testament, suggests irresistibly vast sunken continents of thought, over which the waves of two thousand years of oblivion are rolling, with here and there grey or green island peaks emerging, a wondrous archipelago.

Herewith, then, the contention of Haupt and Harnack and their peers, that the new school neglects the great historical factor of personality, seems to be completely refuted. We do not overlook nor omit this factor; on the contrary, we insert it in far higher potency than do our opponents.

18. But someone will say that we employ many personalities, whereas there is need of a single all-controlling personality. This latter proposition we deny *in toto* and with all emphasis; and for various reasons, each in itself sufficient. It is not true that the great critical events and movements of history have been always or even generally determined by single personalities; it has often happened that there has been no one all-dominating individuality, but that several or even many have conspired in the expression of some one over-mastering ideal. Take the case of the French Revolution. How many leading spirits, all measuring up nearly to the same line, not one shooting up into any very great elevation either absolutely or relatively! Not until the Revolution was accomplished and had ceased wholly to move forward did the wonderful Corsican appear and begin to roll it backward.

19. Here in the New World we celebrate two events as of world-historical importance: the Revolution of 1776 and the

Civil War of 1861–64. In neither of these does any single personality tower up in overshadowing proportions. Washington and Lincoln were officially most conspicuous, and by some are regarded as pre-eminent; but at most they were only slightly taller than numbers of their peers. Consider the Renaissance. What a long line of giants march in the first rank! Possibly Leonardo is the most perfect in his proportions; but no one can claim for him that he was the ruling spirit. Consider even the case of the great Reformation. Luther towers herein conspicuous; but he was by no means without precursors, by no means without peers. Indeed, his personality would seem to have been in many ways over-estimated. This thought need not be pursued further.

20. Of course, it is not for an instant denied that great single personalities may lie behind and initiate great world-historical movements, *though they can never do this except where the springs are already set*, the train laid, and all the necessary pre-conditions already arranged in the antecedent actually existing historical circumstances of the case; but where such pre-arrangement is already complete, then it is not true that a single determinate personality is either always necessary or even generally actually present. The initiative may and often does actually proceed not from one but from many nearly co-equal individualities.

21. This is not nearly all, however. In the case actually under consideration there is a high *antecedent probability* that it must have proceeded *not* from *one*, but from *many*. For if it had proceeded from one single personality even half so dominant as the prevailing theory supposes Jesus to have been, then the movement would have had some very distinct and unmistakable unity, some entirely unambiguous imprint of this one individuality. Of course, it is true that great teachers have been misunderstood in many minor details. There are even now several theories as to the central aim of the *Critique of Pure Reason*. Men may perhaps wrangle for ever over the interpretation of Plato or of Spinoza. But such cases are not nearly parallel to the one in hand. These strifes concern matters of detail or else of extreme subtleties of thought, where either language was inadequate to exact expression, or else the thinker had not himself come clearly

into the light, or perhaps in the course of his own intellectual development had fallen into some inconsistencies such as naturally attend upon growth. None of these explanations will fit the case in hand. In a ministry that must have lasted at most only two or three years there could not have been any notable incongruences due to gradual evolution. The matters were not metaphysical subtleties hard to think, harder to express, easy to misstate and misapprehend. Nevertheless, the great patent obtrusive fact is that by supposition at least 150 years of unintermittent strife followed upon the preaching of this single personality. From the very start he would seem to have been understood or misunderstood in an endless variety of ways. Nor is it possible to detect in his supposed teaching any bond of individuality, any stamp of a single incomparable personality. The impressive fact, admitted even by the liberal critics themselves, is that Christianity is pre-eminently not single-natured, but is above all else syncretic. There is, indeed, a clear and unmistakable thread of unity running through the whole doctrine, the whole propaganda, which has in fact held Christendom together in a kind of unity from that day to this—namely, *the worship of Jesus as God, the doctrine that Jesus was Lord, in some way one with Deity*. Cut this cord of union, and the whole body of doctrine unravels and falls to pieces, the whole distinctive structure of our religion fades away and vanishes. If Jesus be mere man, then he is only one of many; he takes his position side by side with Socrates, Mohammed, and others, and it may be that the only reason he seems so grand and so beautiful is because he looms upon us from the horizon of history : his form may be enlarged and his features softened by the mist and the distance. That a system of world-religion should have as its permanent distinguishing mark the pre-eminence accorded to any mere man seems to be infinitely preposterous.

22. This, however, is not the main point in mind, which is that this dogma, which alone imparts essential and age-lasting unity to the Christian teaching, is precisely the dogma that the critics themselves cannot attribute to this unique teacher. If Jesus were a mere man, we cannot think of him as himself believing that he was God or Lord, nor of

his teaching the same to his disciples. This dogma, then, must have been a later accretion to his original doctrine. But this doctrine, this worship of the Jesus as divine, is the *one* infrangible bond of *unity* in the countless variety of creeds of Christendom. And this, we repeat, is precisely what could not have proceeded from this *one* Personality!

23. Here, then, we are met by a double question: How shall we account for this golden thread of union that has held together for so many centuries the complex web of Christendom? How shall we account for the infinite and immediate lack of unity (this thread excepted) if the teaching indeed proceeded from a single incomparable teacher?

24. Hereto the answers given by the new theory are exceedingly simple and entirely satisfactory, while no answer ever has been given, and apparently none ever can be given, by the older theory, which we here reject. We affirm, namely, that the worship of the One God under the name, aspect, or *person* of the Jesus, the Saviour, was the primitive and indefectible essence of the primitive preaching and propaganda. Infinitely though they may have varied from place to place and from time to time in various particulars, the original secret societies were united in one point—namely, the worship of the One God under this name or some nearly equivalent name and aspect. In fact, the terms "The Nasaree" and "The Saviour"[1] seem to have vied at first with "The Jesus"; and there may very well have been— and admittedly were—other terms, such as "Barnasha," "Baradam," "Son of Man," "Mighty Man," "Man from Heaven," "Second Adam," and the like, that were preferred here and there. This early *multiplicity of designations* testifies eloquently to the primitive wide-rootedness of the cult, and is scarcely at all explicable in terms of the prevailing hypothesis. But there were abundant reasons why the name *Jesus* should be the Aaron's rod to swallow up all other designations. Its meaning, which was *felt* to be Saviour, was grand, comforting, uplifting. The notion of the World-Saviour thrust its roots into the loam of the remotest antiquity; it made powerful appeal to the universal

---

[1] ὁ Ναζαραῖος, ὁ Σωτήρ.

consciousness.   A Saviour was then and there, all around the Mediterranean,

> The pillar of a people's hope,
> The centre of a world's desire.

On this point one need not dwell, for the reader may be supposed to be familiar with the relative writings of Soltau and others, and especially with the compendious treatment of Lietzmann in his *Der Weltheiland* and of Hoyer in his *Heilslehre*.

25. The word *Jesus* itself also made special appeal to the Jewish consciousness; for it was practically identical with their own Jeshua', now understood by most to mean strictly Jah-help, but easily confounded with a similar form J'shu'ah, meaning *Deliverance, Saviour.   Witness,* Matthew i, 21. Moreover, the initial letter J, so often representing Jah in Hebrew words, must have powerfully suggested Jehovah to the Jewish consciousness. Hardly less direct was the appeal to the Greek consciousness. The word Ἰάομαι means *I heal;* the future forms (Ionic and Epic) are Ἰησ-ομαι, ἰήσ-ῃ, etc. The word Ἴησ-ις (genitive Ἰήσ-εως) means *healing,* and Ἰασ-ώ (genitive Ἰασ-οῦς) was goddess of health and healing. The name *Jusus* (Ἰησ-οῦς) must then have suggested *healing* to the Greek mind fully as forcibly as *Saviour* suggests *saving* to the English. Even this was not all, however. The name was closely connected in form and sound with the divine name IAO, regarded in early Gnostic circles with peculiar reverence. It is not necessary to decide whether this latter is to be regarded as the equivalent of the tetragram *JHVH*, or as meaning Jah-Alpha-Omega (Rev. i, 8; xxi, 6; xxii, 13; *cf.* Is. xliv, 6). It is enough that in Hellenistic early theosophic circles the name was, in approved use, a favourite designation of deity. In view of all these facts, the triumph of the name *Jesus* seems entirely natural.

26. On the other hand, the notable, and even unparalleled, diversity of early Christian doctrine seems equally natural, and, in fact, almost inevitable, in accord with the new theory which is here advocated. If you ask why there were so many shades and types of teaching, the answer is, because there were so many types of mind active over so wide a region of country. The "new doctrine" was necessarily vague in its

outlines, just as the preaching in Acts is vague. As we shall see, it was essentially a protest and *insurrection of the monotheistic against the polytheistic consciousness;* but this protest and insurrection could, and did, take many forms, while always substituting for the multiplicity of heathen gods the one healing, saving, and protecting God, the Jesus.

27. This diversity of detail, held together in unity by the one all-dominating dogma of the new deity, the Jesus, the Christ, is and must be explained in similar fashion even by the adherents of the old hypothesis; the only difference is that their explanation is just as forced and artificial as ours is ready and natural. For no man can fail to recognise the wide interval between Mark and John, between James and Hebrews, between Paul and the Apocalyptist. How shall we explain them? The answer must be sought in the diverse individualities of the men concerned. There is precisely where we seek it and find it, and there is nothing to make this answer in any way hard to understand; on the contrary, the whole phenomenon appears natural and inevitable in the light of that other important fact—the propaganda did *not issue exclusively from Jerusalem*, but almost simultaneously from a *number of foci*, both geographically and culturally distinct, and imparting each its own peculiar local colour. Here, then, there seems to be nothing in simplicity and naturalness left to be desired.

28. Altogether different is the case with the elder theory of the one all-dominating, all-originating Personality. Here, again, it must be held that the discrepancies and contradictions of the New Testament writings are due to the diverse individualities of the writers; but where, then, do we find place left for the one overruling character? This question it is absolutely impossible for the critics to answer; this obstacle they can never overcome. By no artifice can they ever make clear how the same individuality could have been reflected so notably diversely as in Mark and John, for instance; these two stereoscopic views will never fuse into one. Hence it has long since become the fashion to reject the latter picture entirely, and depend solely on the former; and of this, to pick out a few features, reject all the rest, and then fill in according to the caprice of the critic himself. Such a method condemns

itself from the very outset; it is irredeemably arbitrary and capricious. But even if it were allowed to succeed in dealing with the Gospels, it would confront even graver and complexer difficulties on drawing the other Scriptures into the circle of consideration. The problem of reducing the Acts, the Paulines, the Apocalypse, the Catholic Epistles, and Hebrews to the measure of the Gospels would still remain, as it does now remain, utterly insoluble. All of these are a unit in teaching the deity of the Jesus, but in nothing else. They are practically devoid of all reference to any human personality whatever bearing that name. By no stretch of the scientific or critical imagination can we discover in the minds of any of these authors any dominance or controlling memory of the life, teaching, example, or influence, in any manner or measure, of a single human personality, the Jesus.

29. Here, then, the prevalent theory is forced to face a contradiction that must annul it in the minds of unbiassed reasoners. On the one hand it assumes a personality so overwhelming, so unexampled, so inconceivably grand, splendid, beautiful, attractive, and ineffaceably impressive that with one accord a group of disciples, after a brief season of companionship followed by a death between malefactors on the cross, are so possessed with memories of this friend and teacher that they have multiplied visions of him as risen from the dead and ascended into glory and seated on the right hand of the Majesty on high. These visions they accept as ocular and even tangible facts; they draw the immediate inference that the man they knew so well in all the aspects of humanity less than two months before, and whom they laid lovingly in the tomb, was really risen therefrom, had overcome all the powers of death and the grave, was really reigning on high in heaven, was really God and Lord, henceforth to be worshipped as the Ruler of the Universe.

30. Now, of itself, all this is absolutely unexampled. No parallel can be found in all the hoary registers of time. That rational men should do this or anything like this, and by their preaching should convert a whole highly civilised Roman Empire to acceptance of such a farrago of extravagances, would itself be a miracle beyond all comparison; nor

need anyone that accepts this theory hesitate for an instant at any wonder of the New Testament: he need not strain out the gnat after swallowing the camel. For his own part, the writer tried many years, for at least a score, with all the help that could be found in the pages of the most consummate critics, from Baur to Wrede, from Ewald to Wellhausen, from Renan to Schmiedel, to make this theory in some way or degree acceptable to the understanding, but only with the result of total failure. He had indeed written many hundred pages of Pauline interpretation, striving with all the powers of exegesis to render this theory intelligible; but, in spite of all and every effort, the inexpugnable absurdity remained and mocked with increasing and more unmistakable derision. Only then it was that he renounced finally the task foolishly begun, seeing that it had already so successfully defied the unsurpassed logical energies of Holsten.

31. Even this, however, does not state the case in its wholeness. Not only must this personality have produced an impression on the disciples entirely without parallel in its intensity, depth, and transformative energy; not only must it, *mirabile dictu*, have hallucinated them, turned them one and all into missionaries and obsessed them for all their following lives with the wildest beliefs imaginable; not only must it have wrought these incredible and impossible effects on the associates of a year; but, *mirabilius dictu*, it must have worked even more astoundingly on an intellect and character of the highest order, with whom it never came into contact at all—who, in fact, seems to have known nothing of it whatever unless by some casual hearsay. For Paul was such an intellect and character, and the accepted fact is that he preached the Jesus with energy, with enthusiasm, with consecration, with success unequalled by any of the alleged personal disciples. Yet, admittedly, he was not a personal disciple; he is supposed to have been a persecutor. Here, then, is *actio in distans*, and in the third degree, more intense than any immediate working. There is here not the least hook on which to hang any shred of personal influence. I yield to no man in admiration of the deep-piercing acumen of Holsten: he possessed an extraordinary logical faculty, the tenth part of which imparted to many a scholar might

make him a thinker; and yet one cannot conceal from oneself the patent fact that all his subtleties are vain in presence of the inherent and eternal absurdity of his central thesis. He has failed, and where he has failed it is not likely that anyone will ever succeed. I hold, then, that the fact of Paulinism and the fact of Paul must remain for ever an insoluble enigma according to the prevalent theory. It is impossible to understand the conversion, the activity, and the doctrine of Paul in terms of the human personality of the Jesus.

32. But still there is more to follow. Not only must this supposed personality have been hallucinating in its immediate action, and still more hallucinating in its remote action on such as never came under its influence; but, *mirabilissimum dictu,* it must have left practically no impression at all precisely where its impression was left the deepest. Here is the everlasting contradiction already mentioned or suggested. For the confounding fact is that the very men whom this Person is supposed to have infatuated beyond all example and all belief have, in their preaching and in their writings, so far as these are delivered and known to us, virtually nothing to tell us of the personality by which they are *ex hypothesi* obsessed. Not, indeed, that they make no mention of the Jesus. On the contrary, their discourse hinges on this mighty concept. But they know virtually nothing of his alleged *human* character. Uniformly they present us this Jesus as a divinity, as a dogma, never as a life. Where in Acts, or the Epistles, or the Apocalypse are we permitted to catch even a faint glimpse of Jesus as a man? By supposition the minds of the speakers and writers must have been crowded to overflowing with anecdotes and incidents and sayings of him who had possessed their minds as never have minds been possessed before or since. Jesus must have been with them a fixed idea, a veritable monomania. Not otherwise can we understand their instant deification and exaltation of him to the throne of the universe. Surely, then, their thoughts would have flowed in the channel carved out by their intercourse with him; their memories would have been laden with the priceless experiences of Galilee and Jerusalem. Reminiscence on reminiscence would have welled up incessantly and formed the burden of their

speech. There is no escape from this conclusion, unless we invert all the known laws of psychology.

33. But what are the facts in the case? What do we meet with in reading these metevangelic scriptures? A virtually absolute dearth of all that we should expect to be present in overflowing abundance! Scarcely a single incident or saying, and absolutely not the faintest indication of human character whatever![1] We are indeed assured that God sent his Son into the world, that he was born of woman, born under the law, of seed of David according to flesh, declared as Son of God with power according to spirit of holiness from resurrection of the dead (whatever such words may mean); that he was crucified, dead, buried, raised again, received up into heaven. Or, as the most ancient formula puts it (1 Tim. iii, 16):—

> Confessedly mighty is the mystery of godliness—
> Who was manifested in flesh, Was justified in Spirit,
> Appeared to angels, Was preached among Gentiles,
> Was believed on in the world, Was received up in glory.

34. We submit it to any fair-minded person: Is this the way that one talks of an intimate personal friend, of a sweet, noble, incomparable character, of a wise, loving, and beneficent teacher, of a life full of deeds of kindness, gentleness, self-sacrifice? Or is it said naturally and inevitably of an unearthly Being, of a Deity, an object of worship and adoration, but not of memory, not of personal acquaintance, nor of human affection?

35. To be sure, we read that "he of Nazareth traversed benefitting and healing those oppressed of demons"; and we also read of the institution of the Lord's Supper, and these passages are discussed minutely in their proper place in this volume. Both are late accessions to the text, and seem only to confirm, and not to shake, the general tenor of the testimony of these Scriptures. But even if such were not the case, even if we could find no reason for otherwise interpreting such isolated scraps of evidence, it would still not affect the general logical situation. For what the

---

[1] It was with this thought that the writer opened the campaign against the liberal theology in an article in *The Outlook*, New York, November 17, 1900.

prevalent hypothesis must demand imperatively is not that there should be here and there at wide intervals, like oases in a desert, two or three, or half-a-dozen, more or less obscure references to an historical life of the Jesus; nay, but that the apostolic and immediately post-apostolic literature should everywhere blossom like the rose with this life and this human character. If such were the case, then we might affirm with some degree of confidence that the character in question must have been historical, in order to furnish the basis for such allusions and reminiscences. But such is as far as possible from being the case. It is the *general tenor* of these scriptures that must decide, and as to this there cannot be the slightest doubt in the mind of the unbiassed. This general tenor gives great dogmatic value to the *Death of Jesus as a God*, but does not recognise at all the *Life of Jesus as a Man*. The very few exceptions are trivial, and only apparent; but even if they were not trivial, and not merely apparent, it would still not matter—they could not weigh against the utterly unequivocal *general tenor*. Many more important isolated statements may have been, and confessedly have actually been, interpolated into the text, no one knows when or how, but the general tenor is unmistakable and determinative. *The general tenor cannot have been interpolated or corrupted.*[1]

36. In view of the extreme importance of this argument, it may be well to state it compactly as a *modus tollens*: If the Jesus of the New Testament had been a human personality who had so profoundly impressed his companions during his life that they became hallucinated immediately after his death, and successfully preached him as risen from the dead and reigning as supreme God in heaven, then such an astounding personality would have possessed the minds and hearts, the imagination and the memory, of these disciples, and their

---

[1] Recently an acute lawyer, a master of the theory of evidence, in speaking with the writer on this general subject, remarked with much emphasis: "A lawyer goes entirely according to the general spirit, scope, and intent of a document; he cares nothing for special isolated phrases and sentences. They may have gotten in there in a hundred ways, through carelessness of thought or expression. The law overrides all such, and goes straight for the general purport." This statement may be rather overstrong, but in the main it seems to be correct. The lawyer in question made no reference to the matter here debated, and has no known sympathy with the writer's views.

preaching and writings would have abounded in recollections of that wondrous life and character, in allusions to his words and deeds and in appeals to his authority. But this *consequent* is utterly false in the widest manner and in the highest degree; on the contrary, its complete opposite is true. Therefore *the antecedent is false.* Here we have made the sharpest issue possible, and we urgently invite the critics to try their teeth on this syllogism.

37. The only possible way of escape from this conclusion, which would seem to be the end of controversy, would appear to lie open in denying that we have any preaching or writing of these friends and companions of the Jesus. But even this denial will not in the least avail. Undoubtedly we have some reported preachments, and we have some writings. Whether these proceed immediately from the first disciples or only mediately through the means of disciples of disciples matters not. If the preaching, the writing, and, above all, the conversation of the primitive disciples abounded in matter taken from the life of the Jesus—as they would have done, according to the current critical theory; if the human personality of the Jesus dominated the first apostolic generation, then this same matter must have passed on—perhaps in augmented volume—into the consciousness and teaching of the next generation; this same human personality must have towered still higher in the imagination of the disciples of the first disciples. Indeed, it is the accepted view that the miracle-stories of the Gospels were mere exaggerations by the second or third generation of incidents natural enough in the narratives of the first generation. To the present writer this view seems to be wholly at fault, but its mere existence is enough to show that there is no escape from the foregoing conditional syllogism in the denial in question and the substitution of the post-apostolic for the apostolic age. Indeed, it is a profoundly significant fact—with which we shall often have to deal—that as we go back to older and older representations we find the human element in the *Jesusbild* fading visibly away, the divine coming more and more conspicuously to the front, until in proto-Mark we behold the manifest God; while, conversely, as we descend the stream of time, this same human element comes more and

more obtrusively to the light, the divine gradually retiring relatively, though not absolutely, into the background, until finally, in modern sentimentalisations, the divine Jesus, the vice-Jehovah of the Jew, the Saviour-God of the Gentile, is reduced to a mild-mannered rabbi or a benevolent dervish. That such has actually been the course of Gospel evolution shall be carefully proved in this volume.

METHOD OF THE FOURTH GOSPEL

38. To be sure, it is not for an instant forgotten or disguised that in this contention there is direct conflict with the prevailing view, as represented, for instance, by Schmiedel in his *Das vierte Evangelium*, according to which the simple humanity of the Synoptics is most subtly sublimed into divinity in the Fourth Gospel. Not for a moment would we deny that such criticism has a certain apparent justification. However, that justification is only apparent, and arises not so much from stressing the divine element in John's Gospel— which is undoubtedly present there, though in a peculiar Gnostic theosophic fashion different enough from the earlier directer concept—as from ignoring or minimising the human element, which is consciously and intentionally paraded by the Evangelist, and far more from overlooking the divine element in the Synoptics, especially in Mark. Precisely at this latter point seems to come to light the prime error of this liberal criticism, so learned and acute, and otherwise so often courageously just in its estimates. In fact, the whole theory of Synoptic interpretation calls for thoroughgoing revision, for which preparation is already largely and effectively made in the frequent concessions that meet us in such works as Schmiedel's, already mentioned. How clearly does this critic recognise that in the Synoptists there is certainly present an important and extensive element of symbolism even in the sayings that he recognises as perfectly genuine "words of the Lord"! Consider what he says of the "leaven of the Pharisees" and of the answer sent to John the Baptist. Repeatedly there forces itself into the mind of the critic the inexpugnable perception that it is simply impossible to understand the Synoptists without admitting that

much of their speech is pictorial and symbolic, and is merely turned into nonsense when it is taken literally. *At some time or other there has intervened a misunderstanding*, not distantly analogous to that far-reaching misunderstanding, that widespread disease of language, to which great philologists would trace back whole systems of mythology.

39. When did this malady begin to assail the Synoptic utterances? It is a question very difficult to answer, perhaps impossible. In different minds at different places the attack doubtless began at different times. Some robust intellects, like the greater Gnostic lights, resisted vigorously and saw clearly to the very last. Irenæus and Tertullian speak of such. With others the invasion was early, the resistance weak, and the confusion present from almost the very outset. Physicians tell us that the tubercle bacillus finds lodgment in nearly everyone very early—that we are all more or less tuberculosic. But in the great majority the disorder never becomes clinic; the defensive forces of the organism hold the morbid microbes in check. In others, alas! the enemy gets the upper hand through this or that contingency; it may be very early, it may be very late, in the life-period of the organism.

40. Somewhat similar, methinks, is the distemper of literalism, of materialising the spiritual, with which all Christianity has now lain on the couch of suffering for eighteen hundred years, attended by throngs of learned and able physicians, who have failed in their prognosis, failed in their treatment, failed everywhere, because from the start they were wrong in their diagnosis. Now at last the truth hidden for so many centuries, dimly divined here and there (but never demonstrated) by many superior spirits from time to time both in and out of the Church—now at last this irrepressible truth shines more and more clearly upon the critical intelligence, and illumines in streaks the New Testament from Matthew to Revelation. But its broad, diffuse light, unbroken and undimmed, has yet to be poured over the whole of these scriptures, especially over the Synoptics. In the case of the Fourth Gospel demonstration is easier. Especially the miracles, like the resurrection of Lazarus, the healing of the blind man, the restoration of the cripple at the pool, the feeding of the thousands, the first sign at Cana—all these

and others are such obvious symbolisms that it seems well-nigh impossible for any enlightened understanding " in a cool hour" to hesitate concerning them.

41. Nevertheless, though there can be no question about the general sense (however much variance as to details), yet the question still presses : Where and when did the misunderstanding begin? It is here that Schmiedel seems, perhaps, to have expressed himself too forcibly. He declares, in spread-type, that John "believed, in all his *accounts of miracles*, that it was *real events* with which he was dealing ; *only by way of supplement* did they become for him symbols of mere thoughts" (p. 88). It appears by no means certain —nay, not even probable—that John, being such a one, deluded himself in any such measure. On the contrary, the whole artistic scheme and method of his Gospel seems to be almost the opposite. The Evangelist had inherited a certain body of symbolism, of obviously pictorial doctrine, such as that the Jesus-cult gave sight to the blind, cured the cripple, raised the dead and corrupting Pagandom to life, cast its net about all the 153 nations of the world ; converted the mere water of Jewish purifications, rites, and ceremonies into vivifying wine of the Spirit ; fed all the souls of believers with abounding bread of life and fish of salvation—all this was but the common property of the Christian consciousness expressed in the familiar phrases of their technical religious dialect. *These notions he proceeded to work up into elaborate narrative.* He sought to make them more vivid and impressive by giving them historic setting and dramatic colouring. This it is that constitutes his main contribution to the representation. He by no means invented the spiritual content ; this was present from the very first, just as the essence, the idea, of a whole man is dynamically present in the microscopic germ, the body itself being but the later unfolding and investiture of that germ—Idea. So the Evangelist has invented no idea, no meaning of any miracle or saying ; all this he found ready at hand. But he has invented the investiture, the historic-dramatic garb in which he has clothed these ideas and meanings.

42. In many cases this seems to be clear as the sun ; in others it may appear less evident, most probably because our

knowledge of the originals from which the Evangelist drew is not so full in these cases. Consider the resurrection of Lazarus. No one needs to be told that the material event is entirely unhistorical; the evasions of many exegetes are merely melancholy and pitiable. But whence comes Lazarus? Clearly from the parable in Luke (xvi, 19-31). Here he seems to symbolise the poor pagan world, waiting for the crumbs to fall from the table of the Jew, rich in the law, the prophets, the promises and the oracles of God. The parable goes on to say that they who had Moses and the prophets would not believe though one (Lazarus) should rise from the dead. On this hint the Evangelist speaks. He recognises this signal truth of history, the stiff-necked rejection of the Jesus by the Semite; and he thinks it deserves to be thrown upon a broad and highly illumined dramatic canvas. Hence the whole story. Not for an instant does he deceive himself, or intend to deceive others. He is simply obeying a certain artistic instinct; he is pressing a metaphor, and, indeed, pressing it rather far.

43. Again, regard the miracle of Cana. In Mark and Matthew, in the primitive doctrine, the presence of the Jesus (the parousy of the new cult) had been spoken of as a wedding feast, the "new doctrine" as new wine that could not be put into old bottles. This hint, too, suffices: it must be elaborated into a story, improved at points, and, of course, slightly modified. Whatever other ideas could be easily and naturally worked up in the same story were also introduced, precisely as a painter, while holding fast his main idea, does not hesitate to introduce auxiliary figures and incidents upon his canvas, if only to fill in and enrich his composition.

44. It would seem to be almost a gratuitous offence to the intelligence of the reader to pursue such illustrations further. It should be added, however, that this, the distinctive, though not peculiar, method of John, is by no means confined to the miracles. It permeates, and even determines, this whole Gospel. Incidents and phrases of every kind strewn through earlier Gospels and expositions he seizes upon, amplifies, magnifies, dramatises at will. Of course, he is not without ideas of his own, and he is not slow to modify the given material in his own sense, to suit his own purposes, to

express his own notions; and he frequently enforces these latter by long expositions put into the mouth of Jesus, whereby he also guards his reader against any misunderstanding of his historisations. But he seems to have builded better than he knew, and to have produced a series of dramatic pictures so full of details, so rich in situations, and withal so lifelike in its characterisations, that, in spite of its obviously symbolic and unhistoric nature, it has deceived full fifty generations of beholders, who have thought to see in it the record of an eye-witness! "Withdraw the curtain," said Zeuxis to his rival, "that I may see the picture"; and Parrhasius smiled, for the curtain was the picture.

45. The twenty-first chapter of John, whether written by the same author or not, is certainly in the same spirit, and contains another excellent exemplification of the Johannine manner, in the account of the miraculous draught of fishes. Clearly it harks back to Luke v, 4–10, even as this itself harks back to Mark i, 17, Matthew iv, 19, and especially xiii, 47 (or their originals). But the writer says that, although there were so many, the net did not break. But how many? He will leave no doubt whatever as to his meaning, so he says there were 153 great fishes. Why not 152 or 154? What virtue in 153? Augustine, following Origen, saw distinctly that this number could not be an accident,[1] that it must mean something; and he found it to be a binomial coefficient, the sum of the natural numbers up to seventeen, and he directs his audience to perform the calculation on their fingers. But why up to seventeen rather than sixteen or eighteen? Because (he says) there were ten Commandments, and seven was the number of the Spirit, as of the Spirits of God, "decem propter legem," "septem propter Spiritum." Here he seems to lose himself in hopeless arbitrariness and artificiality. He might as well have added that $153 = 17 \times 9$, and there are *nine Muses*. Meaning there must be in the number, but it must not be trivial nor far to seek. On turning back to 2 Chronicles

---

[1] "Numquam hoc Dominus iuberet nisi aliquid significare vellet, quod nobis nosse expediret. Quid ergo pro magno poterit ad Jesum Christum pertinere, si pisces caperentur aut si non caperentur? Sed illa piscatio nostra erat significatio" (Serm. 248, i). For this whole observation concerning Augustine I must thank the instructive monograph of Professor E. A. Bechtel on *Finger Counting Among the Romans in the Fourth Century* (1909).

(ii, 16), the matter becomes clear. There it is said that "Solomon numbered all the strangers that were in the land of Israel......an hundred and fifty thousand and three thousand and six hundred." Now, the word "'eleph" ("'alaphîm"), here correctly rendered thousand (s), means often enough tribe (s) or clan (s), and on the basis of the text the Jews reckoned 153 as the number of the nations of the Gentiles.[1] These, then, are the great fishes gathered into the all-embracing net of the Church, of the new faith. On this point, it seems, there can hardly be any doubt. The numerical correspondence can scarcely be accidental, and the explanation it yields is perfectly simple, natural, and satisfactory.[2]

46. Perhaps no one will be minded to quarrel over the six hundred. As not a thousand or tribe, it could not be counted as a great fish. *De minimis non curat lex;* neither does a symbolist. However, it may be gravely suspected that the fraction was really in the mind of the writer, else it is hard to understand the triple use of "little fish" (ὀψάριον) (xxi, 9, 10, 13), and especially the "great fishes" of verse 11 —a phrase elsewhere found in Scripture only at Jonah i, 17.

---

[1] This statement rests upon a study made twenty years ago; but, though visualising now very vividly the page of my authority, I cannot recall the title of the work and so verify the implied reference. Accordingly, I do not now maintain the correctness of the statement, which is retained only because it stands in the German edition. It is a well-known fact, which I have elsewhere cited, that the Rabbis commonly regarded 72 or 70 as the number of the nations. The whole matter is trivial, for the general meaning of the symbolism is transparent. However, it seems to me clear that 153 must have been regarded by some as the number of the nations, in order to explain 153 as the number of species of fish; for surely this latter number must be significant, and whence could it come but from the passage in Chronicles?

[2] In all ages it has been felt that the number must be explained, but all other explanations seem forced or fanciful. Thus Cyril of Alexandria sees in it a symbol of the Church (100 for Gentiles, 50 for Jews) and the Trinity! That the number in some way imaged pagandom was very early perceived, and seems to have given rise to the notion, attributed by Jerome to the Cilician poet Oppian and others, that there were just 153 species of fish. Volkmar (*Himmelf. Mose*, 62) and Keim (*Jesus von Nazara*, III, 564), following Egli, must, of course, have another opinion, and sum the letters of Shimeon (71), Bar (22), Jonah (31), Kepha (29), and of Shimeon (71), Jochanna (53), Kepha (29). Still otherwise, Eisler, in *The Quest* (January, 1911). But what sense in any such gematria? Only the interpretation of Hengstenberg (II, 336) sets the mind at rest. However, for the purposes of this argument it is quite indifferent what symbolic interpretation be adopted; it is important only that some such interpretation is necessary; the literal interpretation is banal and ludicrous. True, Godet is still content therewith; but this fact merely registers the declension from Augustine.

THE PRIMITIVE MISUNDERSTANDING

47. Returning now to the contentions of Professor Schmiedel, we note that he raises the question "whether John held the miracle of loaves to have been an actual event." If so, then certainly "erroneously." "But inasmuch as there had been a time when it was still known that it was not an actual event, it is not entirely unthinkable that John also had inherited this perception from that time" (p. 84). This seems not only "not entirely unthinkable," but, in view of the thoroughly self-conscious method of the Evangelist, as just illustrated, it seems positively necessary, and the contradictory unthinkable. Strangely, however, Professor Schmiedel adds : "On the other hand, however, this, again, is scarcely probable, since the Synoptists in any case no longer had any such perception, and John wrote after them and derived from them." But here must be placed more than one question mark. Very possibly, in some parts of the Synoptists, the original correct view of all these incidents as symbols has been lost ; but in other parts it is still found distinctly preserved ; in others it may be doubtful. So, too, the fact that John wrote later proves nothing, as we have already seen. In more enlightened Gnostic circles the original symbolic sense of the Gospel narratives was long recognised ; and, as we have seen, traces of it may be found even in Jerome and Augustine. Thus one of the most patent of all symbols is found in the healing of the withered hand, on the Sabbath, in the Synagogue. Manifestly the man is Jewish Humanity, lamed by the letter of Jewish law and tradition, but restored to strength and power for good by the emancipating cult of the Jesus. So clear is this that even Jerome could not fail to see it. In commentary on the Matthæan parallel, he says : "Up to the advent of the Saviour, dry was the hand in the Synagogue of the Jews, and works of God were not done therein ; after he came to earth, the right hand was returned to the Jews that believed on the apostles, and was restored to service." Just at this point we think that Schmiedel has hardly done the Synoptists justice. He seems to have minimised unduly their consciousness of the symbolic nature

of their narratives. We suspect they saw matters far more clearly than he thinks, though we by no means would say there has been no such misunderstanding crystallised in the Gospels.

48. This, however, is not essential; whether the Evangelists or their successors misunderstood is comparatively unimportant. The weighty fact, distinctly admitted and even accented by Schmiedel, is that *somebody misunderstood :* (that *original symbolism* has been *misconstrued into history*.[1] Here is the very inmost nerve and core of this book and the exegetic theory it sets forth. We are glad to find such recognition, at least partial, of its correctness by such as Schmiedel, who, of course, represents many. His great predecessor, Volkmar, has made much of *Sinnbilder*. My own thoughts on the subject have been originated and developed entirely independently of Volkmar even, who, I am free to admit, has anticipated them at a number of points, as above, in explaining the withered hand (*Marcus* 206, *R. J.* 224). But Volkmar and Schmiedel and the rest are very far from pressing this just recognition to its logical issue. They have no doubt whatever that Jesus actually lived and spake; that his sayings were misunderstood, and hence the immense overgrowth of legend and thaumaturgy. Moreover, Schmiedel is convinced that such a story as that of Lazarus was in the first place actually misunderstood, and under that misunderstanding actually elaborated into the Johannine account. He would, in fact, relieve the Evangelist from the reproach of having invented the whole story; though he questions whether it need really be a reproach, on assuming that the resurrection was really "handed down" to him as a fact, some person—perhaps a woman!—having misunderstood the symbolic statement that Lazarus really arose, but still the Jews disbelieved. To our mind, this view, while right at so many points, is yet in its entirety incredible, for it reduces John to a mere cipher, whereas he was a deep thinker and a great literary artist, and it overlooks the intense self-consciousness

---

[1] That such misconstructions characterised early Christian thinking is well-known and sometimes frankly recognised. Says Conybeare (*Myth, Magic, and Morals*, p. 231): "Here we see turned into incident an allegory often employed by Philo." And again: "What is metaphor and allegory in Philo was turned into history by the Christians."

THE PRIMITIVE MISUNDERSTANDING 33

that his Gospel betrays in almost every verse. The central thought he did, indeed, take from Luke; the elaboration appears wholly and consciously his own.

49. But the main point of difference with Schmiedel concerns the *nine pillars*—a matter so important, as already observed, that in this book there is dedicated to it an entire chapter. Only one observation remains here to add—namely, that Schmiedel rightly recognises that the question of these pillars is a question of the standing or the falling of the whole modern critical theory of the purely human Jesus. "On the other hand, it is only such passages that give us surety that we may rely upon the Gospels in which they occur—*i.e.*, upon the first three—at least in some measure. Were such passages wholly wanting, it would be hard to make head against the contention that the Gospels showed us *everywhere* only the picture of a saint painted on a background of gold; and we could, therefore, by no means ever know how Jesus had in reality appeared—nay, perhaps, whether, indeed, he had ever lived at all" (p. 17). We shall see these seeming pillars crumble—that "such passages" are "wholly wanting."

50. It has been noted that it is very emphatically held by the school against which these pages are levelled that the Jesus spoke in pictures that were then misunderstood. The proof of this mode of utterance (though not, of course, of any literal speech of Jesus) lies open on nearly every page of the Gospels, according to which the parable was the favourite form of his speaking. The words of Mark (iv, 33, 34), "And with many such parables spake he the word unto them, as they were able to hear it; and without a parable spake he not unto them," cannot be too strongly emphasised. Here is unequivocal testimony that the primitive teaching was exclusively in symbols, and the significance of this fact is beyond estimation. For why was this earliest teaching thus clothed in symbols? To make it intelligible? Assuredly not! It is distinctly said that it had to be explained privately to the disciples (Mark iv, 34), and that it was to keep the multitude from understanding it. "Unto you is given the mystery of the kingdom of God: but unto them that are without, all things are done in parables: that seeing they may see, and

D

not perceive"; etc.[1] It appears hardly possible for language to be clearer. Here seems to be described a secret cult of a secret society; they understand each other as they speak in symbols, but it remains a mystery and incomprehensible to "those without"—to all but initiates, members of the kingdom of God.

"ESOTERISM" IN THE GOSPEL

51. Herewith there is laid bare not only the fact of the practically exclusive or at least prevailing use of symbols in the early cult, but also its reason as well: *It was the dialect of a secret order, intentionally unintelligible to outsiders.* There seems to be no other possible interpretation of this unambiguous passage. What says the orientalist, Wellhausen? Evidently he is bewildered; verse 10 (Mark iv) is an utter puzzle to him, and from his standpoint most naturally. "That would not agree with iv, 33, 36."......" That is hardly possible."......"Finally, the plural τὰς παραβολάς [the parables] can scarcely be understood at this point." Commenting on iv, 11, 12, he says: "A parable serves indeed primarily to visualise some higher truth by means of something more familiar. Since, however, the point must be sought and found, it serves also as well to excite attention and reflection as to put them to the test. That Jesus employed it for this purpose, just like Isaiah and other teachers, there can be no doubt. However, this is still not the esoterism that is implied in iv, 11, 12, and halfway also in iv, 33, 34. This esoterism is not merely excluded by iv, 21, but it also contradicts even the sense of the first parable; they all understand the word, but they take it in very unequal measure home to their hearts. Not even to mention the compassion of Jesus for the ὄχλοι [multitudes], which is elsewhere so conspicuous." These are words of gold, worth remembering by every student of the Gospels. They characterise and illustrate most admirably the spirit and procedure of the critical school. Note first that the real object of the parable, as given by Mark, is quite overlooked, and instead thereof

---

[1] Mk. iv. 11, Mt. xiii. 11, Luke viii. 10.

another entirely different object is assumed. Why? Only because it seems natural that Jesus would act like Isaiah and others! Then it is declared that he did so! An *a priori* concept of the Jesus is formed, and then it is held beyond all doubt that he lived up to that concept! What may not be proved by this method? Of course, Wellhausen is perfectly honest, and will not deny the obvious and necessary sense of verses 11, 12, 33, 34. He concedes it, but only in one word— "esoterism"—and then rejects it utterly. Why? Because he thinks it is excluded by verse 21, contradicts the sense of the first parable, and does not consist with the compassion of Jesus for the multitudes! Suppose all this were correct— what reason would it be for rejecting the obvious sense of the four verses? Why not just as well accept the four verses and reject the three reasons? The only answer is that Wellhausen must maintain his concept of the Jesus at all hazards; he accepts what he can reconcile therewith, he must reject what he cannot so reconcile. Hence he must and does reject the four verses. But would it not be far better to reject the concept? Methinks so, and this book shall prove it.

52. Meantime, what about the three reasons? Are they valid as against the four verses? Very far from it. The first is that the "esoterism" of the verse is excluded by verse 21; let us add verse 22, and it becomes clear that, so far from being excluded, it is necessarily implied by these verses 21, 22: "Is the lamp brought to be put under the bushel, or under the bed, and not to be put on the stand? For there is nothing hid save that it should be manifested; neither was anything made secret but that it should come to light. If any man hath ears to hear, let him hear." Could there be a plainer declaration that the primitive teaching *was* secret, that subsequently the teaching was to be made public? What other possible meaning can attach to such words as *hid* and *made secret, manifested* and *come to light?* The reference of verse 21 is also palpable: the Jesus doctrine is the lamp that is now to be put upon the stand to enlighten the world. Of course, the cult was not intended to remain, and did not, in fact, remain secret; it was at length brought into the open; the writer of these verses is evidently defending this publication, which had perhaps been criticised by some

of the more cautious as premature. Mark also the oracle, "If any man have ears to hear, let him hear." This points unerringly to a secret lore, clothed in words unintelligible to the outsider, but vocal to the instructor. It was like the Masonic grip, which only the Mason can recognise. The words mean simply *only members understand.* The following verses 24-34 confirm the foregoing at every point. They all point more or less directly at the same great fact, that the primitive teaching was secret and was intelligible only to initiates, yet that it was never meant to be so permanently, but only until the time was ripe to proclaim it openly to the world. So far, then, from contradicting verses 11, 12, as Wellhausen thinks, the following verses confirm them fully.

53. But Wellhausen holds that verses 11, 12 contradict the sense of the great first parable, according to which he thinks that "all understand the word, but take it very differently to heart." If, indeed, all understood it then, they were certainly far wiser than men are now. But it is not said that all understood the word; nothing like it is said; nothing is said whatever about understanding. The distinction Wellhausen makes between understanding and "enhearting" the word is foreign to the text and to the thought of the parabolist. "'Twere to consider too curiously, to consider so." Moreover, this interpretation is itself comparatively late; we have no reason to put it in line with the parable itself. Even if there were a contradiction, it would not break nor set aside the obvious meaning of verses 11, 12, for it would arise merely from the addition of another scribe, who need not have been in accord with the first. On the whole subject of this chiefest of the parables the reader is referred to the essay "The Sower Sows the Logos," in *Der vorchristliche Jesus*, where the older form of the parable is restored, and it is shown that the Logos was by no means the preached word, but the Spermatic Logos of ancient Stoic and Jewish philosophy, and that the parable was originally an allegory of Creation. Matthew hints very broadly at the new form and significance given the old Mashal in saying (xiii, 52), "Therefore every scribe discipled for the kingdom of heaven is like unto a man, a householder, who brings forth out of his treasure things new and things old"— a most instructive verse, from which it would clearly appear

"ESOTERISM" IN THE GOSPEL

that this instruction in parables, in the secret dialect of the "new doctrine," was a regular part of the discipling for the kingdom of heaven; and this latter can be nothing (in New Testament usage) but another name for the secret organisation itself, destined to embrace the whole earth converted to the knowledge and worship of the One God.

54. Lastly, Wellhausen finds the admitted esoterism of verses 11, 12, 33, 34 at variance with the compassion of Jesus for the multitudes (ὄχλοι, though Mark uses always—unless x, 1—the singular, ὄχλος, multitude). Well, what of it? Must we, therefore, reject or discredit these verses? Assuredly not. Wellhausen seems to think that Jesus could not have taught in parables unintelligible to the people, and to be afterwards explained to the disciples, because that would not have shown his compassion. *Yet this is precisely what he did*, unless we discredit not merely these verses, but the whole story—yea, the whole Gospel. For the parables are a fact, and since they have certainly puzzled the finest intellects of Christendom, from Origen and earlier to Jülicher, it is simply certain that they could not have cleared up matters for the peasantry of Galilee. The parable—the parable not understood by the multitude—is far more strongly attested than the compassion, and it is purely arbitrary to yield up the former in favour of the latter. Besides, the actual existence in the text of the explanation of the parable proves incontestably that it was originally conceived as a riddle by no means easy to interpret—in fact, impossible even for disciples unaided.

55. But does the compassion of which the Jesus-biographers make so very much really contradict the esoterism? Not in the least, save only in the critic's imagination. A close study of this compassion shows that it is always a divine, and not a human, attribute ascribed to the Jesus: it is the compassion of the new Jehovah, the healing divinity, for the *multitude*, the mass of humanity, idolatrous pagandom ignorant of the true God. This is clearly shown in the Greek word by which it is uniformly expressed—σπλαγχνίζομαι—which word Hellenises the Hebrew רחם (viscera, in plural), which is regularly and almost exclusively used in the Old Testament of Jehovah, just as the Greek equivalent is used specifically of the Jesus or the Lord. Never do we find ἐλεέω (though such a Gospel

favourite) used of the Jesus; never συμπάσχω, which would seem very natural; never οἰκτείρω; never μετριοπαθέω—only this most peculiar σπλαγχνίζομαι, which itself almost needs an interpreter, and for the obvious reason just given. What, then, is meant by this divine compassion? Plainly, it is the *pity of God upon the heathen world*, because of its polytheism, its straying afar from the worship of the true Deity. It is precisely the same pity that is ascribed to Jesus in the ancient pre-Christian Naassene Hymn quoted in *Der vorchristliche Jesus* (pp. 31, 32). It was exactly to save the pagan multitude from idolatry that Jesus came into the world—that the Jesus-cult (in the hymn called the *Gnosis*) was instituted and propagated.[1] Such is also the Gospel idea, as is clearly expressed in Mark vi, 34 and Matthew ix, 36: "He had compassion on them, because they were as sheep not having a shepherd: and he began to teach them many things." To suppose that a human Jesus actually beheld great multitudes following him, and pitied them as sheep scattered and torn, and then began to *teach them many things*, is unspeakably absurd. Manifestly, it was spiritual error and wandering from which they were suffering, and this was to be, and could be, corrected only by *teaching*. Elsewhere and frequently these same multitudes are represented as overwhelmed with all manner of bodily disease, "and he healed them all" (Matthew xii, 15). Clearly, such a state of virtually universal physical invalidism is wholly impossible. Clearly, the condition of the multitude in one case must be practically the same as in the other: if in Mark vi, 34 he expressed his compassion by *teaching them*, in Matthew xii, 15 he must have done the like also. Every index, then, points to the fact that it was spiritual maladies, and only spiritual, that he was healing, and healing by the "new doctrine." It was

---

[1] As late as Lactantius (A.D. 300) this was distinctly felt and avowed: "For when God saw that wickedness and cults of false gods had so prevailed throughout all lands that even his name was almost effaced from the memory of men (seeing that the Jews also, to whom alone the secret of God had been entrusted, forsaking the living God, ensnared by the deceits of demons, had turned aside to worshipping images, and would not, though rebuked by prophets, return to God), he sent his Son [Prince of Angels] as legate to men, that he might convert them from vain and impious cults unto knowledge and worship of the true God" (*Div. Instit.* iv. 14). That Lactantius regarded the "Son" as a mid-being between man and the Highest God is irrelevant.

spiritual blindness, deafness, lameness, leprosy, death, that he overcame, and all in the same way—by preaching the Gospel to the poor (the Gentiles). Here, then, is the full and satisfactory explanation of the much-misunderstood compassion of the Jesus, which in no wise opposes the esoterism of the primitive cult. There was no lack of sympathy in the early secrecy; it was in the main a prudential measure, well enough justified, but intended to be only temporary.

56. The objections of the Göttingen critic are, then, one and all, invalid at every point; they are completely vitiated by a false notion of the humanity of the Jesus. Moreover, they are bound up inextricably with that notion, and when they fall the notion itself goes down with them. For notice that the esoterism, the primitive secrecy of the cult, is unescapably involved in the four verses 11, 12, 33, 34, as Wellhausen himself admits. He finds himself driven to practical rejection of these verses, for the reasons we have examined. But none of these reasons are valid, and therefore the verses, and therewith the esoterism, the cult-secrecy, must stand. But such esoterism does flatly contradict the Jesus-character of the critics, which is thereby shown to be only caricature. As the logician of Marburg has so powerfully put it: "This Either-Or goes deep: either the Evangelists or Jesus." With perfect consistency and admirable honesty, he flatly rejects the Evangelists, as Wellhausen does, and declares: "He who places Jesus higher, who will not pluck out the diamond from his imperishable crown of honour,[1] he will break off a pebble from the bulwark of tradition and confess that the aim of the teaching in parables, in spite of Mark and the other Evangelists, is still simpler than the teaching itself" (*Die Gleichnissreden Jesu*, I. 148).

---

[1] In view of the indisputable fact that the critical humanisers of the Jesus cannot at all agree upon the most essential features of the "Jesusbild," it seems impossible at this point not to recall the famous lines of Milton :—

"The other shape,
If shape it might be call'd, that shape had none
Distinguishable in member, joint, or limb,
Or substance might be call'd that shadow seem'd,
For each seem'd either ;......
......what seem'd his head
The likeness of a kingly crown had on."

57. This seems to be one of the most important passages in modern criticism. The expositor of parables here openly admits that the liberal criticism at this most vital point must defy (*trotz*) Mark and the other Evangelists; he avows, in eloquent terms, that the dilemma is before us: either the Evangelists or Jesus; and he accepts the latter, rejecting the former. Yes, if we had to choose, there being no third choice, we should certainly prefer Jesus to the Evangelists— only *what* Jesus? Surely not the Jesus of the Evangelists themselves; in rejecting them you reject the Jesus they offer. No, it is not the Jesus of the Evangelists; it is *the Jesus-figure of the liberal critics* that stands opposed to the Evangelists in Jülicher's dilemma. This latter is a pure, noble, beautiful man—nothing else, nothing more. We admire it greatly, but we must at the same time recognise that it is not the Jesus; it is only "a liberal Jesus-idea." It is a mere chimera, a creature of fancy, not really thinkable, and wholly destitute of historic validity or justification. Without hesitancy we must reject this Jesus-figure, *but not therewith do we reject Jesus*. On the contrary, we substitute for Jülicher's dilemma a single lemma: we affirm and maintain that the only real Jesus is the Jesus of the Evangelists, the *purely divine Jesus*, who in the Gospels has "cast about him the shining semblance of a reverend man."

Let it, then, be repeated, with emphasis that can never be excessive, that these two representative liberal critics have here admitted unequivocally the final irreconcilability of their theory of the human Jesus with the fundamental New Testament fact of the teaching in parables. On the other hand, the theory of the divine Jesus and of his pre-Christian secret cult harmonises with this fact perfectly, and explains it completely.

58. On the basis, then, of this passage alone we may confidently affirm the primitive secrecy of the Jesus-cult. But it is very far from being alone. Over a score of times do we find reference to *secrecy* and *hiding* of something, the most of which can hardly refer to aught else than the primitive esoterism that is admittedly present in Mark iv, 11, 12, 33, 34. Of course, it is quite impossible to treat these passages in detail in this connection. Besides these there

are many other passages of similar implication. The word *mystery* (that which is known only to initiates) occurs twenty-seven times in the New Testament, especially often in 1 Corinthians, Ephesians, Colossians, Revelation. It seems impossible for it to refer to anything less than secret knowledge, hidden lore, though the reference may often be to something more included in this. The Apostle says (1 Cor. ii, 6, 7): "But we speak wisdom among the perfect"; "But we speak God's wisdom in mystery, the concealed wisdom, which God foreordained before the æons unto our glory, which none of the archons of this æon knew; for if they had known they had not crucified the Lord of Glory." We ask, with all possible directness and emphasis, Can it then be that a secret doctrine is not here in the mind of the epistolist? Assuredly not! Consider the words *mystery*, the *concealed wisdom*, and, most of all, the word *perfect*. The Greek term τέλειος cannot have reference to moral or spiritual perfection; surely no one will contend that there was such a class among Paul's converts, unto whom he discoursed this concealed wisdom in a mystery. The τέλειος or *perfect* was one that had reached the τέλος or end, that had completed the whole course of instruction in this secret lore; as one says of a Mason, that he has taken all the degrees; he might almost be termed a *graduate*. So ἱερὰ τέλεια are sacrifices perfect or performed with *all* the rites (Thuc. v, 47). It is (as it were) a graduate course that the epistolist has in mind. Moreover, we know that these "perfects" formed, among the Gnostics, a class of whom there is frequent talk in the heresiographers.

59. Furthermore, this passage seems to hint at still deeper matters, which cannot here be adequately discussed. Can it be that the authorities in Jerusalem are meant by "the archons of this æon that are coming to naught"? Improbably, as Schmiedel has clearly seen. They are rather the archons or kin to the archons so conspicuous in Gnostic cosmic theory. We may understand the crucifixion of Jesus, but who can understand the crucifixion (*by these archons*) of the Lord of Glory? Surely not Calvary nor any earthly mount, but the supernal hills of heaven, are in the lofty thought of the author. Consider also the remarkable

citation ("as it is written") in verse 9 : "Things which eye saw not, and ear heard not, and which entered not into the heart of man—whatsoever things God prepared for them that love him." This would apparently hark back to Empedocles : "Neither seen are these things by men, nor heard, nor by mind comprehended" (i, 8, 9a ; Plut. *Mor.* 17e) ; yet the last clause, "whatsoever," etc., seems to show that in descending to our epistolist it had received accession as well as modification *en route*, and Zacharias of Chrysopolis declares (*Harm. Evan.*, p. 343) that he had read the words in the Apocalypse of Elias. There appears no escape from the conclusion that they are cited from some such source, here regarded as authoritative. The epistolist, then, was familiar with such apocryphal works, and if he moved in such a circle of thought it seems hard to assign any limit to the extravagations of his fancy ; he may very well have dealt in mysteries, in which the deep Gnostic philosophy, "God's wisdom," was taught, both otherwise and by symbolic rites and ceremonies, one of which may very well have been some representation of the Divine Sufferer, the self-sacrifice of the Great High Priest after the order of Melchizedek, or the like.

60. There are not a few other Pauline passages that strongly suggest a similar state of the case, as those that speak of bearing about always the dying of the Jesus, of bearing the stigmata of the Jesus, of being con-crucified and consepulchred with Jesus—all of which seem to mean more than is commonly suspected. But this subject is too extensive to be broached at this stage of the discussion. Enough that the keenest exegetes are quite unable to agree upon the exposition of the whole passage under consideration, opposing one another at every point ; that they fail one and all to do any adequate justice to the solemnity and sublimity of the wide-circling thought of the author ; and that the evident general reference, lying on the open hand, is to the secrecy and mystery with which the early doctrine was taught in graded classes of catechumens.

61. Similar, too, seem to be the allusions in the Pastoral letters: "O Timothy, guard the deposit" (1 Tim. vi, 20); and again, "Guard the good deposit" (2 Tim. i, 14); and

again, "I am persuaded that he is able to guard my deposit unto that day" (2 Tim. i, 12). At the time of the composition of these Pastorals the propaganda had indeed long been preached more or less publicly; nevertheless, naturally enough the old forms of speech appear to have been still maintained.

62. Far more convincing, however, is the manifest force of the remarkable deliverance (Matthew x, 26, 27): "For nought is covered that shall not be revealed, and hidden that shall not be known. What I tell you in the darkness, speak ye in the light; and what ye hear in the ear, proclaim upon the housetops." All possibility of doubt is here finally and for ever excluded. Zahn and Holtzmann both recognise the reference to secret instruction, but apparently without feeling its significance. Zahn devotes about thirty pages, about thirteen hundred and fifty lines, to "The Co-operation of the Disciples," ix, 35–xi, 1, forty-seven verses, nearly twenty-seven lines per verse. But to this immensely important verse (27) he gives only six lines of text, really merely repeating the verse itself: "Jesus must, in order not to cut short the possibility of the efficacy of the Gospel, practise great reserve, must hide much from the light of publicity, and whisper it into the ears of the disciples. This they were —of course not now, but in the future, to which the discourse from verse 17 on refers—to speak out and preach in full publicity." Such is the comment of this orthodox exegete! One may well wonder what could have been the "much" that Jesus taught by "whisper in the ear," whereof we hear not the faintest hint "in the future," neither in the first nor in any following century. But verse 26 fares far worse at Zahn's dexterous hands: "But at the same time also the hostility towards Jesus and his disciples, now still possible only because of the concealment of the coming kingdom of heaven, will be brought to light, convicted, and condemned for its falseness and untenability." Here the reference of the hidden and covered, which is manifestly the same as in verse 27—namely, to the secret new doctrine—is turned away to the hostility of the world, an utterly impossible reference, as appears doubly clear on comparing the parallel in Mark iv, 21–23, already discussed. Holtzmann, one of the

sanest of all critics, merely speaks of "the passage of the truth from the narrower into the wider circle." Both these treatments, if such they may be called, merely exhibit the despair of exegesis. The passages cannot be explained on the ordinary suppositions, and yet their meaning is transparent. They voice the argument of the eager and enthusiastic party, who were urging the open proclamation of the cult, against the more timid policy of the conservatives, who still would continue to develop it in secrecy. Of course, there were two such parties in the Kingdom; there will always be progressives and stationaries while human nature remains what it is.

63. At this point in the Gospels the progressives have got the floor. But the others also make themselves heard. In Matthew xi, 12 we read: "But from the days of John the Baptist until now the kingdom of heaven suffereth violence, and men of violence take it by force." These words have been a standing puzzle to commentators, ancient as well as modern, who often "slip away over it lightly without touching"; and nothing better seems to have been said than Wetstein's word concerning these Stormers: "I understand them, therefore, to be publicans and soldiers." Zahn admits: "The movement of thought must, to be sure, remain dark as long as we retain the ordinary passive meaning of βιάζεται [*vim patitur, cogitur*]." Hence, "βιάζεται must rather have the very common intransitive sense of *use power, press forward* or *press in with power.*" "With power like a storm-wind[1] it comes upon us, with might it bursts in." Certainly, βιάζεται often means as much; but Holtzmann is right in declaring, "the medial signification, possible in itself, is wrecked on the explanatory clause, 'the men of violence take it by force.'" Such has always been the verdict of common sense, which even Zahn defies in vain. But he is right in holding the movement of thought then to be obscure, and Weizsäcker is justified in throwing the whole verse into parenthesis. However, in the light of the foregoing

---

[1] It is the "Kingdom" of which Zahn is speaking!—the same Kingdom that grows stilly and steadily as the mustard plant, invisibly as the hidden leaven, the Kingdom that "cometh not with *observation.*" Here in the New World we find it discreet to *observe* these "storm-winds" rather carefully.

discussion it does not seem very dark. The violent seem to be the progressives, who insisted on immediate proclamation of the Kingdom, on coming boldly into the open, instead of any longer maintaining the old policy of secrecy. A powerful representative of this radical party might have been John the Baptist; and the conservative seems rather to complain that since John's day the radicals are overmastering the Kingdom, are obtaining the upper hand. However this may be, one thing appears now made perfectly clear—namely, that the original propaganda was a secret one, that it was whispered into the ear long before it was proclaimed on the housetops.

64. It remains only to add that this secrecy was maintained in some measure for many years, for generations even. Especially in the Gnostic portions of the New Testament we meet with the word *mystery;* and in the Twin Epistles, Ephesians and Colossians, it is found six and four times respectively. In the refutations of the heresiographers we find the Gnostics dealing continually in mysteries and secret lore. It seems superfluous to make references, but it may be permitted to quote Epiphanius (*Hær.* lxii, 2) concerning the "so-called Egyptian Gospel": "For in it many such things are reported as in a corner, mysterywise, from countenance of the Saviour." Also in the Gospel (John xix, 38) we read of one Joseph, who was a disciple, but secretly, for fear of the Jews. Even in so late an author as Origen may be found many references to the secret worship and the "mysteries" of the Christians. Thus, in *C. Cels.* iii, 59: "Then, and not till then, we invite them to our mysteries (τελετάς). For we speak wisdom among the perfect (τελείοις)."

CONTENT OF THE GOSPEL

65. We are now brought face to face with a question of vital interest and importance: Why, then, was this Jesus-cult originally secret, and expressed in such guarded parabolic terms as made it unintelligible to the multitude? To answer this we must first propound and answer another query, even more significant and fundamental: What was the essence, the central idea and active principle, of the cult itself? To this latter we answer directly and immediately: It

was a *Protest against Idolatry;* it was a *Crusade for Monotheism.*

66. The proofs of this last proposition are various and abundant. The one that first impressed the mind of the writer is found in a consideration of the general spirit of the apologists. Consider, for instance, Athenagoras—177 A.D. (?) —who seems to represent Christian apology at its best. Of what does his plea consist? Practically of an assault upon the prevailing polytheism. After three or four pages of introduction, in which he protests against the condemnation of Christians for the mere name, Athenagoras proceeds to answer the charges brought against them, of which he mentions three—atheism, Thyestean banquets, Œdipodean intercourse. He then advances to an elaborate refutation of the first, showing that Christian doctrine does acknowledge one God, who has made all things through the Logos; that poets and philosophers alike testify to this unity of the Godhead, to which Christians add the witness of the prophets; that polytheism is intrinsically absurd, as attested by these Hebrew prophets; that Christians cannot be atheists, since they acknowledge one God, increate, eternal, invisible, impassible, incomprehensible, illimitable, etc., who has created the universe through his Logos, also called his Son for good reasons; who admit also the Holy Spirit, effluent from and recurrent to God like a ray of the sun. He further shows that the moral maxims and practice of Christians, particularly as to enemies, confute the charge of atheism; and he explains why they offer no sacrifice to God the Framer of the Universe. He then explains why Christians cannot worship the local gods, like others, who do not distinguish God from matter, and why they cannot worship the Universe. He then comes to closer attack upon the gods, showing their names and images to be recent; that they are themselves creatures, as the poets confess; that the representations of them are absurd; that the poets describe them as gross and impure; that the physical interpretations of the myths are vain, since in any case such nature-processes are not gods; and then he criticises Thales and Plato (and pseudo-Plato). He then discourses at length of demons, whom he regards as the active principles in idolatry. " They who draw men to

idols, then, are the aforesaid demons, who are eager for the blood of sacrifices, and lick them; but the gods that please the multitude, and whose names are given to the images, were men, as may be learned from their history. And that it is the demons that act under their name is proved by the nature of their operations." He amplifies this doctrine of the allurement of demons to idolatry, and insists that the names of gods were derived from men, and calls the poets to witness, and finally attempts to show why divinity was ascribed to men, concluding that "we are not atheists, since we acknowledge God the Maker of this Universe, and his Logos." In six or seven pages he then briefly refutes the other two charges. So, then, almost precisely three-fourths of this plea (chs. iv–xxx) is consecrated to an attack on polytheism and a defence of Christian monotheism, the remaining one-fourth being given up to prologue (chs. i–iii), minor charges, and epilogue (chs. xxxi–xxxvi). Virtually the whole argument is occupied with monotheism *versus* polytheism. Most noteworthy is it that there is no mention or remote hint of any New Testament history. There are repeated assonances to the Gospels (as to Matthew v, 46; Luke vi, 32–34; Matthew v, 44, 45; Luke vi, 27, 28; Matthew v, 28; Matthew xxii, 39; Matthew xix, 9); but, strangely, the only sign of citation is *says* (φησί), where the understood subject is the Logos; for once it stands: "For again the Logos says to us, 'If anyone kiss a second time because it has given him pleasure, [he sins]'; adding, 'Therefore, the kiss, or rather the salutation, should be given with the greatest care, since, if there be mixed with it the least defilement of thought, it excludes us from eternal life.'" The word "again" shows that in the previous quotation in the same chapter the understood subject of the *says* (φησί) was the same Logos. Evidently the apologist has drawn from fountains unknown to us. The Christianity of Athenagoras appears in this plea to consist practically of a philosophic monotheism tempered with some familiar theories, Stoic and other, about the Logos and the Spirit, and with some acquaintance with old-Christian literature.

67. Turn now to the *Apology and Acts of Apollonius*, who is supposed to have suffered about A.D. 185. The story is

nearly the same; his answers to the Prefect are mainly a bold attack on the prevailing idolatry. But he adds that "The Logos *of* God, the Saviour of souls and of bodies, became man in Judea and fulfilled all righteousness," etc. He adds also the invaluable verse 40: "But also one of the Greek philosophers said: The just man shall be tortured, he shall be spat upon, and last of all he shall be crucified." The reference is, of course, to Plato (*Rep.* II, 361 D), and shows clearly that this passage was in the Christian consciousness that wrought out the story of the Passion. The liberal critic does not hesitate, when he finds something done "that it might be fulfilled which was spoken by the prophet," to interpret these words strictly; to declare that the incident was invented to fulfil the prophecy. Precisely so here we have a prophecy by the greatest of the Greek seers, and the incident framed to fulfil it. It is noteworthy that, according to Harnack, no other reference to this celebrated passage is found in old-Christian literature.[1] Why? Because Christians were not familiar with it? Impossible. The silence of the Christians was intentional, and the reason is obvious. The passage was tell-tale. Similarly we are to understand their silence about the pre-Christian Nasarenes and many other lions that were safest when asleep.

68. We return from this important digression to the Apologies. Consider now that of Aristides, famous in antiquity, as witnessed in many ways—by its use in Barlaam and Josaphat, its apparent use by Celsus and by Justin, and by the mention of it by Eusebius in *Hist. Eccl.* and in *Chron.* Here the case is even more evident. In this apparently earliest Apology there is virtually nothing but a most elaborate attack upon the whole system of ancient polytheism, of Barbarians and Greeks, and, most remarkably, even of the Jews.

> The Jews then say that God is one, creator of all and almighty; and that it is not proper for us that anything else should be worshipped, but this God only. And in this they appear to be much nearer to the truth than all the peoples, in that they worship God

---

[1] But it seems to have been in the mind of James, who says (v, 6): "Ye condemned, ye murdered, the Just; he resists you not"; and of Justin, when he says (*Dial.* 16 B): "Ye slew the Just One." This title, "the Just," seems to hark back to the *Republic*, but may have been transferred from Israel.

more exceedingly, and not his works......Nevertheless they, too, have gone astray from accurate knowledge, and they suppose in their minds that they are serving God ; but in the methods of their actions their service is to angels, and not to God, in that they observe Sabbaths and new moons, and the Passover, and the great fast, and the fast, and circumcision, and cleanness of meats, which things not even thus have they perfectly observed.

Amazingly the Christian Aristides attacks the Jews as not being yet quite monotheistic enough ! He continues :—

> Now the Christians, O King, by going about and seeking, have found the truth ; and, as we have comprehended from their writings, they are nearer to the truth and to exact knowledge than the rest of the peoples. For they know and believe in God, the Maker of heaven and earth, in whom are all things and from whom are all things ; he who has no other God as his fellow ; from whom they have received those Commandments, etc.

There is no reference in aught that follows or in the whole Apology to the *New Testament or to the evangelic life of Jesus*.[1]

69. There is, indeed, a so-called Christologic passage, which varies so widely in the Greek, Syriac, and Latin versions that little confidence can be put in any of the text forms. We may metaphrase the Greek thus :—

> But the Christians are descended from the Lord Jesus Christ. But this, the Son of the God the Most High, is confessed in [by] Holy Spirit [as] from heaven descended for the salvation of men and of a virgin holy born, both inseminally and incorruptibly, flesh assumed and appeared plain to men, *in order that from the polytheistic error he might recall them*. And having fulfilled his wondrous dispensation, by a cross death he tasted by voluntary counsel according to mighty dispensation ; and after three days he came back to life and into heavens ascended. Of whom the fame of the Parousy from the (among them so-called) Evangelic Holy Scripture it is possible for thee to know, O King, if thou light thereon. This one had twelve disciples who, after his ascent into [the] heavens, went out into the eparchies of the habitable [earth] and taught his greatness,

---

[1] It is worth remark that the Greek text indeed declares, "The Jews betrayed to Pilate," but not the Syriac. That the Greek text has suffered at this point seems corroborated by the fact that it has been transferred to chap. xiv from its proper position in chap. ii. It appears likewise plain that in the Syriac the original description of the Christians consisted of the single first sentence, as in the parallel descriptions of Barbarians, Gentiles, and Jews. The following christologic passage looks like an afterthought. But the text-critical question is too intricate for discussion here. Compare the thorough work of Geffcken, *Zwei gnechische Apologeten.*

E

even as one of them went round these lands of ours preaching the dogma of the truth. Whence those still yet ministering to the righteousness of their preaching are called Christians.

70. Critics discern in this important passage the beginnings of a creed, the Apostolicum. We are concerned only with two or three observations. First, the use of the word ὁμολογεῖται (is confessed, allowed, admitted). The writer seems conscious that he is not affirming an historic fact, but merely something that is *agreed on* or *granted*—a kind of postulate of faith. Similarly in the Syriac version it reads: "And *it is said* that God came down from heaven and from a Hebrew virgin took and clad himself in flesh"; whereas in the later Armenian and Latin versions all this is declared as fact—there is no such modification as "it is said" or "confessed." Secondly, we note the unequivocal statement of the reasons for the incarnation and manifestation of this Son of God the Most High: *In order that from the polytheistic error he might recall them.*[1] Such, then, seems to have been the original conception of the mission of the Jesus or the Jesus-cult—namely, *the overthrow of idolatry*, as even Origen much later attests scores of times.[2] Very characteristically, we find precisely these words omitted from the later Syriac, Armenian, and Latin versions. They told their story too plainly. Thirdly, the term "Parousy," ordinarily taken to mean the "second" coming, is here properly used of the one presence of the Jesus in the flesh, as detailed in the Gospels. The "second" coming is a later fancy. Fourthly, "Throughout this great Christological passage it is worth noting how the actual phrases of the New Testament are not introduced" (J. Armitage Robinson, p. 84).

71. It would seem, then, that the testimony of this Apology, dating apparently from "the early years of the reign of Antoninus Pius" (Harris), *is strongly and unambiguously* in favour of our thesis, that the prime movement of the propaganda was distinctly and especially against the prevailing polytheism.

72. What now says the Martyr? Two Apologies go under his name, apparently modelled in a measure on others

---

[1] ὅπως ἐκ τῆς πολυθέου πλάνης αὐτοὺς ἀνακαλέσηται.
[2] Still later, Lactantius. See p. 38, footnote.

CONTENT OF THE GOSPEL

that preceded, as that of Aristides. These Apologies speak of a great variety of matters in rather disorderly fashion. The plane of intelligence is sensibly lower than in the pleas of Aristides and Athenagoras. Great attention is given to a very fantastic exegesis of the Old Testament in support of the Christian doctrines championed. The general position of Justin is that the Old Testament prefigures the Christian dispensation in a thousand ways, and that all of it has been or will be fulfilled or repeated in Christian history. "Since, then, all things that have already happened we proved to have been predicted by the prophets before they happened, it is necessary also concerning the things similarly predicted but yet going to happen to have faith that surely they will happen. For in what way the things that have already happened, having been predicted and being unknown, came to pass, in the same way also the rest, even though they be unknown and disbelieved, shall come to pass" (i, 52). Of course, we cannot dwell on any such theory. It is only necessary to observe that Justin does not fail to attack idolatry vigorously, and that he states explicitly that the mission of the Jesus was "for the sake of believing men, and for the destruction of demons" (ii, 6). Inasmuch as his witness on this and other points is elsewhere discussed minutely in this volume, it may be passed over here with the general observation that it accords with the thesis we are defending.

73. We pass now to the Exhortation of Clemens Alexandrinus (Λόγος προτρεπτικὸς πρὸς Ἕλληνας), and we find it consists almost entirely of a rather wordy but withal eloquent protest against Greek polytheism and a recommendation to accept in its stead the worship of the one God and his Logos, which is evidently only an aspect of God. We note particularly the mission of his "Song": "But not such my song, that comes to loose and that not slowly the bitter bondage of the tyrannising demons, and as leading us back to the mild and man-loving yoke of the worship of God (τῆς θεοσεβείας), again to heaven recalls those that to earth had been prostrated (ἐρριμμένους)." Note carefully the Greek word, for it is precisely that used by Matthew (ix, 36) to describe the forlorn condition of the Galilean multitude likened to harassed

sheep. Clement here employs it to describe the condition of the Greeks, led away by their poets to the degrading worship of "idols," of "blocks of wood and stone"—*i.e.*, "statues and images"; and so subjected to the "yoke of extremest bondage" "of the tyrannising demons." It is needless to pursue this thought further. Clement's testimony is the strongest possible—that he considered Christianity, at least the original Christian movement, as a Crusade, as a Holy War, against the stupefying idolatry of the Empire, conceived as the worship of demons. This was the very essence of his conception. The doctrine of the Logos was with him far from unimportant, but it was secondary, and disturbed his monotheism no more than the same doctrine disturbed the monotheism of Philo. How absolutely Clement identifies[1] Jesus, the Word, and the Christ (as mere aspects) with Deity is vividly shown in this sentence : " Now John, the herald of the Logos, for this cause exhorted to become ready for God's the Christ's Parousy (εἰς θεοῦ τοῦ χριστοῦ παρουσίαν)." Of course, he also speaks of this eternal Logos as having appeared to men and even as "become man." Remarkable is his expression : " Verily I say, the Logos, the Logos of God, having become man (ναί φημι ὁ Λόγος ὁ τοῦ θεοῦ ἄνθρωπος γενόμενος)." This is mentioned merely to show that we are not suppressing nor neglecting (though not discussing) the Christology of Clement—not that it bears on our argument.

74. We pass now to the celebrated *Octavius* of Minucius Felix, written at latest before the end of the second century. The testimony of this Ciceronian dialogue is as full and explicit as the most exacting could desire. The reasoning by which Cæcilius is converted is virtually nothing but a plea for the purest monotheism as opposed to the prevalent polytheism. This monotheism is affirmed and re-affirmed, is urged and re-urged, in the strongest possible terms. Of course, it was necessary to repel the slanders current in regard to the morals and worship of the Christians, to wash

---

[1] For similar bold identifications of these Ideas and Beings compare Col. ii, 2, "unto full knowledge of the mystery of (the) God Christ (τοῦ θεοῦ χριστοῦ)"; Titus ii, 13, "looking unto the......appearing of our great God and Saviour Jesus Christ"; Jude 25, "to (the) only God our Saviour." So, too, Clement himself, referring to Psalms xxxiv, 8, quotes Paul as pleading: "Taste and see that Christ is God (ὅτι χριστὸς ὁ θεός)."

away the stain of Cæcilius' bitter reproaches in the waters of truth ; but this flat denial cuts no great figure in the discussion. It is on the Christian monotheism as against the absurd and degrading Pagan polytheism that the whole high argument turns. "Nor seek a name for God, for God is his name......for God, who is alone, God is the one and only name (Nec nomen Deo quæras : Deus nomen est...... Deo, qui solus est, Dei vocabulum totum est)." Referring to the fact that the people in prayer say merely "God," he asks : "Is that the natural speech of the people, or the formula of the confessing Christian ? (Vulgi iste naturalis sermo est, an Christiani confitentis oratio ?)" "Therefore neither from dead men (do) Gods (arise), since God cannot die, nor from men born, since all dies that is born : divine, however, is that which has no rising nor setting." Enough. Octavius is a pure monotheist, nothing less and nothing more. He fights the battle of Christianity as the battle of the One God against the many gods of Rome. He never hints at any New Testament story, nor even at an incipient creed or Apostolic symbol. And with such weapons, and only such, he converts the polytheist Cæcilius. It seems impossible there should be a more exact proof of our fundamental thesis.

75. If now we turn to Tatian's *Address to Greeks*, to Justin's *Exhortation to Greeks*, to the three books of Theophilus to Autolycus, we find one and the same story, the one already so often repeated. It would be wearisome and superfluous to dwell on these, but it is interesting to note Tatian's account of his own conversion (c. 29). It was effected not at all, as we should imagine, by preaching of the cross and of the incomparable life in Galilee, but by study of certain "barbaric scriptures" (Jewish), containing among prophecies and excellent precepts the "Declaration of the Government of the universe as centred in one Being," scriptures that "put an end to the slavery that is in the world, and rescue us from a multiplicity of rulers and ten thousand tyrants"—these are, of course, the "tyrannising demons" of Clement, the divinities of the pagan world, as Tatian repeatedly affirms. Quite similarly was Theophilus converted, according to his own account (Bk. 1, c. 14), nor

can we think of Justin's conversion as different. One or two phrases from Theophilus are worth quoting. Of God he says: "If I call him Logos, I name but his sovereignty." Again: "Entrust yourself to the Physician, and he will couch the eyes of your soul and of your heart. Who is the Physician? God, who heals and makes alive through his word and wisdom."

76. Up to this point the testimony of Origen, as being considerably later (A.D. 250), has not been mentioned. But it is altogether too important to be omitted. In his work *Against Celsus*, on the whole the ablest Apology for Christianity ever published, he presents the case in every aspect that offered itself to his extraordinarily comprehensive and wide-ranging intelligence. Yet nowhere does he betray any consciousness of the modern point of view, nowhere does he advance the human personality of Jesus to the front, nowhere does he ground any argument upon its uniqueness or even its superiority. But everywhere he stresses the sole rationality of monotheism, everywhere he is arguing against the error of polytheism, everywhere he is contending that the heathen gods are demons, that idolatry is demon-worship, to overthrow which and to lead humanity back to the one true God is the especial and peculiar mission of Jesus and the Jesus-cult. Repeatedly he quotes the Septuagint version of Ps. xcvi, 5: "For all the gods of the heathen are demons." In iv, 32 he speaks of Jesus as "having overthrown the doctrine about demons on earth"; in vii, 17 he sees "pledges of the demolition of the devil in those who, through the coming of Jesus, are everywhere escaping from the demons holding them down, and through deliverance from bondage under demons have dedicated themselves to God, etc." *Quid multa?* That Origen conceived of Christianity and the mission of Jesus as primarily intended to recall the heathen world from the great error and disease of the demon-worship of polytheism back to the faith and service of the one true God, is superfluously manifest in every book and almost in every chapter of this chief of all Apologies.

77. Herewith, then, we close the argument derived from the Apologists.[1] It seems hardly possible to imagine it more

---

[1] Their testimony might, indeed, be produced at much greater length; but no attempt is here made to present it fully.

CONTENT OF THE GOSPEL 55

cogent, more explicit, more self-consistent, more absolutely demonstrative. We must remember that the Apologists are not arguing with one another, not speaking a tongue that outsiders might not easily understand; but are reasoning with the heathen around them, and hence must be using such arguments as were common in the great controversy, must be presenting the staple proofs of the Christians in their high debate with pagandom. We may affirm, then, with the highest degree of certainty attainable in such matters, that the central and essential demonstration of the Christian was a vivid exhibition of the colossal absurdity of polytheism and a powerful appeal to the immanent monotheistic (monistic) instinct in every man.

78. On the negative side the silence of the Apologist is profoundly impressive. *He tells absolutely nothing whatever* of the beautiful pure human life in Galilee and Judæa; not a single incident has he to mention, not a single argument, not a single illustration, not a single exhortation, not a single suggestion—not a single motive has he drawn from that incomparable life that is supposed to have hallucinated the disciples and even the slaughter-breathing Saul. The modern minister, even the modern critic, at the distance of nineteen hundred years, fills all the buckets of his discourse from this clear-flowing, exhaustless well of the Jesus-personality and the Jesus-life. But the ancient Apologist under the Antonines, before the canon of the New Testament was formed, in debate with kings and emperors and philosophers and the intimates of his own circle, knows nothing whatever of this fountain. He draws never a drop from its waters; often he does not allude to it even remotely. Almost it would seem to exist for him, if at all, only as an esoteric and not as an exoteric doctrine. We do indeed find a few scant allusions to certain dogmas that were "confessed," but these are all of more or less metempirical nature, like the "mystery" in 1 Tim. iii, 16; we find no recognition whatever of any such human life as modern theology, both liberal and orthodox, lays at the basis of its whole New Testament theory.

79. Against this broad-sweeping averment, the vague references (even if they were far less vague) of Justin to

Memoirs of the Apostles cannot be called in evidence. We have seen that Justin had a theory according to which the Old Testament was an elaborate type, whose antitype must be found in Christian history; he argued not from actuality, but from necessity; such and such must have happened, therefore it did happen.[1] The testimony of such a theory is worth very little. Moreover, the text-critical question concerning Justin is very large and very difficult. The interpolations seem to be so extensive that any argument drawn from him alone must be received with exceeding caution.

80. We hold, then, that the general state of mind revealed in the Apologists, as shown in their virtually uniform method of procedure in controversy with their heathen neighbours, is forever and totally irreconcilable with the theory of the human life. If these men knew and accepted the Gospel story in its literal sense, if they believed in the human life of Jesus as the modern Christian and critic believes in it, then it is scarcely possible to understand why they ignored it so utterly in their debates with their fellows. The full force of this argument cannot be brought home to any man that is not acquainted at first hand with at least one of these apologies. No amount of citation will suffice. Let the reader, then, take down some one of them, as *Octavius*, and read it through carefully, and yield himself to the natural reaction; he will no longer have any doubt of the general correctness of the propositions here maintained.

81. We have digressed intentionally from the main thesis—namely, that primitive Christianity was essentially a revolt against the gods. The argument from the Apologists may be supplemented by a similar one drawn from the Acts of the Apostles, as, for instance, from Paul's speech on Mars' Hill. In this famous harangue the first nine verses move precisely along the lines of the apologists; it is nothing but monotheism *versus* polytheism. The tenth verse (verse 31) switches the thought off upon another track, and is inconsequential in its present context. Says Holtzmann (p. 393): "So also the

---

[1] Even so keen and capacious a mind as Origen's gave to the argument from prophecy easily the first place, and Chrysostom, commenting on Acts ii. 16, says none can be more cogent, since it "outweighs even the historical facts themselves." If these latter contradicted, so much the worse for them!

discourse of Paul takes a sudden turn at verse 31." As it stands, it is palpably unhistorical. This thought, however, we need not pursue further at this point, since we have given a separate and elaborate treatment of Acts (in a MS. not yet published).

82. Equally weighty are the considerations drawn from the Gospels themselves. In the activity of the Jesus and the apostles as there delineated, the one all-important moment is the *casting-out of demons*. Thus, in the commission of the apostles (Mark iii, 14, 15): "And he made Twelve......that they might be with him, and that he might send them forth to preach, and to have authority to cast out the demons"; (Matthew x, 1): "And having summoned his twelve disciples, he gave them authority over spirits unclean, to cast them out, and to heal every disease and every sickness." Again, in Luke x, 17-20, when the seventy (who certainly symbolise the general mission to heathendom) return and joyfully exclaim, "Lord, even the demons are subject to us in thy name," the answer is, "I was beholding the Satan like lightning falling from heaven." It seems amazing that anyone should hesitate an instant over the sense of these words. When we recall the fact that the early Christians uniformly understood the heathen gods to be demons, and uniformly represented the mission of the Jesus to be the overthrow of these demon-gods, it seems as clear as the sun at noon that this fall of Satan from heaven can be nothing less (and how could it possibly be anything more?) than the headlong ruin of polytheism, the complete triumph of the One Eternal God. It seems superfluous to insist on anything so palpable. All that is necessary is for the reader to dwell for a moment on these and similar passages, and let their obvious sense lay hold upon his mind. Let him also ask himself the near-lying question: If such be not the meaning of these verses, then what is their meaning? What other possible significance, that is not trivial, can they have? Can any rational man for a moment believe that the Saviour sent forth his apostles and disciples with such awful solemnity to heal the few lunatics that languished in Galilee? Is that the way the sublimest of teachers would found the new and true religion? And would he describe the cure of a few such

wretches as the downfall of Satan from heaven? Such an idea cannot command the least respect or attention. Are there any scholars that really entertain it? If so, *non ragioniam di lor*. At this point, then, our contention would seem to be so self-evident as to call for nothing but mere statement. Nevertheless, it is so supremely important in its consequences that it has been thought worth while to devote a separate section to its demonstration.

83. We may also look at the matter from another viewpoint. If by the expulsion of demons be meant the overthrow of the heathen gods, their dislodgment from the minds of their former servile worshippers, then this mighty task, certainly by far the greatest that the new propaganda could propose or could accomplish, and certainly by all odds the chiefest of all its actual achievements, this supreme task receives in the Gospels foremost and perfectly proper recognition—yea, in Acts x, 38 it is specified as *the* mission and activity of the Jesus. This, then, is perfectly what we should and must expect. It seems wholly inconceivable that the first propagators of a new religion, annihilating all others, should never make the slightest allusion to any of these, but should direct their chief attention to healing a few defectives, an enterprise merely philanthropic, impossible of any marked significance, and having in it no proper religious element or importance whatever. On the other hand, if the exorcisms be taken literally, if they do not symbolise the conquest of the pagan gods, then, indeed, in the Gospels, in the life, death, and teaching of the Jesus, in the foundation-laying of the new faith, we find no reference of any kind to the overtowering fact of idolatry, to the very state of the case with which the new religion was far more vitally and intentionally concerned than with any and all others. There is, in fact, an immense apparent vacuity in the Gospel, which must be filled, which is actually and completely filled by the hypothesis here set forth, and which can be filled in no other conceivable manner. It seems hardly reasonable to demand a more stringent verification of an hypothesis.

84. We now advance a step, and maintain that it is unthinkable that a great world-religious movement at that era

should not have been aimed first and foremost at the prevailing idolatry. For this latter lay directly across the path of any feasible religious reform. It was utterly absurd to talk of renovating the face of the earth ("The old things are passed away; behold, they are become new") as long as the prevalent polytheism remained unshaken. What other imaginable way lay open for God to "reconcile the world to himself" than by routing the pagan gods; by driving them out of man into the swine, their fitting habitation, and whelming all in the sea? Hence the sublime depiction in Mark v, 1-13. The notion that God was reconciling the world to himself by the conversion (to an unintelligible dogmatic system) of some individuals here and there is inexpressibly puerile; it is, in fact, Individualism run mad. The thought and schemes of the primitive preachers were incomparably grander.[1] They aimed—magnificently aimed—at the re-constitution of all society, at least in its religious aspects; and this involved, first and foremost, as a *sine qua non*, the overthrow of polytheism. In the light of this fact, the Apologies, which represent clearly the attitudes of Christian and Pagan towards each other, become perfectly intelligible; nay, more, we see distinctly how it was absolutely necessary for them to be just what they were. When in modern times a practical and zealous, not merely dreamy and speculative, reformer arises, like Luther or Calvin, or Knox or Fox, or even Parker or Eddy, it becomes unavoidable for him to assume some position with respect to the prevalent faith and worship. So, too, it was unavoidable in the case of the early Christian propagandists. Nor had they any choice of position. Their monotheistic dogma ran directly counter to the idolatry of the day, and between the two, from the very start, it was war to the knife, and the knife to the hilt. Hence the intensity of the struggle as soon as the propaganda was made public.

---

[1] At this point Ramsay's conception of the preaching of Paul presents an important element of correctness.

THE SECRET OF PRIMITIVE CHRISTIANITY

85. We may now also see clearly why the propaganda was at first a secret. This, too, was a necessity, but a necessity of prudence. Had the Christians from the start proclaimed their crusade against the gods, not in the ear, not in the dark, but in the light and on the housetops, they would very soon have been extinguished; for they would have come into instant conflict with the State authorities, which studiously tolerated the gods as the conservative forces of society, and they would have been suppressed speedily and effectively. Hence the extreme prudence that marked the early efforts of the missionaries. Hence, too, the admirable injunctions in Matthew x—a most important chapter, which no man can understand save on the hypothesis of the primitive secrecy of the cult, and that, too, a monotheistic cult of a holy war against idolatry. "Behold, I send you forth as sheep in the midst of wolves: be ye therefore wise as serpents, and harmless as doves." This maxim the early Christians seem to have laid close to heart, and it is really wonderful how successfully they avoided collision with the State authorities; it constitutes a high tribute to their general intelligence and the wisdom of their methods. Not until the second century, when their numbers had greatly multiplied, when they began to feel some confidence in their waxing strength, do they begin to lay aside the counsels of prudence, and attack polytheism more and more openly, and not unnaturally involve themselves in sharp conflict with the police, and finally bring down upon themselves systematic persecution.

86. It seems to have been this necessary secrecy of the cult and this imperative prudence in its first proclamation that forced upon the propagandists a distinct dialect, a parabolic or symbolic mode of speech, that is still preserved in our New Testament, especially in the Gospels, and has been the source of endless misunderstanding. Such is the esoterism that Wellhausen recognises in the famous four verses (Mark iv, 11, 12, 33, 34), and that meets us, in fact, at almost every turn as we pick our way through the earliest Christian literature. Such is the explanation, and the only possible explanation, of the parables, or at least of their

astonishing prominence in the speech of the Jesus. Even if we were to grant everything else to the modern critics, it would still remain for ever incomprehensible why any teacher should employ the parable to such an extraordinary extent and degree; above all, why he should teach intentionally in a manner that not even his intimate disciples, much less the multitude of outsiders, could understand. We must repeat with Jülicher: "Either the Evangelists or Jesus"—that is, the liberal "Jesusbild." This latter is absolutely and admittedly irreconcilable with the Evangelists. But these latter are equally irreconcilable with common sense, so long as they are understood literally. They must, then, be understood, not literally, but symbolically, esoterically, *precisely as they themselves demand* in those priceless four verses.

87. More specifically, we now see why the Gospels never speak of heathen gods and their overthrow, but so continually of the *casting-out of demons*. This phraseology was part and parcel of the parabolic dialect they had found it wise to use. It would have been rash, and might have been disastrous, to talk or even to write about the overthrow of Zeus and Apollo and Artemis and Minerva and Juno and Serapis and Isis and Attis and a legion of others. It was far safer, as well as far more forcible and poetic, to speak of Man as possessed by a legion of demons, who are expelled and annihilated by the omnipotent word of the Jesus, whereupon Man himself, clothed and in his right mind, seats himself (as a learner and follower) at the feet of his Saviour. That it was the especial mission of the new cult to vanquish the prevailing idolatry is expressed in symbolic terms of startling vividness in Mark i, 24. At the very opening of his ministry, as his first miracle, in Capernaum, the Jesus expels the demon, who, speaking in the plural, cries out: "What to us and thee, Jesus Nazarene? *Thou art come to destroy us.* We know thee who thou art, the Holy One of God." This demoniac, mark you, is in the synagogue, and very properly, because it was among the Hellenists, the half-Judaised Greeks and half-Grecised Jews, that the great movement took its origin.

88. We now arrive at the explanation of the name Jesus, which has triumphed over every other name under heaven. The original crusade, even down through the third

century, as the apologists witness, was against polytheism; and one might think that the bare doctrine of the one God, whose name is God, might have been brought forward, as, in fact, it is in *Octavius*. That, however, was not possible without making a more or less open attack on the countless gods; and this, we have just seen, was what prudence forbade as impracticable. If the new doctrine was to be expressed guardedly and symbolically, then nothing else lay nearly so nigh as to speak of the infinite error of humanity as a disease, as possession by demons, who were regarded as actual beings and the active principles in the gods themselves. The incitement to such a metaphor, if any were at all needed, was given in the Old Testament language, where the backsliding of Israel, his reversion to idolatry, is represented as a disease which Jehovah heals. But, in fact, the metaphor lay so close at hand that it could hardly have been avoided. If, now, this paganism, this possession by demons, was conceived as a disease, then whoso overthrew the paganism, expelled the demon, cured the disease, must be conceived as a healer, a physician, a Saviour. Of course, this same power was really God or the worship of God; but it was conceived personally, and in the symbolic dialect it had to be designated by a proper name and represented as a man, according to universal usage. But what should be the name? It needs little additional argument to show, for the considerations already brought forward have made clear, that the name to be preferred above all others was none else than the world-conquering name of Jesus. Both in its Greek and in its Hebrew form it was perfectly adapted to the end in view—to serve as a name for Deity under the aspect or person, not of King, nor Creator, nor Judge, nor even Father, but of the healing, the saving, God; and it is under precisely this aspect, which is at the same time an aspect of eternity, that he appears upon the scene in the Gospels, particularly the more primitive, as Mark, and there enacts the grand *rôle* of Salvation, of triumph over all the demon-gods of the earth.

89. It must not be supposed, however, that this highly pictorial representation would please every mind that was in hearty sympathy with the general idea. By no means. The diversity of individual natures is far too great. There were

doubtless many who would not fall in fully with this depiction, precisely because it had not originated with themselves. We all know the conundrum : What is a Professor? Answer : A man that has some other opinion. Doubtless there were many such among both Jews and Greeks, in whose Talmud and whose philosophies not a few opinions seem to have as their only *raison d'être* their difference from all others. Unless, then, we suppose human nature to have been entirely peculiar in those early Christian circles, we must be prepared to find many diverse representations of this same central concept of God as Saviour. In fact, we do find a very great diversity, even within the lids of the New Testament itself ; and as soon as we pass beyond this canon the diversity becomes almost measureless. So great, indeed, it is that nearly eighteen hundred years of firm ecclesiastical coercion have failed to reduce it to anything like harmony ; and over one hundred years of untiring efforts, of boundless learning, and piercing acumen have been unable to discover and exhibit the supposed original unity of a central personality. In fact, the differences penetrate to the very root of the whole doctrine, and leave absolutely nothing on which there is agreement beyond the one conception of the one God, as in some way and under some form coming to the rescue of afflicted and erring humanity.

90. These deep-reaching diversities seem to show of themselves convincingly that there was at the start no one commanding and all-compelling intellect or personality, but that many minds of many types, ranging from the highly sensuous, pictorial, and imaginative to the deeply pensive, subtly argumentative, and cosmic-philosophic, were from the very first at work upon the same great problem of a universal monotheistic religion. To be sure, there were not merely independent and widely separated points of view; there would also be many eclectics and syncretists, who recognised a certain amount of beauty or propriety or truth in alien doctrines, and sought to harmonise them—to fuse them together into one. Our New Testament scriptures are very largely the result of such well-meant efforts. A striking example is afforded by the fourth Gospel, which seeks to melt into one the representations of the Salvation-God as the eternal Logos

and as the Jesus of the Synoptists—with how much success it is needless to discuss.

91. It should be added that one form of speech was virtually necessitated by the essential nature of the whole movement as aimed at the overthrow of polytheism and the introduction everywhere of the worship of the one God. The goal of endeavour was to *make God known*,[1] to *reveal* him to men. In the new cult he was made known, was revealed; in one word, he *appeared to men*. But not only did he thus appear to men: in this appearance, in this revelation, in this new doctrine, he was (for purely pictorial and symbolic purposes and reasons already set forth) spoken of as a man, as going hither and thither proclaiming the new doctrine, as casting out demons, and performing the whole work of salvation that was actually accomplished by the cult itself. Thus, to take a striking illustration, when Gentile proselytes were admitted into the Kingdom on equal terms with the Jews, though some narrower conservatives at first opposed, the Jesus is represented as blessing "little ones" (as such proselytes or converts were called), and saying: "Suffer the little children to come unto me, and forbid them not, for of such is the kingdom of God." That the reference here is exclusively to such proselytes is elsewhere proved in this volume. Everyone must admit that the symbolic statement of this fact, as an act of the Jesus, is incomparably more impressive than any mere prosaic and literal statement could ever be.

92. But such metaphors carried with them an important corollary—namely, that the Jesus *appeared as a man, in the flesh*.[2] This corollary was merely a piece of poetic or pictorial consistency, and had no further historic validity than the original picture-phrase itself. However, when once a riotous imagination started on such a path there was no telling where it would stop. Some might be content with the

---

[1] Hence the genuine proto-Christian terms *Gnosis* and *Gnostic*. Knowledge of God and worship of God are the two pole-stars of the proto-Christian heavens.

[2] In fact, the idea of the Logos or Word dwelling in men had already been naturalised in extensive circles. "The habitation of the Word is Man" (*Odes of Soloman* xii, 11). It matters not to say with Harnack, "there is no thought here of the Hellenic Logos"—the passage from one to the other was too easy and tempting.

declaration that he appeared as man, appeared in the flesh; others would want to know where, how, and when, and answers would be supplied in varying fashion and in varying degrees of minuteness. Mark and John might resign themselves to silence concerning birth and infancy, while Matthew and Luke devised mutually exclusive pre-histories. But not only might it seem necessary to give an account of the birth, it would certainly in any case seem necessary to give some account of the departure from earth and return to heaven, whence he was in this fullness of time revealed. On this point there could not be so much diversity of fancy, though there might be a great deal. The notion of a Divine Sufferer, even of a dying God, was given in the ancient mythology, with which such students of religion, as the first Christians were, would naturally be acquainted. Still more, the famous Isaian passage on the suffering and death of the servant of Yahveh (Is. lii, 13–liii, 12) lay open at hand, nor could it nor did it fail to impress the earliest Christian consciousness and fancy, as the case of Philip and the Eunuch clearly shows (Acts viii, 27–40).

93. This was not all, however. Perhaps even more determinative was the wonderful passage in the *Republic* (II, 361 D), where they found vividly portrayed the persecution and crucifixion of the ideal Just One. Hence the Jesus could be called directly the Just. Once the death on the cross was elaborated in this great quasi-historic picture, the resurrection and ascension could not linger. To express this resurrection the same word, Anastasis, was used that had already been employed (it would seem) to denote the establishment or inauguration[1] of the new Saviour-God on the throne of the universe. Of course, the resurrection and ascension were not naturally conceived as two things, but as one, as a rising up and ascent to the heights of heaven. The previous use of the term Anastasis, in the sense of setting-up, explains why the resurrection was unnaturally distinguished from the ascension.—In the foregoing sketch we find expressed or implied all the elements of the primitive faith found in that earliest symbol, 1 Tim. iii, 16: "Confessedly

---

[1] Compare the essay "Anastasis" in *Der vorchristliche Jesus*.

great is the mystery of godliness: who was manifested in flesh, was justified in spirit, appeared to angels, was preached among Gentiles, was believed on in the world, was received up in glory." But it must be remembered that they who first sang these lines understood what they were singing, and were clearly conscious that the import was symbolic.

94. It could not be expected that an elaborate parable could be pursued to the end without falling into many contradictions, and even absurdities. All rhetoricians warn us not to press metaphors. In the Gospels the metaphor has been pressed rather hard, and with tremendous consequences to human history.

95. It is by no means forgotten that there are many other important notions in the Gospels, as of the Son of Man, the Son of God, and the Christ, which we have thus far not introduced by name. In some respects these are easy enough, in others not so easy to understand. No discussion of them is at present necessary, for they are in any and every case ideas and nothing else than ideas, conceptions of celestial beings. Whatever be their genesis, and however they were finally though imperfectly fused with the notion of the Jesus, the Saviour-God, it cannot affect seriously our general verdict upon the matter already treated. In particular, the marriage of the concept of the Jesus with that of the Christ, which seems in large measure the work of the Jewish scribe Saul, is a difficult problem of great interest. But its solution cannot disturb the results thus far attained. We may, then, postpone its treatment for the present.

96. In the development of the drama of salvation there were many mythologic elements that lay at hand, not a few venerable in their antiquity, descended from Nippur and Babylon, from the Tigris and the Euphrates, and possibly even from the Indus and the Ganges. It would be strange if these had not suggested or shaped or coloured some of the incidents and delineations and even thought-elements elaborated in the Gospels, in the New Testament, in early Christian literature, faith, and worship. The deep researches of Assyriologists in particular will doubtless bring more and more of these to light, and such illumination is most welcome and valuable. But it would be a mistake (in my opinion) to

ascribe to these more or less passive elements an originative or actively formative power. They were not themselves vivifying; they needed to be vivified. They lent themselves readily to the creative activity of the new spirit, the new teaching, the new religion. It was this creative idea that intussuscepted and assimilated them, and transformed them into the living tissue of the Gospel, the creed and the ritual, even as the formative idea of the organism seizes upon and converts into its own organic fibre the nutritive material that lies within its reach. It appears, then, forever inadmissible to explain Christianity from the Gilgamesh Epos or from Babel or India or elsewhere, though all of these may have contributed more or less food to the organic idea that has unfolded itself in the historic church and creed and scriptures. But for the germ, the growing idea, all of these elements and millions more would have continued to lie inert and lifeless, as they had lain for a thousand years.[1]

THE ACTIVE PRINCIPLE OF CHRISTIANITY

97. Do you ask what was this germ? The answer must be that already given: It was the monotheistic impulse, the instinct for unity that lies at the heart of all grand philosophy and all noble religion.

The Christian fathers did not err in dedicating so much time and thought to the doctrine of *Monarchy*, the sole sovereignty of God; nor was Schleiermacher wrong in saying of the chief of modern Monists that he was "full of religion and full of a holy spirit"; nor Novalis in calling him a "God-intoxicated man." The heart and soul of primal Christianity was an impassioned, sustained, and well-reasoned protest against the prevailing idolatry, as degrading, immoral,

---

[1] Compare my words in the *American Journal of Theology* (April, 1911, p. 265): "As the planet speeds sweeping round the sun it gathers up showers of meteoric masses, the dust of shattered worlds, and imbeds them in its own crust. So, too, as the great idea of the Jesus, the healing, saving, demon-expelling God, circled round through the circum-Mediterranean consciousness, it could hardly fail to attract and attach to itself many wandering fragments of dismembered faiths, and the identification of these may well engage the attention of the orientalist and the comparative philologist; but the nucleus and central mass of the 'new doctrine' would seem to lie nearer home, and need not be sought for on the banks of the Ganges or the Nile, in the Gilgamesh Epos or in the inscriptions of Crete."

irrational, and wholly unworthy of man, who was the sublimest creature in the universe, and ought to worship only the one supreme God, forever one, though revealed to man under a variety of aspects or persons; and it was precisely this plea for monotheism that won for the new religion its sudden and surprising victory.

98. But no germ can grow, or even live, unless the environment be favourable, and the degree of perfection in the development will depend in great measure on the degree of favour shown by the environment. If we apply this truism to the case in hand, we shall quickly perceive that all the conditions were present in the beginning of our era, or even before, in measure and degree never equalled, for the germination and growth of precisely such an idea as we have found embodied in Christianity. For it is well known and freely recognised that there was all around the Mediterranean an immense and intense yearning for a Saviour. The evidence is already printed, and accessible, and referred to, so that we need not dwell on the point longer.

99. Far more important is the fact that the existing conditions were such as to arouse the monotheistic instinct to almost feverish activity. As long as some kind of political independence, or at least separation, attached to geographical isolation or removal, and to racial or linguistic distinction, the dominion of local or ethnic gods was not deeply disturbed by the convulsions of war and the revolutions of empire. The intuition of the One, of whom even the planetary deities were only partial manifestations and embodiments, here and there asserted itself (as Delitzsch has taught us) thousands of years before among the elect by the rivers of Babylon. But only at wide intervals did such Teneriffe-peaks of thought shoot up above the dead level of the many waters of polytheism. Even amid the race-destroying transportations that formed part of the imperial policy of Asshur and Babel, the local gods held their seats unshaken; the new-comers were merely their new subjects, who adopted their cult and submitted themselves to their lordship. A striking example is afforded in 2 Kings xvii, 24–33, where the five nations transported to Samaria are taught "the manner of the God" of their new land, and learn to "fear

Yahveh," though still cherishing the cults of their elder gods. There was a powerful action and reaction at the appulse of Judæa and Persia, but the contact was brief and far from world-wide.

100. Far more significant every way were the planet-ranging conquests of Alexander. That overthrow of Asiatic empire and civilisation by Europe, the vehement refluence eastward of the wave of conquest that for so many centuries had rolled westward, the rout and ruin of the monstrous gods of the Orient before the beauteous divinities of Greek mythology—all this produced a religious fermentation profounder and more important than any political revolution. But the mighty work of Philip's warlike son was prematurely arrested, and his colossal empire fell instantly to pieces amid the strife of his successors.[1] Nevertheless, the spread of Hellenic thought, culture, and speech over all the east was a unifying agency of incalculable moment. To be sure, there was reaction as well as action: Greek culture was debased, Greek speech enervated, Greek ethics and religion corrupted by amalgamation.

101. Still more important—indeed, of decisive influence—were the all-subduing arms and the all-ordering law of Rome. The Roman conquests and, above all, the Roman peace involved the final confutation and condemnation of polytheism. For although the glorious gods of Greece might have been allowed, with some show of reason, to have triumphed over the grosser cults of Asia, yet no one could explain why they themselves, incomparable in beauty and unsurpassed in power, should go down before the borrowed forms and colourless abstractions of Italy. Besides, the universal empire of Rome and the universal intermingling of the peoples, coupled with the universal toleration on equal terms of all forms of faith and worship, not only made all religions known to all men, but at the same time made all of them nearly equally ridiculous. It was a general *reductio ad absurdum*. How could two priests, of Isis and of Artemis, exchange courtesies in the Forum without a smile?

---

[1] How powerful was the subsequent reaction of the religions of the East, Cumont has recently made clear in his *Les Religions orientales dans le Paganisme romain*.

102. Long before this, however, the widely-current philosophies of the pre-Socratics, of Plato, of Aristotle, of the Stoics and Epicureans, and of the later Academy, had completely undermined, and even overthrown, the national faiths in the minds of the cultured, and had even aroused a spirit of indignant rebellion against the degrading slavery imposed on them by the many-headed hydra of superstition, a feeling voiced in verses of immortal beauty by Lucretius, celebrating Epicurus as the deliverer of men.[1] But the contribution of philosophy towards the liberation of the human mind, great as it was, by no means sufficed; for it did not free the enslaved masses, for whom Protagoras and Democritus and Carneades were but the shadows of mighty names. The true Deliverer was yet to come.

103. How keenly this humiliating servitude to demons was felt by the ancient mind is amply attested by Christian as well as by profane writers. Through all the Apologies rings loud and clear the bugle-call to freedom. The same clarion note is heard in the New Testament. In Rom. viii, 19–21 we have a striking description of the state of heathendom (ἡ κτίσις, the creature, here evidently means the Gentile world, as in Mark xvi, 15, "Preach the Gospel to all the creature"; which equals Matthew xxviii, 19, "Disciple all the Gentiles")[2]: "For the yearning expectation of the creature awaits the revelation of the sons of God. For unto vanity the creature was subjected, not of its own will, but through Him that subjected it, in hope that the creature itself shall be freed from the slavery of corruption unto the freedom of the glory of the children of God. For we know that all the creature groans and travails in pain together until now." "Vanity" and the "slavery of corruption" mean here idolatry and polytheism, so fiercely assailed in the first chapter, verses 18–32. "Vanity," under many forms in

---

[1] Mallock in his paraphrase would almost outwing the Roman Eagle:—
"Him not the splintered lightnings, nor the roll
Of thunders daunted. Undismayed, his soul
Rose, and outsoared the thunder, plumbed the abyss,
And scanned the wheeling worlds from pole to pole."

[2] "In my name," as Conybeare seems brilliantly to prove from Eusebius that the earlier ante-Nicene text read (see Preuschen's *Zeitschrift*, 1901, 275-288; also Usener, *Rhn. Mus.*, 1902, 39 ff. *Contra*, Riggenbach, *Der trin. Tauf befehl*, 1903).

Hebrew, is a regular term for idols and idol-worship, and it is also used similarly in Acts xiv, 15; Eph. iv, 17. "Slavery of corruption" means clearly servitude to images, to corruptible stocks and stones, the same bondage against which we find such a powerful protest in Gal. iv, 8, 9, and elsewhere. "The glorious freedom" is nothing but monotheism, the service of the one true God, called the Truth in the Johannines, as in the famous oracle (viii, 32): "And ye shall know the Truth, and the Truth shall make you free." "What?" says an objector, "were not the Jews already the strictest monotheists?" Certainly, they *thought* so; but some enthusiastic Christians would not admit it, as we have already learned from the Apology of Aristides.[1] Neither will the Fourth Evangelist; he denies it in chap. viii, verse 42, and in verse 54 he declares: "Of whom ye say that he is your God, yet ye have not known him." In Gal. iv, 8, 9 Christianity and heathenism are directly opposed as "knowing God" and "not knowing God."

> 104.   Yet, Freedom! yet thy banner, torn, but flying,
>   Streams like the thunder-storm against the wind.

It is political freedom of which the Titan-poet speaks, at sight of whose banner "men have crowded the road to death as to a festival." It was a far more "glorious freedom of the sons of God" that the early Christians proclaimed; it was redemption from a far more terrible "tyranny of demons," which had trodden down humanity in dust and mire since the first syllable of recorded time. It would have been strange if such a banner had not been unfurled precisely at this crisis in the history of our race; it would have been strange if it had not aroused immense enthusiasm in all ranks of society; if it had not inspired its followers with a new sense of the dignity of man and the infinite worth of personality and the human soul, as well as of the universal Fatherhood of God and brotherhood of man, ideas which the ablest critics have regarded as most nearly expressing the essence of Christianity. But these critics have never logically related these ideas to the early propaganda, because they have never thought of this propaganda as a prudently veiled and

---

[1] And from Lactantius. See footnote, p. 38.

cautiously guarded, but none the less intense and determined, crusade against idolatry.

105. If such a rebellion against polytheism was natural, and even inevitable, under the given conditions, it was no less certain that it should find its focus in the Dispersion, among the proselytising Jews and their Gentile proselytes, in that border region where the Jew and the Greek joined hands. For the Jew was unquestionably the one conspicuous representative of monotheistic theory and practice, and his sacred books afforded the most ample arsenal of arguments in the long controversy with pagandom. The writings of the Greek philosophers, moralists, and poets were by no means to be despised; nor were they. On the contrary, the New Testament is vocal with echoes from Greek literature; while in the apologists, as Clement, we hear the full-voiced choir of Hellas. Nevertheless, even Socrates offered a cock to Asklepios, and even Æschylus and Sophocles recognised, though they might have explained away, an endless multiplicity of deities. It was only in the Hebrew Scriptures that the absolute oneness of the Godhead was enounced and maintained clearly, consistently, and unequivocally. Hence, these same Holy Scriptures formed the indispensable *point d'appui*, the base of operations, in the sacred campaign against All that fell by One who rose.

106. Nevertheless, it was in the main a Greek and not a Hebrew consciousness that delivered the tremendous battle. The arms were the arms of Jacob, but the sinews were the sinews of Japheth. It was most natural that the Jews in general should never have felt that this warfare was their own. To be sure, it championed their central dogma, but only in a sense different from the original, a sense to which the great majority of them had never attained, and which involved concessions and renunciations they were naturally very slow to make. This attitude of reserve on the part of the Jew has found frequent expression in the New Testament, to which explicit attention is called in the following pages. He is, *e.g.*, the Rich One of Mark x, 17–31; the Dives of Luke xvi, 19–31. It was hard indeed for him to enter the Kingdom into which Gentiles were admitted on equal terms. He has never been able to do it. Neither could the call to

Freedom awaken in his soul the same echo as in the Gentile's, for it did not smite upon the same reverberating consciousness of servitude to demons. The Gospel message could not have been laden with its full import for Jews who were justly proud of their immemorial henotheism.

107. This fact and this feeling are set in bold and striking relief by the fourth Evangelist (viii, 32–33): "And ye shall know the Truth, and the Truth shall make you free. They answered unto him, We be Abraham's seed, and never yet have been in bondage to anyone." What bondage is meant? Surely not political, for the race had passed most of its history, and was even then, in political bondage. Nor yet moral, in spite of the allusion in verse 34 to sin. The bondage is religious. The Jews boasted of their monotheism, their knowledge of the true God, derived from Abraham. They had never served any false god. It is this that the Evangelist denies, as did Aristides. He will not admit that they are true monotheists, true God-worshippers (viii, 39, 40). Nay, they are not God's children, that is, worshippers of God.[1] They are the devil's children, worshippers (in some way) of the devil, whose works they do (viii, 41). Undoubtedly the Jews here suffer gross injustice, but they never fare well at Johannine hands. This long passage, however, merely elaborates a synoptic idea very briefly expressed (Matt. iii, 9; Luke iii, 8): "And think not to say within yourselves, We have Abraham to our father: for I say unto you, that God is able of these stones to raise up children unto Abraham." Again the monotheistic boast; but a vain one! For God could make the stones sons of Abraham. This can mean nothing (as Zahn, who is so often right, perceives, p. 135) but the conversion of the heathen.[2] Precisely the same sense is found in Luke xix, 40: "The stones will cry out"— *i.e.*, the heathen will accept the Jesus-cult with acclamation.

108. To the Jew the glorious doctrine of monotheism

---

[1] Whether there lies hidden therein any Marcionitic contrast between the Jewish God and the true Good God is a subtle question that need not now be broached.

[2] In Greek and other mythologies stones were turned into men, and stone was not an uncommon word for a dolt; it might well be used to denote such as actually worshipped stocks and stones. Here, however, it seems to be used in a play on words: For *sons* would be *b'nayya'*, and *stones* would be *'ab'nayya'* —the difference in pronunciation is hardly more than perceptible.

belonged of right by inheritance from Abraham, who first of men (in Jewish story) had faith in the one God and went forth a true monotheist from the land of idolatry. But the new monotheism they did not accept; they were shut out from the Kingdom, though themselves its children; and the Gentiles from every quarter of the compass, carried by angels to Abraham's bosom, enter in and share it with the ancient Faithful. This "great refusal" of the Jews is represented again in more fearful colours as a "*Surrender*" (not Betrayal) of the Jesus by Judas (*i.e.*, Judæus) (I)Scariot (*i.e.*, *Surrenderer*, ὁ παραδούς, as is proved in proper place). It is, indeed, the greatest of all national tragedies, stretching out its tremendous length through all succeeding centuries.

109. Herewith the circuit of thought marked out for this Introduction is nearly completed. It is now seen that the title *Der vorchristliche Jesus* given to the earlier work is every way far more than justified. The central fact demanding explanation is *the worship of the Jesus*, a worship that did not grow up gradually, but is full grown from the very earliest New Testament times. Unless this be explained, all other explanations, however interesting, lose their importance, for we cannot be sure of the correctness of any detail until this central all-regulative fact is fully accounted for. Now, since this fact meets us at the very threshold of Christianity, it must find its explanation in something pre-Christian. Even if we had no evidence whatever of a pre-Christian Jesus-cult, we should be compelled to affirm its existence with undiminished decision. A cult of a deity could not have sprung up in a day or in a year. No conceivable series of events, even though they were miracles, in a short or even a long human life, could account for the worship by his disciples of a mere man Jesus, as the highest God, immediately following his execution and burial, and still less for his worship as such and exaltation to the throne of the universe, as eternally pre-existent God, by the persecutor Saul. There must have been a pre-Christian cult of a pre-Christian divinity. This hypothesis is absolutely unavoidable. It meets you full in the face whatever way you turn. Moreover, it is overwhelmingly attested by the New Testament itself, which clearly shows that the cult was

esoteric long before it became exoteric, that what is commonly supposed to have been the beginning of the cult was merely its bursting into full and perfect bloom. "First blade, then ear, then full corn in the ear" (Mark iv, 28). It is wholly unallowable to omit or to reduce the preliminary stages.

110. Finally, the proclamation of monotheism is the only adequate essence that can be attributed to Christianity. The notion that this essence consists in any kind of moral teaching is utterly impossible. The instinct of man has always rejected, and will always reject, any such minimisation and degradation of the Gospel message. The Andean, the Himalayan summits of ethics, are not reached in the New Testament. No such dizzy altitudes of unmixed morality are there attained as in the second book of the *Republic* of Plato. No! The error of criticism at this point is fatal; its malady is immedicable. As against the critics, the Church is in this regard eternally right. Christianity is not morality; it is religion, it is *theoseby*—the worship of the One God.[1] "If anyone be *theosebes* and do his will, him he hears" (John ix, 31).

111. Moreover, it is this content, and this alone, that can account for the swift and tremendous triumph of the everlasting Gospel. What was that "everlasting Gospel" borne on angel wings through mid-heaven, and proclaimed by angel voice to all dwellers upon earth? It was exactly what we have found at every turn to be the one and only original content of Christianity: "Fear God and give him glory" (Rev. xiv, 7). Behold the *Summa Evangelii!*

112. No wonder that such a gospel, at such a time, broke the deep slumber of idolatry like a clap of Dantean thunder. And what other proclamation could thus have roused a world, dissolved the fetters of the tyrannising demons, set free the prisoners of superstition, poured light upon the eyes of the blind, and called a universe to life? Could any moral precepts or ethical example have developed such miraculous powers? Assuredly not! Nay, even if there had been proclaimed a new and superior rule of life and sociologic system,

---

[1] For the contrast of the religious with the ethical point of view compare the Gospel doctrine of the first commandment (Mark xii, 29, 30) with Lucan's mighty line (*Phar.* i, 128): Victrix causa deis placuit, sed victa Catoni.

it might have offered themes for learned and acute discussion, or even provided a basis for wise legislation and righteous judgment, but nothing more. Never could it have renewed the face of creation, never have inspired whole armies of martyrs, never have chased the demons into the sea. Who has ever been enthused by a doctrine of ethics—no matter how stern and awful, like the categorical imperative of Kant; no matter how persuasive and winning, like the sentimentalism of Shaftesbury?

113. And only consider how utterly absurd and nugatory would have been any other publication of a world-religion! Let anyone imagine the Apostles, like the Apologists, proclaiming the One God as against many idols, under the name and attributes of the all-healing, all-saving, demon-expelling Jesus. At once we see that arguments must have poured in upon them from every side; the arrows of thought must have leaped in eager tempest from their minds. But now figure them setting forth the life and character of a Galilean peasant, no matter how beautiful and attractive; let us fancy them preaching that they had visions of him after his death on the cross; let us suppose that they called upon their hearers to believe in these visions, and to worship this peasant as God himself, throned in the highest heavens; and let us imagine them trying to work all manner of miracles in his name. Would it have been possible for any man of even ordinary intelligence not to regard such preachers as madmen? Would he not at least have called on them for some slight semblance of proof of these amazing pretensions? And what proofs could they have produced? Beyond their own statements, *absolutely nothing whatever!* For such a gospel to have swept over all the highly cultured Roman Empire, resistless as "a flame through fields of ripened corn," would have been a miracle, beside which the resurrection of Lazarus would vanish into nothingness. No! The original everlasting Gospel was the proclamation (veiled at first, but afterwards open) of a sublime and inspiring faith and worship, the cult of the One God, the Jesus, the Christ, the Saviour, the Guardian, the Lord of heaven and earth, whose name is Everlasting.

PART II.
TESTIMONY OF THE NEW TESTAMENT

ἅτινά ἐστιν ἀλληγορούμενα.—Gal. iv, 24.

PRELIMINARY

1. RECENTLY the earnest suggestion coming from high sources has reached the writer, that he should make accessible to the public some of the more readily intelligible portions of the long since accumulated, and still accumulating, proofs of the original pure Godhead and non-humanity of the Founder of Christianity. The wisdom of such a suggestion seems indisputable on reflection that no one knows how nigh Azrael may be standing, and it would certainly be better to leave in print some indications, however inadequate, of the line of argument than to leave practically none at all. For in *Der vorchristliche Jesus* it was only a few "positive assertions" that were established "irrefutably," only a few positive tokens of a pre-Christian Jesus and Jesus-cult that received any attention. Studiously the "negative phase" was kept out of sight, or at least as far in the background as possible. Only in one passage, in the "Vorrede," did this "negative phase" come to half-way explicit statement, and then not as anything whose proof was to be attempted in the book in question. In the author's mind, indeed, it was far less immediate and important than the "positive assertions." That the Jesus was divine in the primitive Christian conception, that from this central and original notion of his divinity the whole Christian movement was to be studied and comprehended—this seemed, and still seems, to the author to be the supremely significant and regulative fact, beside which the "negative phase," the fact that he was not an historical man like Napoleon or Mohammed, sinks into a very secondary position. However, it was not unnatural, nor indeed unexpected, that the

majority would exactly reverse this relation, that they would pass lightly over the positive and dwell fixedly on the negative element.

2. Such being the case, this latter could not, of course, be permanently neglected. On the contrary, it called loudly for the minutest and most painstaking treatment, nor could it ever have been in the mind of the author to let the reader wait long for some publication touching this more interesting aspect of the matter. But just because it was felt that this "negative phase" required far more thorough-going treatment than was possible in that book, the discussion of it was adjourned, and consideration was confined strictly to the "positive assertions." So conscientiously was this programme carried out that more than one distinguished critic failed to see the "negative phase" at all—*e.g.*, the Abbé Loisy in the *Révue Critique* and the Rev. Newton Mann in the revised edition of his *Evolution of a Great Literature*—however much both were impressed with the "positive assertions." Nevertheless, the majority have undoubtedly seemed to perceive this "negative phase," if only as a reticent and unregistered corollary from the affirmative; and some have even allowed that perception to cloud their judgment, as Wernle, who roars at the book in five columns of the *Theologische Literaturzeitung*.

3. But, however near-lying this corollary, they are right who hold that it is not contained immediately in the positions established in the book. Indubitably myths and legends[1] do gather like clouds round the mountain-high personalities of history. So much one may concede freely and fully, though setting little store by the Napoleon myths, whether of Pérès or of Whately, which are to be regarded as trivialities quite unworthy of their authors. The fact that a myth, or several myths, may be found associated with the name of an individual by no means relegates that individual into the class of the unhistorical. Far less, however, does it weigh in favour of his actual historicity. If the mountain-top be

---

[1] Hereby it is not implied that the present writer regards the narratives concerning Jesus as either myths or legends; he regards them as *symbols*, consciously chosen at first and in some cases afterwards consciously elaborated and dramatised, always with didactic purpose.

there, the clouds will indeed gather round it: we may often explain the legends from the presence of the historic personality, *independently known to be historic*. But the mere existence of the clouds can never attest the presence of the mountain; for clouds also gather over plains and over seas. So, too, the legends cannot of themselves bear witness to some central underlying historic personality; for they often enough engirdle a name that is name only, perhaps of a great Idea, but not of any flesh-and-blood personality. The arguments, however, that do seem to establish "the negative phase" have not yet been put into print—at least to my knowledge—and are of a nature, perhaps, as yet rarely conjectured. Some few of them only, for their name is legion, it is the object of this work to exhibit.

4. It will be conceded that if the Jesus was an historic man of flesh and blood, then he must have been a most remarkable personality. Eucken would certainly be justified in speaking of "the supreme personality and the constructive life-work of Jesus," and of his "incomparable spiritual individuality." We may not be able to say just in what his distinction lay, but there can be no question that it must have been real and without any historical parallel. For *such* supposed myths and legends of miracles, of supernatural birth, sacrificial death, resurrection, ascension, divine power, and the like, could certainly not attach themselves quickly in that age and clime to any man even of extraordinary stamp, unless he were beyond measure notable and distinguished from all other men. Peter, Paul, John the Baptist, John the Evangelist, and their peers were remarkable men, imposing personalities. Yet we do not hear very soon of any independent supernatural exploits of these men; the miracles imputed to them were comparatively insignificant, and performed by them in the Name of Jesus, or else as his representatives. It must be clear as noon to any unprejudiced eye that the Jesus stands altogether alone in early Christian story.[1]

5. Even such a character as Paul, whom some regard as

---

[1] Some of the present considerations have already been advanced under another guise in this volume; a brief restatement here is necessary to introduce the minuter argument.

the real founder of Christianity, and all admit must have been a most noteworthy person; even he and the Baptist, who was remarkable enough to receive notice from Josephus and to hold together for some time a body of disciples; even they and Peter, who attained such conspicuous leadership among the disciples and such unparalleled authority in the traditions of the Church—even these cannot for an instant be named in the same line with Jesus, nor in the second nor in the third line after him. Everyone must perceive that they do not belong in the same class; the Jesus is entirely *sui generis*, altogether unique and incomparable.

6. Now, if the orthodox position be correct, this is perfectly intelligible, and exactly as it should be; we are not, however, contesting orthodoxy, nor concerned with it now and here. But if the critical or Unitarian view be correct, then this uniqueness in the representation of the Jesus in early sources *must be accounted for*, must be made understandable. The only way to account for the utter singularity of this early conception and representation is to suppose that the Jesus was, if not a wholly unique personality (which would hardly differ from a divinity), yet at least an every way wonderful personality, in kind and degree far surpassing any other of which we have any record.

7. Such is, indeed, the thesis of modern liberal criticism,[1] which cannot find terms quite strong enough to express its conception of this amazing individuality, which was indeed (*ex hypothesi*) only a man, and yet in some mysterious way surpassed all other men, so far as to be deified shortly after his humiliating death, and to inspire his most intimate disciples with unshakable faith in his Resurrection from the grave, his ascension into heaven, and his co-equality with God himself in the government of the universe. Hence the infinitely minute and loving care with which the *character-picture* of the Jesus, as supposedly given in the New Testament, has been studied, to discern and to lay bare and to exhibit just what was the peculiar distinction of this

---

[1] But in its very latest pronouncements, frightened at the obvious consequences of its own conception of the over-mastering personality of Jesus, it begins to hedge, and gravely to question whether he was so very wonderful after all! whether not merely an eschatological enthusiast!

wondrous man, that made him so unexampled in his influence over men, and, if not strictly divine, yet so surpassingly great, beautiful, sublime, attractive, fascinating—away with words!—so infinitely superior to all other men that even his disciples, who did not at all understand or appreciate him, could yet not refrain from worshipping him as God.

8. We all know what desperate and devoted endeavours of this kind have been made, how such men as Harnack have struggled to discover and express the essence of Christianity, how Chamberlain has tried to fathom the secret[1] of the Christus, and Keim, and Volkmar, and Renan, and Bousset, and Schmiedel, and von Soden, and a hundred others. It is impossible not to admire the learning and devotion, the zeal and the acumen, that they have displayed in such endeavours; it is equally impossible to deny or to disguise the fact that, one and all, they have been absolute failures; the results have been absurdly and ridiculously disproportioned to the immense powers enlisted in the attempts. *Parturiunt montes, nascitur ridiculus mus.* Never did this line find more perfect application.

9. It is forever impossible to find in the Gospel narrative—if we eliminate the supernatural element, as these critics uniformly do—more than (at the utmost) a very wise, amiable, admirable, spiritual, kind-hearted, deep-thoughted, heavenly-minded, somewhat mystical and God-intoxicated Jewish Rabbi.[2] Such men, like Gautama, have lived and died, have gathered disciples about them, and been venerated

---

[1] This secret he discovers—*mirabile dictu!*—in the oracle, "The Kingdom of heaven is within you"—misunderstood to mean "in your hearts, your inmost selves." That such a meaning is impossible is clear, from the fact that the Jesus is here (Luke xvii, 20, 21) addressing not his disciples, but the hostile Pharisees. The word ἐντός here means not *within*, but *among, in the midst of*. The Kingdom, at first a secret society, was indeed unobserved among them. The notion that this "Kingdom of heaven" is a *state of mind* (like Boston), on which Chamberlain bases his whole interesting chapter on the "incomparable phenomenon of Christ," is indeed magnificent, but contradicted scores of times in the New Testament.

[2] Not even *such* a character has been deciphered or restored from the New Testament records with persuasive, not to say convincing, clearness. The genial biographers and interpreters of the Jesus, gazing steadfastly into the crystal sea of the Gospels, have beheld each his own image transfigured in those placid depths. No wonder, then, that their *Jesusbild* vibrates between the "sweet reasonableness" of Arnold and the "folie dissimulée" of Binet-Sanglé.

by these disciples for many years; at death they have been mourned for many days and months, their memory has been cherished, their *ipse dixit* has become authoritative, and perhaps exaggerated stories, or even miraculous legends, have gradually gathered about their names. Had the disciples of the Jesus done any or all of these things, or even much of some similar kind, then the theory of the noble and lovable Rabbi might be readily accepted.

10. But the fact is that they did (so far as we can ascertain) nothing of the kind at all. The criticism we are criticising discloses in the conduct of the disciples none of the features that would have been natural and inevitable in the conduct of Jewish disciples of a beloved Rabbi. Neither the record as it stands nor the record as purged, purified, and recreated by the critics can show any natural procedure on the part of these supposed loving disciples of a loving Rabbi.

11. What (according to the critics) do they do? They have visions of their master; they believe he has risen from the dead and ascended to heaven; they begin to preach an elaborate system of salvation, and to work miracles in his name! All attempts to understand such a procedure as the result of impressions made on the minds of the disciples by a few months' conversation with a Jewish Rabbi are worse than futile. As well might we suppose that under the delirium of their memories they would have tried to jump to the moon!

12. This is not nearly all, however. It happens that we have positive proof that this association and resulting impression had *absolutely nothing* to do with personal discipleship, with devotion to the Christian propaganda and consecration to the cause and worship of Jesus. For the greatest of all the Apostles, who in zeal and self-sacrifice, as well as in success, far outran all the rest, the Apostle to the Gentiles, was *not* a personal disciple of the Jesus, whom apparently he never met in the flesh, against whose ostensible personal following he is represented as violently enraged. Here, then, is demonstration that the very strongest personal attachment to the Jesus, the very liveliest affection for the Jesus, did *not* imply any *knowledge whatever of him as a man*. Now, we ask, if we must explain the unparalleled enthusiasm of Paul for the Jesus as enthusiasm for a

heavenly Being, whom he had never known as an earthly man, why *may* we not explain the milder enthusiasm of Peter and John similarly? What do we gain by imagining a wonderful human personality to account for *their* devotion, when we must account for a higher devotion without reckoning with any such personality at all? This consideration seems perfectly decisive against the supposed need of a wondrous human personality to explain the conduct of the disciples.

13. But an even weightier consideration is yet to follow. The critics would outvie each other in exalted conceptions of this man, the Jesus. No one denies or will deny that the human personality, if such there was, must have been in the highest degree extraordinary. If the miracles were actually performed, then the fame of the wonder-worker must have been very great. It must have reached the ears of Jews and Gentiles alike throughout Palestine, as indeed is expressly said in the Gospels. In that case it would seem exceeding strange that no hint of such a prodigy meets us anywhere in contemporaneous records, especially nowhere in Josephus. Some early Christian must have felt this lacuna keenly, for he has filled it up with the well-known interpolation (*Ant*. xviii, 3, 3), wherein the hand of the Christian is plainly to be seen. Josephus has not failed to tell us of John the Baptist, and behold a greater than the Baptist is here. Why, then, did he not mention some of the astounding events that mark the career of the Jesus? The only answer is that he was unfriendly to the Christians, and did not care to honour them with any notice. But such an inadequate answer would be neither suggested nor accepted, except in the case of dire need and the lack of any other. Similar and of similar significance is the silence of the contemporary Jewish historian Justus, as attested by Photius, and of Philo, the Jewish Plato.

14. However, the critics whom we have in mind will reply that the mighty works of the Gospel were wrought only in the imagination of the writers, that Josephus and Justus and Philo did not allude to them, for the very good reason that they were later inventions of the evangelical fancy. Even though as much should be granted, it would still

remain true that *the personality must have been all the more remarkable, it must have been superhumanly wonderful*, to have gathered round it so speedily such an unprecedented nimbus of miracles. The elision of the many miracles does not mend matters at all; it merely makes the One Miracle still more stupendous. Well, such a marvellous character must have attracted wide attention, and his crucifixion must have been a notable occurrence: why, then, does not Josephus, why does not Justus, why does not any profane authority mention it?[1]

WITNESS OF ACTS

15. All this, however, is only preliminary. We come now to the vital point. Such an unexampled personage as the Jesus is universally assumed to have been must have made the deepest impression on the minds of his disciples. *Why, then, do we find no traces of any such impression?* It is a fact that in the preaching of the Apostles, as recorded in Acts, we can discover practically no marks whatever of any personal acquaintance with the Jesus. The preaching of Peter and Stephen and Philip stands upon the same footing, revolves in the same circle, with that of Paul. They appeal to the Scriptures, to certain necessities of exegesis, but never to any biographical facts of their own knowledge. They never say, We heard the Jesus say this and this, nor We saw him do so and so. No one can get the impression from reading Peter's speeches that he is talking about a marvellous man, the Jesus, whom he had known and loved. The allusions to "signs and wonders" and the "hanging on a tree" are merely perfunctory or else dogmatic.

16. In one single passage, strongly interpolated and quite unparsable, the Jesus is indeed described in these words: "Jesus, him of Nazareth, how God anointed him with holy spirit and with power, who traversed benefiting and healing all those dominated by the Devil, because God was with him, and we (are) witnesses of all that he did, both in the land of the Jews and in Jerusalem, whom also they

---

[1] Elsewhere in this book the reader will find the "Silence of Josephus" discussed at length.

executed, having hung upon wood. This one God raised on the third day and gave him to be made manifest, not to all the people, but to witnesses, those predesignated by God, us who ate and drank with him after he arose from (the) dead." So it is written. But that Peter never pronounced it thus is certain; for he would hardly have spoken even in that presence of the deeds of Jesus "in the land of the Jews and in Jerusalem," since those deeds were not done in "the land of the Jews" (even if Peter could have used such an expression), but were practically peculiar to Galilee.

17. Moreover, the critics against whom these lines are levelled cannot admit that Peter could speak of eating and drinking with the risen Jesus; by no stretch of the imagination could he and the rest ("we") eat and drink *with a vision* (such as these critics esteem the Risen to have been). Plainly the passage has been worked over by a later hand, and illustrates the extremely significant fact that the earliest documents contain in effect no reference to the human but only to the divine Jesus, whereas the humanisation of this divinity proceeds apace as we descend the stream of tradition. This fact is vividly exemplified in the Gospels. What clearer indication could be given of the primitive divinity of the Jesus?

18. The main point, however, lies in the two words "traversed benefiting" (went about doing good).[1] This phrase is supposed to be peculiarly descriptive of the Jesus as pre-eminently the *good man*, going hither and thither, doing good wherever opportunity offered. It is true that the Gospels supply no basis for this conception, but it certainly is the conception not only prevailing at present, but established and almost exclusive.

19. Let us consider, however. The Greek word[2] does *not* mean "went about";[2] it means "went through," "traversed." It would be hard to find a certain example in Greek literature of this word used of a person in the sense of "go about," though it may in a very few cases have some such object as *the land* or *his life* omitted, to be supplied from the context. Thus in Acts viii. 4 we read: "They therefore having been scattered went through (the land)

---

[1] διῆλθεν εὐεργετῶν.   [2] διῆλθεν.

preaching the word,"[1] and the verb should perhaps be rendered *departed*, as it was rendered in Acts xiii, 14, where the revisers render it by *passing through*, as also in viii, 40. If the word means this and not "went about" in Acts xiii, 14, and viii, 40, it seems hard to find good reason for rendering it by "went about" in viii, 4 and x, 38.

20. Be this as it may, the kernel of the matter is this: the term "benefiting"[2] is a favourite technical word in the Gnosticism of Basilides, where it is continually used in connection with the "Sonship." In describing the function of the Jesus, he declares (according to Hippolytus, *Ref.* vii, 27): "And through him was purified the Sonship the third, that had been left behind for the benefiting and being benefited,[3] and ascended toward the blessed Sonship through all these traversing."[4] Again (vii, 26), he says that "all the Sonship that had been left for benefiting the souls in Formlessness[5] and being benefited, having been transformed followed the Jesus," &c. Again (vii, 22): "Basilides calls such not wind, but holy spirit, which the Sonship benefits, having put it on, and is benefited." Again (vii, 25), speaking of the entrance of the Gospel into the world (which is little different from the entry of the Jesus), Basilides declares, it "traversed[6] every Principality and Authority and Dominion and every Name named, and it came in reality though nought descended from above." These few examples show that the terms "benefiting" and "traversed" were technical with Basilides in speaking of the Sonship. The same notion of "traversing" is found in Heb. iv, 14: "Having therefore a great High Priest that has traversed[7] the heavens, Jesus the Son of God," &c.

21. Of course, these notions were not original with Basilides, great organiser of thought though he was. In the Naassene Hymn,[8] which such as Harnack and Preuschen recognise as "very old," which there is no reason whatever for regarding as post-Christian, we read of this same Jesus,

---

[1] Though here ℵ reads ἦλθον and not διῆλθον, so that either the ℵ-scribe is correct, in which case διῆλθον is an error, or else is a corrector of διῆλθον, which he felt to be an error—for mere carelessness on his part is unlikely.
[2] εὐεργετῶν.   [3] πρὸς τὸ εὐεργετεῖν καὶ εὐεργετεῖσθαι.   [4] διελθοῦσα.
[5] εἰς τὸ εὐεργετεῖν·   [6] διῆλθε.   [7] διεληλυθότα.
[8] Hilgenfeld (K.d. U., p. 260): "Welcher freilich der älteren Gnosis noch näher steht"; and this "elder Gnosis" was *proto-Christian*.

in the bosom of the Father, viewing sympathetically the woe of the world (polytheism), and declaring he will descend through all the æons to the rescue of humanity (from idolatry) :—

> Therefore send me, Father;
> Bearing seals I shall descend,
> Æons all I shall fare through,[1]
> Mysteries all I shall open up,
> Forms of gods I shall show;
> And the secrets of the holy way,
> Having called it Gnosis, I shall deliver up.

Here the case is presented in elemental form, with all desirable clearness; the Jesus is to issue from the bosom of the Father, is to fare through all the æons on his mission of mercy, and descend to men on earth below to save them through the holy way of the Gnosis, or, as we should now say, of the Gospel (compare "Gnosis of salvation," Luke i, 77).[2]

22. Inasmuch as it seems morally certain that these oldest of the Gnostics were pre-Christian,[3] it would appear established that this idea of traversing (or faring through) benefiting is a pre-Christian idea, and refers primarily, not to going about the country of Galilee doing little deeds of kindness (a relatively modern conception of which there is no sign in the Gospel), but to the infinitely sublimer outward transit of the divine Jesus earthward, through the æons that envelop like so many concentric spherical shells the central Godhead Supreme. Here is a thought really worthy of those ancient profound theosophists who said "Beginning of perfection is knowledge of man, but knowledge of God is perfection consummated"; whereas the ordinary notion, which degrades the Jesus into

---

[1] διοδεύσω.
[2] In *Theol. Rundschau* (Oct., 1911, p. 384) the editor, Professor Bousset, in an article notable for its concessions to "D. v. J.", suspects the text of this Hymn, and suggests "Spake then Nus" (δὲ(ὁ)νοῦς) in lieu of "Spake then Jesus" (διησους). A counsel of despair, but, as Bousset himself "lays no weight" thereon, enough to remark that, if he were right, Nus, like Logos, would be only another name for Jesus, and the situation would hardly be altered. B. thinks the Naassenes certainly "Christian"; and if he means proto-Christian, who would deny? They were the first Gnostics, "and as, indeed, is self-evident, progenitors of Gnosticism" (Badham, *Theol. Tijdsch.*, 1911, p. 420); and the Gnosis was an early name for the Christian movement.
[3] "So out of this conception arose the pair of notions 'pneumatic' and 'psychic,' even before Paul; that Gnosticism, in its fundamental conceptions, antedates this apostle is also lexically established" (Reitzenstein, *Die Hellenistichen Mysterienreligionen*).

something like a benevolent dervish, seems to be a positive profanation.

23. Some will, of course, say that Basilides took these terms from Acts x, 38; but this is entirely inconceivable. The evolution of the Gnostic systems from the New Testament is quite unthinkable, and unbiassed critics are perceiving every day more clearly that Gnosticism antedates Christianity; and the writer seems to have proved clearly in a work (yet in MS.) on "Gnostic Elements in the New Testament" that the New Testament parallels to preserved Gnostic passages are almost without exception younger than their Gnostic correspondents. This is shown by the fact that the connection is uniformly better in the Gnostic context, and the passage much more intelligible.[1] Now, the context in

[1] This proposition seems quite too important to be left hung on the air; the supports are to be found in a careful analysis of scores of parallels in the Gnostic writings and the New Testament, which is, of course, impossible in this connection. One striking example is given later (p. 133) in the discussion of the Ektroma. A single additional illustration may suffice to show the nature of the proof elaborated in the unpublished work already mentioned.

In Col. ii, 8-15 occurs a passage of deepest darkness. It seems really amazing that anyone could write sentence after sentence of such impenetrable obscurity; in fact, it appears psychologically impossible that any teacher such as the epistolist certainly was should address such things to a consciousness that had not long been familiar with a great body of doctrine in which the mysterious phrases used were catchwords, meaningless to us, but full of meaning to the persons addressed, faintly suggesting the technical terminology now current among the followers of Mrs. Eddy. It is especially verses 13-15 that we must now consider: "And you, being dead through your trespasses and the uncircumcision of your flesh, you did he quicken together with him, having forgiven us all our trespasses; having blotted out the bond written in ordinances that was against us, which was contrary to us: and he hath taken it out of the way, nailing it to the cross; having put off from himself the principalities and the powers, he made a show of them openly, triumphing over them in it." Notice the want of connection in thought. Verse 14 speaks, apparently, of the abolition of the Law, abolished through the death on the cross; this might be understood. But v. 15 straightway turns the thought into a wholly different channel: "having stripped off (as a garment) the principalities," &c. The text is very uncertain, as might be expected. Some witnesses omit "the principalities and the powers," others add "the flesh." So the Fathers understood it, as testify the phrases *exuens se carne, spolians se carne, exutus carnem, exutionem corporis*. This putting off the flesh on the cross seems intelligible, but putting off principalities and powers—! Again, the nailing of "*the manuscript*" (of the Law) to the cross is a bewildering phrase. Such treatment of a manuscript looks far more like publication, official proclamation, than annulment. Common sense seems to cry out that it was his body that was nailed to the cross, and that the original reference must have been to the *body*.

Now turn for a moment to the Docetic doctrine reported by Hippolytus, *Ref.*, viii, 10: "Having come from above, he put on the begotten (body) and did all things just as has been written in the Gospels; he washed (himself) in Jordan, but he washed, having received type and seal, in the water, of the

which the passage can be best understood is the original context; it is transference and adaptation to new surroundings that make it unnatural and bewildering. Hence we conclude that the phrase "traversed benefiting" has been taken from Gnosticism and applied to the Jesus in this ostensible speech of Peter. That such spiritual benefiting was really in the writer's mind is shown further by the following explicative clause: "and healing all those dominated by the Devil"—where the "and" seems to be emphatic and to mean "that is"; and the casting-out of demons (as we shall see) is nothing less than the overthrow of idolatry, the conquest of the heathen gods, which is here, as everywhere in the early apologists, correctly reckoned as the specific mission and activity of the Jesus.

WITNESS OF REVELATION AND HEBREWS

24. When now we inquire of the Apocalypse, the report is not different. However many details about this book may

body begotten from the Virgin, in order that, when the Archon should condemn his own proper figment to death, to the cross, that soul nourished in the body, having put off the body, and having nailed it to the cross, and having triumphed through it over the principalities and the powers, might not be found naked, but might put on, instead of that flesh, the body typified in the water when he was baptised."

Surely no fair-minded man can deny that this passage, however fantastic, is clear as noonday, compared with the Colossian text. The Docetist held that the baptism in the Jordan was a symbolism expressing the putting on by the Jesus of another (spiritual) body, the type and seal of the body derived from the Virgin; when this latter (body) was nailed to the cross, the Jesus stripped it off from himself, but was not left a *naked* (disembodied) spirit; on the contrary, was still clothed in the spiritual body that he had put on in baptism; and by means of this spiritual body he triumphed over all the principalities and powers led by the Archon, which had thought to end his life on the cross, but had merely succeeded in destroying a flesh-body, leaving the true spirit-body intact and triumphant. The doctrine is so plain and self-consistent as to need no further commentary.

Notice, now, that the Docetic and the Colossian passage cannot be unrelated—the verbal agreements are altogether too close. Such extraordinary phrases as "having stripped off the body, and having nailed it to the wood" (ἀπεκδυσαμένη τὸ σῶμα καὶ προσηλώσασα πρὸς τὸ ξύλον), and "having triumphed through it over the principalities and the powers" (θριαμβεύσασα δι' αὐτοῦ τὰς ἀρχὰς καὶ τὰς ἐξουσίας), could never have originated twice independently. They are not difficult, but perfectly natural in the Docetic context; they are not only unnatural, but virtually incomprehensible in Colossians. The inference is obvious. Moreover, that the Docetist is not quoting from the Epistle is clear to see in the fact that no allusion is made to it, but instead there is a very different reference—namely: "This it is," he (the Docetist) says, "that the Saviour speaks, Unless one be born of water and spirit, one shall not enter into the kingdom of the heavens, because the begotten of the flesh is flesh"—closely agreeing with John iii, 5, 6.

remain in doubt, despite the most learned and illuminating labours of a host of savants, it is enough for our purpose that it represents, at least in part, a comparatively early stage of the Propaganda. Now what is the figure of the Jesus in this volume? Four times the name appears with the suffix Christ, and ten times without. In none of these cases is there the slightest allusion to the personality or the life-history of the Jesus. Six times the phrase is "witness[1] of Jesus"; once it is "Jesus Christ the witness,[2] the faithful"; once it is "those keeping the commandments of God and the faith of Jesus"; twice it is "the Lord Jesus"; once "the blood of the witnesses of Jesus"; once it is "Revelation of Jesus Christ"; once it is "I Jesus sent mine angel"; once it is simply "In Jesus." This witness, then, to the human personality of the Jesus is zero.

25. But far more conspicuous than Jesus in this Apocalypse is the Little Lamb,[3] occurring twenty-eight times. This

---

The state of the case now seems plain enough: the Docetic doctrine and phraseology were known to the epistolist; the latter pleased him, the former did not. He attempted to bring in the high-flown Docetic expressions in speaking of a wholly different theme, the abolition (by the Jesus-cult) of the religious distinction of Jew and Gentile. Hence he talks of him as having nailed the hand-writing (the Law) to the cross (which is utterly inappropriate), and of having stripped off the principalities and the powers (which is senseless), of his having triumphed over them (where αὐτούς is of wrong gender and the whole is unthinkable), and finally he throws in the enigmatic " he patterned in frankness" (which is words). The Fathers felt that the thing "stripped off" could not be the principalities, but must be the flesh or body; yet the instant you insert such a term you are thrown back upon Docetic ground—the Jesus is represented as stripping off his body (or flesh) on the cross, and hence leaving it nailed there to the wood.

That some such idea was animating the author of Colossians is also seen in a phrase in ii, 11: "And ye are fulfilled in him, who is the head of every principality and power, in whom also ye were circumcised with circumcision not made with hands, *in the stripping off of the body of the flesh*, in the circumcision of the Christ, having been consepulchred with him in the baptism." These lofty-sounding but discordant phrases have little meaning in their own context. On their face it appears that they have been transplanted from their native soil to their present surroundings, where they look odd and do not thrive.

Possibly someone may cavil at the Docetic statement "that soul nourished in the body, having stripped off the body and having nailed it to the wood," and may object that the executioners, and not "that soul," nailed it. Let such an one reflect that the sublime primitive conception was that of the self-immolation of a suffering high-priest, and that in any case "that soul" might easily have been spoken of as nailing, had it only permitted the nailing.

This example, only one of many, shows unmistakably that favourite expressions have been borrowed from the Gnostics, appropriated by the epistolists, and converted to strictly ecclesiastical use.

[1] μαρτυρία. [2] μάρτυς. [3] ἀρνίον.

Lamb is introduced (v, 6) as a sacrifice, "a Lamb standing as having been slain, having horns seven and eyes seven, which are the seven spirits of God sent forth into all the earth." Here the suggestion of the Gospel narrative and the modern Unitarian conception seems to be vanishingly slight. But in xiii, 8 the whole matter is made reasonably clear: "And shall worship him all the dwellers on the earth of whom hath not been writ his name in the book of the life of the Lamb that hath been slain from the foundation of the world." Here the whole evangelic story, conceived as history, seems forever excluded. By no possibility can the supposed death of the Jesus a few years before be described as a slaying from the foundation of the world. To say that he had been slain in the counsels of God is imposition, not exposition, of meaning. Of course, the critics refer the phrase to "hath been written," transposing so as to read "whose name hath not been written from the foundation of the world." But this is only a makeshift, a forced exegesis, and does not really mend matters. The notion of the names being written from the foundation of the world in the Lamb's Book of Life still leaves the Lamb and his Book of Life there in heaven since the foundation of the world, which in no wise rhymes with the conception of the Gospel as history.

26. Turning now to the first chapter, we find another different conception of the same character, "one like Son of Man clothed full length and girt at the breasts with golden girdle; and his head and hairs white, as white wool, as snow, and his eyes like flame of fire, and his feet like burnished brass, as refined in a furnace, and his voice as voice of many waters, and having in his right hand stars seven, and out of his mouth a sword two-edged sharp proceeding, and his visage as the sun shines in his might." This fearful vision describes himself thus: "I am the First and the Last and the living—and was dead, and lo, living am I unto the æons of the æons—and have the keys of death and Hades." Without detailed interpretation it is plain that this being is supernal, over-earthly, and in no particular suggests the so-called historic Jesus.

27. But does he not say "I was dead"? Certainly. True, the whole clause, from "and was" to "æons," is

perhaps interpolation; but the death, the sacrificial death of the Jesus, is certainly part of this whole tremendous doctrine. Yet this by no means implies that there is any reference to the crucifixion of a man Jesus at Jerusalem. The Jesus being a divine personality variously and titanically conceived —now as a Lamb, now as a High Priest, now as Alpha and Omega, now as Son of Man, amid the candlesticks—this sacrifice, this death, this resuscitation are all to be understood as supernal, over-earthly transactions, extra-spatial and extra-temporal, and by no means necessarily carried out here on the Palestinian stage.

28. If one asks just *how* this sacrifice was effected, the answer must be that the question is unreasonable. The writers themselves had no clear ideas on the subject. They were dealing with vast and vague notions of heavenly happenings, of which it was impossible to form any exact Gaussian "constructible mental image." Deity dying and coming to life, the great High Priest offering up himself, the Lamb slain from the foundation of the world—such gigantic conceptions defy the limitations of sense-presentment. What happens when serious attempt is made to depict them historically may be seen in the Gospels.

29. This self-immolation of the great High Priest is treated at length in the Epistle to the Hebrews, but I hardly think that even Delitzsch or Harnack would contend that any idea has been made quite clear. The point is that the representation therein given, as everywhere in the New Testament outside the Gospels, does not seem to presuppose any knowledge of the Gospel or of the Gospel story. It is *far vaguer than this latter*, nor does it make the faintest allusion to the Gospel delineation. It is not merely that the writers do not seem to have read the Gospels, they have no conception of the existence of any Gospel account, nor is there the slightest reference to any such personality as we find depicted in the Gospels. Thus the letter to the Hebrews has much to say of this great High Priest, who offers up himself, who suffers in the days of his flesh, &c. But he is "an High Priest after the order of Melchizedec," who, being "without father, without mother, without genealogy, having neither beginning of days nor end of life, but made like to

the Son of God, abideth a priest continually" (vii, 3). Clearly, then, we are dealing in this High Priest with a strictly supernatural being; we see here the beginning of a doctrine that this being had to become flesh and offer himself up; but no such stage is anywhere reached as is found in the Gospels, and there is no hint of any knowledge of such a personality as is supposed to be there painted. In particular, it is only the *suffering of the Divine Being, the self-immolation of the High Priest*, that is mentioned, and not at all the supposed lovely human personality of which the critics make so much account.

30. It is impossible in this sketch to enter more minutely into this matter, already considered from a neighbouring point of view in the foregoing chapters. But the cardinal points thus far made in this statement may be summarised thus:—

(1) If the Jesus was merely a man of flesh and blood, as the critics assure us, then to have produced the Christian movement he must have been a most amazing and every way memorable personality.

(2) Any such personality would have made, must have made, the deepest impression as a man on his immediate and intimate following.

(3) Such a personage would then have bulked largely in the preaching of the early Christians, which would in fact have taken its tone and colour in great measure from that personality, from things that he said and did.

(4) But the fact is that the case is exactly the reverse: the personality, his deeds and words of love and wisdom, are entirely absent from the early preaching. The Jesus-character cuts no figure at all in the primitive propaganda. This latter pivots on and swings about certain great *ideas*, as of the coming judgment, the Son of Man, the self-immolating High Priest like Melchizedec, the Lamb slain from the foundation of the world, the dying and re-risen Christ, the installed Son of God, the Faithful Witness,[1] and

---

[1] This phrase and this notion seem to be peculiar to the Apocalypse, and the prevalence of the word "witness" (μαρτυρία) in the Johannines is remarkable. It occurs in John fourteen times, in 1 John six, in 3 John one, in Apocalypse nine, or thirty times in all. Elsewhere it occurs in all the New Testament only

various others; but the human personality, the "meek and lowly Jesus," is simply nowhere to be found; it is absolutely absent from the original proclamation.

31. Hence we must insist that the hypothesis of this wondrous human personality is positively excluded. It explains nothing that calls for explanation. No amount of amiability and "sweet reasonableness" can be any ground for ascribing to a mere man a series of astounding miracles, for receiving and believing visions indicating his resurrection, still less for basing thereon a highly elaborate, artificial and, in the main, transcendental structure of philosophy and religion. These actual effects stand entirely out of relation to the hypothetic causes.

32. It is not likely that a finer logical intelligence than Holsten's will soon be brought to bear upon the problem of the Gospels of Paul and Peter, yet the failure of his superb effort is now apparent and admitted. In fact, as already indicated, the hypothesis of the colossal personality merely makes matters worse. In proportion as this human form towers higher and higher, more and more evident becomes the impossibility that it could have failed so completely to leave any impress on the teaching and preaching of the early propagandists. This point cannot be stressed too strongly

seven times, sporadically and without special significance. In the Apocalypse Jesus is twice called "the Witness the Faithful" (i, 5; iii, 14—"the Amen, the Witness the Faithful, and [the] true"). The term "witness" ($\mu\acute{a}\rho\tau\nu s$) is used in thirty-three other New Testament passages, but without important reference. So, too, the verb witness ($\mu\alpha\rho\tau\acute{\nu}\rho o\mu\alpha\iota$) is found five times, and the noun $\mu\alpha\rho\tau\acute{\nu}\rho\iota o\nu$ about twenty-one times, without giving occasion for remark. But the exceptional prevalence of "witness" in the Johannines, and especially the "witness of Jesus," peculiar to the Apocalypse, *are* important as illustrating the striking fact that the New Testament writings are strongly characterised, and often sharply distinguished, by favourite ideas and catchwords current most probably in particular groups of Christians or circles of Christian thought. It is not strange, but rather enlightening, that the Jesus should have been variously conceived as Lion, as Lamb, as Witness, as Vanens, as Demon-destroyer, as Son of Man, as Messiah, as Alpha and Omega, as Was-and-Is-and-Will-be, as Man from Heaven, as Second Adam, as Logos, as Lord, as Spirit, *et al.* It would be idle to seek to unify or even to reconcile these divergent conceptions. The important thing is to recognise clearly the true ground of the divergence, as lying in the diverse mental temperaments, in the varying conceptive or imaginative processes of the writers or of the schools they represent; a diversity unavoidable on the hypothesis that the Jesus was at first an ideal and divine personality, but inexplicable on the hypothesis of a purely human Jesus. Noteworthy is the definition the Apocalyptist himself gives of "the witness of Jesus" as "the spirit of prophecy"—an enigma that Volkmar strives to unravel, with more energy and ingenuity than success.

or *repeatedly*, for it seems to be decisive. Let anyone realise vividly the historical conditions of the problem; let him read again and again the New Testament outside of the Gospels, and yield himself to the natural total impression, and he will find the *absence* of the human personality of the Jesus to be by all odds the most conspicuous feature of the whole situation.

WITNESS OF THE GOSPELS

33. But someone is ready with the objection: "The Gospels, however, the Gospels—they are full of this human being; they present a vivid picture of a noble man, a supremely beautiful character, unique, incomparable, unimaginable, which the ignorant disciples could never have invented, which they have merely inadequately reproduced." Here, then, the issue is joined sharply. I deny each and every one of these confident time-honoured and timeworn contentions. At nearly every point the real state of the case is exactly the reverse. It is *not* true that the earliest Gospel narratives describe *any human character at all;* on the contrary, the individuality in question is *distinctly divine and not human,* in the earliest portrayal. As time goes on it is true that certain human elements do creep in, particularly in Luke and John. In the latter, indeed, there begins that process of sentimentalisation which has been carried to such lengths in this modern, and particularly this recent, age. The received notion that in the early Marcan narratives the Jesus is distinctly human, and that the process of deification is fulfilled in John, is precisely the reverse of the truth. In Mark[1] there is really no man at all, the Jesus is God, or at least essentially divine, throughout. He wears only a transparent garment of flesh. Mark historises only. Matthew also historises and *faintly humanises.* Luke more *strongly humanises,* while John not only humanises, but begins to *sentimentalise.*

---

[1] Of course, in these pages the reader will not look for any polemic with Weiss or Mueller or Wendling or Nicolardot or Loisy, about the Synoptic question. Fortunately the large questions here raised do not depend for their satisfactory general settlement upon delicate determinations of priority and dependence of Synoptic elements. Otherwise they would have to be postponed from the beginning to the close of the century.

34. Thus far these are mere assertions, but they repose upon careful analysis, which indeed cannot be reproduced here in detail.[1] Only a few salient features of the situation can be presented, and the reader must be advertised in advance that it is the general consensus of indications that constitutes the strength of our position, and not any two nor any half-dozen single indications, be they never so direct and telling. Since, then, it is quite impossible to discuss these minute matters exhaustively in this connection, the reader will please take the following as samples only:—

(1) Mark says naught about any early history of the Jesus; apparently he knows of none; in fact, it is demonstrable that the accounts both of Matthew and of Luke are pure imaginations. Now the fact that these elaborate and thoroughly contradictory stories were invented proves that fantasy played round the theme, that there arose a demand at least for ideas concerning it; but if there had been any facts in the case these must have been in some measure accessible; that none were ascertained indicates that none were ascertainable, that such facts did not really exist.

Moreover, Mark does not claim to be telling an historical tale; he is concerned avowedly with the *doctrine*—"Beginning of the Gospel of Jesus Christ" (i, 1). Certainly he gives this an historical form; he historises, but he does not profess to write history.

If the Jesus was such an impressive human personality, it seems strange that the earliest narrator should think solely of a body of dogma, and not at all of the character of that marvellous human being.

(2) Mark nowhere applies to the Jesus any term that would indicate any impressive or even amiable human personality, or in fact any human personality whatever. On the contrary, the distinctive terms are such as would naturally be used of a God, in fact of Jehovah, and not of a man. The few apparent exceptions will serve to prove this rule.

(*a*) Three or four times (in Mark) the Jesus is said to have "had compassion" on the people (i, 41; vi, 34; viii, 2;

---

[1] The writer completed in September, 1909, a minute discussion of Mark, verse by verse; since then the importunacy of professional duties has prevented final revision and preparation for the press.

ix, 22), in Matthew five times, thrice in Luke; this "compassion" is one of the *two* chief traits of Jesus according to Schmiedel, and is perhaps *the* chief in the general conception. Surely compassion is most human. Yes, but it is also divine; in fact, it is the *especially* divine attribute in the Oriental conception: "Allah, the Compassionate, the Merciful." And now mark well. The Greek word[1] is not idiomatically employed in this sense; it is a mere imitation in Greek of the Hebrew *raḥam* (*raḥamim* = bowels, mercies). Now this Hebrew term is continually and almost exclusively used (in the Old Testament) of or in connection with Jehovah. With only a few exceptions, it is solely Jehovah that is made subject of the verb, and these exceptions rather strengthen than weaken the rule. We may say, then, that the Greek word, as merely rendering the Hebrew, though it might be used of a man, is far fitter applied to Deity; is, indeed, distinctive not of man, but of God; as is also seen in the fact that it is used *only of the Jesus*, with only three even apparent exceptions in all the New Testament: Matthew xviii, 27, where "the Lord of that servant" represents Jehovah; Luke x, 33, of the Good Samaritan (symbolising a divine Being?); Luke xv, 20, where the Father is God or the Jesus. Its practically exclusive predication of the Jesus clearly indicates, though it does not positively prove, that he was from the first conceived as Jehovah, or at least as a Vice-Deity.

(*b*) The term "rebuked"[2] is used in Mark six times of the Jesus (also frequently in the other Gospels). It is also used of others (thrice), and so in the other Gospels. Hence it, too, appears distinctive of the Jesus. Now, however, it merely renders the Hebrew *ga'ar*, which, again, is used distinctively, though not peculiarly, of Jehovah (about eighteen out of twenty-four times). Here, then, the indication is the same as in the foregoing case, though not so strong.

(*c*) The term "snort at"[3] is used four times of the Jesus (Mark i, 43; Matthew ix, 30; John xi, 33, 38), once of the disciples (Mark xiv, 5). The word is most rare, and seems extraordinary as applied to any man, most especially puzzling

---

[1] σπλαγχνίζομαι, from σπλάγχνα = viscera.   [2] ἐπιτιμάω.   [3] ἐμβριμάομαι.

as applied to the gentle Jesus, particularly as it is hard to find any good reason for this "snorting." However, the explanation is not far to seek. The word merely renders the Hebrew *naharah* (snorting, Jer. viii, 16), or *neshamah*, used regularly of the "blast of the nostrils" of Jehovah. Here, then, the application of the repellent word to the Jesus appears as natural and almost inevitable, *only if the Jesus be thought as like Jehovah*, so that the predicates of the latter are transferred to the former; otherwise it remains perplexing and offensive.

(*d*) But is it not said that the Jesus "loved"[1] the Rich One? Yes, indeed, in a most important pericope (Mark x, 21), the *only one* in which such a sentiment is ascribed to the Jesus, outside of the sentimentalising Fourth Gospel. Let us look narrowly at this instructive passage. This love for the Rich One appears very human, and yet is it not strange that such a feeling should well up *only once* in the life of the Jesus of the Synoptists? The phenomenon is certainly worth pondering. Now, in another connection I have proved beyond contradiction that the Rich One is and can be nothing else than Faithful Israel; the mysterious figure is symbolical purely and only. Detailed proof cannot be given here, but clear indications may suffice.

(1) This One[2] meets the Jesus just at the entrance into Judea (Mark x, 1, 17). It is highly unlikely that an individual Jew would have met the Jesus in the manner detailed, while the typical Jew, the Jewish people, could be so described with great beauty and propriety.

(2) The features of the One suit Faithful Israel; the use of the bare term *One* seems noteworthy.

(3) Hitherto in Galilee (of the Gentiles) the Jesus seems to have met only multitudes of invalids, particularly demoniacs; "great multitudes followed him, and he healed them all." No such persons meet him in Judea, only blind Bartimæus forms an exception confirming the rule. Now Galilee was certainly as healthful as Judea. Why, then, such countless throngs of sick folk in Galilee and none in

[1] ἠγάπησεν.   [2] εἷς.

Judea? Only one answer is possible: *The maladies of Galilee were purely spiritual;* they were *paganism, false worship, polytheism.* The gods and idols, those were the diseases he cured and the demons he cast out. His career in Galilee is only a brilliant poetic picture of the progress of the Jesus-cult. "Go tell John what ye hear and see; blind men look up and lame men walk, lepers are cleansed and deaf men hear, and the dead are raised and the poor are evangelised." All these works stand in line. It is the same great deed expressed under six forms—the conquests of the Jesus-cult among the Poor, the Gentiles and the Gentilised Jews. Now, in Judea the true God was worshipped, true religion prevailed. Hence such cures as those wrought in Galilee of the Gentiles were impossible. But spiritual blindness prevailed, alas! even among the highly-honoured people of God; hence the cure of blind Bartimæus, who symbolises the spiritually blinded Jew. If such be the proper interpretation of those facts, then there is no other choice: we *must* regard this *One*, who meets Jesus at the gate of Judea, as the symbol of Jewry.

(4) That the writer was actually thinking of Jacob the chosen lies plain to see in the language used of the One in verse 22: "But he with lowering look at the word went away grieving";[1] as compared with Isaiah lvii, 17: "And he was grieved, and with lowering look went on in his ways."[2] Now the prophet here speaks of Israel, and of Israel only, and it seems impossible that the Marcan writer was not thinking of this Isaian passage. Especially to note is the word στυγνάσας ("with lowering look"), corresponding to the Septuagint "lowering" (στυγνός). This extremely rare στυγνάζω (now rejected from Matthew xvi, 3) is a Septuagint word rendering the Hebrew *shôbab* (froward, apostate); outside the Septuagint it seems to be found just once, in a scholium on Aesch. *Pers.* 470.[3] We may safely say, then, that the Marcan writer had the Septuagint, or some similar translation, of the Isaian verse in his mind, hence he must have been thinking of Israel. In fact, he seems to have quoted

---

[1] ὁ δὲ στυγνάσας ἐπὶ τῷ λόγῳ ἀπῆλθεν λυπούμενος.
[2] καὶ ἐλυπήθη, καὶ στυγνὸς ̓ πορεύθη ἐν ταῖς ὁδοῖς αὐτοῦ.
[3] Its use by Eumathius (A.D. 1100?) hardly counts.

thus from Isaiah, to make his own symbolism clear and unmistakable.[1]

(5) The requirement to sell all goods and give to the poor is unreasonable, and unwarranted by precedent. It acquires sense and reason only when taken, in its proper historic setting, to be the demand of the Jesus-cult that Israel should renounce his "many possessions," his spiritual privileges and prerogatives, should share them with the Gentile by admitting this latter on equal terms into the Kingdom. No wonder he hesitated.

(6) The reported conversation between the Jesus and the disciples is to be understood only in accord with the foregoing: "How hardly shall they that have the possessions enter into the Kingdom of God! And the disciples were amazed at his words." Notice the language: "They that have the possessions."[2] A distinct and definite class appears to be meant. And why the amazement of the disciples? There seems nothing amazing in the notion that the rich should find it harder than the poor to enter into the Kingdom. On hearing that it is "easier for a camel to go through the needle's eye than for a rich man to enter the Kingdom of God" they exclaim, "Who, then, can be saved?" That is, *if the Jew cannot;* otherwise the question lacks point. Their attitude seems strange, as well as that of the Jesus, if *rich* be meant literally. The Jesus replies: "With men this is impossible, but with God all things are possible." This means, if anything, that the salvation of the rich is really impossible, save by a miracle. Applied to a rich man, this looks unreasonable; applied to the Jewish people, it looks reasonable enough. Note, too, the closing words: "But many last first and first last." A perfectly natural interpretation refers this to the Jew (naturally first, really last, in accepting the new cult, or the Kingdom) and the Gentile (naturally last, really first). What other worthy interpretation has revealed itself to the eyes of the commentator?

(7) Lastly, that such is really the thought of the Evangelist is made clear by the exactly parallel thought

---

[1] Compare the learned remarks of Abbott, *Corrections of Mark* [439]-[442].
[2] οἱ τὰ χρήματα ἔχοντες.

in Romans ix–xi. What a prodigious puzzle this inversion of relations (of Jew and Gentile) to the Kingdom presented to the early Christian consciousness is distinctly visible in this most elaborate argument on the paradox of Jewish rejection and Gentile acceptance of the Gospel. Now note the conclusion. The apostle insists, in the teeth of all the facts in the case, that the rejection cannot be real and permanent, and that the honour of the Almighty is pledged to the salvation— nay, the glorification—of Jacob, that the incoming of the Gentile is only the prologue to the stately drama. "So then all Israel shall be saved," he concludes (xi, 26); and, intoxicated with the splendid vision of *all* the Jews redeemed, of the glorified *People of God*, he bursts out into the magnificent apostrophe: "O depth of riches and wisdom and knowledge of God! how unsearchable his judgments and inexplorable his ways!" Such is precisely the view of the evangelist, but shadowed forth by symbolism, not recommended by passionate rhetoric.

35. Let the reader notice the great number of marks by which we identify this Rich One and determine the interpretation of the whole passage—no less than seven, and some of these not single, but multiple. It is most unlikely that any interpretation fitting so accurately at every point can be incorrect. If you put together a very complex machine, as a watch, so that it functions perfectly, you may be practically *sure* that you have put it together right, even though admitting the *abstract possibility* that the maker intended it to be set together otherwise. But probability is the guide of life. We may know, indeed, *a priori* that this paradoxical relation of Jew and Gentile must have vexed the wits of the first Christians, even as it is now inexplicable to such as disregard the essential Hellenism of Christianity; and it would have been strange had it not received treatment in the Gospels as well as in the Epistles.

JEW AND GENTILE

36. In fact, it has received more than one treatment. The parable of Lazarus and Dives is an interesting presentation of the matter. Dives is the rich Jew, Lazarus the miserable Gentile, "poor and needy," "sick and sore"—

obviously and certainly, as is seen in more than one circumstance. Thus Lazarus lay at the gate, waiting for the falling (crumbs) from the rich man's table. Precisely so, the Syrophenician woman (Mark vii, 28) declares wisely that the dogs eat of the children's crumbs. Now no one doubts that by the children are here meant the Jews, and by the dogs the Gentiles; hence the presumption that the same is meant in the other parable. Again, Lazarus is carried to Abraham's bosom, and Dives cast into hell. Exactly so in Matthew viii, 11, 12 it is declared that many from east and west (Gentiles) shall sit down with Abraham in the Kingdom, while the children of the Kingdom (Jews) shall be cast into outer darkness. Again, Dives asks that Lazarus be sent "to my father's house" to warn his "five brethren." What does this mean? "My father's house"—*i.e.*, Jehovah's house—is an Old Testament name for Palestine. Thus in Hosea viii, 1: "As an eagle (Assyria) swoops upon Jahveh's house" (Canaan); Hosea ix, 3, 4, 5, 6: "Thou shalt not dwell in Jahveh's land, but Ephraim shall return to Egypt, and they shall eat unclean (food) in Asshur......for their bread, for their hunger, shall not come into Jahveh's house......Egypt shall gather them up, Memphis shall bury them"; ix, 15: "Out of my house will I drive them" (the people out of the land of Israel). But the "five brethren"? Plainly the five nations of Samaria (2 Kings xvii, 24–41), the five husbands of the woman of Samaria (John iv, 18), who have "Moses and the prophets." Observe, further, the utter disconnection of this parable (Luke xvi, 19–31) with its context; omit it, and the flow of thought is quite as smooth as before. *It is not even put into the mouth of the Jesus.* Obviously it is a parable quite independent, inserted here, but having its own *raison d'être.*

37. The fourth Evangelist has seized upon Luke's statement that they would not believe even though one (Lazarus) should arise from the dead, and developed it into an elaborate story in which a certain Lazarus does actually arise from the dead—with the predicted result: they do not believe, are merely hardened in their unbelief (xi, 46, 53). That such is the interpretation of this minute narrative seems certain, for Lazarus is known to the Synoptic story only in Luke xvi,

20, 23, 24, 25. Now, had Mary and Martha had such a brother, and had such a stupendous miracle taken place under such conditions, it is altogether inconceivable that the Synoptists should have failed to notice it, especially as it was (according to John) precisely this prodigy that was the prime cause of the arrest and execution of the Jesus (xi, 53).

38. We can now see clearly who were the ten lepers healed in Luke xvii, 11-19. Why ten? Why in passing through Samaria? Why did they stand "afar off"? All these indices point to the scattered Ten Tribes of Israel, leprous from contact with heathen idolatry. It seems, indeed, astonishing that anyone can fail to perceive instantly that this story cannot be historic, cannot be a legend, that it must be a symbolism freighted with meaning. Does anyone ask who was the typical solitary Samaritan that gave thanks? Is not his name found in Acts viii, 13? Is it not Simon Magus?[1] This, however, parenthetically and without insistence.

39. Returning to the notion of the rich-feasting Jew and the poor crumb-craving Gentile, we find it beautifully set forth in the parable of the Prodigal Son, the emphasis falling on the joy in heaven at the return of humanity to the true God after its long carousal with the false religions of heathendom. The elder son who looks on so grudgingly, almost as displeased as was the fatted calf itself, though not with such good reasons, typifies most vividly the jealous Jew, so unwilling to share his possessions with his younger Gentile brother—the Jew who had served God so many years, nor ever transgressed a commandment, and who had, indeed, suffered much, and had made merry but rarely in so many centuries. His reluctance was not unnatural. Note, however, that, although he now refuses to enter into the Kingdom, yet his right of primogeniture is not really forfeited. Says the Father: "Child, thou art always with

---

[1] Whose sublime transfiguration is Simon the converted, the penitent, the Apostle, the so-called Peter. Does some one object that this leper could not at one and the same time symbolise a lost tribe and an individual, Simon Magus? But nothing was more familiar to the oriental mind than this representation of a people by a person—the notions of the general and the particular were continually flowing into each other. However, it seems very likely that vv. 15-19 are by a later hand, an expansion of the original simpler idea in view of the prominence of Simon Magus in the early days of the Church. *Simonians*, as we learn from Origen (*C. Cels.*, v, 63), was one of the names applied to Christians.

me, and all that is mine is thine." Again we hear the voice of the Apostle: "So, then, all Israel shall be saved."

40. A still subtler and more elaborate, though far less sympathetic, picture of the Jew is found in that notorious character Judas Iskariot, the Jew the Surrenderer. That such is the meaning of Iskariot seems to be proved, with at least as high probability as commonly attaches to such matters, in another chapter (see *infra*). The term *v'sikkarti* ("and I will deliver up") is actually found in Isaiah xix, 4, and the form Skariotes seems to be only a very slight disguise formed after the analogy of such a Greek word as *stratiotes* (soldier) passing over into Syriac in the form "estratiota." The suffix "he that delivered up (or surrendered[1])" seems to be merely a translation of (I)Skariot, and does *not* mean *who betrayed*. The Jew (Judas) is called the Surrenderer because he surrendered the Jesus-cult (his natural prerogative, monotheism, the true worship) up to the Gentiles. Of course, in this connection, I make no attempt to prove these statements. This idea has, to be sure, undergone much elaboration and some deformation, but it is still distinctly recognisable in the Gospel story. The interpretation of (I)Skariot as "man of Qerioth" is impossible, as Wellhausen (*e.g.*) expressly admits.

41. But by far the most pleasing picture of the Gentile and the Jew in their relations to the new Jesus-cult is given by Luke (x, 38–42). In the two sisters Mary and Martha (Lady), the former sitting at the feet of Jesus (gladly adopting the Jesus-cult), the latter cumbered with much serving (Jewish rites and ceremonies), and demanding similar service from her sister, it seems impossible not to recognise the Gentile and the Jewish world. Consider that it was the habit, many centuries old, to speak of a people as a woman (daughter of Zion, daughter of my people), and then say how the early Christian mind, brooding continually over the knotty problem of the Jew and the Gentile in the Kingdom, could have narrated such an incident *without thinking* of the patent allegory.

42. That the great dramatist John was conscious of the

---

[1] ὁ παραδούς.

true import seems clear from his famous eleventh chapter: "There was a certain invalid, Lazarus of Bethany,[1] of the village of Mary and Martha her sister. It was Mary that anointed the Lord with myrrh and wiped his feet with her hair, whose brother Lazarus was sick." As Lazarus can be nothing but the Gentile world, so, too, his sister Mary. There is no inconsistency, only harmonious variety in the symbolism. This brother is sick even to death—how true of heathendom! All three (both Jew and Gentile) are beloved of the Jesus. Lazarus is designated as "Whom thou lovest" —plainly pagan humanity. Could such an individual favourite of Jesus (the man) have absolutely escaped through the sieve of Synoptic tradition? Impossible! Note, further, the various delicate touches of the artist. The Jesus knows that his "dear Lazarus" is sick, yet delays two days till death intervenes. Why? Whence this strange *motif?* Is it not the long delay of history, the thousand-year patience of Jehovah with the malady of pagandom, that the symbolist sets forth? Again, it is Martha, not Mary (the Jew, not the Gentile), that goes to meet the coming Jesus (in the Law and the Prophets). She is clearly designated as the people of God by the words put into her mouth: "I know that whatsoever thou askest of God, God will give it thee"; "I know that he will rise up in the resurrection at the last day"; "yea, Lord, I have believed that thou art the Christ (Messiah), the Son of God, that cometh into the world." Notice, too, how exquisitely the faith of the Jew is supplemented by the *doctrine of the Jesus:* "I am the Resurrection and the Life," &c.—words that have proper meaning only when understood, not of a person, but of an Idea, a soul-quickening Teaching. Notice, still further,

---

[1] This *Bethany* is in the Syriac and therefore in the Aramaic *Beth* "*ania*," and this latter word has been variously interpreted incorrectly. The corresponding Hebrew stem recurs continually in the Old Testament in the primary sense of *vex, afflict*, and the derived sense of *poor* ("ani"). Now in Luke x, 40, it is said that Martha *was vexing herself*, and the Syriac word is precisely this same "*ania*," as it is also in the Sinaitic Syriac at John xii, 2 (as noted by Nestle, *Phil. Sac.*, p. 20, and as it now stands in Burkitt's monumental *Evangelion da-Mepharreshe*, p. 492), where the received text in all the languages now presents *served*. Bethany, then, means *house of her that vexes herself*, and we see why John has made it the home of the self-vexing Martha. Whether there ever was such a village need not here be discussed. The obvious suggestion is that the name designates Judea or the Jewish nationality, the home of her that received the Jesus when he came thither from the Dispersion.

the very different meeting and conversation with Mary, who falls at the feet of Jesus—*i.e.*, worships him—as Martha did not. Note, too, that Jesus *calls* Mary (the "calling of the Gentiles "), that he never enters into the house of Martha, who *leaves Jesus where she met him*, and *objects to opening the sepulchre.*

43. From childhood the writer could never read this chapter without a feeling of unrest, of bewilderment, as to the parts played by the two sisters, which seemed almost to invert the relations natural in the case; nor was this wholly involuntary mental reaction ever relieved till the symbolic significance of the characters was revealed.

43*a*. John is careful to identify Mary, the sister of Lazarus, as "the one who anointed the Lord with ointment and wiped his feet with her hair." In xii, 2 he emphasises that "Martha served" (rather, "*was vexing herself*" with service—*war bemüht mit der Bedienung*—Merx). It is Mary that overwhelms Jesus with worship, against which Judas (*i.e.*, Jewry) protests. Now, on its face this scene is compounded out of the Synoptic scenes given in Mark xiv, 2-9; Matthew xxvi, 6-13; Luke vii, 36-50, x, 38 42. Perhaps no one will deny this. In Mark and Matthew the scene is laid in Bethany, in the house of Simon the leper; in Luke it is in the house of Simon the Pharisee; but John takes one important item from the scene in the home of Martha in Bethany. In Mark and Matthew it is merely a woman; in Luke she is a fallen woman—a sinner. The writers are perfectly conscious that they are dealing with symbols, and not with history, for they modify the statements freely, to suit the purposes of their thought. Particularly in Luke it seems clear as day that the writer means to set forth the sharp contrast between the receptions accorded Jesus (the Jesus-cult) by the Jews and by the Gentiles. The Pharisee receives him with no mark of honour or worship; the sinful woman overwhelms him with both, and with affection besides. Loisy thinks nothing easier (*rien de plus facile*) than to explain the incident in Capernaum or a neighbouring village—the courtesan could readily enter, thanks to the tumult and freedom that accompany great feasts in the East! (*Ev. Syn.*, I, 684). Is it Loisy or Renan that is writing? About as easy to explain such an intrusion at a dining in honour of a bishop in Boston. Loisy admits a "certain indifference" in the Evangelists as to "mere matter of fact," as well as the presence of what "one might almost call a trace of religious worship." Nor would he seem to hold firmly to the historicity of the incident in Bethany. Other acute biographers of Jesus have remarked the conspicuity of women, even of erring women, in the Gospel narrative, and have shrewdly surmised that the Christ must have been an uncommonly handsome and winsome Rabbi—in fact, "a dear, charming man," such as the Jewish race not seldom perfects in beauty —and must have had a peculiar attraction for the eternal feminine. Nor is it, indeed, easy to do justice to the Gospel narratives as history without some such supposition, for their statements certainly indicate as much, nor are these to be understood as mere gratuitous inventions. On the other hand, how such a marked trait of character is to be set in any even half-way plausible or acceptable *Jesusbild*, without fatal offence to the religious consciousness, has not yet been demonstrated. Thus between Krethi and Plethi the liberal theory of the purely human Jesus goes to pieces utterly.

43*b*. Now, however, the whole explanation is obvious and transparent. In the Old Testament, as well as in the New, an erring woman is the standing symbol for an idolatrous or apostate people. One need only think of the prophet Hosea, of Jeremiah iii, of Ezekiel xxiii (of Aholah and Aholibah), of Matthew's and Mark's "adulterous generation," of the Jezebel of Revelation. As soon as the suggestion is made it becomes clear as light that the sinful woman who anoints the Jesus and bathes his feet with her tears, and covers him with caresses of reverence and affection, can be none other than the *converted heathen world*, so long given up to the shameless service of polytheism. When a riddle or rebus is proposed, one may cudgel one's wits in vain to unravel it. Once, however, the solution is stated, there is no longer any doubt whatever; we see it clearly and distinctly enough to satisfy the most rigorous Cartesian.[1]

---

[1] In his wondrously learned *Biblische Liebeslieder* Professor Haupt has made this observation, and has illustrated it most felicitously by this example: $2 \times 2 = 4$ (*Nichts neues vor Paris*).

Critics need no longer wonder how Jesus exerted such a marvellous magnetism over village Cyprians.

In one case the symbolist, playing on his favourite theme, seems to have fairly outdone himself. Of course, the reference is to the famous pericope now printed in brackets (John vii, 53-viii, 12). The symbolism is perfectly obvious, but the colouring is almost too high; hence it very early gave offence, and never quite established itself anywhere, neither in John nor in Luke, codically. Very likely it was an elaboration of the incident mentioned in Papias, also in the Gospel according to the Hebrews, of the woman accused of many sins and brought before Jesus (Eus. *H.E.*, III, 39). Reuss thinks "the authenticity of the fact appears sufficiently established"! Godet thinks it an "inimitable feature of the life of Jesus"! And yet, long before them, Hengstenberg (as I have just observed) had clearly perceived that the story was the invention of a believer hostile to Judaism, who would depict the pardoning grace of God towards the Gentile world. Such critics refuse to see the most obvious spiritual figure, and obstinately insist upon the most deadening letter of historic fact. One cannot blame them. They are guided by a faithful logical instinct. They feel that they must resist the beginnings—that even a small concession to the symbolic would entail ultimately the surrender of their whole historic theory.

SYMBOLIC INTERPRETATION NECESSARY

44. It seemed proper to dwell at length on this idea of the rich Jew and the poor Gentile, to show how full the Gospels are not only of this thought, but of thought in general; how symbolism of the most pregnant kind constitutes their very warp and woof. Far more than this, however, there is a logical virtue in such elaboration. A symbolic interpretation, however satisfactory in itself, might still be quite unconvincing if it stood alone. When, however, so many fairly obtrude themselves at so many points and call so urgently for acceptance, the demands support each other. We cannot reject *all*. If the improbability of any one be as much as two-thirds, the simultaneous improbability of half-a-dozen (independent) such would be only $\frac{64}{729}$,

or less than $\frac{1}{12}$; there would hardly be one chance in twelve that all six would be erroneous. Now, however, the number of such obvious symbolisms is not six, but rather sixty; yea, more (as analysis of the Gospel clearly shows). We may, then, be practically sure that symbolic interpretation is imperiously required in many cases, here and there, everywhere in the Gospels. But if such interpretation be required at any considerable number of independent points, then it becomes at once antecedently probable that it should be employed wherever easily possible. For, mark you, we have become morally sure of frequent symbolic interpretation; we are not yet, and apparently never can be at any point, morally sure of a matter-of-fact historical interpretation.

45. The liberal critic is challenged to point out a single passage dealing with the Jesus where such a simple historical interpretation is certainly, or with very high probability, required. Note carefully, then: in many cases the historic interpretation is excluded with practical certainty; in many cases the symbolic interpretation is imperiously demanded; in no case (under consideration) is the historic interpretation certainly correct or imperiously demanded; in no case is the symbolic interpretation positively or with compelling probability excluded.

46. I say "in no case," not implying that we can actually make out the symbolic sense in every case. Certainly not. It may very well be that such a meaning may often elude us, for our comprehension of the mind of the Evangelists is only very imperfect; our knowledge of the facts in the case, of all the elements that entered into their thinking, of the views, dogmas and theories they wished to express, is notoriously incomplete. When, then, we fail to find any satisfactory symbolism, it may very well be due to our ignorance of the subject, an ignorance to be gradually enlightened by continued study.

47. Since, then, we have one certain and one uncertain principle of interpretation, it follows that we must employ the certain one as long as and wherever possible; nor dare we invoke the uncertain except in case of necessity, except where the certain proves positively to fail, to be impossible of application. Such is the Razor of Occam, the principle

of Parsimony : *Entia non sunt multiplicanda præter necessitatem.*

48. This logical situation, this location of the burden of proof, must be carefully heeded. It is the object of the New Testament analysis upon which the present writer has been long engaged to bring out in clear and bold relief this large element not of mythical, not of legendary, but of symbolic matter that is certainly present, in the Gospels especially and in Acts. He has never hoped to be able to present a perfectly satisfactory symbolic interpretation of the total content of the quasi-historical parts of the New Testament. Such a result lies perhaps beyond human power, at least under present circumstances of grossly defective human knowledge. But it is certain that a large, a very large, percentage of that content not only may, but even must, be interpreted thus symbolically, as he thinks may be proved to the satisfaction of every competent and open-minded scholar —no other is addressed at present.

49. Moreover, there is no part of that content (touching the Jesus) that anyone has yet made any serious pretence of proving to be certainly historical, if we except the Nine Pillars of Schmiedel; and even these the reader will elsewhere find lying prostrate and crumbling. We are then logically, and even morally, bound to exploit the symbolic method to the utmost, as far as possible, and to reject it—not when *we* have actually failed to succeed with it—but only when it becomes clear that in the nature of the case *no one* can ever succeed with it; in other words, that the historic explanation is positively demanded. There is nothing strange in the form of argumentation here adopted, for it is merely the approved scientific procedure universally recognised and employed as the only proper method of interpreting natural phenomena. Now the existence of the New Testament and of Christianity is also such a natural phenomenon (since history is a nature-process and psychology is the fundamental science); in fact, it is the sublimest, most important, and most fascinating of all phenomena.

EXAMPLES OF SYMBOLISM

50. That there is no cause to lose heart, even though

EXAMPLES OF SYMBOLISM

some features of the Gospel narrative should long resist analysis, is clearly illustrated by the case of the "young man clothed in linen" (Mark xiv, 51, 52). For nearly 1,800 years this youth has been the despair of exegesis. Wellhausen thinks he was merely some unknown fellow in the neighbourhood who heard the racket of the arrest, jumped out of bed, with only a nightrobe around him, and rushed to the scene as young America hastens to a dog-fight. How such a widely learned and keen-sighted scholar can for an instant entertain such a banal view of an item in this succinct, compressed, thought-laden Gospel seems incomprehensible. Zahn (following Olshausen?) has the notable merit of having perceived clearly that this youth was not a mere nobody, that the mention of him must be charged with some kind of deep significance. Accordingly Zahn discovers in him no other than Mark himself! The two verses, he thinks, are in fact Mark's sign-manual, to identify him as author, hid like a painter's in a modest, unpretentious way in a dark corner of his great historical picture! It is impossible not to admire Zahn's ingenuity and the vigour of his imagination. But his suggestion can hardly be taken seriously. Inasmuch as there is no hint of authorship anywhere in the Gospel, that seems a queer kind of signature and identification which consists of a wholly unintelligible mark without even the trace of a *fecit*. Wohlenberg refines on Zahn, and fancies that Mark wished "to conceal and at the same time to reveal himself" as author; and he assumes further that the soldiers had already explored Mark's house in search for Jesus, where Jesus, as Wohlenberg thinks, had just eaten the Passover!

51. These verses appear at first sight to be quite inexplicable, and yet they yield their meaning readily enough.[1] We

---

[1] Curious the bewilderment of Strauss (*Das Leben Jesu kritisch bearbeitet*, § 127). Bacon "paraphrases" thus: "But a certain man was there who had *followed him thither from his bed*, having the sheet wrapped about him." It would seem that a sense of humour should have saved any man from paraphrasing συνηκολούθει αὐτῷ in such a grotesque fashion. The Greek verb is very emphatic; besides, it is imperfect, and is properly rendered by "was habitually accompanying." In Aristotle it is used to designate *necessary accompaniment*, logical involvement. The term is peculiarly unfit to denote the accidental or casual presence imagined by Wellhausen. Volkmar, followed by Keim, Holtzmann, Loisy, Reinach, and others, recalls Amos, ii, 16: "And the stout-hearted among the mighty shall flee naked in that

note that the term "young man"[1] is not frequent in Mark; it occurs only here and in xvi, 5. In both cases it is a "youth wrapt all round about";[2] in this case in fine and costly linen cloth,[3] especially used for cerements; in xvi, 5, in a white robe.[4] Even Leibnitz would have admitted the two figures to be almost *indiscernibles*. The garment in both cases is white, and is the only garment.[5] In the first case the young man is "following along with," in the second he is "sitting on the right." These two passages, xiv, 51, 52, and xvi, 5, are not far apart; the phraseology is strikingly similar—the youths seem strangely alike. Are they related?

52. Let us turn to the Old Testament and see if we can find any prototype. At once we light on Ezek. ix, 2, where we find "one man among them clothed with linen, with a writer's inkhorn by his side"; the same "man clothed with linen" (*'îsh labûsh baddîm*), with no significant change in phraseology, occurs also in ix, 3, 11; x, 2, 6, 7. In Daniel x, 5; xii, 6, 7, we again meet *with the same phrase*. Nowhere else is the phrase found in the Old Testament. In all these nine cases the "man clothed in linen" is a technical phrase denoting a celestial being, an angel or divinity. Evidently in Ezek. ix, 2 he is a Secretary (or Recording Angel), and Zimmern (*K.A.T.* 404) does not hesitate to identify him as "manifestly the Babylonian Planet- and Secretary-God Nabu," akin to the Greek Hermes, whence may be explained very naturally the term "young man" used by Mark. It seems, then, that we are dealing with a technical expression for a celestial personage.[6] In Mark xvi, 5, the "youth clothed in white robe, sitting on the right" of the open sepulchre is unquestionably such a being; in ten cases out of eleven we know certainly the meaning; what, then, is the meaning in the eleventh case? We need

---

day"; in the lxx.: "the naked shall be pursued in that day." But this is *Hamlet* with Hamlet left out; there is no "youth wrapt all round about." Besides, there is no point, no propriety, in the allusion, which would have been possible only for a writer dead set on fulfilling the most out-of-the-way Old Testament passages; such a writer Mark was not. Volkmar's suggestion does not explain that which most needs explaining, though the Amos-passage *may* have been in the mind of the author.

[1] νεανίσκος.   [2] περιβεβλημένος.   [3] σινδόνα.   [4] στολὴν λευκήν.

[5] ἐπὶ γυμνοῦ, xiv, 51; γυμνός, xiv, 52.

[6] Compare Rev. xix, 14, where the heavenly hosts appear "clothed in fine linen, white and pure."

not invoke the tedium of the calculus of probabilities. Sound human understanding does not wait an instant, but says at once that the meaning must be the same in the solitary eleventh, unless there be insuperable obstacles in the way. But there are no obstacles at all. On the contrary, it is plain sailing. The Celestial is the Angel-Self of Jewish anthropology, the Persian *ferhouer* (represented on an extant coin as Sapor II., the rival of Julian the Emperor), a kind of astral body that "follows along with" the Jesus, robed in fine linen to abate its intolerable splendour. The soldiers try to seize it, but it flees away naked, leaving only the linen investiture behind. The fact that such an idea was not strange to the Evangelists is clearly witnessed by Matthew xviii, 10 ("their angels do always behold"—*i.e.*, have access unto—"the face of my Father").

53. What does the Evangelist mean to say by these perplexing words? Thus far he has represented the Jesus exclusively as a god, a being of infinite power; and now this divinity is arrested and carried away to trial and condemnation and death! Arrest, judge, condemn, execute a god! How can these things be? Apparently the Evangelist would give us a hint that he is not to be taken literally. He would whisper to his reader: "Of course, the God-Jesus could not be arrested, but only the garment concealing his divinity, the garment of flesh that he has put on in this my symbolic narrative." Hence the repeated use of the word "naked," both in 51 and 52. Now "naked" (γυμνός) is the equivalent of *disembodied* when applied to a spirit, as in 2 Cor. v, 3. Of the exact shade and shape of the Evangelist's thought we may not, indeed, be quite sure, but there seems to be no doubt of the general identification of the "young man" as a supernatural being.

54. Here, then, is a decisive example of a deep symbolism in this Gospel, and that, too, in the very centre of a mass of seeming historic details. It is noteworthy that the other more humanising Gospels seem to have taken offence at this Marcan passage—at least, none has repeated it. Not strangely. Here, indeed, we may gather a hint at explanation of the absence of the proper conclusion of the Marcan Gospel. Originally it may very well have squinted towards Docetism,

I

have thus incurred the disfavour of the Church, and have fallen a victim to the zeal that in one small diocese (says the Bishop) destroyed such mildly unorthodox documents as Tatian's *Diatessaron* by the hundred.

55. Another most vivid example of Mark's symbolism is found in the Barren Fig Tree (xi, 12-14, 20, 21). Surely no one can for a moment understand this quite literally. To curse a fig-tree, to blast it and wither it, because it did not bear figs out of season ("for it was not the season of figs"), is inconceivable in any rational being, much more in a perfect man or a man-god. If one asks, What, then, is the symbolism? the answer is by no means so certain. It might seem to be a condemnation of some premature endeavour, of some promise without fulfilment. It was once my notion, held subject to revision and correction, that it was aimed at the movement headed by John the Baptist, which seemed to force Messianism and the Jesus-cult prematurely into the open. It is noteworthy that scant words of praise for the Baptist are to be found in Mark. Certainly the movement might be not ineptly likened to a leaf-laden fig-tree suddenly withered from the roots. Matthew and Luke would seem to have thought better of the forerunner, and the apology they introduce (Matthew xi, 7-15; Luke vii, 24-28) might appear to be a perfectly conscious correction of Mark. On such a conjecture one need not insist; it is important only to recognise that the whole story is certainly a symbolism.

56. Matthew has given this incident a still more emphatic form (xxi, 17-22), in which the tree withers instantly ($\pi\alpha\rho\alpha\chi\rho\tilde{\eta}\mu\alpha$, on the spot) at the curse of Jesus. It is impossible even for Zahn (*Ev. d. Matt.*, p. 616) not to recognise herein a symbol; but, with the strange perversity of an acute intellect, he still regards the whole as historical! He rejects, justly, the pretence that the Jesus merely "simulated his futile search for fruits for pedagogical reasons"; neither was his wrath inconsiderate. But his experience with the tree instantly became for him the emblem (*Sinnbild*) of what he had to experience in Jerusalem, of which city the fig-tree was the symbol. Inasmuch as "Jesus did not explain the symbol to the disciples," and they seem not to have understood it, he would appear, in Zahn's exegesis, to have been virtually

talking to himself and acting out parables that no one could comprehend.

57. On turning to Luke xiii, 6, 7, we find the parable of a certain one that had a fig-tree planted in his vineyard, and came seeking fruit on it that he did not find, and therefore ordered its destruction. Naturally, we do not meet with the Matthæan-Marcan incident in Luke; his allegory of the vineyard seems to take its place. Luke declares openly that this is a "parable," and the application to Jewry lies plain on its face. It seems hardly possible that the Lucan and Matthæan-Marcan incidents should not be variants upon one and the same general idea, since the central facts of seeing the fig-tree, coming to it for fruit, and getting none, are the same in all. As illustrating how a symbol may quite innocently and naturally undergo metamorphosis into history, this parable is highly interesting and instructive. It looks as if Matthew and Mark had taken this "parable," worked it up, and then narrated it as historical—of course, with no intent to deceive anyone, but very properly persuaded that anyone might see at a glance that it was purely symbolical. But Zahn and his school will have it that even the most obvious allegories were historical, that the Jesus literally acted his sayings.

58. On this point it may be well to pause for a moment. There may be those who would not deny the often obvious symbolic meaning of a Gospel incident, but would yet hold that the incident did really take place. In 1 Kings xxii, 11 (2 Chron. xviii, 10), we read that Zedekiah ben Chenaanah made him horns of iron, and said: "Thus saith Jahveh, with these shalt thou push the Syrians, until they be consumed"; and there are other such symbolic actions mentioned in the Old Testament. But everyone will admit that Zedekiah (if he really did as recorded) most surely wasted his metal and his muscle, and must have cut a ridiculous rather than an impressive figure. Besides, Zedekiah and the rest explain their emblematic deeds, which, without such explanation, would remain entirely inoperative. But we hear of no such explanations in the Gospels. Consider the case of the healing of the withered hand. Jerome, as already observed (p. 31), perceived the patent symbolism; it was Jewish

Humanity lamed by Tradition, healed by the new Doctrine. No one can deny that the symbolic statement in Mark is a bold, beautiful, poetic metaphor. For the purposes of a circle familiar[1] with such allegories it seems admirably chosen. But suppose the incident had actually occurred. What would have resulted? Amazement, doubtless; but would anyone have dreamed of the symbolic meaning? Certainly not. Even supposing the Jesus had followed up the miracle with an explanation of its significance, it could have made no impression. Everyone would have thought of the astounding miracle itself; no one would have cared for the explanation, which would have seemed trivial. While, then, a man might (foolishly enough) go through some queer performance (in itself meaningless), and then explain it as typifying this or that fact or idea, yet it is quite impossible that anyone should perform some confounding miracle, some wonder in itself highly significant, and then explain it typically. Such an act would defeat its own object, for the marvel of the emblem would rivet all the attention, and leave the emblematised significance quite forgotten. We may, then, dismiss the conceit that the Jesus performed emblematic wonders, as merely puerile. Nor can it be said that the symbolism was intended not for then, but only for now, to

[1] To any one that may doubt this familiarity and the abundant use of such symbolism, it may be recommended to consider these passages taken from Cohen's *Les Pharisiens:* "Not daring to attack openly the tyrants and enemies of Judea, they maintained the popular hatred towards them by a war of allusions which, intelligible only to their auditors, impassioned them against the oppressors of their country. In this way, from the time of the Zealots, Edom and Esau, as types of tyranny and atheism, became the personification of Roman rule. There was invented and put into circulation, against these two foes of Israel, a host of legends applicable to contemporary events; and these have been preserved, although their hidden meaning was lost in the course of time. They preached also the Holy War, in veiled words, and that form of warfare, as earnest as a pitched battle, inflamed the popular enthusiasm" (Vol. II, p. 282). Similarly, others assailed the Hasmonean house, under guise of the academic question: Would pure water lose its purity in passing from a pure to an impure vessel? The Pharisees said Nay, and ascribed to the Sadducees the opinion that water might be pure though issuing from a field strewn with corpses. Now, says Cohen: "The pure water is the Hasmonean succession, which, though present in the person of heirs less worthy than the first Maccabees, is none the less unaltered, whatever the Sadducees may say in their zeal to legitimate the usurpation of Herod by discrediting the later Hasmoneans. The field of corpses signifies the massacres on which Herod had founded his power, which power the Sadducees hold to be legitimate and respectable, despite its criminal origin" (I, p. 362). *So it appears that such symbolism as we find in the Gospels was not merely a native plant, it was a rank growth in the soil from which they sprung.*

teach us. Impossible; for, unless we already have the ideas symbolised, we cannot understand the symbol. No! These incidents, so often miraculous, are *merely* symbolisms; they do nothing but state, in more or less conventional form, frequently with vigour and vividness, some truth or doctrine held by the symbolist, and attributed to the Jesus as the source of all authority.

59. Still more transparent is the bold and powerful account of the demoniac of Gerasa (Mark v, 1-20), which so provoked the indignation, contempt, and merriment of the militant Huxley. Understood as history, myth, or legend, it is certainly utterly impossible, an offence to all reason; but as a symbol it is little less than sublime. Immediately as the Jesus issues from the ship upon the shore, behold! meets him (a) *Man* (notice the single word ἄνθρωπος) coming out from the tombs with spirit unclean. Then follows the vivid description, which we need not repeat. The Man is possessed by a host of foul spirits whose name is Legion. All are expelled, sent into the swine, and with these hurled headlong into the sea; whereupon the demoniac seats himself at the feet of the Jesus, clothed and in his right mind. Is it possible not to recognise herein Humanity—heathen Humanity—possessed by its legion of foul, false gods, unsubduable to the laws and ordinances of Jehovah, which the Jesus-cult restores to its right mind and subjects to the mild dominion of truth and reason? It seems that the mere statement of this interpretation is almost an unanswerable demonstration, while its perfect harmony with the rest of this great symbolic poem-Gospel merely makes assurance doubly sure. Will he who doubts this interpretation suggest some other?

60. Once more we repeat that there is *not a single distinctly human trait or act ascribed by Mark to the Jesus*. Perhaps the example that will instantly arise to the heart and lips of everyone is the blessing of the little children (Mark x, 13-16; Matthew xix, 13-15; Luke xviii, 15-17). Certainly this is by far the most tender human deed described in the Gospels, and has determined more than aught or even all else the current conception of the gentle Jesus. However, only consider. *These "little ones" were believers!* "Whoever scandalises one of these little ones that believe (on me)."

Note, also, that the question is about the admission of these little children to the Kingdom; and it is declared that the Kingdom is (composed) of such[1]—that is, of *them*, not of persons like them. Note, further, that the disciples rebuke those that bring the children to the Jesus, which is quite unintelligible if ordinary babies or children be in contemplation. What sense in scandalising a little child? None whatever.

61. Now turn for a moment to the Talmud and read Jebamoth 22a, 48b, 62a, 97b, Bechoroth 47a: "sojourner who becomes a proselyte is like a little one who is born."[2] And, again, Maimon. Mishneh Torah, Issure Biah, chap. xiv, par. 11: "Gentile that is proselytised and the slave that is free, behold! he is like a little one new born." Here, then, the matter is made perfectly clear. These "little children" or "little ones" are neither more nor less than Gentile proselytes or converts; the question is about their admission on equal terms with the Jew into the Kingdom, the difficult question that so vexed the early Church. The writers are all liberal; they insist on the equal rights of the Gentile; and Matthew, with his wonted splendid rhetoric, denounces ruin upon whoever would scandalise them—that is, make them offend by imposing upon them Jewish rites and ceremonies or restrictions which they would fail to observe, and so would catch them as in a trap. Especially noteworthy is the use of the term "little ones" six times in the New Testament (Matthew x, 42; xviii, 6, 10, 14; Mark ix, 42; Luke xvii, 2), always in the sense of Gentile converts, in

---

[1] Compare herewith the saying of Heraclitus (*Hipp. Rel.*, ix, 9): "Æon (life? Zeus?) is a child sporting, playing draughts; of a child (is) the Kingdom." It seems to have been famous, and is surely "dark" enough to satisfy the most fastidious. Note also that the "little ones" and the "children" are the same, as is clear from Matthew xviii, 1-6.

[2] Compare herewith *I. P.*, ii, 2: "As newborn babes long for the doctrinal undeceiving milk, that by it ye may grow unto salvation, if ye have tasted that *Chrestus is the Lord*." *Chrestus* is here only another form for *Christus*, as Clemens Alex. and Augustin perceived. Similar is the sense of "babes" in the great Gnostic Hymn (Matthew xi, 25-30): "I thank thee, O Father, Lord of heaven and earth, that thou didst hide these things from the wise and understanding, and didst reveal them unto babes." It is the rejection of the Jesus-cult by the Jews, and its acceptance by the Gentiles. Note that it is a doctrine on which the new-born feed and thrive. The ordinary translation, "The Lord is good" or "gracious," cannot be correct, because not in accord with the context.

exact accord with the Talmud, which does not say *child* (*yeled*), nor *suckling* (*yanik*), nor aught else but *little one* (*qaton*).

62. We see now with perfect clearness the noble and beautiful meaning of this passage, and we see further that it bears not the faintest nor remotest witness to the humanity of the Jesus; on the contrary, it testifies eloquently in favour of the system of interpretation it illustrates. The question as to whether Paul the apostle be obliquely hinted at in the *little child set in the midst of the disciples* may be left undiscussed.

63. The prevailing symbolism repeatedly exemplified in the foregoing pages is so deeply interwoven in the intimate texture of the Gospels that to illustrate it adequately would call for a verse-by-verse interpretation, such as already mentioned on p. 96, but quite impossible in this connection. However, it must not pass unnoticed that the failure to observe the often thinly-veiled sense of these scriptures has betrayed the most learned critics into fallacies they would easily have escaped. Thus, in a very recent interview (*Baltimore American*, February 13, 1910), the renowned Assyriologist of Johns Hopkins, rejecting the positions of Professor Drews (known then, perhaps, only through the very inadequate, and even misleading, reports of the daily press), declares that some "one man," some commanding personality, lies behind every world-stirring movement, and that therefore the Jesus was historical—which sounds like a rectification or specification of the well-known Bacbuc oracle of Hegel, that "individuals stand at the head of all actions, and therefore of the world-historical also." Yet the ordinary view is that "in the Hegelian system ideas supersede persons"; and the lamented Professor Friedrich Paulsen, in his well-known *Introduction to Philosophy*, pp. 3, 4, affirms exactly the opposite, referring "mythico-religious" phenomena to the "collective mind": "Nowadays no one speaks of a founder of the Egyptian or the Greek religion." True he says, "The Christian and Mohammedan religions have their religious founders"; these he mentions as peculiar and exceptional—and very naturally, for he had not then read *Der vorchristliche Jesus* and been "blinded by the multitude

of new views," as he wrote shortly before his too early passing.[1]

64. But, to take a single decisive example, one would like to know who was the human personality, "the committee of one," back of Mithraism, which neared or touched Christianity at so many vital points, and which for so many years disputed with it the Roman Empire—at last, indeed, unsuccessfully, but in large measure because it was a man's, a soldier's, religion (as protector of warriors Mithra received for his companion *Verethragna*, or *Victory*—Cumont), and failed to make provision for the Eternal Womanly. Was Mithra, whose worship, as witnessed by monuments, girdled the whole Roman Empire from the Black Sea to the lochs of Scotland and the Desert of Sahara—was Mithra really an historic personality? Or was he an immemorial divinity, the Light "ever waking, ever watchful," "the Lord of wide pastures"?

65. In the same interview we find a liberal interpretation of the miracle of Cana. The jars held water, not wine. The guests grumbled at such a "dry" feast; but afterwards, recalling how beautifully Jesus talked to them, they said it was really wonderful; no one minded the drought; it seemed "as though a miracle had been performed, and he had turned the water into wine." "Thou art so near and yet so far." It seems strange that interpretation can go so widely astray and yet touch the right path at an important point. By such exposition the whole miracle is reduced to the utmost triviality, and the Jesus is equated with some charming post-prandial speaker. That such a thing could have been in the mind of the Fourth Evangelist, profound and solemn as the ether itself, the far-flying eagle of New Testament Scripture, is about as if Hegel should have incorporated the Ballad of Nancy Bell in the second chapter of his *Science of Logic*. Yet the meaning of the Gnostic Evangelist is really not far to seek. In the

---

[1] Some well-disposed reader may instance Buddhism and Confucianism; but neither of the Buddha nor of Reverend Master Kung do we know enough to estimate his personal contribution to the system that bears his name. We may be sure, however, that the doctrine was, like the Gospel commandment, made for those that could receive it—that it was indigenous to the soil in which it thrived.

Synoptics we read: "And no one puts new wine into old bottles" (Mark ii, 22); and again: "Can the sons of the bride-chamber fast while the bridegroom is with them?" (Mark ii, 19, 20). Here, then, we have the presence of Jesus with his disciples figured as a wedding feast, and his "new doctrine" as new wine that could not be put into old skins, which it would burst. In the Fourth Gospel we find these same ideas worked up into a distinct account of a miracle, precisely in the painstaking, artistic fashion of the Fourth Evangelist. In comparison with the wine of the "new doctrine," the old formalism of the Jews was mere water in the jars "of stone set there after the Jews' manner of purifying." At his command the wine gushes forth in abundance, such wine as the guests had never drunk before. What wine, do you ask? The same wine contemplated in the Synoptics—the wine of the "New Doctrine." Hereat, indeed, the world wonders; hereby the new God did, indeed, manifest his glory; and no marvel that his disciples believed on him.

66. Such is the miracle of Cana, the transformation of the Jewish formal doctrine of rites and ceremonies, working outward purifying, into the new spiritual doctrine of the Jesus, cleansing, reviving, and inspiring "the inner man." The abundance of this great "gift of the spirit" is clearly hinted in one little feature of the narrative: the water-pots were filled to the brim. They were six, each of two or three firkins—that is, of 18 or 27 gallons; the six would have held from 108 to 162 gallons—certainly a full supply in any case, especially after the "wine of the marriage had been consummated."[1] Very queer sounds this clause of the Sinaitic Codex, confirmed by countless authorities, for which as many others have the wholly different "wine having failed";[2] whence it appears that the clause is a later insertion, designed to explain the succinct original statement, "and wine they had not"—that is, the "new doctrine," the Jesus-cult, was not yet theirs. Now we see clearly who is this "Mother of the Jesus"—none other than the Jewish Church, as Jerome long ago clearly perceived;[3] the same mother who with "his

---

[1] ὅτι συνετελέσθη ὁ οἶνος τοῦ γάμου.   [2] ὑστερήσαντος οἴνου.
[3] For in commenting on Galatians i, 19 he says: "Now let this suffice, that on account of his high character and incomparable faith and extraordinary

brethren stood without" (the Kingdom), calling him and seeking him (Mark iii, 31-35).

67. This great marriage feast at Cana is, then, nothing less than the introduction of the Jesus-cult into the world, the wedding of the Greek and Jewish religions into the "new doctrine" destined to rejuvenate the earth. Most appropriately, it is called the "beginning of the signs," where we may almost translate σημείων by "symbols." Of course, in all such elaborations certain details are introduced merely for artistic effect, and it would be puerile to dwell on such or to attempt to force an interpretation; but it seems really surprising how accurately the symbolism is carried out, and how vividly the general situation is delineated. Kindred remarks hold of all the Gospel narratives. Hosts of particulars may be only delicate touches of the author's pencil, designed simply to heighten the colour or to improve the dramatic setting; and occasionally some ancient mythical motive may have been active, or some historical reminiscence (*not* of the Jesus); yet it is astonishing how large a fraction of the Gospel total urgently invites symbolic interpretation.[1]

68. The foregoing exegesis of this passage seems so very obvious that little honour can attach to originality, or even to priority. It may, however, not be amiss to remark that it was worked out fully by the present writer in a paper written some twenty years ago on *Numerical Symbolism in*

---

wisdom he was called the Lord's brother, and because he was the first that presided over the Church which, the first to believe in Christ, had consisted of Jews. The other apostles are also called brothers (John xx, 17, Psalm xxii, 22); but he pre-eminently is called brother to whom the Lord, at his departure to the Father, had committed the sons of his mother" (*i.e.*, the members of the Church at Jerusalem, as is manifest and is stated in the words *Hierosolymae, scilicet* in the *Index locupletissimus* to Jerome's works).

[1] The foregoing paragraph seems to be important. To disregard the contribution of the poetic faculty, and to insist on the emblematic interpretation of every detail, would be fatal to any proper comprehension even of avowed allegory. As an example, take the famous parable of the People Israel as a vineyard, found in Isaiah v, 1-7. Here the general sense is straightway obvious, and the interpretation is expressly given in verse 7. But who can interpret the various details of verse 2? No one. They serve merely to make vivid the main idea that Jehovah had been very kind to Israel; they are mere *filling*. Scores of similar instances present themselves in the Gospels. We must be content to recognise the general content in the broad outlines, in the diagram of the symbol, and not seek to trace it in the more delicate shadings.

EXAMPLES OF SYMBOLISM

the Fourth Gospel (not published, but circulated privately), and was with him original. Since then he has read Thoma's discussion in *Das Johannes-Evangelium* (1882), pp. 411-418, where the story is interpreted symbolically with great minuteness; while, strangely enough, the heart of the matter, the identification of the wine with the "new doctrine," is omitted. Kreyenbühl, in his *Evangelium der Wahrheit* (1905), glances at this "sign" repeatedly, understanding it quite correctly (i, 441, 587 *ff.;* ii, 372, 481-483). Indeed, for one that has feeling for the atmosphere of thought that envelopes this Gospel it appears not easy to go far astray.

69. It remains to observe that the notion of wine instead of water is very familiar, and is found in Philo (*Leg. Alleg.*, ii, 76a): "But let Melchisedek bring forth wine instead of water, and drench and fortify souls, that they be possessed of divine intoxication more sober than sobriety itself. For a Priest is Logos, that has the Ens as lot, and sublimely thereof and importantly and magnificently speaketh. For of the Highest he is Priest......"

70. Here, then, is a well-marked example of evangelic symbolism, plain beyond all reasonable doubt. Almost equally clear are all the other (six) signs in this "spiritual" Gospel. Thus, consider the miracle of the loaves and fishes, given also in several forms in the Synoptics. Professor Paul Haupt thinks that the hearers of Jesus listened as in a trance, "none thought of luncheon," and "this story, told and retold, came to assume the evidence and character of a miracle"—an interpretation of which it would be hard to find even a faint suggestion in any of the texts (Matthew xiv, 17-21; xv, 32-38; Mark vi, 34-44; viii, 1-9; Luke ix, 12-17; John vi, 5-71). Even more serious, the essence of the matter is again evaporated or made utterly trivial. Who could have any reverence for a religion that originated in such silly misunderstandings and exaggerations? Are the four Gospels to be interpreted as specimens of Rocky Mountain humour? Sincerely and unreservedly as we admire the learning and ability of such expositors, we must reject their expositions without hesitance, as inadequate

historically and unequal every way to the psychological demands of the case.¹

71. John is himself the earliest interpreter of the Synoptics; and his interpretation, while, of course, it must be interpreted, is nevertheless a trustworthy and unambiguous guide. We notice the long discourse with which he supplements his brief account. The Jesus himself figures therein as the bread of life, the bread that came down from heaven. To eat him is to sate hunger forever. "Except ye eat the flesh of the Son of Man and drink his blood, ye have not life in yourselves." "For my flesh is true meat, and my blood is true drink." It seems that language could hardly be plainer; that the meaning must be patent to the dullest sense. It is simply certain that this bread and wine of the spirit must be a doctrine, an idea, a cult. To eat, to feed on learning, is a form of speech familiar to all times, modern as well as ancient. "Eat this roll, and go speak unto the house of Israel" (Ezek. iii, 1), is the angel's command to the Son of Man. "And I took the little book out of the angel's hand and ate it up" (Rev. x, 10).

72. This weighty thought of complete appropriation of the "New Doctrine" under the emblems of wine and bread (of life) has found impressive symbolic expression in the Eucharist, and is still preserved under such names as trans- or con-substantiation—*quantum mutatus ab illo!* Notice that it is the disciples, the first learners of the "New Doctrine," that distribute it to the multitude; nor is there meant any personal teaching received from the Jesus, for nowhere in the New Testament, nowhere in the apostolic or even immediately post-apostolic age, do we find any such teaching in any measure the burden of their proclamation. On the contrary, it was not any teaching *by* the Jesus, but a doctrine *about* the Jesus,² that they everywhere published from shore to shore, as did the eloquent missionary Apollos

---

¹ Most interesting is the "solution" given by Schweitzer (*Quest of the Historical Jesus*, p. 374), "that the whole is historical, except the closing remark that they were all filled." Far from being "filled," "each received a very little"; it is a "morsel of bread which he gives his disciples to distribute to the people." There would seem to be little magic in such a miracle; but how would it have pleased the hungering multitudes? Would they have hoped much from the kingship of such a wonder-worker?

² τὰ περὶ τοῦ Ἰησοῦ.

all round the Mediterranean long before he had heard of the New Testament story, " knowing only the Baptism of John " (Acts xviii, 24, 25).

73. As already stated, space is wanting to discuss further the miracles of the Jesus, and to exhibit the deep symbolism that pervades them all. But before concluding these specimens let me insist once more that it is on the Gospel of Mark that the issue is most sharply joined. "The main data of his life as enumerated in the Gospels, especially in Mark, may have actually occurred" (*Open Court*, January, 1910, p. 30)! Nay, it is precisely in this Gospel that the humanising process has scarcely begun, that we can see the divine lineaments most unmistakably, the human scarcely at all. "And then," says Pindar's Medea, "the lonely-faring god came suddenly upon us, having cast about him the shining semblance of a reverend man." There is, in fact, in this earliest extant evangelic story not a distinctive human feature; it is indeed hardly even in any guise of man, but openly and unambiguously as God, that the Lion of the tribe of Judah strides through this Gospel. Who will overturn this universal negative by producing a single unequivocal affirmative instance?

THE DIDACTIC ELEMENT

74. As to the "Sayings" (Logoi, Logia), descended from a source higher up than the narration, they have been assembled from every point of the literary compass. Thus, for Matthew v, 25 (Luke xii, 58) we must turn to the Twelve Tables, I ;[1] that a Roman consciousness is speaking is plain from the word *quadrans* (κοδράντην), which Luke naturally turns into λεπτόν (though D, with others, retains κοδράντην). For the justly famous saying (Mark ii, 27), "The sabbath was made for man, and not man for the sabbath," we revert to 2 Maccabees v, 19 : "For not the race for the place, but the place for the race the Lord elected." The antithetic sentiments, "He that is not with me is against me" (Matthew xii, 30; Luke xi, 23), and "Who is not against us (you) is for us (you)" (Mark ix, 40; Luke ix, 50), were uttered the

---

[1] Si in ius vocat, ito. Ni it, antestamino ; igitur em capito.

first by Pompey, the second by Cæsar, and most appropriately by each, at the beginning of the Civil War, as we read in Cicero, *pro Q. Ligario*.[1] "There is none good but one, God" (Mark x, 18; Luke xviii, 19) recalls the Pythagorean maxim,[2] "There is none wise but God"; while the very significant form, "Why askest thou me about the good? One is the Good" (Matthew xix, 17), repeats the doctrine of the Megarean Euclid: "One is the Good, though called by many names" (*Diog. Laert.* ii, 106). True, the gender is masculine in Matthew, but the sense and pertinence of the answer to the question require the neuter, and the two genders were not distinguished in the primitive Aramaic. Merx renders the Syriac: "Was fragst du mich über das Gute? Denn einer ist der Gute (oder: der Gute ist einer, oder: Das Gute ist eines)." Plainly only the last is relevant to the query.

75. The profoundest recesses of ethical character are laid bare in the famous verse of the Sermon on the Mount, Matthew v, 28; but the same depths had already been fathomed 400 years before by the second head of the Academy: "Xenocrates, the companion of Plato, used to say that it matters not whether one put the feet or the eyes into the house of another; for the sin is the same when one views regions, and when one enters places one ought not" (Aelianus, *Variæ Historiæ*, xiv, 42). The difference between the two pronouncements is not ethical, but rhetorical; and the writer has no quarrel with anyone who prefers the rhetoric of the Evangelist to that of the philosopher.

Naturally, the thought became a commonplace in Greek ethics, and even much earlier. "What a beautiful boy!"

[1] 33: "Valeat tua vox illa, quæ vicit: te enim dicere audiebamus nos omnis adversarios putare, nisi qui *nobiscum* essent; te omnis, qui *contra te non* essent, tuos." It is peculiarly gratifying to find in Preuschen's *Zeitschrift für die neutestamentliche Wissenschaft*, 1912, I, pp. 84–87, a careful discussion by W. Nestle, who reaches precisely the conclusion here enounced as obvious on bare statement. But when he says, "Certainly neither our evangelists nor their source knew Cicero's oration," he would seem to be wise above what is written, though he is right in regarding these sayings as "wingèd words" flying round the Mediterranean. It matters little that Nestle does not mention the priority of *Ecce Deus* at this point. Such omissions are no less frequent than trivial. Critics may not like to disfigure their pages with such personalities.

[2] Reproduced by Plato (*Phaedrus*, 278, D): τὸ μὲν σοφόν, ὦ Φαῖδρε, καλεῖν ἔμοιγε μέγα εἶναι δοκεῖ, καὶ θεῷ μόνῳ πρέπειν.

said Sophocles; but Pericles answered, reproachfully: "An official must hold, not only his hands, but also his eyes in check."

The doctrine of self-abasement (as it stands written, especially in Matthew xxiii, 11, 12) seems at first blush altogether peculiar to the Gospel. In fact, however, it was known well enough even in Roman imitations of Greek moralists, as appears from Cicero, *De Officiis*, i, 90: "So that they appear to teach rightly who admonish us, the higher we are, the more humbly [*summissius*] to deport ourselves." Yea, we may confidently maintain that, if we possessed the Greek ethic in its original form and entirety, including the writings of Antiochus and his Fifth Academy, instead of merely meagre remnants or dim and confused reflections thereof, we should find anticipated practically the whole ethics of the New Testament. Even the dogma of the duty of Universal Love to man must have found expression therein, for it is only an immediate and obvious corollary from that other still deeper dogma of Common Humanity, of Man as Man, which Cicero so loves to re-echo in his favourite word, *humanitas*. Hence, it followed directly that one should treat *every* man, even the unworthy, even one's enemies, with kindness—yea, with affection; for were they not one's fellowmen? Assuredly, it is not to persecutors as persecutors, but as our brother-men, that we are to do good. Exactly to this point of view had Aristotle already attained; for when reproached for doing a good deed to a reprobate, he answered: "Not to the man, but to the human."[1]

It is this same dogma that forms the basis of the Law of Reciprocity, the Golden Rule (Matthew vii, 12), as well as of the doctrine of the equality of all men in the eyes of the God of nature (Matthew v, 45).

75*a*. The doctrine of the tree to be judged by its fruits is conspicuous in the Gospels (Matthew vii, 16–21; Luke vi, 43–46). But it was a commonplace far older than the Sermon on the Mount. Says Ovid (*Ars Amat.*, I, 747): "If any one hopes this, let him hope tamarisks will bear apples, and let him search for honey in the river's mud." Plutarch

---

[1] Stobæus, 37, 32: οὐ τῷ ἀνθρώπῳ ἀλλὰ τῷ ἀνθροπίνῳ.

also (*De Tranq. An.*, xiii) : "We do not expect the vine to bear figs, nor the olive clusters." How idle, then, to ask whether the question in Matthew vii, 16 or Luke vi, 44 be the original. Both—and neither.

75*b*. At this point it becomes necessary to note the fact that the most distinctive feature of the Gospel, or at least of the discourses of Jesus, is their prevailing sententious character. More than all else, it is the gnomic allied with the parabolic element that impresses the reader, and has shaped the current idea of the uniqueness of these compositions and their incontrovertible testimony to a single incomparable originative personality. In fact, however, it is precisely this self-same stylistic quality that stamps these writings as *not* emanating from one remarkable individual, but as the aggregated product of the collective intelligence of nations and ages. A teacher may, indeed, intersperse his discourse with occasional aphorisms; but living speech, almost exclusively aphoristic, would be unnatural, and would repel rather than attract. The poems of such as Phocylides and Theognis, the Maxims of a Rochefoucauld, the Lacon of Colton, and other such "Proverbial Philosophies," are the laboured outputs of years of solitary reflection. A proverb is, indeed, the wisdom of many, but it is rarely the wit of one. He who examines even a dictionary of quotations, or collates saws in various languages, must soon perceive that their perfected forms have nearly always been gradual growths that may be traced back through cruder and more cumbrous stages. Even in the Gospels themselves we find many examples of more and of less consummate artistry. Witness the energic grandeur of Matthew vii, 24–27; how superior to Luke vi, 47–49! Compare also the more primitive Lucan Sermon in the Plain with the far more elevated and spiritualised Matthæan Sermon on the Mount. Compare likewise that brilliant cluster, the Beatitudes, with its constituent gems lying scattered in Isaiah lv, 1, lxi, 2; Jeremiah xxxi, 24; Psalms xxiv, 3, 4, xxxvii, 11, cix, 28, cxxvi, 5, 6. Surely it is not hard to forgive the scribe who, by omitting a single letter (σ), has sublimed the primary angelic song, "Glory on high to God, and on earth peace among men of (His) good-will" (*i.e.*, His people Israel), into "Glory on high to God, and

THE DIDACTIC ELEMENT

on earth peace, among men good-will." Such cameo work abounds in these scriptures. The starry words of the New Testament are evidently stones that have been polished to perfection by the attrition of the ages.

75*c*. There can hardly be a more serious error than to ascribe this purely literary quality to the personality of Jesus, or, indeed, to any other. Aside from the fact that he would in all probability have spoken Aramean, the literary style—so far ranging from Mark to John—stands in no relation to the supposed individuality. Jesus and John are thought as contrasted, and even antipodal; yet their styles are the same. The great speech of the latter (Matthew iii, 7-12), with slight changes, would fit as well the lips of the former. Indeed, both denounce the Pharisees as a "brood of vipers" (Matthew iii, 7; xxiii, 33); both use precisely the same words about the Tree and the Fire (Matthew iii, 10; vii, 19); they proclaim the Kingdom in identical terms (Matthew iii, 2; iv, 17).

75*d*. In this connection the recent papyrus finds, with their new "Sayings of the Jesus," are of striking interest. Though each introduced by the solemn formula, "The Jesus says"—apparently exactly in line with the Old Testament preamble, "Thus saith Jehovah"—they seem often to have nothing in common with the Gospels but the unmistakable gnomic stamp—the hall-mark of the earliest Christian literature. Clearly they are *disiecta membra* of a once imposing organism. Such Logoi may have existed aforetime in almost countless number. Oblivion has swallowed them up with so much else of ancient literature. Here and there some few have escaped, and are seen *rari nantes in gurgite vasto*. The salvage of our canonics is like the seven tragedies of Sophocles—seven out of eighty! We may suspect, however, that what has survived is the best—not all of it the best, nor all of the best, but on the whole the most worth saving. The Christian consciousness has sifted and re-sifted, has tested the spirits whether they be of God; it has polished and refined, has set and re-set, the precious stones, until the great citadel of its faith gleams and flashes like the bejewelled gates of the New Jerusalem.

75*e*. Illustrations of the foregoing theses might be multiplied interminably. Take one additional, to which Eisler (*Weltenmantel und Himmelszelt*, p. 733) has already called attention. In Herodotus (I, 141) Cyrus answers the request of Ionians and Æolians for terms they had already rejected with the "saying" of the fisher who, having caught in a net the fishes he had vainly tried to lure ashore by piping, on observing their leaping about, said to them: "Cease dancing for me now, since when I piped you would not come out and dance." Evidently this was a familiar fable, to which the Gospel parallel (Matthew xi, 17; Luke vii, 32) harks back, in expanded and more rhythmic form, though in being diverted to its new application its edge has been somewhat turned. Such "Æsopic sayings" (Logoi) abounded, and formed a staple of cultured Hellenic table-talk, just as the Italian interlards his speech with proverbs and the American with humorous exaggerations. The Evangelists did not, indeed, take from Herodotus, but from the common treasury of ancient wit and wisdom. To attempt to deduce the character of Jesus from the "Sayings" ascribed to him is like trying to make out the features of the man that sat for a composite photograph.

76. In still further illustration let it be noted that the remarkable and important statement of the method of Jesus (Mark iv, 33, 34), "And without a parable spoke he not unto them, but privately to his own disciples he expounded all things," seems echoed back from the *Theætetus* of Plato (152, C), where Socrates exclaims: "Well, then, by the Graces, was not Protagoras an almighty wise one, who spake this in enigma to us the mixed multitude, but to his disciples in secret spake the truth?" For the celebrated oracle concerning the two ways (Matthew vii, 13, 14) we revert to the Eleusinian mysteries; for the saying about measures (Matthew vii, 2) to Hesiod; for the terrible picture of social conditions preceding the impending cataclysm (Mark xiii, 12, 13; Matthew x, 21) to the cuneiform inscriptions. Similarly, in 1 Cor. ii, 9 we hear a clear echo of Empedocles (I, 8, 9a, *Plut. Mor.* 17E): "So neither seen are these things by man, nor heard, nor by mind comprehended."

77. In the mysterious utterance, 1 Cor. xv, 28, "that

THE DIDACTIC ELEMENT

God may be all things in all,"[1] we meet with the famous doctrine (homœomery) of Anaxagoras, that all elements or "seeds of things" were so completely mixed that something of each appeared in each, "all things in everything."[2] So, too, the extraordinary combination in Eph. iii, 18, "the breadth and length and height and depth," is a *formula* recurrent in the magic papyri.

78. Likewise the pathetic exclamation in Romans (vii, 24), "Me, miserable man! who shall deliver me from the body of this death?" is heard again in Epiktetus, quoted by M. Antoninus (iv, 41), "Thou art a little soul carrying a corpse," as is also the notable verse (vii, 15) describing the inner conflict of natures, "For not what I would, that do I practise; but what I hate, that I do." So Epiktetus declares (*Diss.* II, xxvi, 4): "(The sinner) (ὁ ἁμαρτάνων) what he will, does not; and what he will not, does." This epistle (not to the Romans, but "to all those that are in love of God"[3]) is, in fact, in high degree Stoical, as witness the frequent recurrence of "God forbid" (μὴ γένοιτο), the logical use of which was peculiar to Stoical disputation. It pervades Epiktetus.

---

[1] ἵνα ᾖ ὁ θεὸς [τὰ] πάντα ἐν πᾶσιν.

[2] καὶ οὕτως ἂν εἴη ἐν παντὶ πάντα, πάντων μὲν ἐν πᾶσιν ἐνόντων, and many equivalent phrases.

[3] So reads the older text of i, 7: πᾶσιν τοῖς οὖσιν ἐν ἀγάπῃ θεοῦ—see the proof in the writer's article in the *Journal of Biblical Literature*, Part I, pp. 1–21, 1901, and the words of Harnack in a following number of Preuschen's *Zeitschrift* (1902, p. 84): "It is the custom to remain content with the Received Text, but Smith is right in declaring it interpolated"; and again, after statement of reasons: "Ἐν Ῥώμῃ is, therefore, to be regarded as a very old interpolation." In his *Einleitung in das Neue Testament*, i, 278 (1897), Zahn spoke of the absence of ἐν Ῥώμῃ "in ancient times" "from an occidental (Nr. 1, 2) and an oriental (Nr. 5, 6) text," but *never suggested* that either was the original text. On the contrary: "We see, therefore, much rather a process of text-corruption, which, having begun in i, 7, has in G developed so much further as to involve i, 16, also." After writing to me twice about it and pondering the demonstration given in 1901 and Harnack's acceptance thereof in 1902, in the third edition of his *Einleitung* (p. 273 *ff.*), he has abandoned his former position, and "has given the exacter proof" that the text with "*Rome*" cannot be "original"; and he repeats and completes the same in his recent commentary on *Romans*, Exc. I., p. 615 *ff.*, still speaking of ἐν Ῥώμῃ (instead of Ῥώμῃ), as interpolated! Similarly Lietzmann, in his commentary just appearing. But neither of the twain mentions the present writer, because, forsooth, as a mere *outlandish* author, he has no rights that they are bound to respect. A queer survival of primitive "group" morality.

THE PAULINE QUADRILATERAL

79. We are thus brought to the "Pauline" epistles, and especially to the "acknowledged" first four—the innermost citadel of liberal criticism. When driven from every other stronghold, the higher critic will certainly take refuge in this redoubtable quadrangle. No elaborate attempt can be made in this work to dislodge him thence. Only a few observations, however, are needed to show that even it is not impregnable.

80. In the first place, it was precisely the long-continued study of these epistles that drove this writer to his present position. In fact, the extremely slight dependence of exactly these four on any biographical theory of the Jesus is, in relation to the present discussion, their most striking feature. We do, indeed, hear of the death and resurrection; but in the only allusion in Romans (*e.g.*) to the crucifixion it is declared (vi, 6), "knowing this, that the old man was concrucified" (with the Christ?); and again, "we were then consepulchred with him" (vi, 4); so, too, in Gal. ii, 20: "I have been concrucified with Christ." Of course, it is easy to say that these expressions are mere figures; but if there was a symbolic burial (in baptism, as all admit), why not also a symbolic crucifixion?

81. Consider, again, the phrase in Gal. iii, 1: "O foolish Galatians, who was bewitching you, to whom before your eyes Jesus Christ was portrayed crucified?" The word προεγράφη (portrayed) hardly admits of satisfactory rendering, but it indicates certainly a most vivid depiction, and apparently a physical representation, and much more than a teaching "most definitely and plainly concerning the meritorious efficacy of the death of Christ"—a thing which Peter and Paul nowhere do in Acts.

82. Consider, again, the Pauline boast, "bearing round always in the body the dying of the Jesus" (2 Cor. iv, 10), and that other, "For I carry in my body the brands[1] (στίγματα) of the Jesus" (Gal. vi, 17); and it will seem hard to resist the

---

[1] Similarly might the follower of Mithras have spoken, for he was branded indelibly with a hot iron (Cumont, *Les Religions orientales*, p. xiv).

suggestion that there was in the very earliest initiations, as part of "the mystery of godliness," some physical representation of the suffering God, in which the initiates shared a symbolic life-and-death history, perhaps not wholly unlike what was enacted in Greek mysteries. Further guesses need not now be hazarded at this point, but reference may be made to 1 Tim. iii, 16 as lending colour to the foregoing.

83. An objector will certainly cite the Last Supper as witnessed in 1 Cor. xi, 23 *ff*. But the remarkable thing is that the apostle does not profess to know about this matter (itself a symbolism, as we have just seen) from any human historic testimony (as that accomplished Grecian, Georg Heinrici, clearly perceives, and sets forth in Meyer's Commentary), but by divine revelation: "For I received from the Lord what I also delivered to you, that the Lord Jesus," &c. We may not be sure what the apostle means, but it is surely not any witness he bears to the supposed historic fact. (See Addendum, *infra*.)

84. Once more, that these epistles are saturated with Gnosticism comes variously to light. A single illustration must suffice. In 1 Cor. xv, 8, we read: "And last of all, as if to the Ektroma, he appeared also to me." Our translators have rendered ὡσπερεὶ τῷ ἐκτρώματι by "as unto one born out of due time"; but in so doing they omit an important word, the definite article τῷ (to the). Their word *one* excludes the Greek article. This translation cannot, then, be correct; it does not give the sense of the original. The subtlest spirit of Protestant exegesis, Carl Holsten, gives half a large page of fine print to explaining this "dark expression"; but in the end he elicits nothing that is less dark, though confident that his "alone" "is the explanation of the whole passage." This same he had evolved from his own inner consciousness, in apparent disdain or ignorance of the fact that *the Ektroma* is a constantly recurring term in the Gnostic doctrine of Sophia and the Æons, where it is entirely in place and quite comprehensible, however visionary. That such a doctrine and application of the term could have proceeded from this passage, to which they are quite unrelated, is in the last degree improbable; that the term should have been imported into our passage and used there as sufficiently definite and

well known to call for no comment is a simple and natural literary phenomenon. (See Addendum, *infra*.)

85. Meyer and Heinrici explain the article τῷ as designating Paul as "pre-eminently the premature birth (*Fehlgeburt*) among the apostles"! Paul, whose birth into their ranks was not premature, but postmature! Nor do they any more than Holsten dream of the Gnostic employment of the term. But when they tell us of "what weight Paul here and in ix, 1 lays on the actual and real appearance of the Lord," we must reply that he does indeed put his own experiences in the same line with those of the others. Hence we may judge of theirs by his own; but his own seem to have been purely intellectual, or at least mental merely: "When it pleased (God)......to reveal His Son in (*or* through) me, that I should preach him in the nations, straightway I conferred not with flesh and blood, etc." (Gal. i, 15-17). Meyer and Heinrici have imported the words "actual and real" out of their own theory into the statement of the Apostle, to whom these appearances were not visions, but spiritual perceptions of the fundamental dogmas of his propaganda.

86. Turn which way you will, then, it becomes ever clearer that exegesis and commentary have hitherto been playing on the face of these wondrous scriptures, that there is everywhere a far deeper primitive sense than even the critics have suspected, that we have been feeding on the husk and not on the kernel, that we have been trying to sound the depths of the ocean with fish-hooks.

87. This remark leads to the further observation that the scheme of interpretation herein sporadically exemplified—an interpretation so strenuously suggested and recommended by the pre-eminence of the parable in the Gospels—could hardly be misunderstood more completely than if supposed directed against the New Testament, or even against Christianity in its original sublime conception. Interpretation, indeed, has strictly nothing to say either for or against; it raises no question of true or false; its sole object is to understand, to reveal the mind of the author, to find out precisely what he meant, what he intended to say. Faith and unfaith have nothing whatever to do with the case.

88. However, it is possible and even proper to lay two interpretations side by side and to ask which is the nobler, worthier, more inspiring, more uplifting, more soul-satisfying. Such a test must not indeed affect in the least our critical judgment, for our allegiance is due, first and last and all the time, to the truth, to the God of things as they are; yet we need not disclaim either preference or aspiration. Accordingly, comparison is boldly invited, comparison of the symbolic interpretation with either the current liberal or the traditional conservative, in the confident anticipation that any unbiassed intelligence will perceive that the interpretation here illustrated is not only historically, philologically, and theologically justified and demanded, but that it renders far superior honour and majesty, power, beauty, and sublimity to the Apostles and to the New Testament, to the Christian religion and to the Jesus the Christ.

ADDENDA

I.—JESUS THE LORD

89. A very plain indication (which, like other matters discussed in these Addenda, could not find a natural place for treatment in the body of the foregoing discourse, but is too important to be passed by unnoticed) of the very early identification of the Jesus with Jehovah is found in the regular application to him of the term *Kyrios* (Lord), which is the uniform Septuagint rendering of the divine name, the tetragram JHVH, in the Old Testament. It is true that this word Kyrios is also employed in the New Testament precisely as is the term *lord* in English, or *seigneur* in French, or *Herr* in German. Nevertheless, in spite of such use as a class name, when used with the article and without specification, as in *the lord*, and *der Herr*, and *le seigneur*, it is perfectly unambiguous, and means Jehovah, God. So, too, in the New Testament: Lord, the Lord, the Lord Jesus, the Lord Christ, all mean one thing, and only one thing—namely, the Supreme Being—the Jehovah of the Hebrew, the God of the Greek.

90. In the case of such a usage, much depends upon the consciousness on which it is based. If any deeply religious western Aryan in this age speaks of the Lord, the Saviour, the Redeemer, the Messiah, no one ever dreams of any other than the one necessary reference. The speaker would be horrified if anyone should misunderstand him. Now the consciousness that speaks to us throughout the New Testament was more intensely religious than perhaps any at the present day; it was saturated with the Septuagint and kindred versions of the Old Testament. The use of the term *Kyrios* to designate God and to translate Jehovah (Adonai) was as familiar to it as indeed it was possible for any use to be. When, then, such a consciousness applies the term regularly to the Jesus, the conclusion is quite unescapable that it would thereby identify the Jesus with Deity.

91. Let it be noted carefully that this application of the divine name is not a late phenomenon. It did not make its appearance gradually; there is no trace of slow and cautious introduction. By no means! The very earliest layers of the New Testament deposit, if we may trust the results of critical inquiry, show this usage as distinctly as the latest. Leaving aside all possibly doubtful cases, we find the Jesus called the Lord in Matthew xxi, 3; xxviii, 6 (not to mention iii, 3); Mark xi, 3 (xvi, 19); Luke ii, 11, 26; vii, 13, 19; x, 1, 39, 41; xi, 39; xii, 42; xiii, 15; xvii, 5, 6; xviii, 6; xix, 8; xix, 31, 34; xxii, 61; xxiv, 3, 34; Acts, i, 21; iv, 33; v, 14; viii, 16; ix, 1, *et passim*. In the Epistles, even the very earliest (supposedly), as Galatians and 1 Thessalonians, the usage in question is so well known and regular as to make citations superfluous, if not impertinent. Similarly in the Apocalypse, as we have already seen.

92. In fact, the term is applied so indiscriminately that it is a matter of difficulty and often impossibility to determine whether the reference is to the Lord God the Jehovah of the Old Testament, or to the Lord Jesus the New Testament Jehovah. This notable and indisputable phenomenon seems to exclude positively every theory of a gradual deification of the Jesus. Had any such process taken place, it appears scarcely possible that no trace of it whatever should have

survived, and that the earliest extant literature in equal measure with any other should have unhesitatingly and without explanation applied to the Jesus a term that on its face identified him with the Supreme Deity.

93. Hereto we must add the further consideration that doubts and questionings concerning the human character of the Jesus make themselves heard both in and out of the New Testament precisely as we might expect, if the notion was not primitive. Thus, no trace of such a scruple is to be found in the great mass of the New Testament scriptures. If the earliest propaganda proclaimed a God, an over-earthly being to whom a certain earthly career was ascribed only symbolically and by way of teaching certain profound, important, and revolutionary truths—if no one at first took this ascription literally, but understood it correctly in harmony with the general religious conceptions of the age and clime—then there is nothing to wonder at: the earliest presentations contain no controversy on this point, because this point was not in dispute; it was fairly and generally comprehended.

94. If, as the days went by, the symbolism began to crystallise and to be taken literally, if increasing emphasis fell upon the human aspect, upon the historic representation, the incarnation or coming in the flesh, then the champions of this materialism would naturally begin to recommend it in writing; they would declare it was the truth, and the only truth, and they would proceed to denounce the non-progressive adherents of the elder view as old fogies, as heretics, and as schismatics.

95. Exactly such denunciation we find in the admittedly late First and Second Epistles of John. In 1 John iv, 2, the test is stated: "Hereby know ye the Spirit of God: Every spirit which confesseth that Jesus Christ is come in the flesh is of God: and every spirit which confesseth not (or annulleth) Jesus is not of God: and this is the (spirit) of the antichrist, whereof ye have heard that it cometh; and now it is in the world already." Similarly 2 John 7: "For many deceivers are gone forth into the world, (even) they that confess not that Jesus Christ cometh in the flesh. This is the deceiver and the antichrist." Here, then, at that comparatively early date, in the bosom of the Church we find these antichrists,

whose offence was not that they denied the Christ, but that they rejected the coming in the flesh *as an historical fact*.

96. Of course, we are told universally that this rejection was a new error just introduced into the Church. Certainly, in all such cases, each side must represent its view as the good old truth, the other as a novelty and false. The "antichrists" whom John denounces would almost surely have replied that theirs was the old truth and his the new error. Which was right? We must weigh the probabilities in the case. Observe that John represents a rather lower view of the Jesus Christ than is familiar to us from the early scriptures. The Jesus is presented almost exclusively as the *Son*, in contradistinction from the *Father*. Such a Son is, of course, divine, but the naïve, unquestioning identification of the Jesus with God is not found. These Johannine epistles nowhere use the term *Lord*.

97. It seems impossible to read these epistles without feeling that the position assigned to the Son is distinctly subordinate to that of the Father. Very different is the earlier language of Acts, of the Paulines, of the Apocalypse, of the Synoptics, where the Son-Father relation is indeed expressed, but not so emphasised, and where the Jesus is continually called by the highest designation of Lord.

98. Now, if the humanity of the Jesus was an integral part of the earliest Christian consciousness, then at the date and stage represented by the Johannines this consciousness would seem to be growing faint, even passing away among many. Along with this there would naturally go an increasingly lively consciousness of the divinity, an exaltation or even an over-exaltation of his Godhead. This, however, we do not find; rather the opposite, at least in the Johannines. Nor can we make it at all clear how the denial of the humanity came about, if from the first it was preached and belonged essentially to the propaganda. No superior wit is required to recognise that the natural desire to make vivid the doctrine and symbols in question would of itself bring forth a host of narratives all contributing to the *humanisation* of the Hero. No one that postulates the fundamental principles of human nature can fail to admit the necessity of such a process, which seems to be attested at countless points in the New Testament

itself, and by universal admission has produced an innumerable host of apocryphal and extra-canonical stories.

99. The current, in all these writings that we know aught of, sets unmistakably and undisputably towards humanisation. Nevertheless, the Johannines (and the same may be said with even stronger emphasis of the Ignatians) witness incontestably the existence of such as denied the humanity, as resisted the humanisation. Either, then, this latter view of the matter originated near the time of the Johannines and Ignatians (say near but after 100 A.D.), or it was itself original, and the humanising view came forward conspicuously about that time. Remember, the humanising tendency is a fact; it is attested by all history, and in this particular case it is superfluously proved and incontestable; whereas the opposite *dehumanising* tendency is entirely hypothetic, unwitnessed by any fact, and devised solely to account for the fact of the existence of those who denied the humanity. As such an hypothesis we must reject it, *unless it be necessary;* it is shaved off by Occam's Razor.

100. But it is not at all necessary; nay, it is not only superfluous, but cumbrous and bewildering. Let us suppose for an instant that the divinity of the Jesus, and not the humanity, was the primitive doctrine; then the observed humanisation follows naturally, almost inevitably, from fixed psychological laws; the championship of John and Ignatius becomes so intelligible as to call for no explanation, and the heretical "antichrists" appear as nothing but familiar old fogies left behind on the primitive standpoint.

101. On the other hand, suppose that the conception of the Jesus as a man was the original; then the course of development becomes oscillatory, and hard or impossible to understand. Following this supposed earliest conception we find that of Mark, in which the key-note of humanity is lost, drowned in the note of divinity. But this latter begins straightway to grow slightly flat, while the human sounds out louder and louder, till suddenly once more it is damped nigh to extinction among the Docetists, while ringing clearer and clearer among the orthodox. These undulations remain scarcely, if at all, intelligible, after infinite efforts to explain them. Strictly rectilinear development we may not in reason

expect, but any imagined evolution from an original doctrine of the humanity of the Jesus seems highly unnatural and improbable.

II.—DIFFUSED LIGHT OF SYMBOLISM

102. The interpretation of the Gospels, particularly Mark's, as symbolic exhibitions of the progress of the Jesus-cult enlightens many a dark point in the ordinary understanding of those scriptures. For example, we are told (Mark vi, 5, 6) that in "his own country" "he could do no mighty work," and that "he marvelled because of their unbelief." Mark here implies what Matthew expresses—that he did not work many miracles there "because of their unbelief." Now, this seems passing strange, that his wonder-working should be conditioned by their belief or unbelief. Elsewhere we find his power easily transcending any such limitations. Surely the stilling of the tempest was not rendered less easy by their "little faith." The son of the widow, the daughter of Jairus, and finally Lazarus, long since committed to the tomb, did not have to believe in order to be revived. In fact, the notion that any power of physical healing or other thaumaturgy possessed by the Jesus was dependent on the faith of anyone seems quite unworthy of the Son of God and the New Testament, and fitter for Mrs. Mary Baker Eddy and the *Science of Health*.

103. Nevertheless, not only here, but almost as explicitly in other places in the Gospels (as in Mark ix, 23), this dependence of the power of the Jesus on the faith of the subject is affirmed, and even emphasised. Incomprehensible as this must be so long as we think of the Jesus as an historic personage, it is not only comprehensible, but almost self-evident, as soon as we think of him as standing for his doctrine, his cult. Plainly the spiritually healing power of such teaching depends essentially, if not absolutely, upon the faith of the taught.

104. Here, then, we see clearly vindicated the supreme position held by *faith* in the Christian system—not *faith in a person*, to which, in spite of all the might of the deep-

eddying ocean of oratory that has been poured round it for so many centuries, no adequate idea can ever attach, but faith in a Doctrine, in an Idea, the Idea of the One God, the Heart of the Universe, the unifying Principle of the Cosmos, conceived and worshipped not merely as King, Creator, Ruler, but also as the Healer, the Guardian, the Saviour of the World. It is this ethical, metaphysical, religious, philosophic, theosophical Idea that meets us in endlessly diverse forms throughout the earliest Christian literature, whether apostolic or post-apostolic, whether in the New Testament or in the Fathers, whether in Apocalypse or Apocrypha, whether in Evangelist or Epistolist or Apologist: an idea quite as conspicuous by its presence in all this literature as the human personality of the Jesus is conspicuous by its absence. It is this Idea that conquered the circummediterranean world for Christianity; that, having almost perished, revived later in distorted and degenerate form, yet still found strength to subdue the Asian and African coast to Mohammedanism. Let no one marvel that an idea should work such wonders. What else but ideas have ever accomplished the really great things of history? Hereby we need enkindle no strife with the hero-worshippers. Ideas must incorporate themselves in personalities.

105. Perhaps no one would forgive the writer even of a slight sketch, should he pass over without any notice the Last Week in Jerusalem. Here such severe analysts as Brandt think they find the very ultimates, the irresoluble elements of the earliest and most veridical tradition. In truth, however, the conditions are not very peculiar; no special difficulties of interpretation are present. It is a great idea, the idea of salvation through suffering, the suffering of a God, that has received most elaborate and, at points, even pathetic dramatisation. This was the very centre of the splendid historic canvas, and most naturally it has been treated with especial care and delicacy of detail. But the guidance of ideas has at no point been abandoned; on the contrary, it has been everywhere followed with noteworthy conscientiousness. The vague general notion of a great vicarious sufferer seems almost as old as humanity itself; certainly it might have been suggested by aboriginal

experiences, even should we not refer it ultimately to the awful phenomenon of an eclipse of a Sun- or Moon-God, which must have impressed deeply the devotees of any astral religion. But for the capital detail of the Crucifixion we should look much nearer home. The notion of the *impalement* of the Righteous found its classical and immortal expression in the second book of the *Republic*, in a context of matchless moral sublimity.[1] Glaukon, putting Socrates on his mettle, draws the liveliest possible picture of the sufferings of the Just who is thought unjust: "He will be scourged, will be racked, will be bound, will have his eyes burned out, (and) at last having suffered every ill he will be crucified" (361 D). The last verb (ἀνασχινδυλεύω) is commonly rendered by "impale," and is rare; but it is the exact equivalent of ἀνασκολοπίζω, which again is exactly the same as ἀνασταυρόω (as in Philo i, 237, 687), which appears in Heb. vi, 6 (where it has been falsely rendered *crucify again*), and is the regular Greek word for *crucify*, shortened also into σταυρόω, the New Testament term. The ἀνα means *up*, and not *again*.

106. How deeply this image of the Righteous crucified had stamped itself on the religious consciousness seems remarkably attested by the fact (to which M. Salomon Reinach has called attention) that in the Psalmist's description of the sufferings of the Righteous (Israel) the LXX have rendered the Hebrew *ka'ari* by ὤρυξαν : "they *dug through* (A. V. *pierced*) my hands and my feet." Now, it is true that the Hebrew is highly uncertain, but in any case we can hardly believe the writer meant *dig* or *pierce*, because the act is attributed to *dogs* (heathen), who might tear or rend or do other cruel things, but would scarcely pierce or dig through hands and feet. Whether or not, then, the LXX understood the Psalm (and particularly this v. 17) messianically, as do the moderns, their translation would

---

[1] If anyone would estimate the uplift in ethical theory during two thousand years, let him compare Plato's treatment with that of the greatest Anglican Church dignitary, Bishop Butler, Sermon xi, 21, *in fine:* "Let it be allowed, though virtue or moral rectitude does indeed consist in affection to and pursuit of what is right and good, as such; yet, that when we sit down in a cool hour, we can neither justify to ourselves this or any other pursuit, till we are convinced that it will be for our happiness, or at least not contrary to it." Consider also the apologetic note suffixed by Gladstone.

ADDENDA

seem to indicate that they entertained the idea of a crucifixion as the climax of the passion of the Just. Such being the case, this form of execution of the Jesus was imposed upon any religious consciousness nourished on the Septuagint, as was the Evangelic. Hence followed with a certain necessity that He should be executed by the Romans, not stoned like Stephen by the people, and thence through natural combinations the story of his surrender by the Jews to the Romans, which afterwards became the account of how Judas delivered him up to the Jews and they to the Romans. But the Passion and the Pillars of Schmiedel must be reserved for another discussion. Only be it remarked here as elsewhere (Preface) that the apparently earliest Gospel-source Q, the "Sayings," as now recognised by Harnack, stops short of the Judæan ministry, which thus appears to have been an afterthought forming no part of the most primitive Gospel.

107. In conclusion, it should be repeated (as too liable to be forgotten) that in showing the Jesus of Proto-christianity to have been a God, and not a man, one by no means depreciates the *rôle* or the importance of personality in affairs human, particularly in the genesis of Christianity. The early propagandists were great men, were very great men; they conceived noble and beautiful and attractive ideas, which they defended with curious learning and logic, and recommended with captivating rhetoric and persuasive oratory and consuming zeal. "The Apostle" (Paul) and Apollos and Peter and John and Stephen and Philip, not to mention Barnabas and the great unknown symbolist whom we call Mark, and *Autor ad Hebræos*, and the learned and eloquent James, with other Epistolists and Evangelists, were striking, powerful, and imposing personalities; they were mighty fishers, but fishers of men. The first, indeed, looms up vague and vast as the bulk of "Teneriffe or Atlas unremoved; His stature reached the sky, and on his crest" he bore flaming the principal mottoes that have formed thus far the main dogmatic content of Christianity, both militant and triumphant. No wonder that Wrede and others have thought him, rather than the Jesus, the founder of our religion. If by the Jesus he meant only the magnified man of modern criticism, the comparison is inevitable, and the judgment of Wrede does

not seem strange nor unenlightened. But the Jesus the God is, of course, quite incomparable with Paul the Apostle.

108. A modern sentimentalist will insist that grand ideas can neither save nor convert men, whose hearts must be touched by the story of the Cross, and the tender gentleness and loving-kindness of the meek and lowly Jesus; and the missionary confidently hopes to be able to render these features so attractive as to draw all people, Asiatic and African, into the Church, whence they will issue to the final conversion of the unfeeling European and American—the Mongolian and the Hottentot will in the end convert us to our own religion!

109. Such expectants seem to forget or ignore many significant truths—as that reason is a topmost flower on the tree of humanity; that history presents frequent examples of suffering and devotion and self-sacrifice perfectly in line with the New Testament narrative; that the earliest depiction of the Jesus is singularly wanting in the very features that the sentimentalist would stress, and instead throws all emphasis on the sterner traits of infinite power and knowledge; that the tenderly human traits belong to the later forms of the Gospel, and are sometimes even interpolations, as in the case of the famous prayer on the Cross: "Father, forgive them, for they know not what they do" (Luke xxiii, 34—of course, it is not less noble and sublime for being late "Western" than if it were early Eastern). They seem also to overlook such characteristic touches as are found in Matthew x, 14, 15, 34, 35; xi, 20-24; xviii, 17 and xxiii, *passim*, not to mention Luke xvi, 1-9; xviii, 1-6, especially in comparison with Matthew vi, 7.

110. Such passages are sore puzzles to the expositor, who finds it almost impossible to treat them with perfect fairness; but they do not bewilder him who once perceives that it was *not* the purpose of any evangelist to *depict a character at all, much less a perfect character*, but to describe symbolically various aspects of the progress of the Jesus-cult, and to express under guise of parable various details of the "new doctrine." The Synoptists were as little concerned to portray a perfect man as were the prophets or the authors of the Pentateuch in their sketches of Jehovah.

111. But there is here still another and far more important lapse of memory; for such expectants forget that the primitive preaching was addressed to a highly cultivated but *polytheistic* consciousness. *Here is the nerve of the whole matter.* The message of earliest Christianity was irresistibly strong and compelling, because it proclaimed monotheism to a consciousness that had lost faith in its own theory and worship of polytheism, because it proclaimed "*God-worship*" ("theoseby"), the service of one and only one God, always and everywhere the same, to minds and hearts that were already on the point of revolt against the ubiquitous but many-coloured idolatry. As the "everlasting Gospel," proclaimed with mighty angelic voice, " Worship Him that made heaven and earth and sea" (*Rev.* xiv, 6, 7), this message reverberated from shore to shore louder than Sinai's thunder and roused to life a waiting world already tossing and restless in slumber; no other conceivable message at that time and place could have wrought such a marvel; the preaching of the Jesus of modern criticism, of a wise and amiable Jewish rabbi, as the God and Saviour of an idolatrous world, would have been justly derided as puerile and ridiculous.

112. Lastly, does someone find it hard to breathe in such a rarefied atmosphere of symbolism, and hard to believe that the first Scripturists would voluntarily choose to express themselves in such fashion? Let such an one consider that for this reason or for that the *Maschal* (symbol, simile, parable) was then unquestionably a favourite in the highest degree,[1] that a *large portion of the Gospels consists of such avowed metaphors*, and that it is expressly said by Mark: " Without a parable spake He not unto them." How deeply the mind of the Scripturist was tinged with this habit of symbolism may be inferred from the story of Sarah and Hagar and Ishmael, which seems to us to be as plainly, simply, and unequivocally historical as anything in literature. Yet says the apostle: "Which things are allegorical" (Gal. iv, 24). If the principal author of the New Testament interpreted such an unvarnished biographical detail as an

---

[1] See the footnote to sec. 58, p. 115.

elaborate allegory, are we wrong in still further widening the circle of symbolical interpretation in the Gospels, where, in any case, it must admittedly be drawn with a radius so exceptionally large?

III.—THE SO-CALLED PAULINE TESTIMONY

Supplementary to Article 83.

113. This passage (1 Cor. xi, 23 *ff.*) figures so importantly in the writings of the critics, they appeal to it so confidently as the "ground-reaching pillar of the lofty roof" of their whole theory of Proto-christianity as emanating from the man Jesus, that it may be well once for all to examine it minutely. In order to do this, we must unite in one view the four accounts found in our New Testament, which accordingly are here presented in parallel columns, and the Synoptics in the oldest (Syriac) form, as translated by Burkitt (*Ev. Da-M.*, I., 231, 157, 397):—

MARK XIV, 22–25.—And while they were eating bread he blessed, and brake and gave to his disciples, and said to them: "Take, this *is* my body." And he took a cup and blessed, and gave to them and they drank from it. And he said to them: "This *is* my blood of the new covenant, that for many is shed. Amen, I say to you that no more shall I drink of the offspring of the vine, until that day in which I shall drink it with you newly in the kingdom of God."

MATT. XXVI, 26–29.—And while they *were* eating Jesus took bread and blessed *God* over it, and brake and gave to his disciples, and saith: "Take, eat this is my body." And he took a cup and gave thanks over it, and gave to them and said: "Take, drink of it all of you; this is my blood, the new covenant, that is shed for many to forgiveness of sins. For I say to you that I shall not drink from now of the fruit of the vine, until the day that I shall drink it with you new in the kingdom of my Father."

LUKE XXII, 17–20.—And he took bread and gave thanks over it and brake and gave to them and said: "This is my body that *is* for you; so be doing for my memory." And he took a cup and gave thanks over it and said: "Take this; divide *it* among you. I say to you that from now I shall not

1 COR. XI, 23–27.—For I received of the Lord that which also I delivered unto you, how that the Lord Jesus in the night in which he was betrayed took bread; and when he had given thanks, he brake it, and said, This is my body, which is for you; this do in remembrance of me. In like

drink of this produce of the vine until the kingdom of God come."

manner also the cup, after supper, saying, This cup is the new covenant in my blood: this do, as oft as ye drink *it*, in remembrance of me. For as often as ye eat this bread, and drink the cup, ye proclaim the Lord's death till he come.

114. No critical intelligence is needed to perceive that Mark and Matthew are here practically identical, the latter adding only the one important phrase "to forgiveness of sins." Plainly, also, the other pair are very closely, though not quite so closely, related. The main, the essential, difference between the two couples is that the second declares the establishment of this Supper as a permanent institution among the disciples ("do this in memory of me"), whereas nothing of the kind is hinted in the first. Now this is a highly important addition. If Mark and Matthew had known of any such institution, at this critical juncture, of the most important sacrament of the Church, it is quite unbelievable that they would have passed it by in silence. Moreover, Luke is in general admittedly later than Mark. It will perhaps, then, not be denied that this vital moment (of the institution of this permanent sacrament) is a Lucan accretion to the older account.

115. In fact, it seems very hard, on reading Mark and Luke consecutively, not to recognise that Mark is more primitive, that in Luke the thought has visibly developed and expanded while the text has suffered dislocation or mutilation. Now pass to Corinthians. Is it possible not to perceive a still further growth? The formula of institution is here repeated, and the second time with especial emphasis: "This do as oft as ye drink, unto my memory."[1] Also the author still further stresses this idea by his own pronouncement: "As oft therefore as ye eat this bread and drink the cup, proclaim ye the death of the Lord, till he come." Here, again, the thought is measurably advanced. Surely no one

---

[1] This turn of expression, with various others, as "table of the Lord," "communicants of the altar," "communicants with demons," was not original with "the Apostle," but was known to the terminology of the cult-unions long before our era. See Heitmueller, *Taufe und Abendmahl im Urchristentum*, p. 71 (1911).

can marvel at the gradual enlargement of dogmatic content, no one familiar in the least with the history of dogmas. But how could anyone understand the shrinkage of content from Corinthians through Luke and Matthew down finally to Mark? If Corinthians gives the original form and sense of the incident, then the same must have been known to Mark and Matthew, as representing the earliest traditions. How, then, shall we explain their fore-shortening, their omission of the very pith and nerve of the whole matter? Plainly nothing but the most compulsive proof could justify us in dislodging Mark-Matthew from their natural precedence and yielding the priority to Luke-Corinthians. Have we any such compulsive proof? *Absolutely none whatever.*

116. What? Is not Corinthians much earlier than Mark? We need not raise here the general Pauline question. That is another matter. For the purposes of this argument (and only for such purposes) we might fully grant that this epistle as a *whole* proceeded from Paul, and was earlier than Luke or even Mark. Such a concession would not for a moment imply that *this particular passage* was earlier than any Synoptic, or that it proceeded from Paul the Apostle. For it is a notorious fact that the original New Testament Scriptures have in general been subject to revision, over-working, and interpolation. Why, then, should 1 Cor. be exempt? Why should it form an exception to the general rule? Even if there were no visible traces of insertion, no internal grounds of suspicion, nevertheless, since the passage presents obviously a comparatively late stage of dogmatic evolution, we should be perfectly justified in regarding it as a late accession to the text. However, there are very cogent internal reasons for holding the verses to be a later incorporation into an elder text, reasons wholly independent of the relation borne to the Synoptics.

117. For, firstly, these verses occur in a region of interpolation. This whole eleventh chapter, from verse 2, is a standing puzzle. The powerful exegesis of Carl Holsten, after long and painful wrestling, is compelled to admit that verses 5b, 6, 10, 13, 14, 15, are interpolations, and must be "expunged," if we are to understand the

Apostle. A still closer study seems to show that even more extensive expunctions are necessary. But if these five verses *must* be elided, what sure patron protects verses 23–25?

118. Moreover, it is hard not to believe that a late consciousness is speaking in verse 2. Paul can scarcely have reached Corinth before A.D. 55; he remained there "many days" over a "year and a half" (Acts xviii, 11, 18), which would bring his departure from Ephesus nearly to 57. About a year or less thereafter, in 58, he is supposed to have written 1 Cor. Yet in this verse he praises "you that ye *hold fast the traditions,* even as I delivered them unto you." Certainly such language sounds very strange addressed to a congregation hardly two years old. And what traditions? Can we really think of Paul's own "insight" or "a revelation vouchsafed to him" as meant by such "traditions"? Consider also the astonishing disorders into which the congregation had fallen in so short a time. Consider the fact that there had been many deaths ("many sleep," xi, 30), which of itself seems to imply necessarily a considerable lapse of time, much more than two years. In fact, the whole atmosphere of the chapter seems charged with suggestions of a long interval, and not a mere twelve- or twenty-month since the founding of the church and the departure of the Apostle.

119. More than this, however. It is plainly not the Lord's Supper proper, but the common Love-feast, the Agape (very like our picnic), that is contemplated in verses 17–22, 33, 34. Contending factions met; it was "*not possible to eat the Lord's supper*"; some hungered, some were drunken; each took his own meal in advance. "So, my Brothers, when ye come together wait for one another" (33). Plainly it is not our sacramental Eucharist, but rather the Agape, that is here in mind. The two were closely related, and are often hard to distinguish. But it is not difficult to perceive that there is a most notable confusion of thought. At verse 23 the key of the composition changes; it is not now the Agape, but the Eucharist.

120. We hold, then, with confidence that all the indicia point to the comparatively late origin of these famous verses

xi, 23–26 (as they now stand).[1] Before they can be used in evidence of the historicity of the event in question, as witnessed by Paul, there must be given some surety that they are not interpolated, that Paul actually did write them as we now read them. No such surety has ever been given—nay, none such has ever been seriously attempted. On the contrary, all the signs are against the Paulinity and against the antiquity of the whole passage in question.

121. We may go even still further. It is well known that the Mithraic Sacrament very closely resembled the Christian, so closely that Justin charges imitation upon the wicked demons, who seem *capable de tout*: "Which, indeed, also in the mysteries of Mithra the wicked demons imitating, taught to be done; for that bread and a cup of water are placed in the mystic rites of him that is being initiated, with certain incantations, either you know or you can learn" (*Ap.* i. 66c). Tertullian bears similar witness (*De pr. haer.*, c. 40). No one perhaps will agree with the Christian worthies in their explanation of the resemblance. In both cases the Sacrament is the expression of a wide-rooted religious idea.

122. Add to this that the venerable and trustworthy *Didache*, while discussing the Eucharist at great length (ix, x, xiv, 1), knows nothing whatever of the Gospel account, nothing whatever of body and blood, nothing whatever of the Gospel ideas. So important is this witness that it should be quoted in full :—

> But concerning the Eucharist thus bless [eucharise]. First, concerning the cup : We bless thee, our Father, for the holy vine of David, thy child [servant], which thou madest known to us through Jesus thy child : to thee the glory unto the æons. Then concerning the morsel[2] : We bless thee, our Father, for the life and knowledge

---

[1] In his *Taufe und Abendmahl im Urchristentum* (64–69) Heitmueller finds in Paul at least "three groups of conceptions" concerning the Eucharist: (*a*) Communion with Christ, 1 Cor. x, 16; (*b*) Communion with one another, 1 Cor. x, 17 ; (*c*) Commemoration of Christ's death, 1 Cor. xi, 23 *ff*. Of these he recognises (*a*) and (*b*) as the earlier, "the fundamental view"; (*c*) as a "more theologising interpretation," in which "reflection begins gently" concerning the "act of the cult." But all this would be quite impossible if 1 Cor. xi, 23 *ff*. were the eldest account and conception of the "symbol and sacrament." Heitmueller's view, however cautiously expressed, cannot fail to confirm strongly our present contention.

[2] κλάσματος.

[Gnosis] which thou madest known to us through Jesus Christ thy child—to thee the glory unto the æons. As was this morsel scattered upon the mountains and was assembled [as] one, so be assembled thy Church from the ends of the earth into thy kingdom; because thine is the glory and the power through Jesus Christ unto the æons. But let no one eat nor drink of your eucharist, but those baptised into name of the Lord; for concerning this hath spoken the Lord: Give not the holy to the dogs. And after being filled thus bless: We bless thee, Father holy, for thy holy Spirit, whereby thou tentedst down in our hearts; and for the Gnosis, and faith and immortality, which thou madest known to us through Jesus thy child—to thee the glory unto the æons. Thou Master Almighty createdst the universe because of thy name; both nurture and drink thou gavest the men for enjoyment, that we might bless thee; but unto us thou vouchsafedst spiritual nurture and drink and life everlasting through thy child. Before all we bless thee that mighty art thou: [to thee] the glory unto the æons. Remember, Lord, thy Church, to save it from all evil, and perfect it in thy love, etc.

In the presence of this extremely ancient Teaching concerning the Eucharist, how is it possible for anyone to maintain that the Gospel story is historical and the Corinthian version primitive? Are they not manifestly elaborate and deep-thoughted symbolisms? Do they not bear the most unimpeachable testimony directly *against* the cause for which they are called into court?

123. When now we turn to 1 Cor. x, 14-22, we hear a *more primitive* note quite in accord with the "Teaching" just quoted. "Wherefore, my beloved, flee from idolatry." Surely this sounds Proto-christian. "The cup of blessing which we bless, is it not communion of the blood of the Christ? The bread that we break, is it not communion of the body of the Christ? Because one bread, one body, we the many are, for we all partake of the one bread." In the Teaching the morsel is the symbol of the unity of the brotherhood, its particles having been scattered in divers grains upon the mountains, but now all gathered into one loaf. With "the Apostle" the idea of unity is the same; but it inheres not in the loaf, but in the participation of all in the same loaf. Prefer which you will. And what is this "body of the Christ"? The notion pervades the New Testament, but the passages most directly in point are these :—

1 Cor. xii, 27 : " But ye are Christ's body, and severally members thereof."

Eph. i, 23 : " And gave him to be head over all things to the Church, which is his body, the fullness of him that filleth the All in all."

Eph. iv, 12 : " Unto edification of the body of the Christ " (the Church).

Eph. v, 30 : " Because we are members of his body."

Eph. v, 23 : " Himself Saviour of the body " (the Church).

Col. i, 19 : " And he is the head of the body, the Church."

Col. ii, 17 : " Which is shadow of the things to come, but the body is the Christ's."

Col. ii, 19 : " Nor holding fast the Head, from whom all the body......increases (with) the increase of God."

124. Here the conception of the Church (or congregation) as the body of Christ is quite too clear for argument. The communion of the loaf symbolised in one way or another the organic unity of the many members. As there was one body, so also there was one spirit (" One body and one spirit," Eph. iv, 4) ; and of this the chosen and fitting symbol was wine, which inevitably suggested blood, even as it is written : " Only flesh with its soul [nephesh], its blood, shall ye not eat " (Gen. ix, 4 ; *cf.* Lev. xvii, 11, 14; Deut. xii, 23). That such was the original idea there seems to be not the shadow of a doubt. How easily it might give rise to a story such as we find in Mark, and how naturally this might develop into the Lucan and Corinthian accounts, and thence into the tremendous medieval dogma, must be clear to every student of history and psychology. On the other hand, it is quite incredible that anyone knowing or having been taught the awful origin and import of the Last Supper, as given in 1 Cor. xi, 23–26, or even in Mark, should ever speak of it in the terms used in 1 Cor. x, 16, 17, and in the " Teaching." Herewith, then, the guns of this boasted battery are not only captured ; they are turned destructively upon the critics that trained them. The simple primitive and long-cherished conception of the Eucharist not only does not prove the historicity of the Last Supper, but it does prove decisively the non-historicity and purely symbolic content of

the incident in question. Since, as Heitmueller has just declared, the passage (1 Cor. xi, 22 *ff.*) is a "theologising interpretation" (of the "fundamental conception" in 1 Cor. x, 16, 17), then assuredly it is *not* an historical narrative.

125. It remains to consider the famous passage in 1 Cor. xv, 1–11. Into the grammatical and textual difficulties that herein so abound we need not enter; certain general reflections may suffice. First, then, it seems very strange that such a chapter should be written to a congregation very recently founded by the writer, from which he had been absent about a year or two, to which he was expecting soon to return. That such controversies should have sprung up almost instantly upon his departure, that they should have been reported to Paul, that he should try to settle them at a distance by such argumentation, seems queerer and queerer the more one ponders it. Moreover, the tone of the opening verses is not at all what we should expect under the circumstances: "Now, I make known to you, brethren, the gospel which I preached unto you, which also ye received, wherein also ye stand, by which also ye are saved, with what word I preached it unto you, if ye hold it fast, except ye believed in vain." Surely this extreme formality is most unnatural. Would Paul "make known" to them by letter the gospel he had been preaching to them nearly two years? Would he have reserved such an all-important matter for the next to the last heading in his letter? Would he have failed to hint at it in the beginning and body of his epistle? Would he have given precedence to the coiffures of the Corinthian women? Would he have described his preaching the gospel as handing down a tradition he had himself received—he that preached from the inner light of revelation, and conferred not with flesh and blood? "For I delivered unto you first of all that which also I received, how that Christ died for our sins according to the Scriptures, and that he was buried," etc. We look in vain through Acts for any such preaching of any apostle, and quite as vainly for any such attitude of Paul handing down a tradition received from others. It seems hard to blink the fact that the Epistolist is rather far down the stream of tradition, that he is addressing a long-

established Christian community, and that he makes little pretence to first-hand authority.

126. Such scruples are nowise allayed by minuter inspection of this "Gospel," which consists essentially of a chronological grouping of appearances of the Risen Christ. Mark well that it is Christ or the Christ throughout, thirteen times, only in verse 31 is it "Christ Jesus our Lord," and in verse 57 "our Lord Jesus Christ," never Jesus. This seems far away from the "Jesus and Anastasis" which he had just preached on Mars' Hill and from the spirit of the proclamation in Acts. It seems to represent a Judaic standpoint distant from any found in the Gospels, and apparently measurably later. Observe also the careful ordering of the appearances. Can we ascribe the like to Paul? Does it not represent a stage of historisation (or tradition, if you will) distinctly later than the Synoptic, reminding us of the Fourth Gospel (xxi, 14), and the Marcan appendix (xvi, 9, 12, 14)? Note, further, that the phrase *The Ektroma*, used as needing no explanation, implies a well-developed Gnostic consciousness, and on this point see *infra*.

127. Looking at the whole body of indicia, we cannot find one that points to Pauline or to early authorship. We find many that point away from both. But even supposing that all these tokens, by which we are here dealing with an appendix to Corinthians, were misleading, and that the paragraph really proceeded from the Apostle, what of it? Would it firmly establish the Gospel record as history? Would it even show clearly that the Epistolist was himself writing history? By no means! For be it noted that the Death was "according to the Scriptures," that the Resurrection also was "according to the Scriptures." The reader need not be taught that this phrase, equivalent to "that it might be fulfilled," characterises the Justinian theory of history also expressed in another appendix, Rom. xv, 3, 4, according to which the Old Testament was a perfect mirror of Christian story, on looking into which one might discover what this story was by seeing what it must be, with little study of contemporaneous testimony. If death and resurrection had been found to be "according to the Scriptures," then such a theorist would without hesitation affirm them, not

indeed as exactly matters of history, but at least as articles of faith, as true in some super-historical sense. There are scores of such historisations in the Gospels, as critics almost unanimously recognise. In order to bring about such a postulated fulfilment of Scripture, Matthew does not shrink from seating the Jesus at the entry to Jerusalem upon the ass and her colt (xxi, 5, 7). This impossibility has worried the Fathers and critics far more than it did Matthew, who was intent solely upon his idea, and would let the facts take care of themselves.[1]

When these things are said to have happened "according to the Scriptures," the reader is clearly informed that they happened in the aforesaid Justinian sense; the statement is a certificate of their dogmatic necessity, not of their historic actuality.

128. But what of the appearances, six in number, upon which the main stress is laid? Does anyone competent to judge in such matters really find herein any testimony to the humanity of the Jesus? It seems hard to believe. What is meant by "appeared" ($\H{\omega}\phi\theta\eta$)? In the case of Paul we have some evidence. Three times in Acts such an appearance is described (ix, 3-7; xxii, 6-9; xxvi, 12-15). At midday a light falls upon him, it is not hinted that he saw anyone; he hears a voice unheard by his companions (xxii, 9) calling him to preach to the Gentiles, to turn them "from the power of Satan unto God" (*i.e.*, from polytheism to monotheism). On its face the whole account seems to point to a purely psychical experience: the light is the light of the truth, brighter than the sun at noon; the voice is that of conviction and resolution, heard only in the depths of the individual soul. This view of the matter is fully confirmed by various passages in the Paulines, as by Galatians i, 16, 17: "But when it pleased God......*to reveal his Son in me*, that I

---

[1] Zahn and Blass meet the difficulty boldly; the former reads "him" ($a\vec{v}\tau\acute{o}\nu$) instead of the first "them" ($a\vec{v}\tau\hat{\omega}\nu$), and applies it to the colt, while referring the second "them" ($a\vec{v}\tau\hat{\omega}\nu$) to the garments; the latter does likewise, except that he more heroically strikes out the second "them" ($a\vec{v}\tau\hat{\omega}\nu$)—both missing the mind of Matthew, who was merely bent on fulfilling literally the prophecy: "Thy King cometh......riding upon an ass *and* upon a colt, foal of a yokeling," and did not observe that the *and* (ו) in Hebrew meant *yea* ("Sitting upon an ass, yea upon a colt, foal of she-asses"). Zech. ix. 9.

might preach him among the Gentiles......" If we render the Greek by "through me" instead of "in me," the case remains as strong. The revelation is still a psychic process brought about by psychic means. Similar is 2 Cor. iv, 6: "Seeing it is God, that said, Light shall shine out of darkness, who shined in our hearts, to give the light of the knowledge (Gnosis) of the glory of God in person of Christ." Not pausing on the heavily freighted phraseology, we see so much clearly, that the light was spiritual—indeed, intellectual illumination.

129. If such then was the "appearance" to Paul, what right have we to suppose that it was aught else to Peter and to the rest? None whatever. We must assume that the appearances were alike, until reason is shown for thinking them different. No such reason is even to be sought *outside* the Gospels, and it is precisely because no reason for supposing any other than psychic revelation is to be found *in* the Gospels that appeal has been made to Corinthians. And here we now find this appeal decidedly rejected, and the case referred back to the Gospels! The fact is that the so-called Pauline testimony strongly confirms the symbolic interpretation of the Gospel. The appearance or revelation of the Jesus or Christ or the Son of God is everywhere the same, and means primarily the intellectual enlightenment that attends conversion to the Jesus-Cult, to Monotheism, to the worship of the One God "in person of Christ," and the voice is the angel voice of right reason, proclaiming the everlasting Gospel, "fear God and give Him glory" (Rev. xiv, 7). As Epicharmus nobly sang, "Reason sees and reason hears: All things else are deaf and blind." We affirm, then, confidently, that the so-called Pauline testimony at every point runs directly against the current dogma of the humanity of the Jesus.

Herewith all the important Pauline "proofs" have been considered. Various others, mainly detached phrases, are indeed sometimes cited, though not worth citing. Careful discussion of all, at request of a correspondent in Europe, shows clearly they have no significance either singly or collectively; to resort to them is to abandon the battle. When the field-forces are routed, the navy sunk, the forts dismantled, the *capital surrendered*,[1] a few desperate fighters may escape to the mountains, and there in dark caverns and inaccessible retreats maintain a tedious guerrilla contest. Such patriotic courage never to submit or yield may indeed be magnificent and admirable—but is it war?

IV.—THE EKTROMA
Supplementary to Article 84.

130. The central problem in Gnostic theory (the doctrine of the *Gnosis*, the knowledge of the One Supreme God) was the venerable cosmologic-theologic one of the relation of the Creator to the Creature, of God to the Universe. Following in the wake of the old Academy, the Gnostics sought to fill in the whole sphere of possible being between the opposite poles of pure Deity or Noumenon (Bythos) and Phenomenon (matter) with a succession of conjugate emanations, projections, or æons varying from six to thirty in number. Of these there was one set of twelve (projected by Anthropos and Ecclesia or Logos and Zoe), of which the last pair were Theletos and Sophia. Of these two the latter (said they) became possessed of an overmastering desire to bring forth or project an æon independently of her conjugate, in emulation of the primal inconjugate activity of the central Godhead (Bythos). This passion (Enthymesis) of this twelfth æon resulted disastrously; the projection or emanation proceeding from her was indeed Substance, but was shapeless and unordered, as lacking the masculine form-giving virtue,[2] and was technically and fitly called *The Ektroma*.[3] The Ektroma was really nothing but the formless stuff (Hyle) of Aristotle, the Tohu-va-Bohu of Genesis i, 2, as is shown by the citation in Hippolytus: "And this is, he (the Gnostic) says, what Moses speaks, *the earth was invisible and unordered*."

131. Inasmuch as all the preceding æons were not only

---

[1] As apparently by Heitmueller in the passage just quoted.
[2] οὐσίαν ἄμορφον, οἵαν φύσιν εἶχε θήλειαν τεκεῖν, *Iren.*, I, i, 3.
[3] ὥσπερ ἔκτρωμα, *Iren.*, I, i, 7; ἐπὶ τῷ γεγενημένῳ ὑπ' αὐτῆς ἐκτρώματι, οὕτω γὰρ καλοῦσιν, Hip., *Ref.*, vi, 31.

substantial, but were heavenly forms, it was perfectly natural for the Gnostic to call this formless emanation of Sophia *The Ektroma* (abortivum). Plainly the notion is derived from, or at least correlated with, the passage in Proverbs (viii, 12 *ff.*), where Hokhmah (Wisdom) is so highly extolled as having assisted the Creator at the founding of the heavens and the earth. This is doubly evident from the other name, Achamoth, which they gave to Sophia (not to Enthymesis, as Tertullian thought), which is manifestly only a thin disguise of the Hebrew name Hokhmah, or the Syriac Hekhmetha, though Tertullian declares it to be "uninterpretable" (*Adv. Val.*, xiv). Thus the Ektroma appears as the *last* and *least* of the æons sent forth, as, in fact, *not worthy to be called* an æon, being defective in its generation.[1] In view of this Gnostic speculation, and *only in view of it*, the self-depreciatory language of the Apostle now becomes perfectly clear and remarkably apposite.

132. Of course, the reply of the critics will be, and must be, that the relation is just the inverse, that the Gnostics took the notion of the Ektroma from this passage in Corinthians. But such a contention it is impossible to maintain. That such an obscure and far-fetched phrase should have given birth to the highly organised and elaborate Gnostic doctrine of æons or emanations would be as marvellous as any of the inconceivabilities of that doctrine itself; whereas the comparison in Corinthians appears natural and almost inevitable *when, and only when, the whole Gnostic* theory is presupposed. I say the *whole theory*, not, indeed, in its details (which varied greatly from thinker to thinker), but in its spirit and general outline. The notion of the stuff of the physical or phenomenal world as an Ektroma, an imperfect projection of a spiritual nature, is a highly abstract cosmologic-metaphysical imagination, evidently the result of prolonged and profound philosophic meditation. It reminds us forcibly of the modern doctrine

---

[1] This queer conceit, of the imperfect æon, was really a thoroughly honest attempt to clear up the darkest of mysteries, the origin of evil, by interpreting this evil as a pure *negation*. This form of explanation has exerted a strong fascination over the profoundest intellects, and has been repeatedly revived in later times, as by Spinoza. We may smile at the bizarre inadequacy of the Gnostic solution; but where the ancient failed, what modern has succeeded?

that one's physical world is one's own ideas, the spatial construct of one's psychic experience. Still more, it is a part and parcel of the general theory of successive emissions or reflections of the primal essence, each (pair) a dimmed and reduced image of the preceding; and this scheme of interpolation goes back at least to the stern and stainless Xenocrates (396–314 B.C.).

133. Perhaps an objector may urge that the æons (or emanations) were figments of the Valentinian fancy, and that Valentinus belonged to the second century. It is answered that only the finer elaborations may properly be ascribed to Valentinus; the bolder conceptions and broader outlines antedate him by generations, if not by centuries. Even in the tradition and polemic of the Fathers (who were eager to bring down Gnosticism to the very latest date possible, to represent it as the most modern innovation, and their own orthodoxy as the long-uncorrupted ancient truth) the origins of Valentinianism are traced back to Simon Magus, the *elder* contemporary of Peter (Acts viii, 9, 11—note the "beforetime" and "long time"). Hippolytus (*Ref.*, vi, 12, 18) tells us that Simon already had his æons and his emanations in pairs, at least three such, some of whom—*e.g.*, Sige (Silence) and Nus (Reason)—agreeing in name, position, and importance with the latest Valentinian characters; Enthymesis, also, the passion of Sophia, whence came the Ektroma, is one of the Simonian æons, paired with Logismos (Ratiocination). Plainly, then, the æonian system was not the origination, but at most merely the elaboration, of Valentinus; and of this system Sophia and her Ektroma must have formed a very ancient part; for the notion of the first and of her creative zeal is given clearly in Proverbs (viii, 12 *ff.*), and the second lies at the threshold of Scripture (Gen. i, 2), in the "Earth without form, and void," which was the first sensible or phenomenal issue of the supersensible cosmogonic energy.

134. Does some one remind us that Irenæus (I, i, 16), followed by Epiphanius, represents the heretic as actually citing the Corinthian text (1 Cor. xv, 8) in support of his own heresy, though wrongly applying it, and infer thence that the heretical doctrine was derived from the text? We answer that such an inference is by no means legitimate.

The Gnostic might, indeed, have used the passage precisely as we have used it, to prove the antiquity of the notion of the Ektroma—a proof that both Irenæus and Tertullian would have found it very hard to rebut, had they ever attempted; and some late Valentinian may have even used the text as the Fathers affirm, though little trust can be put in the accuracy of their affirmations; but all this does not even begin to imply that the Corinthian verse preceded the original Gnostic conception.

135. Lastly, it is plain as day that the Apostle speaks of "the Ektroma" as something *requiring no explanation, and hence familiar to his readers*. It is certain, then, that his language reveals a Gnostic consciousness addressing a consciousness that is Gnostic. This conclusion may be heavy-laden with consequences, but it is none the less unavoidable.

It is gratifying to find the foregoing view of the priority of Gnosticism to Paulinism, already set forth in *Der vorchristliche Jesus,* and even earlier in my article on New Testament criticism in *The Americana*, explicitly affirmed by Reitzenstein in his recent book, *Die Hellenistischen Mysterienreligionen:* "So out of this view even before Paul there arose the pair of concepts, ' pneumatic ' and ' psychic '; that Gnosticism in its fundamental notions antedates the Apostle is also lexically demonstrated."

V.—THE GOSPEL PORTRAIT

136. A great lawyer, in this case as good a judge as a great critic, writes me that his main difficulty in accepting the new theory lies in the extremely vivid portraiture in the Gospels of a highly attractive personality. This portrait seems to him to have been drawn from life, and impossibly the product of a religious philosophising fancy. Other distinguished thinkers have written me in similar strain, and therewith seem to have laid bare the very heart of the matter as it lies in the minds of many highly intelligent laymen.

Von Soden also insists that the Gospel image is quite too fresh, original, and uninventible to be intelligible otherwise than as taken directly and photographically from life.

ADDENDA

Inasmuch as this contention is endlessly repeated in the liberal apologies of to-day, it would not be fair to the reader to pass it by without careful consideration.

137. An obvious and sufficient answer would seem to be that if any Evangelist really aimed to depict a thoroughly noble and beautiful personality—perfect, indeed, according to the Evangelist's standard—there seems to be no reason why he might not have done so; it would be merely a question of literary skill, and there is no ground for setting any narrow limits to the abilities of the Evangelist. If some one urges, however, that there were three, and even four, such artists, and that their agreement is decisive proof that they were drawing from the same living model, the answer is that in the case of the three it is admitted and certain that none of the portraits is strictly primitive, but that all are elaborations of the same original or originals; whereas the fourth is confessedly so divergent from the other three as to make even the most stout-hearted despair of harmonisation.

If, now, it be urged that the perfection of the character delineated goes beyond the power of any literary artist and beyond the conception of any philosophic genius of that period, the answer is that this is mere assumption, no matter how surpassing the perfection in question be supposed to be. The Judæo-Greco-Roman consciousness was perhaps the most intensely religious that this earth has ever seen. Moreover, for centuries it had wrestled with ethical problems with energy, persistence, and determination that command admiration and excite wonder; the Sage, the Perfect Man, had long been the object of its plastic imaginings; and immediate inner communion and even identification with God had long been the goal of the strivings of many more or less exalted spirits. That, under such well-known and recognised conditions, especially *with the transcendent model in the Second Book of the Republic in full view*, the Gospel-writer should have been able (if he desired) to depict a personality of altogether surpassing beauty, nobility, and excellence, seems to afford no occasion whatever for exclamation.

138. But we have not yet touched the heart of the matter. The latent difficulty lies in a most erroneous view commonly entertained of the century in question and the one immediately

preceding. We are prone to think of them as sunk in intellectual sloth and moral turpitude; as wholly given up to the senses, to degrading lusts, to revolting crimes, to effeminacy, triviality, and bestiality. Now, for this view of the border centuries there is no justification. Undoubtedly such repulsive elements were actually present in that day and civilisation, even as they have been in every other. But that they were dominant, that they excluded their very opposites, is false and calumnious. Indeed, the presence of conspicuous vices would almost imply as natural reaction the presence of almost equally conspicuous virtues; and that such virtues did indeed abound, that very high moral ideals were frequently set up and not infrequently approached, is the unambiguous witness of history. The eloquent indignation of the satirists attests the probity as well as the improbity of the age. No general inference lies from occasional examples of unnatural crimes; precisely such examples come even now occasionally to light in the highest walks, intellectual and even official, of our modern life. Moreover, that the heart of the Roman world was still sound and its pulse steady, is proved decisively by the sudden triumph of Christianity, explain that triumph as you may. The multitudinous converts to the new faith were already in the main good men and true, whether God-fearing heathen or Israelites without guile. In general, it was their virtue that made them converts rather than their conversion that made them virtuous. They were already "not far from the kingdom of God." Consider the centurion and the eunuch and Dorcas and Lydia and Timothy and the "devout women" and "God-worshippers" that throng the Book of Acts. The divine flame of Protochristianity fed upon an immense mass of long-prepared and highly combustible material.

139. Neither was the age intellectually contemptible. Posidonius, and still more Antiochus, were learned and vigorous thinkers. Only a little earlier Chrysippus was the most prolific and Karneades the subtlest of all Greek philosophers. Roman poetry sought not only to follow in the steps of Homer and the dramatists, but also in Horace essayed ethical, and in Lucretius cosmological, flights. In fact, philosophy, since Socrates become more and more emphati-

cally ethical, had deeply tinged the whole current of human life; and men of action, like Brutus, Cicero, Cato, Sergius Paulus, and the Antonines, devoted far more time to speculative reading and to converse with philosophers than does the modern member of Congress or Parliament or the Reichstag or the Chambers. In the first century Philosophy positively mounted the imperial throne, and in the second she ruled for two generations with splendour and beneficence scarcely equalled in the annals of man. Nor dare we forget the great birth of Neo-Platonism, for which a long period of fitting preparation must have been necessary. On this same point we cannot dwell longer in this connection. In a future volume we hope to return to the matter, and to submit the conclusive proof in all desirable detail. Regard it, then, as you will, it seems sufficiently clear that the border centuries (150 B.C.–150 A.C.) presented every conceivable condition requisite to account for an imaginative delineation of virtue just such as the modern reader fancies he finds photographically reproduced in the Gospels. Even then, should we concede that he has read these Scriptures aright, it would still be unsettled whether the character delineated was historical or an ideal.

140. But we are as far as possible from making any such concession. It is *not* in any sense or measure true that the Evangelists, at least the Synoptists, have sought either to reproduce or to create *any human character at all*, either actual or ideal. This is a most radical contention, concerning which, however, we can entertain no doubt whatever, and it must be grounded solidly and unshakably. In the foregoing pages the minuter philologic proof has been submitted, and it has been shown that precisely the terms that seem to denote most distinctly the personal character of Jesus have no personal human reference at all, but are specially selected to indicate his divinity and non-humanity. At this point it is now in place to indicate certain much broader facts that bear exactly the same testimony.

141. In the first place, that no faithful or vivid portraiture is present in the Gospels is clear enough from the fact that no human genius has yet been able to say convincingly what the character of Jesus really was. The various conceptions

are just as different as the various minds that conceive them. It is common enough to read in the books without end, of celebrated critics, that Jesus was this, that, and the other; such affirmations are made most confidently, as if there were and could be no doubt whatever. But such writers are no more prodigal of assertion than they are frugal of proof. I have never been able to find any even plausible reason that they did or could assign. Apparently each one has formed his own idea of what Jesus ought to have been, and he has interpreted everything in accordance with that idea. Hence their constructions of the human character of Jesus have been almost wholly reflections of their own ideals. Their exegesis has been imposition rather than exposition. As a result these loving interpretations have been notoriously inconsistent; no two have agreed essentially. Of late it has become the fashion to abandon all attempt at depiction proper, and to rest content with the dimmest outline. Jesus, until recently, supposed to be portrayed so vividly is now regarded as a "Great Unknown." The indication is unmistakable. If the Gospel portrait loses so markedly in colour and definition on nearer approach and on carefuller study, it can hardly have been drawn originally from life, nor indeed originally intended to represent a man.

142. We may also understand, and without grave difficulty, just why it is that even the highly cultured and not uncritical *imagine* they find such a convincing character sketch in the Gospels. The faithful Mohammedan finds everywhere in the Koran the highest perfection of literary art. To the infidel Aryan the work makes no such appeal. Wading through its Surahs in quest of gems of thought or expression seems like hunting for pearls among the oyster beds of the Delta. The difference is subjective. Moslem and Christian bring entirely diverse forms of consciousness to face the fact of the Koran. Somewhat similar is the case with the reader of the Gospels. He brings to his perusal an immense weight of prepossession. He is enveloped and permeated by the atmosphere of ages, shaping and tinging the image he beholds in the Gospel, which is thus in large measure his own reflected consciousness. He accepts and rarely questions his first impression, and never suspects that it is mainly a

subjective product. But had any such documents been suddenly brought to light in Central Africa he would most probably have formed an entirely other judgment, and scarcely have received them as strictly historical.

143. Indeed, on close inspection, it seems quite impossible that the Synoptics were aiming to depict *any character at all*, either real or ideal. Else why is the picture so stript of human attributes? How shall we explain the utter absence of plausible and obvious anecdote, and especially of *words and deeds of kindness*, and above all of *self-sacrifice?* Surely this latter is the very touchstone of a noble character, and is an essential element of attractiveness and amiability Yet we never hear of a single instance of the least self sacrifice on the part of the Jesus. The Passion is not in point, for its contents are purely dogmatic. He finds Peter's mother-in-law sick of fever; he touches and heals her. It is an act of divine power, simply and solely. There is no suggestion of love, of kindness, of human affection. She arose and served—such is the whole story. On the tempest-tost deep he sleeps calmly at night. His disciples wake him up saying, "Master, carest thou not that we perish?" Surely a most natural question, in no way hinting any lack of faith. Yet the answer is harsh: "Why are ye craven, ye of little faith?" Certainly there is naught in such an incident or in similar displays of temper to attract one's fellows. Such remarks as the foregoing apply, practically, to all the deeds of the Jesus. His tenderness towards fallen women is an apparent exception, an exception quite impossible to understand literally as biographical. In fact, the fallen woman is in the New Testament as in the Old a symbol for an idolatrous or apostate people; the sinful women that worship the Jesus are the pagan peoples that adopt his cult. See *supra*, p. 106.

144. Someone may mention the famous Doxology in Matthew xi, 27-29, as showing the gentle, loving nature of the Jesus, especially the invitation "Come unto me, all ye that labour and are heavy laden, and I will give you rest. Take my yoke upon you, and learn of me; for I am meek and lowly of spirit; and ye shall find rest unto your souls. For my yoke is easy (chrestos), and my burden is light." It seems strange

that anyone with literary feeling should stumble at these rhythmical, almost metrical, verses. In the mouth of a human Jesus at any time of his supposed ministry they are simply meaningless and impossible. Let anyone try to imagine the benevolent rabbi uttering such words, and he will perceive the incongruity straightway. We have long since ascribed to them a purely dogmatic content, and hence feel no difficulty; but such a sense could not have been understood, nor intended, at the supposed time of utterance. None the less, the quotation is not only beautiful, but is perfectly intelligible. It is the voice of *Wisdom* that we hear, the Wisdom already mentioned just before (verse 19). It was common enough to represent this Wisdom, this Child of God, as preaching, as exhorting, as inviting men to her paths of pleasance and life. Proverbs and Ecclesiasticus are full of such representations. "Doth not Wisdom cry?" "She uttereth her voice on the streets." In Proverbs viii the divine creative functions of this Wisdom are eloquently set forth. In fact, in later Jewish thought she became a kind of deity, easily passing over into the Divine Logos, the Son of God. This is too well known to call for either proof or elaboration. Hence it is not at all strange that this invitation, along with the Doxology, is here ascribed to the Jesus, a closely kindred aspect of one and the same God.[1] Raising no unnecessary question as to the original form of the verses, we perceive clearly that the passage is a fragment of a Gnostic hymn (such as we elsewhere meet with in the New Testament), and testifies strongly to the deep religious feeling that dictated it, but not for an instant to any humanity of Jesus.

145. A very striking proof that the human qualities with which we deck out the hero of the Gospel played no part in the primitive conception of our religion is this noteworthy fact that we find no mention of them, no allusion to them, in the oldest Christian writings. Paul and Peter and John, the

---

[1] In fact, the identification of the Jesus with Wisdom is not only common enough elsewhere, even frequent in Origen, but is found also in the Apostle (1 Cor. i, 24, 30), and especially in Luke xi, 49, where the words of the Jesus in Matt. xxiii, 34, are ascribed to "the Wisdom of God." Compare the commentary of Wellhausen (*Evan. Luc.* p. 52): "Jesus is to be sure the Achamoth"—the Gnostic Sophia (Wisdom), which Origen holds to be the "Son of God," *in spite* of the feminine gender (*C. Cels.* v, 39).

author of Acts, the early apologists know practically nothing of this character supposed to be so vividly set forth in the Gospels. Their interest centres solely in the divine aspect of the Jesus, in the dogmatic purport and consequences of his cult and message. The modern Christian in controversy with a heathen would certainly have dwelt on the perfection of the man Jesus and his striking elevation in character over Moses and David and Elijah, over Socrates, Plato, Epaminondas, and the rest, and would have expatiated on the measureless superiority of his ethical ideal to that of Zeno, of Antiochus, of Epicurus, of Cato, of any and of all the worthies of Greek philosophy and Roman history. Some such course of argument seems unavoidable for anyone occupying the standpoint of modern Christianity, whether orthodox or heterodox, whether conservative or liberal. But the ancient did nothing of the kind. He is dead silent precisely where and when the modern would have been most strenuously insistent and eloquent. The author of *Hebrews* does, indeed, compare the two covenants, and is very eager to show the higher excellence of the New and the incomparability of the great high-priest Jesus. But it is with him solely a question of official dignity, of precedence in rank and authority, of cosmical sway and sovereignty—in a word, of divine power and heavenly exaltation. He nowhere insists upon the human perfection, the exemplary character, the ethical virtue of the supernatural high-priest after the order of Melchizedek.[1] Similarly throughout the long array of Old Christian Scriptures, canonic and uncanonic. The occasions were countless on which the writers might naturally have expatiated on such inviting themes; that they did not do so is a demonstration that their consciousness was widely different from the modern. Yet they had at least our own present sources in which to behold the alleged vivid portrait of Jesus. That they practically never avail themselves thereof is proof conclusive that they did not recognise therein the lifelike picture in question. Hereby they showed themselves much more objective and much less subjective

---

[1] The allusions to temptation (ii, 18; iv, 15) are not real exceptions, being merely vague and casual, and with only dogmatic import, with no clear reference to anything historic.

interpreters than their present-day followers. The matchless Jesus-character of the Gospels is, in fact, a modern invention, born of the necessity of supplacing with something highly respectable the genuine evangelic figure of a God, which criticism has striven so long with such plausibility and apparent success to remove from the Gospels and the early faith. The earlier (not the earliest) Christian centuries did, indeed, rejoice in the idea of the man Jesus, but they frankly created their hero in a host of palpably fictive Gospels and legends; unlike the modern, they did not find him already portrayed with inimitable and convincing fidelity and power in the pages of the "Four Biographies." In the same spirit they also invented characters and lives for Mary and Joseph and numerous others. All such imaginations count for nothing in history, but the Scripture witness to the human personality of the Jesus is really much weaker than its witness to any secondary figure, because it is not merely negative, but very strongly positive *against* any such personality.

146. In his eight books *Against Celsus* the most alert mind of the early Church, Origen, has passed the ploughshare of his argument over the whole field of controversy. He has anticipated in substance nearly all the pleas of seventeen centuries of apology, and he is discussing Jesus and the representations of the Gospel on nearly every page. The acute and ruthless heathen, who had so alarmed Ambrosius and stirred him up to demand a word-by-word refutation from Origen, Celsus by no means spares the character of Jesus, but assails it at every point. Origen understood his logical responsibilities thoroughly, and he seizes eagerly upon every point of argumentative vantage. Had he perceived in the Gospels the vivid portrait of a unique, majestic, and beautiful man, it is inconceivable that he would not have mentioned it, that he would not have stressed it with all emphasis. But he does naught of the kind. He is unwearied in proofs from prophecy, to which he gives the first rank, in proofs from miracles and from the amazing triumphs of Christianity; but he never argues from the human character of Jesus. When Celsus (in the person of his imaginary Jew) charges harshness upon Jesus, Origen's answer is most remarkable: the Jehovah

of the Old Testament was equally harsh and threatening! Here, indeed, he seems to have come very near the exact truth in his *argumentum ad hominem*. In his summary (ii, 79) and everywhere else the favourite modern argument from the matchless character of the Gospel hero is conspicuous only by its absence. Yet Origen is greatly concerned to vindicate in some way the humanity of Jesus, which he evidently regards as the Achilles' heel in his whole system of doctrine. He recurs to it continually, is ever advancing new forms of defence and recommending the dogma by new subtleties and plausibilities. That he never employs the favourite, yea, almost the exclusive proof of the modern liberal, seems to show with all desirable clearness that for his mind that proof did not exist. Origen did not perceive in the Gospel story the vivid portrait of a matchless, unmistakably human character; yet no man has ever studied the Scriptures more deeply, or mastered their contents more comprehensively. It seems impossible that such a genius of exegesis should have failed to observe what the modern liberal sees lying plain as day spread out over the whole surface, if indeed it be really there, if it be not a figment of modern fancy. The observations just made concerning Origen may be repeated *mutatis mutandis* of all the great scribes of Old Christian literature. Save as a mere dogma, the human character of Jesus seems to form no appreciable element of the early Christian consciousness; and as a dogma it is never defended in the modern fashion by appeal to the lifelike depiction of the Gospels. Yet unquestionably this early Christian consciousness stood far closer to the supposed human personality in question in every respect, racially, geographically, socially, intellectually, than does any modern West-European consciousness. Moreover, be it repeated, that early consciousness (from A.D. 100 on) was as intensely interested in establishing that humanity as is the modern in Germany or Britain. There is then one and only one possible conclusion, the one already recommended by numerous and decisive independent considerations: The *alleged vivid human portraiture is not really present in the New Testament;* it is a reflection, from the Gospel mirror, of the consciousness of the modern Christian reader. As the ancient believer beheld the whole story of the Gospels, the whole new Dispensation, foreshadowed in its minutest details in the Old Testament, so the modern believer beholds all the features of his Ideal Man delineated in the evangelic writings. We know now that it was wholly an illusion in the first case; we shall soon recognise that the illusion is quite as complete in the second.

147. As a further and final general demonstration, we enter what might be called the topographical argument, hitherto unhinted. It is simply this: If Jesus was a great, impressive, commanding, human personality, in terms of which must mainly be understood the message and mission of Christianity; if his personal influence and ministry, whether merely natural, though wonderful, or supernatural, whether pure-human or superhuman, initiated and determined that great religious movement, then of necessity would the region of his personal activity, where he taught and preached and healed and gathered about him his first devoted disciples, have been the centre and hearthstone of the " new teaching," there we should find the earliest and perhaps strongest churches, with that region would tradition connect the oldest and most distinguished disciples. Let no one cite at this point the saying that a prophet is not without honour, save in his own country and among his own people. Even granted the truth of the saying, it would have no relevance. For we are not talking about "his own country and his own people," but about the chosen region of his successful activity; not where he could do no mighty work, but where he is reputed to have done many and practically all his mighty works, and captivated the multitudes, and won his first and only faithful following, and achieved all of his personal triumphs. True it is, if Jesus had changed the scene of his activity, if he had gone elsewhere and there established a new school, and gathered round him a still more numerous and enthusiastic band of believers, and had prolonged his stay in this new capital till the end, then, indeed, this new theatre might have taken the place of the old, and figured in history as the emanative focus of the new faith. However, nothing of the kind took place, according to the Scriptures. The deeds of might were confined

practically to Galilee. There was the preaching heard, there the healing done, there were the demons expelled, there the disciples called and charged and instructed, there the multitude gathered and cried out in amazement, "Never man spake like this man." By all the laws of human psychology, by all the precedents of human history, this same rich and populous Galilee, the exclusive scene of the personal ministry of Jesus, should, and indeed must, have been the principal theatre of the first activity of the Galilean disciples; there should have been proclaimed first of all the gospel of the resurrection, there wrought the first miracles of the new spirit, there formed the first congregations, there established the first churches. Thence, in an ever-widening circle, the waves of the gospel mission should have issued and spread themselves all over the empire. But what are the facts in the case? They are all reversed as completely as possible! With the departure from Galilee for Jerusalem, Galilee vanishes from the horizon of the Scriptures, never to appear again. The poor peasants never view again the shores of their native lake. Never do they revisit the scenes made sacred to them by the life and doctrine of Jesus; never do they see again where his feet trod, where his voice resounded, where his miracles were wrought, where the peoples thronged him, where the waves were stilled and the multitudes fed; never do they bear back word to their friends, to their kinsmen, to those that believe on him there. Galilee is deserted and forgotten completely and forever; no gospel is preached there, no church founded, no letters addressed to the saints. The disciples proclaim their message in Jerusalem, in Cæsarea, in Antioch, in Joppa, in Crete, in Corinth, in Thessalonica, in Galatia, in Rome—yea, everywhere, but not in the one place where of all places in the world the proclamation would have been most natural and most effective—yea, in the only place where it could have been either natural or effective. Had the Galilean disciples proclaimed the resurrection and exaltation of Jesus to Galileans in Galilee, where Jesus had already laboured and captivated all men by his personality and marvellous deeds and doctrine, it is at least conceivable that the preaching might have found some acceptance among his former admirers and adherents; a cult might possibly have sprung up in such circles. But for them to abandon this most promising of all fields for their mission, and to *open* their grand campaign in the heart of the enemy's country, where they had no friends, where there was no sentiment already that favoured them or Jesus, where they could not summon a single witness in their own behalf, where all was indifference or positive hostility, where not a single favouring condition was present and not a single unfavouring circumstance was absent—this would have been an absurdity that no rational man, no matter under what possession or prepossession, could have perpetrated. Beyond the shadow of a doubt, had Galilean disciples opened this great campaign as is described in Acts i, ii, it would have been said, "These men are full of new wine," and that would have been the end thereof. No person would have paid them any attention. The author of John xxi seems to have felt the necessity of restoring the disciples to their homes in Galilee, so he has them go a-fishing in the sea, and there catch the miraculous draught of one hundred and fifty-three great fishes—that is, capture the heathen world in the unbreaking net of the Church. Nevertheless, the fact remains that Galilee cuts no figure at all in the actual tradition of the first preaching of the Gospel; and this fact negatives finally and forever the notion that Galilee was the scene of a life in which that Gospel was grounded, from which it sprung, and to which it returned as to its one and only source of authority and inspiration.

148. Of all the religious movements of which we have any exact knowledge (for the history of Mormonism offers no such parallel), the recent rise and career of Lazzarettism in Tuscany furnishes by far the closest and worthiest parallel to primitive Christianity as conceived by the liberal critics. Renan, Rassmussen, and Barzellotti, among others, have perceived and stressed the remarkable likeness, and have thought to find in the carefully-ascertained and verified facts of this recent case (1878) a thoroughly satisfactory commentary on the so-called Galilean movement of nearly two thousand years ago. Now it is exactly at this capital and vital point that the two stories repel each other to opposite poles, that they contrast as sharply as could be imagined. In the case

ADDENDA

of Lazzaretti the course of events is exactly what common sense requires as natural and necessary, whereas in the case of Jesus and the Gospel it is reversed precisely and in every particular. For the minuter particulars the reader may be referred to the excellent work of Barzellotti, *Monte Amiata e il suo profeta (David Lazzaretti)*, reviewed by me in the *International Journal of Ethics* (October, 1911), from which review it will suffice to quote the following:—

> As to the scientific value of Barzellotti's and similar works, and the importance of the spirit and method of investigation which they exemplify, we shall not raise any question. But at one point of vital significance we must register a wide dissent and the most emphatic protest. Even though one accept with very slight reserve the analysis of the general religious consciousness and of many of its most notable active manifestations in the genesis of cults and sects and orders, even granted that the pre-Christian and proto-Christian religious consciousness must be measured in some dimensions with the one universal standard, it still remains true that the parallel, whether express or implied between the *Saint* and the Jesus, is wholly imaginary and misleading, and that any and every attempt to interpret the origin of Christianity in terms of Lazzaretti or St. Francis, or any and all human personalities, must fail henceforth as hitherto, flatly, hopelessly, and ignominiously. For all such interpretations begin and end with a strange neglect of the central and pivotal fact of proto-Christianity—namely, that it was a monotheism, begotten, born, and reared in an intensely monotheistic consciousness, directed squarely and firmly against the prevailing polytheism, which was the one supreme religious fact of the day, and of necessity formed the point of attack for any religious movement emerging from Greco-Jewish circles. It is this one overshadowing fact that separates the Christian and the Lazzaretti movements as far apart as the poles, that forces them apart by the whole sphere of experience. In the presence of this broad and decisive diversity, the multiplied similarities in detail that appear in connection with the current superficial and systematically false interpretation of the Gospels must all sink into insignificance, while the deeper and correcter interpretation shows them to be but shadows, void of any substance whatever. Let one illustration suffice. The strength of Lazzarettism lay in the personality of David. In what his charm consisted it is superfluous to inquire. Suffice it that few of his fellows could resist the spell, still less could any one break it once cast upon him. So far forth he was indeed the exact counterpart of the "Jesusbild," as it flourishes in the fancy of liberal critics. But now mark the difference. Naturally and necessarily, since it was the personal fascination exerted by David that won him disciples, these latter were found from first to last in the circle of his immediate acquaintance. Says

our author (p. 339) : " Not everywhere on Mount Amiata, but in Arcidosso and in the neighbouring hamlets, in those nearest to Mount Labbro in the fields that face the Maremma, where the prophet found from the start the majority of his followers, there remain still faithful nearly all the survivors of the societies founded by him, his apostles and some of the younger disciples, of those called later to the faith." Beyond this charmed circle of his own personality the faith of the Lazzaretti has never extended, and we may safely say can never extend itself perceptibly. Not only is this precisely as it should be, it seems precisely as it must be. Now had the Christian propaganda resembled Lazzaretti's in its origin, had it welled out from a single pure-human source, as the critics maintain, then surely something similar would have happened. The region of the personal influence of Jesus, the fertile and populous shores of Galilee, would have formed the radiant focus of his gospel mission, thence it would have spread itself in widening waves, and always at the front we should have found the historic names of the immediate primitive disciples. However, in the case actually presented all this is exactly reversed. Galilee is practically unknown in the early preaching. The primitive churches or groups of disciples spring up in remote regions, in Damascus, in Antioch, in Crete, in Libya ; we find Epistles to Corinthians, to Galatians, to Romans, to the Dispersion, and to many others, but none to the saints in Capernaum, or in Chorazin, or in Bethsaida, or in Nazareth, or even in Jerusalem. Neither are the historical primitive propagandists the friends, fellow-citizens, and personal disciples of the Jesus. Saul of Tarsus, Ananias of Damascus, Apollos of Alexandria, Prisca and Aquila of Rome, Barnabas of Cyprus, Stephen the protomartyr, Philip the deacon, and various other missionaries—none was ever acquainted with a human Jesus. The twelve Apostles stand forth but as shadows of mighty names. The earliest traditions find nothing for them to do, can tell nothing of their activity. This is notoriously true of eleven, and is, in fact, also true of the one apparent exception, Simon Peter. Thus the supposed similarity between the two origins of the two movements turns out to be a dissimilarity and contrast so complete as of itself to show the impossibility of explaining the two similarly. Since Lazzarettism was admittedly an emanation from a purely human focus, we have no choice but to admit that primitive Christianity was not such an emanation in any such sense. So far, then, from corroborating and verisimilating the modern critical theory of Christian origins, the example of David must shatter and disprove it utterly. Barzellotti and his peers have indeed rendered a great service to science by their intense study of this recent religious phenomenon, but in a sense exactly the reverse of the intended. They have builded better than they knew.

This argument seems to be decisive. The geographic

facts of the first proclamation and expansion of Christianity negative conclusively the liberal theory of the wonderful Galilean carpenter. No critic thus far has met the argument in *Der vorchristliche Jesus* on the multifocal origin of Christianity. The considerations here adduced strengthen that argument to positive irrefragable demonstration. What will the Liberals do about it?

PART III.

THE PILLARS OF SCHMIEDEL

ἀμφοῖν γὰρ ὄντοιν φίλοιν ὅσιον προτιμᾶν τὴν ἀλήθειαν.—ARISTOTLE.

THE BULWARKS OF LIBERALISM

1. THE manner in which the deepest, the most difficult, and by far the most important problem of the New Testament is almost uniformly treated by the most accredited spokesmen of the Higher Criticism is cavalier to a degree that must make the judicious grieve. It is only with an impatient air of undisguised condescension that they will deign so much as to admit it into the arena of debate, and, once admitted, it is adjudicated in the foregone sense with a speed, not to say precipitation, that reminds one of the *ad patibulum, ad patibulum* of the awakened judge in the good old days of Alva. In the German edition of this book it was thought well to devote some seven pages to the complacent arguments advanced by Renan, Réville, and Keim, before the historicity of the Jesus had really become a burning question. Such a discussion promised to be instructive, at least in showing how closely the more recent had been compelled to follow the elder apologists, how little real advance the latest and most learned liberalism had been able to register. However, these pages have been omitted from this edition to make room for matters of graver moment, and because the bulk of the considerations therein gathered together may now be found in equivalent though more elaborate forms distributed at proper places in this volume, so that its argument in no way suffers from the omission.

2. There is, however, one exception to this rule of inadequacy—an exception so noteworthy as to merit especial and minute consideration. Professor Paul Wilhelm Schmiedel of Zürich, the great successor of the great Volkmar,

understands the case perfectly, and in his most notable article on "The Gospels" in the *Encyclopædia Biblica* (§§ 131, 139, 140, 141) he has developed a real argument that calls for the closest scrutiny along with unreserved admiration.[1] So important is this formal and serious attempt to show the historicity of the Jesus that its basis deserves to be quoted *in extenso*. Schmiedel rightly declares it "unfortunate that the decision as to the credibility of the Gospel narrative should be made to depend upon the determination of a problem so difficult and perhaps insoluble as the synoptical is." Very true. To adjourn a problem till the "synoptic question" is settled is to adjourn it to the Greek calends. But we must observe that the question of the historicity of Jesus, as we conceive it, is not at all the same as the question of "the credibility of the Gospel narrative." To maintain that the Gospels are in the main a conscious and elaborate symbolism, is not to say anything against their credibility. We may speak of the force, the beauty, the propriety of a simile or metaphor or parable, but never of its credibility or incredibility. This is a distinction essential to bear in mind. To forget it is to become incapable of any proper appreciation of the matter in hand.

3. Schmiedel continues: "The examination of the credibility must from the beginning be set about from two opposite points of view. On the one hand, we must set on one side everything which for any reason arising either from the substance or from considerations of literary criticism has to be regarded as doubtful or as wrong; on the other hand, one must make search for all such data as, from the nature of their contents cannot possibly on any account be regarded as inventions.

4. "When a profane historian finds before him a historical document which testifies to the worship of a hero unknown to other sources, he attaches first and foremost importance to those features which cannot be deduced merely from the fact of this worship, and he does so on the simple and sufficient

---

[1] Of course, it is not meant that Schmiedel's argument is without anticipations or parallels of any kind—so much could rarely be said of any scientific procedure. Nonetheless, by just accentuation and painstaking development he has made it peculiarly his own.

ground that they would not be found in this source unless the author had met with them as fixed data of tradition. The same fundamental principle may safely be applied in the case of the Gospels, for they also are all of them written by worshippers of Jesus. We now have accordingly the advantage—which cannot be appreciated too highly—of being in a position to recognise something as being worthy of belief even without being able to say, or even being called on to inquire, whether it comes from original Mark, from logia, from oral tradition, or from any other quarter that may be alleged. The relative priority becomes a matter of indifference, because the absolute priority—that is, the origin in real tradition—is certain. In such points the question as to credibility becomes independent of the synoptical question. Here the clearest cases are those in which only one evangelist, or two, have data of this class, and the second, or third, or both, are found to have taken occasion to alter these in the interests of the reverence due to Jesus. If we discover any such points—even if only a few—they guarantee not only their own contents, but also much more. For in that case one may also hold as credible all else which agrees in character with these, and is in other respects not open to suspicion. Indeed the thoroughly disinterested historian must recognise it as his duty to investigate the grounds for this so great reverence for himself which Jesus was able to call forth; and he will then, first and foremost, find himself led to recognise as true the two great facts that Jesus had compassion for the multitude and that he preached with power, not as the scribes (Matthew ix, 36; vii, 29). Let us, then, proceed to test in the two ways indicated some of the leading points in the synoptic gospels."

5. Professor Schmiedel now goes forward with this critical testing, and at first with only negative and unfavourable results touching the "Chronological framework" (132), the "Order of the narrative" (133), "Occasions of utterances of Jesus" (134), "Places and persons" (135), "Conditions belonging to a later time" (136), "The miracle-narratives" (137), "The Resurrection of Jesus" (138). At last, however, after this weary pilgrimage through the desert of negation, he reaches the promised land of affirmation and certainty,

and confidently exclaims in joy: "139. Absolutely credible passages: (*a*) About Jesus in general. 140. (*b*) On the miracles of Jesus."

6. It is with lively interest that one hears this announcement, though the terms are not perfectly reassuring. It is one thing for a passage or statement to be "absolutely credible," and quite another for it to compel belief, for its contradictory to be incredible. With regard to many narratives, we may have to admit that they are "absolutely credible"; there may be no reason for disbelieving, and yet there may at the same time be no reason whatsoever for believing them. Judgment in such cases would have to remain balanced until some decisive external consideration should be thrown into the scale. This observation deserves to be made at this point, because of its pertinence, not so much to the case in hand as to scores of critical works that are thoroughly vitiated by this fallacy of assuming that, if a Gospel incident be not in itself nor in its context unbelievable, it should therefore be believed—a principle that would compel us to accept as history whole libraries of fictitious literature. Of course, it may be taken for granted that Professor Schmiedel does not entrap himself in such a paralogism. In his article we must suppose that by "absolutely credible" is meant absolutely coercing belief, compelling acceptance; in which case our lively interest becomes intense.

7. What, then, are these passages of such transcendent importance? Under (*a*) we find five: (1) Mark x, 17 *f*. ("Why callest thou me good? None is good save God only"); (2) Matthew xii, 31 *f*. (that blasphemy against the Son of Man can be forgiven); (3) Mark iii, 21 (that his relations held him to be beside himself); (4) Mark xiii, 32 ("Of that day and of that hour knoweth no one, not even the angels in heaven, neither the Son but the Father"); (5) Mark xv, 34 ("My God, my God, why hast thou forsaken me?"). Under (*b*) we find: (1) Mark viii, 12 (where Jesus refuses to work a sign); (2) Mark vi, 5 (Jesus able to do no deed of might in Nazareth); (3) Mark viii, 14-21 ("Take heed, beware of the leaven of the Pharisees," etc.); (4) Matthew xi, 5—Luke vii, 22 (answer to message from John the Baptist).

8. Such are the nine pillars of the Gospel conceived as history. The falcon eye, the sleuth-hound scent of the Zürich professor has espied and detected these nine—no more. Certainly they are, in number at least, enough. It is claimed for them that they "might be called the foundation-pillars for a truly scientific life of Jesus"; that "they prove" ("that in the person of Jesus we have to do with a completely human being.")....they also prove that he really did exist [as an historic man], and that the Gospels contain at least some absolutely trustworthy facts concerning him." Elsewhere, as in his luminous Introduction to Arno Neumann's *Jesus*, the Swiss critic has expressed himself even more unequivocally. He speaks of supplying "the proof of the historical existence of Jesus in a manner that shall be wholly immune from possibility of objection." Refuting Robertson, he holds that the latter "is thinking of texts which in themselves considered are equally applicable to a demigod and to a man; while my 'foundation' passages, on the other hand, are appropriate only to a man, and could never by any possibility have been written had the author been thinking of a demigod" (p. xvii). Most distinctly of all, p. xviii: "We are thus brought to a simple question of fact: Has the distinctive peculiarity of the foundation-passages been correctly stated? Could worshippers of Jesus, such as by universal consent the writers of the Gospels were, possibly have invented for him such words as 'Why callest thou me good? None is good, save God alone' (Mark x, 18)......And so forth. If they were led by their worship for Jesus alone, they could not. They must, therefore, have been led by a tradition. But, further, this tradition was itself really handed down by worshippers of Jesus; and, accordingly, these texts cannot have been invented even in this preliminary stage of Gospel composition, but must rest upon a faithful reproduction of facts. Mr. Robertson has not gone into the question whether this be so or not."

Lastly, and most pointedly, p. xxi: "In reality my foundation-texts were in no sense sought out by me for any purpose whatever; they thrust themselves upon me in virtue of one feature, and of one feature only: the impossibility of their having been invented, and their consequent credibility."

9. Surely the reader must now understand clearly this argumentation. Prof. Schmiedel maintains that nine passages written and preserved by the worshippers of Jesus are so directly opposed to their conception of Jesus as a being to be worshipped that they could not have been invented by these worshippers; hence he concludes they must have been part of a tradition concerning the Jesus, in which tradition he appeared, not as a being to be worshipped, but as a man. This tradition, as lying behind all written gospels, we should have to accept as original and trustworthy, at least as to its central point, the historic manhood of Jesus.

This seems to be an admirable piece of critical thinking, and to deserve the highest tribute that can be paid to controversial dialectic — the tribute of minute, exhaustive, and impartial examination.

EMINUS

10. Before proceeding to the detailed exploration of these pillared bases, it may be well to premise certain general observations. It will be noticed, in the first place, that in this demonstration Prof. Schmiedel essays to show forth an *impossibility*. He maintains that the Christian authors *could not possibly* of their own accord impute certain words and deeds to the Jesus, that the same *must* have been imposed on them by a tradition against which, indeed, they kicked, but in vain. Now an obvious reflection in the presence of this contention is that it is certainly a very large contract. All universal affirmatives are hard to establish—full as hard all universal negatives; this one seems particularly inaccessible to rigorous proof. In order to see clearly that *no one* worshipping Jesus as a deity *could* have attributed to him such and such words or deeds, one would have to make a pretty accurate inventory of the psychic contents of the nature of many thousand Jews and Gentiles during the border centuries (150 A.C. to 150 P.C.). Such an inventory is plainly impracticable, and has never been attempted. But of one thing we may rest well assured—those contents were in any case extraordinarily varied. To prove this we need not refer to the vast library of the countless sects that adorn the pages of the early heresiographers and the historians of primitive

Christianity. It is enough to flutter through the leaves of the New Testament, where there are not, indeed, just as many views as there are writers or writings, but, in fact, far more, for the same Gospel or Epistle offers often abundant irreconcilable varieties of teaching.

11. Nor are these species and sub-species always close akin; often enough they seem thrust asunder by the whole diameter of doctrine. At one place it is faith without works that justifies; at another this same faith without works is dead; often, too, the conceptions are not so much contradictory as almost entirely unrelated, having apparently little more to do with each other than algebra and geometry, or than music and painting. Witness Romans and Hebrews, Galatians and Ephesians, Colossians and the Apocalypse, John and Mark. It seems superfluously evident that it is with a most manifold wisdom that we have to deal, and that it is altogether vain to look for any sort of consistency. In such a heterogeneous mass we may expect to find a little of almost everything, both Jew and Gentile, both Scythian and Greek. If occasionally the most bizarre imaginings meet us, as (Hebrews vii, 3) of the historic High-Priest Melchizedek, fatherless, motherless, undescended (like a Linnæan species), eternal; or some Stoic dogma, as the universal conflagration (ἐκπύρωσις, 2 Peter iii, 10); or some Babylonian astronomical conception of the restoration of all things (Acts iii, 21); or some Persian fancy of the accompanying angel or astral self (Mark xiv, 51, 52)—none of such encounters need move us greatly. All of these things must come to pass, but the end is not yet.

12. At first blush, then, it seems to be an act of logical hardihood to declare it was impossible for anyone worshipping Jesus to speak or write thus and thus. Verily many things were possible to the many-coloured religious consciousness of that era—many, doubtless, that have not yet been dreamed of in our philosophy. It is not easy to comprehend our fellows even in the present day. Certain of us stand completely nonplussed by the phenomena of Christian Science and its practical deification of Mrs. Eddy. Other examples hardly less striking offer themselves in abundance. How, then, can we pretend to fathom or exhaust the

possibilities of the Greek-Roman-Egyptian-Syrian-Judæan consciousness of nineteen hundred years ago? Most moderns think of God as One, in whom is naught but peace—no strife at all; yet even such a philosopher as the late lamented Friedrich Paulsen tells us "that God's life is not without inner conflicts." If such a statement had been made of Jesus's life, how easy to have inferred that he could not have been conceived as God! The mixed multitudes of Hither Asia thought endlessly contrarious things of their deities; and it seems most hazardous to affirm that certain "passages are appropriate only to a man, and could never, by any possibility, have been written had the author been thinking of a demigod." Strong words are these and others already quoted; but their strength rather rouses than allays a suspicion of their correctness.

13. Even if we could not conceive how they could have been so written, what would that prove? That no one could have so written them? By no means! But only that *we* could not have so written them. Now, is the impossible for us necessarily impossible also for the Jew-Greek, for the Palestinian, of nineteen centuries past? Assuredly not. "*Du gleichst dem Geist den du begreifst*"; but certainly not the religious spirit of that border-land and time.

14. Here, then, at the very start we detect a fatal flaw in the seductive syllogism. The impossibility so confidently asserted cannot, in the nature of the case, be satisfactorily made out. Herewith we have not called to help a second observation—namely, that Professor Schmiedel has assumed that these pillar-passages are primitive and not later accessions. This assumption would have to be vindicated by careful examination of each case. The mere fact that a passage occurs in Mark is no guarantee of its primitive character. Even though Mark be the oldest narrative, yet there is much reason to regard the Logia source, so extensively exploited in Matthew, as still older; and rarely can one say with *certainty* that a particular passage is of primary and not of secondary origin. Neither can one say with certainty that a given Mark-form (just because it is in Mark) must therefore be older than the parallel form in Luke or Matthew. We may prefer Mark's form in general, in the

majority of cases, and yet recognise that Luke's or Matthew's may be preferable in special cases. On this point we need not dwell, since it will come up in the detailed discussion of the various pillars; but it is touched here because we hold that the original relations of the human and the divine elements in the delineation of the Jesus have been exactly reversed in the minds of the Higher Critics: the divine was the primitive; the human is the addition of a later fancy.

15. Once more, this Schmiedelian argument seems embarrassed by a very stubborn difficulty of fact. In order to give force to the contention that certain passages seem to treat Jesus as a man, we must suppose that these passages passed through the revising hands or consciousness of such as worshipped him not as a man, but as God. Plainly, nothing could be inferred from texts that express the Unitarian view, if these texts came to us only through Unitarian mediation. The whole edge of Schmiedel's reason is laid bare in his own words: "This tradition was itself really handed down by worshippers of Jesus"; while these pillar-passages (as he holds) were inconsistent with "their worship of Jesus." It is this supposed inconsistency that seems to him to make it impossible that they should have been inventions; hence, he concludes, "they must rest upon a faithful reproduction of facts."

16. Let us look at this argument narrowly. Note, in the first place, that the question is not about whether such and such words and deeds *are* inconsistent with divinity, but only whether they appeared inconsistent in the minds of the Gospel writers. Of course, since no one, neither then nor now, *knows* what God really is, no one *knows* what is and what is not incongruous with His divinity. The most that anyone can say is that "such and such agrees or does not agree with my *conception* of God—with the idea of Him in my mind." Accordingly, the question is: Did the passages under consideration contain elements incongruous with notions of divinity entertained by all the Gospel authors? We have already seen that there is no way to prove the affirmative conclusively; our knowledge is not adequate. Now, however, one may take a long stride forward, and affirm that the *fact* assumed by Professor Schmiedel, that

these passages were preserved and transmitted by these *worshippers* of Jesus, is decisive proof that in *their* minds the passages were *not* inconsistent with the Jesus-cult, were *not* inconsistent with divinity; however they may seem to *us*, they certainly were *not* inconsistent therewith in the minds of the Gospel writers (who were Jesus-worshippers). And the reason is obvious. If the passages had been felt as inconsistent with Jesus-worship, with the cult of the Jesus as God, they would have been altered, and the inconsistency would have been relieved. This conditional proposition we affirm with perfect confidence. The whole structure of the Gospels shows that the material at hand or supplied has been handled with the greatest possible freedom. Of course, no man knows this better than Professor Schmiedel. More than mere mention would seem to be almost an affront to the intelligence of the reader. Let anyone take down a *Harmony*[1] of the Gospels, and consider carefully any page. He cannot fail to perceive that no language can exaggerate the liberty with which the Evangelists deal with all their material, whether it be words or deeds of the Jesus.

17. Consider the case of the birth and compare the stories of Matthew and Luke, which are mutually exclusive in every detail. Consider the Resurrection and Ascension, note the radical divergence of Luke and Acts from the rest in the all-important matter of topography. Behold how John develops the Lazarus of Luke and transforms a parable into a history. Think of the hopeless diversity of form and of content in the story of the anointing of the Jesus. Compare Matthew's Sermon on the Mount with Luke's Sermon in the Plain. So on throughout. It is plain as day that the Gospel writers have felt themselves wholly untrammelled either by tradition or by precedent. It is equally plain that their over-workings have not been at random or careless. In countless cases a motive is unmistakably disclosed; in many others, where not evident, it may by analogy be presumed. The Evangelists were not writing for fun, nor even for fame. Their object was to *teach*, to supply their readers with "undeceiving milk of doctrine" that they might grow thereby (1 Peter ii, 2).

---

[1] *Lucus a non lucendo.*

Their sentences are surcharged with meaning; they felt they had to give account of every idle word. The notion that they were simple folk, naïvely jotting down what they heard or indulging in pleasing reminiscences of good old days, is quite too absurd for consideration.[1] They had ideas and knew excellently well how to express them, how to slur and how to accent, how to hint guardedly and how to enforce with emphasis. A certain common stock of sentiments and conceptions is on all hands in evidence, but no Evangelist hesitates for a moment, if it suits his own purpose, to modify or even to reverse the statement of any or all of the others. Nor does he do this covertly or in a corner. He does it with openness and accentuates it by repetition. Thus the Synoptics (Matthew xxvi, 69; Luke xxii, 55, 56) tell us that Simon was *sitting* by the fire; but John three times insists that he was *standing* (xviii, 16, 18, 25).

18. In view of these facts we affirm with all boldness, as beyond contradiction, that the tradition, whatever it contained, whether of word or of deed, was as far as possible from being a sharp-angled crystal or a fragile vase; on the contrary, it was malleable as tin, it was plastic as wax in the hands of the Evangelist. Not until far down in the second century was it labelled "Handle with care." "A faithful reproduction of facts"—such would have been accounted the very least among the virtues of an early Gospel. "The letter killeth: it is the spirit that makes alive."

19. We make bold to repeat, then, that the very fact that a certain word or deed is ascribed to the Jesus by a Gospel author is proof positive that it was not in conscious discord with that author's idea of the Jesus; nor was it likely to have been in unconscious discord, for these Gospels are pre-eminently deliberate compositions, the words have been laid carefully in the scale, and even far down in the centuries we find the manuscripts consciously modified in the interest of subtle cogitation. The stricture is made upon the great Vatican MS. B, that the scribe has considered too curiously.

20. Well, then! The Evangelists were admittedly Jesus-

---

[1] For their rhetorical accomplishments see the important monographs of D. H. Mueller: *Die Bergpredigt im Lichte der Strophentheorie*, and *Das Johannes-Evangelium im Lichte der Strophentheorie.*

worshippers, they believed and earnestly propagated the doctrine that the Jesus was divine; in their minds, then, the passages were *not* demonstrations of his mere humanity, they were *not* pillar-proofs "that the divine is to be sought in him only in the form in which it is capable of being found in a man." Professor Schmiedel's notion that these tell-tale passages have been preserved out of reverence for the very words and very deeds of the Jesus is caught out of the air; it is contradicted by everything that we know of the composition of the Gospels.

21. If now it be urged that, although the Gospel writers themselves might have felt no discord between these "fundamental passages" and the worship of the Jesus as a divinity, and so might have *preserved* the passages, yet the original writers, half-a-century older than the Gospels,[1] must have felt the discord, and so could not have written the passages in a Jesus-worshipping frame of mind, but must have written them regarding the Jesus as human—we answer that such a contention is gratuitous assumption. There is no reason to believe that human nature changes greatly in fifty years, nor that a discord unfelt in the following generation would have been felt in the preceding. Since it was Jesus-worshippers that preserved these pillar-passages, we may rationally believe that it was Jesus-worshippers who originally wrote them.

22. How easy it was for such an adorer of Jesus as a God to reconcile apparent contradictions is strikingly shown by an example that might well fill out the decade of pillar-proofs of the humanity and historicity of the Jesus. The prophecies of the imminent coming of the Son of Man at the destruction of Jerusalem, and of the prodigies on prodigies connected therewith, none of which were verified, would seem to be a crowning demonstration of humanity, and even widely errant humanity. Surely one might reason that no worshipper of the Jesus could have written such predictions; surely they must have been uttered essentially as given, and preserved only by the reverence of the biographers intent upon a

---

[1] If, indeed, these pillars do all belong to the oldest stratum of the Gospel deposit—which is far from certain, and is here granted only provisionally, for the sake of argument.

"faithful reproduction of facts." At first glance this seems to be plausibility itself. However, it is nothing more; it is far from being fact. On turning to 2 Peter iii, 4, 8, we discover two things: that the difficulty was actually raised by certain "scoffers," and that it did not disturb the serenity of the epistolist. The discord that jarred so harshly upon the "willingly ignorant" his faith readily resolved into a higher concord. By the simple and elegant device of introducing a constant multiplier (or divisor, as required), namely, 365,000 (neglecting some odd hundreds), he brings the prophecies into harmony not only with experience, but also with the loftiest previsions of stoical speculation. Perhaps someone may think such treatment a trifle heroic, but nay, not so! It shall appear as mild and modest to a degree, on comparison with the manipulations of modern exegesis in handling the exact chronometry of Genesis i, whereby a day defined by one complete rotation of the earth on its axis ("and was evening and was morning, day one") is expanded into a geologic age. And are there not millions of highly enlightened persons who even now find the Petrine reconciliation quite *comme il faut?*

23. It seems, then, that the strong-winged shaft of Swiss argument has overshot its mark, because in aiming no allowance was made for the personal, the national, the temporal equation. Professor Schmiedel has not unnaturally, but yet unfortunately, judged others by himself; he has projected his own highly-trained, sequacious, and scientific modes of thought across the sea of centuries into the minds of the deep-musing theosophists who organised the Christian system. The conclusions he has drawn might possibly hold for a consciousness like his own, but not for a consciousness like theirs. Such is the result to which we are guided by general reflections upon the whole matter and manner of this argument, without any special investigation of any passage adduced.

COMINUS

24. It is now time to grapple more closely with these pillars of historic faith. Inasmuch as the arrangement is logically quite indifferent, we shall follow an order that seems

more convenient than that given in the *Encyclopædia Biblica*, and the reader will readily recognise the guiding principle.

Mark iii, 21: "And he cometh home.[1] And there comes together again a multitude, so that they could not even eat bread. And having heard it, his friends[2] went out to overpower[3] him; for they said that He was distraught."[4] Now the idea in the *Encyclopædia* seems to be that here we have preserved a genuine trait; that the Jesus here appears as an enthusiast, whom his friends held to be mad;[5] that such an incident could never have been invented by a Jesus-worshipper—hence that it is an original, preserved by the artless Mark, and priceless in its revelation. But notice that this construction takes the Marcan verses precisely at their face-value, as mere biographic notes or reportorial items. Now I hold this whole mode of interpretation to be radically and incurably wrong. It does the grossest injustice to the work of the second evangelist. A minute examination of Mark, verse by verse, proves incontestably that the work is *essentially a symbolism from beginning to end*. Symbolic interpretation is absolutely demanded in a host of important instances; it is preferable in many more, and it is excluded in none. The literal biographic exegesis of these verses is, then, by no means certain in advance; quietly to assume it is to assume nearly everything in dispute.

25. On careful scrutiny, this prevailing construction of the passage turns out to be entirely inconstructible. Let anyone imagine the situation. The Jesus goes into a house. Again, the crowd assembles in such numbers that they cannot so much as eat bread! Understood as history, this is nothing less than puerile absurdity. We may not be perfectly sure what the evangelist means to say, but we must believe that he means to say something of significance, that more is meant

---

[1] εἰς οἶκον, into a house. [2] Those alongside of him, οἱ παρ' αὐτοῦ.
[3] κρατῆσαι. [4] ἐξέστη, stood out.
[5] It is painful to read the attempts of modern pathography to throw light on the "life" and "character" of the Jesus. It is enough to mention the names of Baumann, O. Holtzmann, Rassmussen, de Loosten, who summon all sorts of neuroses to their aid, and Schaefer, who opposes them all. But what else is possible than just such divagations in the erroneous wood of liberal theology? "Che la diritta via era smarrita." For the logical crest unto the crest, the perfect flower and ripened fruit of this more recent "eschatologie" theory, at present in such favour, the reader is commended to *La Folie de Jésus*, which were more fitly entitled *La Folie de Binet-Sanglé*.

than meets the ear. Again, who are these friends "beside him"? One would naturally think of his disciples as his friends "beside him." But can we think of them as overpowering him? Assuredly not. And what has been done to indicate or even suggest the insanity? Certainly nothing in the text. Possibly someone might think the multitudes insane, if not able to eat bread; but they are not so charged withal. Notice also the queer word ἀκουσάντες (having heard), used without any object, and used of the "friends"—as if these "beside him" were not near him, but had received from afar some report of the situation. Observe still further that there follows an account of a strife over *casting out demons*, in which the charge is brought that the Jesus has a demon, and that he casts out demons by Beelzebul, the prince of demons. Finally, note that the text is at this point peculiarly and hopelessly uncertain. The great Codex Bezæ has the tempting variant: "And when they heard about him, the scribes and the rest went out to conquer him, for they said that he dements them (ἐξίστα ταιαύτούς). And the scribes, those from Jerusalem,[1] having gone down, said that he has Beelzebul," etc. The form is, of course, not active; but the accusative "them" (αὐτούς) requires the active sense. Since the spelling in D is particularly bad, we may conjecture that the verb is misspelled; the active form is implied in the Latin translation *exentiat* (*exsentiat*) in many MSS.

26. Of course, it is not possible to settle any text-critical question here with certainty. But common sense, which has some voice in such matters (*pace* Bengel), declares that the D-text, while itself corrupt, seems to have preserved a rationality that has been lost in the received form. It appears impossible not to recognise that the verses 20–21 are not complete in themselves — that they merely introduce the following sections. The form "concerning him"[2] appears far preferable to "beside him";[3] and herewith his "relations," suddenly dropped down from the sky, are evaporated and return thither. Now, consider this fundamental fact. *The*

---

[1] This phrase is important. It was not the scribes in general, but those from Jerusalem, from the centre and heart of Jewish orthodoxy, that rejected the new cult, born in the Dispersion, as paganism and its deity as a heathen god. Precisely as we might expect!

[2] περὶ αὐτοῦ.   [3] παρ' αὐτοῦ.

demons of the New Testament are nothing but pagan gods; casting-out demons is nothing but converting from heathen worship to Jesus-worship. "But what they sacrifice they sacrifice to demons, and not to God," says the Apostle (1 Cor. x, 20). Justin Martyr too bears witness, saying (*Dial.* 30 C): "For from the demons, which are alien from the service of God, which formerly we worshipped, we pray God always to be preserved through Jesus Christ, that after conversion to God through him we may be blameless." Here, in plain prose, the adoption of the Jesus-cult converts from the worship of the demons. In the bold and splendid poetry of the New Testament the demons are cast out of Man by the word of the Jesus. That such is the meaning of the Gospel, it seems, there cannot be the shadow of a doubt. In the light of this fact we must explore the meaning of this pericope. The multitude throngs the Jesus. What is it but the rush of the world towards the Jesus-cult? But the scribes declare that the Jesus himself hath a demon, and that he casts out demons by Beelzebul, prince of demons—that is, they maintain that the Jesus-cult is itself pagan; that it is merely supplanting one heathen worship by another. This charge was so near-lying, containing as it did a certain element of truth, that it seems impossible it should not have been made. In Matthew xii, 27, Luke xi, 19, we find the *argumentum ad hominem:* "If I by Beelzebul cast out the demons, by whom do your sons cast them out?" which may refer to the fact that the Jews did drive out demons by proselyting, by converting from idol-worship to the service of the true God.[1] The charge that the Jesus-cult was really idolatry must have stung the Christians to the very quick, and must have been resented with the fiercest energy.[2] Hence it is here solemnly declared to be unforgivable. "Amen, I say unto you that all shall be forgiven the sons of men, the sins and the blasphemies whatever they may blaspheme; but whoso shall blaspheme against the holy spirit has not

---

[1] Hereby it is not denied that some Jews may have attempted exorcism by magical means.
[2] Allusion to some such charge seems to be heard in the strange words of the Apostle (1 Cor. xii, 3): "Wherefore I give you to understand that no one speaking in the spirit of God saith ANATHEMA JESUS; and no one can say LORD JESUS but in the Holy Spirit."

forgiveness unto the age, but is guilty of age-lasting sin. Because they said, A spirit unclean hath he." The phrase "the holy spirit"[1] is rare in Mark, occurring only three times —here, xii, 36, and xiii, 11; only iii, 29, and xiii, 11, are strictly parallel, and both seem clearly late comparatively. The term "holy spirit" seems used only in contrast with "unclean spirit." They say he hath an unclean spirit, but we Christians say he hath the Holy Spirit.

27. In Matthew xii, 32, we find the statement that "Whoso shall speak a word against the Son of Man, it shall be forgiven him"; and in Luke xii, 10, that "Everyone who shall say a word at the Son of Man, it shall be forgiven him." This clause is clearly stamped in Matthew, and still more clearly by its dislocation in Luke, as a commentator's addition to the simpler Marcan original. The Son of Man looks here like a mere variant on Mark's "the sons of men." As to the statement about not being able to eat bread, it seems to mean that the harvest was great, the labourers few; that the eager demand for the bread of life (the doctrine of the Jesus) could not be adequately met by the first preachers, enumerated immediately before. The "house" or "home" referred to may be Judea. But on none of these minor points do we insist. The main thing is that verses 20–29 form a whole; that the general subject is the thronging towards the new cult, which the Jewish officials admit is casting out pagan deities, but only (say they) by introducing another pagan deity in their stead. While we may never be able to establish the primitive text, we may be sure it said nothing about his "relations," nor about His being insane.

28. The symbolic character of this whole passage is attested by the symbolic character of the immediately following (iii, 31–33). Wellhausen recognises the two as organically related. The mother and the brethren standing without appear plainly to be the Jewish people holding aloof from the Jesus-cult; and the passage would teach that no race-privileges hold in the new religion, that all are on equal footing, that all are one in Christ.

29. The next pillar-passage has already been considered:

[1] τὸ πνεῦμα τὸ ἅγιον.

"Whoever speaks a word against the Son of Man, it shall be forgiven him" (Matthew xii, 32; Luke xii, 10). To Professor Schmiedel such a sentiment seems impossible as the invention of a Jesus-worshipper. This may or may not be so; but, in any case, what of it? Does Professor Schmiedel really think that Jesus uttered such words?—that the Jesus called himself the Son of Man? Surely not. It was recognised as early as 1569 by Gilbert Génébrand that "Son of Man" here means only "man," as commonly in Syriac. Grotius, followed by Botten in 1792, attained the same position. More recently the learned Orientalists Meyer (1896) and Schmidt (1906) have powerfully maintained it. Holtzmann thinks that the "reference to the Son of Man has been spun out of the reference to the sons of men in the fundamental passage Mark iii, 28," as Pfleiderer had already declared in a footnote (*Das Urchristentum*, p. 376). Wellhausen (*Ev. Marci*, p. 62) regards Matthew xii, 31-32, as a conflation of Mark iii, 28, and Luke xii, 10 (the Q-source)— "variants of one and the same saying." The priority he assigns to Mark, holding that in Q the Messias is meant, but in Mark men in general—*man*. He thinks it probable that Q found "son of man" instead of "sons of men" in Mark iii, 28, and misunderstood the singular, which really meant *man*—a singular that was later changed to the present plural. In his *Skizzen und Vorarbeiten*, vi, p. 204, Wellhausen, following a hint of Marcion, suggests that the original reading was: "Whatever is said by man."

30. We are not called on to pronounce positively in such a case. It is enough that the pillar-passage is admittedly late—how late no man can say; that it forms no part of the earliest Gospel, that its reference is very uncertain, that its text is far from sure. Such a pillar is too frail to bear the least weight of inference, and is worthless for the contention it is intended to sustain.

31. Mark x, 18: "Why callest thou me good? None is good, save God only." Schmiedel reasons that a Jesus-worshipper could not have invented this disclaimer of goodness, hence he concludes that the report is absolutely trustworthy, that Jesus must have used these words, hence must have been an historic man. In this form the argument

crumbles instantly, for it may be proved, and the writer has already proved in this volume that this famous incident is an elaborate symbolism, the Rich One being none other than the People of Israel, whom the Jesus (the new Jehovah) "loved" (verse 21), according to the prophet, " when Israel was young I loved him " (Hos. ii, 1). With the historicity of the whole incident vanishes the historicity of the saying, and therewith the argument based thereon. But perhaps some one may interpose : " Never mind the incident; the saying still reveals a consciousness that could not have belonged to a Jesus-worshipper ; hence it must have been preserved through reverence, and shows that the older consciousness from which it proceeded must have thought of the Jesus as human (not in the highest sense good), and hence not as divine." This interpretation has pleased the Higher Critics immensely. It shows them a Jesus precisely after their own hearts, modest and lowly and intensely human, and they will not tolerate any other conception. Yet the Fathers did not see it in any such light. They regarded it as an argument *for* the divinity of the Jesus, a syllogism with suppressed conclusion : You call me good ; God alone is good ; therefore you call me (and correctly call me) God, "not protesting against himself being good," says the ancient exegete. And how will anyone prove that the Fathers were wrong? The very naïveté of the ordinary conception seems rather suspicious. Moreover, the original form of the saying is doubtful. Luke, indeed (xviii, 19), reproduces the Marcan form, but Matthew presents quite another (xix, 17) : " Master, what good shall I do that I may have life everlasting? But he said to him, ' Why questionest thou me about the good? One is the good.' " The Greek here gives the masculine,[1] but the sense requires the neuter, the good.[2] In the Syriac the distinction of genders is lost as in English, hence Merx gives the three equally justified renderings of the Sinaitic (the oldest) text : Einer ist der Gute, Der Gute ist einer, Das Gute ist eines. Of these only the last is possible in the context, of which the Greek would be ἓν (ἐστὶν) τὸ ἀγαθόν. Now this is precisely the form assumed by the dogma of the Megarean Euclid, as we

---

[1] εἷς ἐστὶν ὁ ἀγαθός. [2] ἓν (ἐστὶν) τὸ ἀγαθόν.

learn from Diogenes Laertius (ii, 106) : " One is the Good, though called by many names."[1] On comparing the many varying text-authorities, manuscripts, versions, and citations, it seems clear not only that this was the primitive form in Matthew, but that it was the most primitive form of the saying of which we have any knowledge, for the variants reveal an unmistakable tendency to depart from this form and to approach the Mark-Lucan form. Thus the Peschita reads, " There is not Good, if not one—God." We can easily understand the derivation of the Mark-Lucan from the Matthæan, but not of the Matthæan from the Mark-Lucan. We must remain content, then, with the probability that the original form of the saying was " One is the Good "—a catchword of Greek ethical philosophy, correctly translated into Aramaic, then incorrectly translated back into Greek.

32. So, it appears, there was in all likelihood no original reference to any good Personality, but only to the universal Principle of Goodness. Herewith, then, the position of the critic seems completely turned. But even if the Marcan text were accepted as original, there would still be allowed from it no inference as to the humanity and non-divinity of the Jesus. We have seen that the Fathers drew the opposite inference ; but suppose we grant that therein they were over-subtle ; let us suppose that the Jesus *is* represented as disclaiming goodness ; it would certainly not mean that he was disclaiming it absolutely, but only relatively (as the Father says), "in contradistinction from the Goodness of God." Very well ; herefrom we could not infer that the original writer was conceiving him not as divine, but merely human. For there are many grades and aspects of divinity. For Jesus to be divine by no means identifies him throughout with the One Supreme God, with God the Most High[2] (Luke viii, 28, Acts xvi, 17, Hebrews vii, 1). With some the Jesus was only a certain mode or aspect of this God alone ; the worship of the Jesus or the Nazarene was not the worship of God *in se*, but under the aspect of Saviour or of Guardian, in relation to men. The ancient mind was perfectly familiar with this notion of definite degrees or

---

[1] ἓν τὸ ἀγαθὸν πολλοῖς ὀνόμασι καλούμενον. [2] ὁ θεὸς ὁ ὕψιστος.

aspects or persons[1] of the Infinite Deity, and hence might very well represent such a Deity as disclaiming Goodness in comparison with the One God Most High. *Test it, then, as you will*, this fundamental passage refuses to bear the testimony for which it was summoned. We pass, then, to the next, which is like unto it.

33. Mark xiii, 32 (Matthew xxiv, 36) : " But concerning that day or that hour knows no one, neither the angels in heaven nor the Son, except the Father." It has no pertinence that many manuscripts omit " nor the Son "; but what possible inference may be drawn concerning the humanity of the Jesus? We can see none. True, a larger knowledge is ascribed to the Father than to the Son, but this is perfectly natural, as we have just seen ; no one claims that the Jesus was originally *metaphysical Deity*, the God Most High. On the other hand, the mere humanity seems implicitly but emphatically denied. The Son is placed above the angels in heaven and next to the Father (for plainly a climax is intended). The witness of this fundamental passage is directly against the position of the liberal critics, for it attests not the pure human and earthly, but the divine and celestial character of the Son (the Jesus).

34. Last among the words attributed to the Jesus we find the cry on the Cross : " My God, my God, why hast thou forsaken me?" (Matthew xxvii, 46 ; Mark xv, 34). It must be frankly and fully admitted that this is by far the most solid-seeming pillar-proof that the skilful research of the critic has been able to produce. At first sight it does look as if the Jesus were here represented as a mere man, an enthusiast abandoned to his fate, and at the last moment realising that he was forsaken both of earth and of heaven. Involuntarily we recall the pathetic lines of Iacopone da Todi :—

> Vidit suum dulcem natum
> Morientem, desolatum,
> Dum emisit spiritum.

Let us, however, consider. In the ancient conception a Deity was a deathless being. It is the " immortal gods "

---

[1] Compare the phrase (2 Cor. iii, 6), "glory of God in person of Christ."

that people Olympus and the whole literature of Greece and Rome as well as the records of Asia and Egypt. Accordingly, when the ancient thought had to deal with a dying god it encountered a very serious obstacle, something indeed like a contradiction in terms. How was this obstacle to be removed or surmounted, or at least circumvented? Some more or less plausible artifice had to be adopted, and different minds would most probably adopt different devices. Perhaps the most obvious and most popular would be to say that the divinity assumed (put on as a garment) a mortal form, which he laid aside at the moment of apparent death. Precisely how this was done no one would inquire too curiously. It is enough that the ancient consciousness was perfectly familiar with the notion of a god clothing himself in the garment of humanity, or even of some lower form of mortality. It would offend the reader to cite instances, they are too numerous and too familiar; but the lofty words of Pindar may be allowed us: "And then a lonely-faring god came suddenly upon us, having cast about him the shining semblance of a reverend man."[1] *The Hebrew Scriptures also are replete with theophanies*, with apparitions of deity and of angels in the guise of men. Now it was precisely to some such device that the primitive Christians found themselves driven when they sought to give pictorial expression to their grand ethical idea of a suffering and dying God. One of the most vivid statements is found in the Epistle to the Philippians (ii, 5–11), a remarkable passage: "Have this mind in you, which was also in Christ Jesus: who being originally in the form of God counted it not a thing to be grasped to be on an equality with God, but emptied himself, taking the form of a servant, becoming in likeness of men; and being found in fashion as man, he humbled himself, becoming obedient unto death, yea, the death of the cross," etc. Here there is no notion whatever of human birth or human history or genuine humanity. The Divine Being Christ Jesus humbles himself, empties himself of his heavenly glory, takes the form of a slave, submits to the shameful

---

[1] τουτάκι δ' οἰοπόλος δαίμων ἐπῆλθεν, φαιδίμαν Ἀνδρὸς αἰδοίου περ' ὄψιν θηκάμενος. —Py. iv, 50.

death of the cross. But only in this human guise, and the momentary humiliation is followed by supreme exaltation. Plainly the writer seems thinking along lines parallel to Pindar's in the passage just quoted. A similar conception is found expressed weakly in Rom. xv, 3, more forcibly in 2 Cor. viii, 9.

35. A most remarkable hint of a related imagination is found in Mark xiv, 51, 52. As is elsewhere proved decisively (p. 112), the "young man wrapped round about with linen," who was following along with (accompanying) Jesus, was a heavenly being, the guardian angel or angel-self, the divine nature of Jesus. This it was impossible for the soldiers to arrest; it fled away, leaving behind in their possession only the linen, the glistening linen, the human flesh, like the "shining semblance" in which Pindar's Poseidon had robed himself. Even so early in the final action Mark found it proper to state in terms vocal to the intelligent that the passion of the Jesus was to be understood as in some sense a symbol, a sublime apparition.

36. Turning now to Hippolytus, we find a luminous statement as to the faith of the Docetæ (*Ref.*, viii, 10): "And he, descended from above, put on the begotten itself, and all things he did so as in the Gospels has been written; he washed himself (dipping) into the Jordan; washed, too, a type and seal having taken in the water, of the body born from the virgin, in order that, when the Archon should condemn his own proper figment to death, to the cross, that soul in the body nourished, having stripped off the body and nailed it to the wood, and having triumphed through it over the principalities and the powers, be not found naked, but put on the body that had been ectyped in the water when he was baptised, instead of that flesh." It matters not how fanciful we may regard this theorising; the point is that it presents clearly and unmistakably a certain thought regarding the human semblance and the part it played in the crucifixion. This form sprung from the Virgin was indeed nailed to the cross; but the soul, the true Jesus, was already clothed upon with another form impressed upon it in the act of baptism; and when the "peculiar figment" (*plasma*) of flesh was crucified, the soul (the Jesus) stripped off the crucified figment,

and, clothed on with the ectypal body received in baptism, it triumphed over all the principalities and powers leagued under the Archon[1] for its destruction.

37. It is vain to say that this is only a very late figment of fancy. The passage just quoted, or at least its idea, with its form of expression, is older than Col. ii, 14, 15, as is elsewhere shown (p. 88, *n.*). In fact, the Colossian passage adopts the Docetic phrases, appropriates them to another use, and thereby makes them unintelligible. The doctrine above set forth may in its elaborated form very well be later than the Gospel, but it is manifest, and it is enough, that the central idea is one and the same—namely, that on the cross the true God, the Jesus, laid aside the form of flesh temporarily assumed, and escaped, whether as a *naked* (γυμνόν) disembodied spirit or as clothed upon with an ectypal or spiritual body. That the ancient mind shrank from the notion of a naked (bodiless) spirit is seen clearly in 1 Cor. xv, where the Apostle argues so powerfully for a *body for spirit* as well as a *body for soul;* and also in 2 Cor. v, 1–4, where he deprecates being found *naked* (a bodiless spirit).

38. Such is the company of conceptions in which this pillar-passage finds its explanation; and we see clearly that it testifies not at all to the historic reality of a man Jesus, but to the high-flown idea of a God who had transiently thrown round himself a vestment of flesh, which *vestment he abandoned* on the cross, and thence ascended, flesh-unshrouded, triumphant to his native heaven. This idea seems natural, and almost necessary (at some stage of evolution), if, and only if, the *primitive* notion was of a God in some way *appearing* to men (even as Jehovah *appeared* in the Old Testament); but it is a confounding case of reversed generation, of "the child the father of the man," if we assume that the primitive notion was of Jesus a pure man, as contended by critical theology. It may not be superfluous to observe that the words (given by the MSS. in three principal forms—Hebrew, *ēli, ēli, lama zafthani;* Aramæan, *elōi, elōi, lama*

---

[1] The same Archon (prince) so conspicuous in John: "Now the Archon of this world shall be cast out" (xii, 31); "Comes the Archon of the world" (xiv, 30), because "the Archon of this world has been judged" (xvi, 11); also mentioned in Ephesians: "The Archon of the power of the air" (ii, 2).

sabachthani; Hebrew-Aramæan, *ēli, ēli, lama sabachthani*) here ascribed to Jesus are taken from Psalm xxii, 1, where they are heard as the cry of the Just and Persecuted (Israel). Their ascription to a deity who had emptied himself of glory and put on a cloak of suffering flesh seems no way strange— nor their utterance on the cross, since Plato had said the Just, thought unjust, would be crucified. That they did not jar with Mark's (and Matthew's) conception of Jesus as God we may be *sure;* for, had they jarred, the way was wide open for him to leave them out—*as did* Luke, supplacing them with the more edifying prayer, "Father, into thy hands I commend my spirit"; and John, substituting the dramatic *Tetelestai* (it is finished); and the "Gospel of Peter," still more neatly altering *ēli* (my God) into *ējali* (my strength). There is no reason to suppose that these three had more reverence for Jesus and less respect for his words than had Mark (or Matthew); it is only different preferences they display in theologising fiction. To the Docetic Mark (followed by Matthew) the cry seemed perfectly fitting, and almost *demanded* as fulfilment of Scripture; had it not seemed so, never would he have imputed it to Jesus. The notion that tradition forced it upon him is baseless, and completely refuted by the procedure of Luke, John, and "Peter."

39. We come now to the deeds of the Jesus that are supposed to indicate his mere humanity. Of these the first is: (I) Mark vi, 5; Matthew xiii, 58: "And he could not there do any deed of might, save that, having laid his hands on a few invalids, he healed them; and he marvelled at their unbelief." Apparently it is thought that only a man could have this power limited by another's unbelief, and that only of a man would such a limitation be reported. Professor Schmiedel says this took place "in Nazareth," but Mark and Matthew declare only that "he came into his fatherland,"[1] which decidedly does *not* signify Nazareth. The meaning of the whole passage is clear, and need give no great trouble. The "fatherland" (*patris*) is, apparently, Jewry, Israel, the Jewish people—specifically the Palestinian Jews. When the

---

[1] εἰς τὴν πατρίδα αὐτοῦ.

Jesus-cult came to them it encountered, and has always encountered, persistent opposition. Among them it has done no deeds of might, for they will not believe. "A few weak ones" have accepted it, but the strong body of the race has steadily rejected it. The passage hints nothing whatever about the humanity of the Jesus, but it exhibits the Jesus-cult as triumphant among the Gentiles and despised by the Jews. Also it represents, and very properly represents, the progress of the cult and its triumph as dependent upon the faith with which it is received. Precisely as we should expect.

40. (II) Mark viii, 12 (Matthew xii, 39; xvi, 4; Luke xi, 29): "Why doth this generation seek a sign? Amen I say to you if there shall be given to this generation a sign" ("but the sign of Jonah, the prophet"—"but the sign of Jonah"—"but the sign of Jonah"). It is not the word, but rather the deed of the Jesus disclaiming thaumaturgy or sign-giving, that the critic regards as clearly indicating humanity, even modest humanity. The sign of Jonah is taken as the preaching of Jonah. In proof we are referred to "the immediate sequel—'the men of Nineveh repented at the preaching of Jonah.'" But of all this the explanation lies on the open hand. It is the Jesus-cult that is wonderfully successful; the Gentiles far and near are falling away from their idol-worship and receiving the "new teaching"; they are repenting even as the people of Nineveh repented. This is, indeed, *the one and only sign* that the Jesus gives that marks the progress of his cult among the nations. But did he not cast out demons? Assuredly! But this preaching of the "new doctrine," this conversion of the heathen, *was* casting out demons, *was* cleansing lepers, *was* healing the sick, the lame, the blind, *was* raising the dead. Once more there is nothing to be found in the passage but the strongest confirmation of the interpretation herein championed and illustrated.

41. In close connection with the foregoing stands (III) Matthew xi, 5 (Luke vii, 22), the answer to the Baptist: "(the) blind look up, and (the) lame walk about, lepers are cleansed, and (the) deaf hear, and (the) dead are raised, and (the) poor evangelised. And blessed is whoever is not offended in me." Professor Schmiedel is impressed with

the fact "that all the miracles mentioned have taken place, either at an earlier date, or before the eyes of the Baptist's messengers. All the more remarkable therefore is it that the list should close with what is not a miracle at all. It would be impossible to counteract the preceding enumeration more effectually than by the simple insertion of this final clause. *The evangelists therefore cannot have added it of their own proper motion.* Neither could Jesus have neutralised the force of his own words—if we assume miracles to be intended —in such an extraordinary way. On the other hand the clause in question fits admirably, if Jesus was speaking not of the physically but of the spiritually blind, lame, leprous, deaf, dead. This is the meaning, too, which these words actually have in the Old Testament passages, Isaiah xxxv, 5 *f.;* lxi, 1, which lie at the root of this; and it also fits very well the continuation in Matthew xi, 6; Luke vii, 23, which reads, 'Blessed is he who is not offended in me' (*i.e.*, *in my unpretentious simplicity*). Here, therefore, we have a case, as remarkable as it is assured, in which a saying of Jesus, *though completely misunderstood*, has been—in its essence at least—incorporated with verbal accuracy in the Gospels."

42. To do no possible injustice, we have quoted in full the argument on this important passage. It contains much that seems to be entirely just. We have italicised what appear to be the unwarranted statements. Professor Schmiedel seems to err in supposing the evangelists have misunderstood anything. They have used the terms "blind," "lame," "leper," "deaf," "dead," "poor," throughout in their proper *spiritual* sense, and perfectly consciously. They meant no physical miracles whatever, and they have quite correctly summed-up the situation in the climacteric, "the poor are evangelised" —that is, the Gospel is proclaimed to the poor heathen—a bold and beautiful characterisation of the primitive propaganda. The passage is quite self-consistent throughout. The "unpretentious simplicity" is simply a fancy. No matter how you interpret the Gospels, *the Jesus was neither simple nor unpretentious.*[1] The meek and lowly Jesus exists only in the imaginations of modern Christians. But the

[1] See Addendum, p. 226.

phrase "whoso is not offended in me" is most significant. What about the Jesus could give offence, could cause one to stumble at accepting him? Manifestly not simplicity, not unpretentiousness. One thing, and one thing only—his half-heathen origin, the fact that the "new doctrine" sprang up, not on the sacred soil of Judæa, not in the bosom of the strict Pharisaic or priestly party, not under the sacred shadow of the temple, but far away in the Dispersion, among the Gentiles; there the great light arose in the deep dark of the nations;[1] and at this fact Israel has always stumbled. It seems, then, that this celebrated passage testifies openly in favour of our contention. Very noteworthy is the use of the term "the Christ" (xi, 2), but we are not at present concerned with its implications.

43. (IV) Lastly, we come to the misunderstanding of the disciples concerning the leaven of the scribes and Pharisees, Mark viii, 14-21 (Matthew xvi, 5-12; Luke xii, 1): "Take heed, beware of the leaven of the Pharisees and the leaven of Herod" (in Matthew, "and of the Sadducees"; in Luke, simply "of the Pharisees"). The pith of Professor Schmiedel's reasoning seems to be disclosed in two sentences: "Both evangelists have previously related the feeding of the 5,000 and the 4,000 as *facts.*" He then goes on to show that only on assuming that the "feeding of the 5,000 and the 4,000 was not an historical occurrence, but a parable," does the language of the Jesus become intelligible; and then continues: "It is exceedingly surprising, yet at the same time evidence of a reproduction of earlier materials, that Mark and Matthew should give the present narrative at all—a narrative which

---

[1] So declares Origen (*C. Cels.* vi, 66) in a passage too important not to quote: "And to this we will reply, that all sit in darkness and are rooted therein who gaze on the wicked handiwork of the painters and moulders and sculptors, nor will look aloft and ascend in thought from all things sensible and visible unto the Demiurge of all things, who is Light; but everyone is in light that has followed the beams of the Logos, who has shown through what ignorance and impiety and unlearnedness concerning the Divine these things were worshipped instead of God, and has led the mind of him that would be saved unto the God unbegotten and over all. 'For the people that sat in darkness'—the Gentiles—'saw a great light, and for them that sat in the region and shadow of death a light arose'—the God Jesus (ὁ θεὸς Ἰησοῦς)." Surely the chief of Church Fathers here indicates with all desirable clearness the two hinges of Proto-Christianity: its Aim—the Salvation of men (especially Gentiles) from ignorance of God and the consequent sin of idol-worship with all its attendant vice; its Means—the monotheistic cult of Jesus, the Doctrine of the Divine Logos, of "THE GOD JESUS."

CONCLUSION

in their understanding of the miracle of the feeding is so meaningless." Again we have italicised the few words to which we must except. Of course, we cannot say who first misunderstood the symbolic narrative of the feeding,[1] but no evidence has been produced that Mark and Matthew misunderstood it, or that they related these feedings "as facts." This prop removed, the argument in the *Encyclopædia Biblica* falls to the ground. The whole passage remains somewhat mysterious; but we are not logically responsible for clearing it up perfectly. It is enough for our purposes to recognise distinctly that it contains nothing to recommend the notion either that the Jesus was a mere man, or that the earliest compilers conceived of him as such.

CONCLUSION

44. Herewith, then, the Nine Pillars have been disintegrated. Not one of them bears witness for the accepted critical position, while some of them bear eloquent witness directly against it. But this collapse and crumbling of these pillars means far more than merely that these particular supports have dissolved into dust. For these were the chosen passages on which the scholar and critic had rested and risked his case, and but for which he would regard that case as hopeless.[2] They supplied him the most plausible arguments that he could find, the least equivocal indications that he could discover anywhere in the Gospels. And these elect witnesses, on cross-examination, produce testimony that is either entirely negative or else positively contradictory of the idea in whose interest they were called into court. When these witnesses thus turn coat, where shall we find any in the Gospels that will remain firm? The answer is, "Nowhere." *There are no texts in the Gospels that indicate that the Jesus was a man.* Of course, he is represented as speaking, as

---

[1] Nor who last, for Schmiedel has himself gone slightly astray. It cannot be "that the bread with which one man in the wilderness was able to feed a vast multitude signifies the teaching with which he satisfied their souls" (Schmiedel). No man can point anywhere to any such soul-satisfying teaching *by* Jesus. On the contrary, the bread distributed *by* the Disciples to the multitude is the teaching *by* the Disciples *concerning the Jesus*. John's interpretation is essentially correct (vi, 32 *ff.*).

[2] See quotation, p. 33.

going from place to place, even as sleeping and (in a transparent parable) as hungering, as working wonders, as being surrendered, arrested, tried, condemned, executed, buried, raised again. But all this is only imagery; it is but the linen cloth that is wrapped round about the divine form of the "new teaching"; it is but the historisation of a system of religious ideas. The deep thinkers who invented these parables and symbols were perfectly conscious of the inner sense, and so were the first who heard them, and repeated them, and wrote them down.

45. Yea, this consciousness survived keen and clear for generations, at least in many groups of Christians. In the first quarter of the second century (according to current chronology), perhaps two hundred and fifty years after the first secret propaganda begun, we find that the fiery Ignatius has his heart set on a strict historic interpretation of the Gospel, at least in its main features, and he fiercely denounces such as oppose him. He has the ardent zeal of one that is advancing something comparatively new, not the calm confidence of a conservative upholding the old. In Justin Martyr somewhat later we find the contentions of the historisers epitomised in a formula that very strongly suggests the Apostles' Creed. In Irenæus and Tertullian, at the close of the second century, we find the historisers battling valiantly against all the more ancient forms of Christian thought, and vehemently denouncing them as heresies of recent growth. The absurdity of their contention is apparent on its face, and yet they succeeded in their strife over much more spiritual and high-minded antagonists. For anyone who reads with impartial sense the works of the heresy-hunters must perceive that Marcion, Basilides, Valentinus, and many others, were far superior to their denouncers in all the loftier qualities of religious intuition and theological speculation. Hereby it is not denied that these noble Gnostics, to whom the illustrious Harnack concedes that we owe so much, were too often visionary and hopelessly fantastic in their daring constructions. Their speculations were dreamy, phantasmagoric, and full of emptiness, not adapted to the general social and religious conditions of the time. No wonder that they went under in the struggle with

CONCLUSION

the concrete matter-of-fact historisations of Irenæus, Tertullian, and the rest. We need not regret that they failed, for they had run off into all manner of extravagance, and did not deserve to succeed. Nevertheless, we owe them an incalculable debt of gratitude, for without their indications it might have been impossible ever to discover the original sense and spirit of the Christian propaganda, so overladen as it now is with the millennial growth of degenerate historisation. This, however, is a digression from which we hasten to return.

46. In closing let attention once more be called to the heavy obligations under which Professor Schmiedel has placed historical criticism by his sharp and accurate formulation of the logical conditions of the problem in hand. By disclosing and signalising the strongholds of the prevalent critical opinion, he has rendered it possible to join issue precisely and definitely, to grapple in hand-to-hand struggle, and to bring the battle to an unambiguous result. As long as defenders of the historicity content themselves with vague intangible rhapsodies on the imposing personality of the Jesus, wherein no two exhibit delineations that bear any recognisable resemblance either to each other or to the Gospel original, so long even the most vigorous and rigorous counter-dialectic must in some measure prove to be merely buffeting the air. Of what avail to smite down such cloudforms that like the ghost of Loda fall shapeless into mist, only to gather themselves together again and resume their voice of thunder and shake their dusky spears? But in the case of Schmiedel's Pillars we encounter something real, tangible, close-reasoned, and subtly excogitated. For these columns to stand means for the historic conception of the Jesus to become a permanent possession of the human spirit, inalienable and indefectible. For them to fall and crumble, as we have seen them do, means the passing of the present structure of Christianity, and the substitution therefor of an older, a sublimer, and a more spiritual temple.

> Mächtiger
> Der Erdensöhne,
> Prächtiger
> Baue sie wieder,
> In deinem Busen baue sie auf!

ADDENDUM I.

Supplementing § 17.

IN Luke ii, 52, we read that "Jesus advanced in wisdom and stature and in favour with God and men." Professor Schmiedel was too cautious or astute to number this passage among his ground-pillars; but his able disciple, Dr. Arno Neumann—who is deeply touched by "the simple, sober, naïve facts of history as we find them in the" Synoptic "Gospels"—has not shown such foresight. With it he heads his list (otherwise agreeing with Schmiedel's) of "Statements which can be nothing more nor less than survivals of the truth, precious fragments," etc., and he adds: "Had the writer been a worshipper of Jesus as a deity, he would have presented him to us as full-grown" (*Jesus*, p. 10). This, too, is a "precious fragment" exemplifying the habits of distinguished critics; it is, indeed, invaluable for the purposes of our argument. One or two features seem to call for careful inquisition.

Dr. Neumann is sure that "a worshipper of Jesus as a deity would have presented him to us as full-grown." But how can he be so sure? Are not the stories of the gods, stories invented by their worshippers, full of accounts of birth and childhood? Has Dr. Neumann forgotten Bacchus and Zeus? Does not Pindar tell us how Leto steadied with her holy foot the vagrant island of Delos, and made it broad earth's immovable marvel, and there brought forth to light and looked upon her blessed brood? And does anyone doubt that Pindar worshipped Apollo and Artemis as deities? The stories of the birth and childhood of the Jesus are quite in line with other theogonies invented by the ancients, all of whom worshipped these prodigious births as deities.

Observe well, however, that these stories in Matthew and Luke *do not belong to the earliest narrative.* It is recognised on all hands that they are late accretions; they are the full flower and almost the ripened fruit of the humanising tendency that has wrought such wreck with the original

ADDENDUM I.

doctrine of the Jesus. To adduce them or any part of them as examples of the primitive Evangelic conception is a notable critical procedure. Perhaps it would have been worthier of the new deity to be introduced on the stage in the full flush of heavenly power, without any enfeebling suggestions of earthly parentage. And this is precisely what Mark does (i, 1–3): "Beginning of the Gospel of Jesus Christ: even as is written in Isaiah the Prophet, Lo I send mine Angel before thy face, who shall prepare thy way; voice of a crier, 'in the wilderness make ready the way of the Lord, straight make his paths.'" It is the Lord (Jehovah) that comes, and comes in might. Similarly the Fourth Evangelist, striking a keynote less highly poetic, but more deeply philosophic. It is only Matthew and Luke that yield to the weakness of human nature, and open the gate for the tiresome procession of Gospels of the Infancy. On account of the hardness of our hearts they did this, but from the beginning it was not so.

This verse, with which Dr. Neumann precedes the Schmiedelian list, is in fact a striking illustration of the process whereby the whole evangelic and apocryphal history has come into being. At first, as in Mark's narrative, there was little thought of humanising the divine figure introduced upon the stage. Still, if there was to be any historisation, dramatisation, or symbolisation at all of the great ideas that seethed in the mind of the Evangelist, then the principle of Xenophanes had to be followed; the *Deity* had to be represented as a *man*—as speaking, walking, sleeping, doing deeds of might, and at last even dying. Similarly, though even in still less degree, in the earliest collection of Sayings (Logoi, Logia) of the Jesus, he is of *necessity* represented as human, as speaking. A Saying was regularly introduced by the phrase "The Jesus says," or the like. This was exactly parallel with the customary preamble of the prophets: "Thus saith Jehovah," "Oracle of Jehovah," etc., and, in fact, presents the Jesus as a new Jehovah, or at least as a pro-Jehovah, the conception that reigns throughout early Christian literature.

Gradually and most naturally the artistic feeling asserted itself more and more, and dramatic situations were devised and then elaborated as settings for the Sayings, which themselves underwent great development and expansion. Of this process the Fourth Gospel furnishes perfect illustrations. At the same time or later there made itself felt the universal tendency to humanise *unnecessarily*, and even unreasonably; to attribute to the God the passions and even the weaknesses of man, and especially to accent the pathetic and the sympathetic. Thus the Fourth Evangelist insists that Jesus loved, and even that he wept; while the late accounts of Matthew and Luke, profaning the sacred reserve of Mark (i, 13), inform us that he fasted, and afterwards hungered. Last and least pardonable, though perfectly natural, are the stories of birth, infancy, and childhood. After the humanising process had triumphed over the solemn and awful divinity of the original conception, it was inevitable that human fancy should ask and should answer the questions: How was he begotten? How born? How nourished? What wonders glorified his early years? In all of this development we recognise the most familiar workings of human nature. "Of all things the measure is man," said Protagoras; in all ages man himself has been the canon that he has laid upon the universe, whereby he has meted, interpreted, and constructed it in thought.

ADDENDUM II.

CASTING OUT DEMONS

The perception that the demons of the New Testament are the heathen gods, and that casting them out means overthrowing the prevailing idolatry by the introduction of the Jesus-cult, is so fundamentally important, and even essential to a proper understanding of the original sense of the Gospel, that it may be well to look at it still more narrowly than has thus far been done.[1]

---

[1] It is gratifying to observe that on pp. 180 *ff.* of his acute and learned work, *De groote Vraag* (1911), Professor Bolland has expressed himself in full accord with the views herein set forth, as well as with the interpretation of the Rich One as the symbol of Jewry. If the philosopher of Leiden has

ADDENDUM II.

The census of the uses of δαιμόνιον (demon, devil) in the New Testament appears at first glance rather formidable. It recurs in Matthew eleven times, in Mark thirteen, in Luke twenty-three, in John six, in Acts one, in 1 Corinthians four (x, 20, 21), in 1 Timothy one, in James one, in Revelation three. Besides, Matthew has δαιμονίζομαι (have a demon) seven times, Mark four, Luke one, John one (x, 21). Quite equivalent seems to be the expression unclean or evil spirit (πνεῦμα ἀκάθαρτον or πονηρόν) recurrent in Matthew four times, in Mark twelve, in Luke nine, in Acts six (v, 16; viii, 7; xix, 12, 13, 15, 16), in Revelation two (xvi, 13; xviii, 2). Besides, we have δαίμων (demon) once (Matthew viii, 31), and divining spirit (πνεῦμα πύθωνα) once (Acts xvi, 16). Hence the idea may be said to occur in Matthew about twenty-three times, in Mark twenty-eight, in Luke thirty-three, in John seven, in Acts seven, with a few scattering and unimportant uses in 1 Corinthians, 1 Timothy, James, and Revelation. Practically it is confined to the Synoptics, for the Johannine uses all refer to the charge of *having a demon, brought against the Jesus* (vii, 20; viii, 48, 49, 52; x, 20, 21). The notion of casting out demons, the real matter in hand, does not occur in John. All the more conspicuous is it in the Synoptics; but here again we find something remarkable: all the references to demons and unclean spirits belong to the Galilean, none whatever to the Judæan, ministry of the Jesus. The last appearance of such a term in Matthew is at xvii, 18, after the Transfiguration; in Mark at ix, 38, in Capernaum; in Luke at xiii, 32, apparently in Galilee, "journeying toward Jerusalem" (verse 22). Here there is something that calls for explanation. The cases of possession and of exorcism in Galilee have been countless; in Judæa there are none at all. Can it be that epileptic lunacy and nervous disorders prevailed so amazingly in Galilee, but found no material in Judæa? Certainly not; for it is an ethnological fact that the Jews are specially subject to such distempers, though otherwise uncommonly vigorous and

---

reached such results independently of this book, which he has read carefully and elsewhere cites repeatedly in its German form, but not on pp. 180 *ff.*, then this coincidence affords a very strong confirmation of the correctness of the views in question.

healthy. There is one and only one explanation of this curious evangelic distinction between these two adjoining regions: the maladies in question were spiritual maladies that afflicted whole multitudes in Galilee of the Gentiles, but not the Jews in Judæa; they were the maladies of false religion, of demon-worship, of Paganism.[1]

Let it not be supposed for a moment that I would deny there were epileptics, lunatics, maniacs, neurasthenics, both in Galilee and in Judæa. Of course, there were, and are, and will be. Moreover, the symbolist, having once determined to represent Polytheism, that multiform aberration of the human mind, as possession by a demon, both naturally and well-nigh inevitably drew the features of his description from his own observation, or at least knowledge, of the course of such attacks in noteworthy patients.

Of course, the ancients had the idea of one's being under the power of a Dæmon, though it was expressed by δαιμονάω rather than by δαιμονίζομαι, which properly means to be *doomed,* or else *deified.* But that any such afflictions overwhelmed the multitudes of Galilee, or that the Evangelist intended to represent the multitudes as so afflicted, seems quite impossible.

It is most remarkable that, although this casting out of demons is represented in the Gospels (and even in their echo in Acts x, 38) as the main activity of the Jesus, though it is the principal power he bestowed on the Apostles, yet we never hear of its exercise. The passages in Acts (v, 16; viii, 7; xix, 12) are the vaguest and merest generalities—symbolic phrases without any specific historic content. It cannot be that an activity of such supreme significance during the life of the Jesus, and of special endowment conferred on his successors, should cease immediately and permanently, not

---

[1] According to Keim (iii, 53; see p. *infra*), at Jericho the curative energy of Jesus was at its height, "in might as a flame of fire"; but Bacon (*The Beginnings of Gospel Story,* p. 146) thinks this flame had sunk low, even to extinction, when the Jesus journeyed southward from Galilee. "The course of events, therefore, does not imperatively demand the rekindling in this sporadic instance of the flame of Jesus' healing power, so far from the scenes of its original activity." That is, one degree's depression of the pole annihilated the miraculous might of the Saviour! And precisely where Keim found the wonder-working powers of the Jesus at their acme, precisely there Bacon finds them quenched and pulseless!

ADDENDUM II.

upon his death, but even before, upon his entrance into Judæa. Had the treatment of such diseases been any part of the activity of the Apostles, we should certainly have heard of it, both in Acts and in the Epistles.

What, then, is the explanation? It is very simple—namely: The Synoptists are poets and symbolists, but the authors of the rest of the New Testament have definitely laid aside that symbolism. They chose to state the propaganda in more direct, literal, and unmetaphorical terms, and less under the veil of symbolic language. Very rarely, as in the cases mentioned, the author of Acts drops back for a moment into the symbolic phraseology of the Synoptists.

We may feel sure, then, that the primitive preachers did not exorcise, and did not pretend to do so. It is a great relief to know that our noble religion did not have as its primal form of activity the magical and temporal alleviation of the condition of hopeless defectives. That a religion that made such charlatanry one of its main features could conquer the intelligence of the Roman Empire stands greatly in need of proof. Herewith it is not forgotten that even Schmiedel has sought to show that such healing of demoniacs prevailed in the early days of the Church; and it is not denied that some enthusiasts may sometimes have undertaken some such cure, and even, under imaginable conditions, with partial or apparent success. Such exceptional cases, sometimes hard or impossible to understand, may occasionally be constated. But that they cut practically no figure in the elder Church is the thing that is plainest to see from Schmiedel's own testimonies. Let us hear them in detail.

Schmiedel says ($E.\ B.$, "Gospels," § 144):—

> According to Mark vi, 5 $f.$ (see § 140b [which we have already considered, p. 201]), we are to understand that Jesus healed where he found faith. This power is so strongly attested throughout the first and second centuries that, in view of the spiritual greatness of Jesus and the imposing character of his personality [all of which is imaginary], it would be indeed difficult to deny it to him. Even the Pharisees do not deny his miracles of healing [only "casting out demons" is mentioned in the texts], though they traced them to a compact [?] with Beelzebub (Mark iii, 22; Matthew ix, 34, xii, 24; Luke xi, 15). According to Matthew xii, 27=Luke xi, 19, the disciples of the Pharisees also wrought such miracles [Jewish proselytism?];

the man who followed not with the disciples of Jesus cast out devils [but only "in thy name"] (Mark ix, 38–40=Luke ix, 49 f.); the same is said of those whom in Matthew vii, 22 f., Jesus rejects in his final judgment [these, too, "cast out demons" "in thy name"—*i.e.*, overthrew idolatry by preaching the Jesus-cult]. Paul asserts that a like power was possessed by himself (2 Cor. xii, 12; Romans xv, 19) and by other Christians (1 Cor. xii, 8–11, 28); Justin mentions castings-out of devils (*Apol.* 26, *Dial.* 30, 35, 39, 76, 85); so also Tertullian (*Apol.* 23), Irenæus (ii, 31 f., Eus. *H.E.* 5), and Quadratus (Eus. *H.E.*, iv, 3_2).

Then in a footnote:—

As for Josephus, cp. *B.J.* ii, 8_6, vii, 6_3, *Ant.* iii, 11_5, viii, 2_5, and *c.Ap.* 1_{31}; for Pliny, *N.H.* 30_2; for Lucian, *Philops.* 16 f. According to Tacitus (*Hist.* 4_{81}), Vespasian effected several wonderful cures (cp. above, col. 1456).

Certainly a formidable array of authorities, which might indeed be greatly lengthened. We need consider only the supposed testimonies to literal casting-out of demons. So far as the Gospels are concerned, the remarks we have inserted in brackets [ ] are sufficient to show that there is no such testimony at all; the passages are far more naturally understood of the banishing of idolatry by preaching the Jesus. As to Paul, we have already seen that he is never named in connection with such exorcism, nor does he ever name it. The first passage cited (2 Cor. xii, 12) merely declares: "Truly the signs of an apostle were wrought among you in all patience, by signs and wonders and powers." In Romans xv, 19 (which I have proved [see *J. B. L.*, 1901, 129–157; 1902, 117–169] to be a late accession to the epistle), the language is still vaguer—"in the power of signs and wonders." There is no hint of exorcism.

In 1 Cor. xii, 8–11, various "gifts of the Spirit" are mentioned, among them "gifts of healing"; also in verse 28, "gifts of healing"—in both cases without further specification. Plainly nothing can be inferred.

Leaping now over nearly one hundred years of silence, in Justin's *Apol.* 26 we read: "That also after the ascent of Christ to heaven the demons sent forth certain men claiming themselves to be gods who not only were not persecuted by you, but were even adjudged worthy of honours: as a certain Simon, a Samaritan from a village called Gittæ, who under

Claudius Cæsar by the art of inworking demons, having wrought magic powers in your city royal Rome, was esteemed a god and was honoured by you as a god with a statue, which statue was erected in the Tiber river between two bridges, bearing this Roman inscription: To Simon God Holy (Simoni Deo Sancto)." On this it seems enough to remark, in the first place, that it hints nothing about casting out demons, and even if it did it would prove nothing, for Justin here condemns himself unappealably. The real inscription was: Semoni Sanco Deo. Fidio Sacrum Sex. Pompeius. S. P. F. Col. Mussianus Quinquennalis Decur Bidentalis Donum. Dedit.

This Semo, whom Justin mistakes for Simon, was a Sabine god of oaths or compacts ("sancus a sanciendo"), hence also called "Fidius a fide," and had no more to do with Simon Magus than with Simon Peter. Most of all, however, it is perfectly plain that Justin himself considers demons the same as false gods.

This fact is fully confirmed by the next proof-text, *Dial.* 30: "For from the demons, which are alien from the worship of God, whom formerly we adored, we pray God always to be preserved through Jesus Christ, that after conversion to God we may be blameless through him. For him we call Helper and Redeemer, at the might even of whose name even the demons tremble, and to-day being exorcised by the name of Jesus Christ the Crucified under Pontius Pilate, who was procurator of Judæa, they are subdued; so that also from this it is evident to all that his Father has given him such power that even the demons are subdued by his name and the dispensation of his passion." Clearly Justin identifies the demons with the heathen gods, and if he means aught else by the exorcism and subduing of these demons to the name of Jesus than the downfall of heathen deities before the preaching of the Jesus, it is only by a *late misapplication* of the old familiar phrase "casting out demons" or "subjecting demons to the Jesus." Manifestly the passage cannot be quoted as witnessing the reality of any such exorcism.

The next citation (*Dial.* 35) does not mention demons, but only "the powers that even now proceed from his name," whereon it seems quite needless to dwell. Neither does the next (*Dial.* 39), but merely speaks of one having the spirit of healing (ὁ δὲ ἰάσεως), perhaps glancing at the passage in 1 Cor. xii, 8–11.

In *Dial.* 76: "And now we that believe on the Jesus, our Lord crucified under Pontius Pilate, have all the demons and evil spirits subdued to us, exorcising them." Remember that Justin has clearly identified these demons with the heathen gods, and you perceive that this passage is at most a rhetorical flourish. Had anyone pressed the Martyr for an illustration, he might have referred to some conversion in which indeed some heathen demon-god was overthrown and cast out by the power of the Jesus (-cult).

Lastly (*Dial.* 85): "For by the name of him, this Son of God and first begotten of all creation, and born of a virgin and made passible man and crucified under Pontius Pilate by your people, who died and rose from (the) dead and ascended into heaven, every demon exorcised is conquered and subdued. But if you exorcise by every name of those among you that have been kings, or just, or prophets, or patriarchs, none of the demons will be subdued; but if, however, anyone of you exorcise by the God of Abraham and God of Isaac and God of Jacob, perhaps it will be subdued. But already I have said that your exorcists, by using the art as do the Gentiles, exorcise and use fumigations and magic ties." I have quoted this long passage because it is the strongest in Schmiedel's list, and because it shows the Apostles' Creed in process of formation. On the great significance of this latter this is not the place to enlarge.

Now it must not be supposed for a moment that the present writer denies or calls in question the bare fact of exorcism at the period under consideration. The word itself is a witness to the fact, and as such is unimpeachable. Yea, more, the immense magic literature of the old faiths, the countless incantations and conjurations, bear unequivocal testimony. Chief of all, certain passages to which the writer has called repeated attention show decisively that the names "Jesus" and "Nasarya" were actually used as names of deities in conjurations at an extremely early date in the beginning of Christianity. In fact, the very phrase, "In the name of Jesus," bears sure witness, as Heitmueller has so admirably set forth, to the use of that great name as a magic spell. That it should have been used for exorcisms of demons as well as for other purposes is antecedently probable, and may be fully conceded.[1] In view of this state of the case, it seems not unlikely that Justin's formula, rapidly expanding into the Apostles' Creed, may have been actually pronounced at some exorcisms, especially as we know that the spell was thought to be strengthened by such quasi-historical recitals. Thus Origen (*C. Cels.*, I, vi): "For they seem not to prevail by enchantments, but by the name of Jesus after the recital of the stories concerning him."

On the other hand, this very formula has become the creed of the Church, a ceremony of admission to the Church itself. So this expulsion of demons is again clearly seen to stand in the most intimate relations with the renunciation of paganism and the adoption of the Jesus-cult. That such must have been at least the controlling sense and use among Christians appears quite manifest from this consideration, that it could have been used at most only in a few comparatively exceptional cases of exorcism of demoniacs, whereas it must have been used in thousands of thousands of cases of conversion from paganism. Even then, when we allow all possible force to these words of Justin, they still fail to point towards actual possession and exorcism as a certain, or at least *prominent*, fact in the early life of the Church; they are found in connection with the formal renunciation of paganism and acceptance of Christianity. This was indeed an exorcism, but an exorcism in the New Testament sense, which we have already found necessary.

---

[1] Inasmuch as the demon-worshipping idolater was conceived as in some sense possessed—*i.e.*, under influence of his demon—it was natural for Christians, especially the more ignorant (as Origen testifies), to ascribe physical infirmities of idolaters to such possession; hence it became quite as natural to speak of all manner of illness, especially mental, as completely healed by Jesus, at invocation of his name—*i.e.*, by the all-saving monotheistic Jesus-cult. Hence such forms of conception and expression, no matter how frequent, stand not in discord but in concord with our understanding of New Testament exorcisms, whose essence is this: *expulsion of demons by Jesus* (and *generally*, later, in his name, by Christians) *is to be understood only in the religious sense of conversion from polytheism to the Jesus-cult.* Compare 1 Cor. xii, 2, 3, where "being led away to dumb idols" stands in sharp contrast with saying "Jesus is Lord"—*i.e.*, with confession, with conversion.

In confirmation of this view we may make still further and decisive appeal to Justin himself; for the most important passage is not cited by Schmiedel, possibly because found in the Second Apology, 6 : " But Jesus has the name and significance both of man and of Saviour. For also a man, as we said before, was he made, according to the counsel of the God and Father, brought forth for the sake of believing men and for dissolution[1] of the demons." Here, then, the nature and mission of Jesus are defined. He is a Saviour, as the name indicates. From what does he save? From demons. Whom does he save? Believers. Here, then, all doubt appears set at rest. It is quite impossible to understand this salvation of believers from demons as referring to the cure of a few sporadic demoniacs. Justin is defining the *general significance* of the Jesus as saviour, and he defines it as for the sake of believers and for the overthrow of the demons. It seems certain that this must mean the conversion of heathen idolaters to the Jesus-cult. Now notice the remarkable terms in which he further specifies and describes such conversion : " And now you can learn from what takes place under your own eyes. For many possessed by demons throughout the whole world and in your city, many of our men, the Christians, exorcising by the name of Jesus Christ the Crucified under Pontius Pilate, by all the other exorcists and enchanters and magicians unhealed, have healed and still now heal, annulling and expelling the demons obsessing the men."

Here the distinctive activity of the Christians is described as this expulsion of demons. That such, in the literal sense of the words, could have been the technical and professional calling of Christians in Rome near the middle of the second century appears incredible. There was but one thing that could have been ascribed to them as their peculiar vocation, and that was the conversion of men to Christianity, to the worship of the Jesus. This, then, is the expulsion of demons, considered by the Martyr. The phrase " not healed by all the other exorcists," etc., would seem to refer to the multitude of creeds and cults with which Rome abounded.

---

[1] Or expulsion, $\epsilon\pi\grave{\iota}$ $\kappa\alpha\tau\alpha\lambda\acute{\upsilon}\sigma\epsilon\iota$ = *ad eversionem*—Otto.

ADDENDUM II.

Moreover, this notion and designation of heathen gods as demons is not occasional, but regular, and even universal in Justin. He declares them to be sons of wicked angels, to have the Devil, Satan, the Serpent as Prince, to demand victims and worship from evil livers, to enslave men, to appear under simulated forms and names preserved in fanes and temples, corrupting and affrighting by prodigies, to be called gods, each choosing his own name, to send forth heretics intent on turning men from God and Christ, to calumniate Christians, to flee from the power of men, and to be subdued by the name of Jesus. On nearly all these points Justin voices the general sentiment of the Christians. Nor was he unsupported in this matter by the heathen themselves, such as Porphyry, the bitter antagonist of Christianity. We may say, then, with renewed and augmented confidence that by the expulsion of demons Justin Martyr meant, in general, if not indeed in every case, the overthrow of polytheism by conversion to the worship of the Jesus.

We pass now to the other authorities cited. In Tertullian's *Apologeticum* (xxii, xxiii) we find set forth his ideas as to the pagan gods, demons, and evil spirits. Already in Cap. xxi he has defined the mission of Christ, not like Numa's, to temper boors and savages to humanity by frightening them with a multitude of gods to be propitiated, but to open to the knowledge of the truth the eyes of men already highly cultured and deceived by their very refinement (*sed qui iam expolitos et ipsa urbanitate deceptos in agnitionem veritatis ocularet*). We must surely admire the largeness and justness of his view. It needs no argument that this means that Numa fulfilled his mission by the passing expedient of pagan worship, and this the Christ came to remove and abolish. Precisely so (as we have seen) thought Justin, who preferred the symbolic expression "dissolution of demons." Tertullian now proceeds (Cap. xxii) to declare :—

> And so we say there are certain spiritual substances. Nor is the name new. Philosophers know (there are) demons......But how from certain angels corrupt of their own free will a more corrupt brood of demons issued, condemned of God with the authors of their brood and with him we called their chief (Satan), in the sacred Scriptures is set forth in order......Their business is the ruin of man. So from the first, spiritual malice has been aimed at the downfall of man......

> with various errors, whereof that is the worst whereby it commends these gods to men's minds entrapped and ensnared......Every spirit is winged, both angel and demon......Their speed is accounted divinity......Or if both angels and demons do just what your gods do, where then is the pre-eminence of divinity?......Is it not more reasonable to assume that it is they themselves (demons) who make themselves gods......than that the gods are equals of angels and demons?......A difference of races is distinguished, I suppose, so that by their temples you esteem as gods whom elsewhere you call not gods......But thus far, words; now comes the demonstration of the thing itself whereby we show the quality to be the same under either name. Let anyone be led out there before your tribunals, who, it is settled, is driven by a demon. That spirit bidden speak by any Christian will confess of a truth himself a demon as elsewhere (he) falsely (confesses himself) a lord (god). Or......let that same celestial Virgin (Carthaginian Juno?), promiser of showers, that same Æsculapius, discoverer of medicines, ready to minister another day (of life) to moribund Socordius and Tenatius and Asclepiodotus —unless not daring to lie to a Christian they confess themselves demons, shed on the spot the blood of that most insolent Christian.

So it glimmers through the nebulous rhetoric of Tertullian that he held a god to be only a demon worshipped in a temple. Moreover, he declares that one possessed by a demon would confess himself a demon if interrogated by a Christian. The meaning of the closing passage is almost hopeless; it may possibly refer to some incident of which we have no knowledge. Says Oehler: " I have restored by conjecture this passage almost desperate for the reason that to what story Tertullian is referring is absolutely unknown." Plainly no argument can rest on such a passage. Perhaps there was no such incident at all. Tertullian's boast that the possessed interrogated by a Christian would confess himself a demon perhaps means only that some person under some such conditions had been or might be converted to Christianity, had renounced paganism and accepted the Jesus-cult. We must remember that Tertullian is a prince of rhetoricians, to whom plain, straightforward speech is almost impossible. After much more declamation, little to the point in this argument, he declares : " Why all our domination and power over them comes from nomination of Christ......Fearing Christ in God and God in Christ, they are subdued to the servants of God and Christ." This seems to be only vague declamation, for which perhaps the only basis is the actual conversion to Christianity of zealous heathen devotees. We note that Tertullian claims nothing for himself personally, and attests nothing as of his own observation. Our suspicion is strengthened by his following remark: "Finally these testimonies of your gods are wont to make Christians; in believing them as much as possible we believe in Christ the Lord." In view of Tertullian's notorious sacrifice of all else to oratorical effect, it seems hard to feel sure that he had in mind aught else but conversions, sometimes of neurasthenics, to Christianity.

It may be remarked that his estimate of demons finds ample confirmation and reiteration in the pages of early Christian literature. Irenæus (ii, 4, 6) declares that "all things are subject to the appellation of the Highest and Omnipotent; and by invocation of it even before the coming of our Lord men were saved, both from spirits most vile, and all demons diverse, and every apostasy......And as, though they have not seen him, nevertheless all things are subject to the name of our Lord (Jesus? or the Emperor?), so likewise (to) his who made all things and established (them) by a word, since no other is there than he who made the world. And therefore Jews even till now by this very adjuration put demons to flight, since all fear the invocation of him that made them." Here Irenæus seems to have in mind the prophetic passage, "Whosoever shall call on the name of the Lord shall be delivered" (Joel ii, 32). Such invocation was an acknowledgment of the god invoked, hence it came to be associated intimately with conversion to his worship. However, Jewish magic and incantation are, of course, not hereby denied. But nothing is yet made out as to actual exorcisms, distinct from conversions, among early Christians. On turning to Schmiedel's reference (ii, 32, 4; Harvey, i, 375), we find the matter somewhat cleared up. Speaking of the spiritual gifts possessed by the Christians, he declares: "For some drive out demons firmly and truly, so that often those cleansed from the evil spirits both believe and are in the church."

Here, then, the secret seems to have escaped. The connection between casting out demons and converting to belief is set forth as so close and intimate that there seems hardly a doubt that the one is but a variant of the other. To be sure, Irenæus does say "often," and does seem to make a distinction; but this is no more than we should expect: it is but a part of the general process of literalisation, of transforming spiritual symbols into material events, which he, along with "Ignatius," did so much to further, and which the Old Catholic Church has to thank in such large measure for its existence.[1]

In any case, this seems a very dangerous passage for Professor Schmiedel. At the most and best it could prove nothing for his cause, seeing that immediately after we read that "even now" "dead men were raised and remained with us for many years." Since he will certainly reject this statement as incredible, in spite of Harvey's note, what credence can he put in the immediately foregoing?

Most illuminative in this connection is the following passage from the learned work of Carl Schmidt on *Gnostische Schriften in koptischer Sprache*, p. 510: "This reminds us only too distinctly of the exorcisms which in the olden time played a highly significant *rôle* at Baptism, *inasmuch as all candidates therefore were thought to be possessed of demons* (*Täuflinge*),[2] in consequence whereof there was in fact a class of exorcists standing in high repute." In this deep descent from the serene heights of the primitive propaganda it seems impossible not to recognise the fact that Christianisation was originally conceived as a casting-out-of-demons, as a conversion from paganism to the worship of the Jesus, the Saviour-God.

The fact is that the more spiritual Christians even of that day—commonly called Gnostics as a term of reproach, though Clemens of Alexandria calls the Christians Gnostics by way of honour—understood perfectly well that all these healings referred primarily and properly to diseases not of the body,

---

[1] Hence, indeed, the testimony of all such literalists, even if far more explicit, could really prove nothing against our thesis; for at most it would attest only *their* interpretation of the New Testament text, but could never prove their interpretation to be correct. Understanding demon-expulsion, like the rest of the Gospels, literally, and recalling that the disciples were to do even greater deeds (John xiv, 12), it was almost positively necessary for them to bear *some* witness to such literal exorcisms. That their witness is nevertheless so extremely vague looks like a clear indication that there was really naught of the kind to witness at all.

[2] Italics are the present writer's.

but of the soul, and taught so explicitly. For their insight and their candour they received sharp rebuke at the hands of Irenæus : " But so much they lack of raising the corpse, as the Lord raised, and the apostles by prayer, and often in the brotherhood for some necessity......(they hold), however, that resurrection from the dead is recognition of the truth that is taught by them " (II, xxxi, 2 ; Harv., II, xlviii, 2). Similarly, but of course more violently, Tertullian, *De Resurr.*, 19 : " Resurrection also of the dead, openly announced, they distort into an imaginary sense, averring that even death itself is to be understood spiritually." As at so many other points, modern thought here also rejects the orthodox and adopts the Gnostic interpretation.

Professor Schmiedel next refers to Eus., *H. E.*, v, 7. This, however, is only an imperfect quotation by Eusebius of the foregoing passage from Irenæus, and hence cannot detain us. His next reference is also to Eusebius, *H. E.*, iv, 3, 2, a quotation by the historian from Quadratus' " Apology for our religion " addressed to Ælius Adrian. It declares only that "the works of our Saviour were always present, for they were genuine—those that were healed and those that were raised from the dead......so that some of them lived even unto our day." Nothing is said of any other works but the Saviour's, and nothing is said about demons at all.

The next citation is of Josephus, *B. J.*, ii, 86, part of the famous description of the Essenes, but containing no allusion to demons or exorcisms or any kind of wonders. But it is said they search out medicinal roots and peculiarities of stones for treatment of diseases, which brings us to the following citation (*B. J.*, vii, 6_3)—a trivial story of a kind of rue, large as a fig-tree, that had lasted from the time of Herod, and would have lasted much longer had it not been cut down ; and of a root called Baaras, from its place of growth, in a valley near Macherus on the north—a root miraculous in every way, but valuable only " because even if only brought near the sick it quickly drives out the so-called demons (and these are the spirits of evil men), entering into the living and killing such as fail of help." All this story can prove, if it can prove anything, is only what has never been in dispute—namely, that magicians did try to exorcise persons supposed to be possessed of demons. Josephus regards these latter as spirits of wicked men—not as divinities, as did the Christians. By this testimony the question of the New Testament conception of casting out demons is not touched.

Passing by the next reference (Jos., *Ant.*, iii, 11$_3$), which speaks solely of certain uncleanness, and not of demons, we come to the classic passage (*Ant.*, viii, 2$_5$). It tells how "God taught Solomon the art against demons for help and healing unto men"; how Solomon "left behind him tricks of exorcosis whereby indwelling demons are driven out so as never to return"—a method valid to this day, for he (Josephus) had himself seen a certain one of his countrymen, by name Eleazar, who, in presence of Vespasian and all his host, by applying a ring, having a Solomonic root under its seal, to the nostrils of a demoniac, draw out the demon through the nostrils, who would then upset a basin of water at Eleazar's command to let all know that he had really gone out. What trickery was here we know not, nor whether the whole story be not a silly invention; in any case and at most, like the preceding citation, it merely proves the undisputed, but does not touch the question of New Testament expulsion of demons.

In the last citation (*C. Ap.*, i, 31) Josephus is defending Moses against Manetho, and seems to make no mention of demons.

Simply to make the story more complete, we proceed to consider the other references. In Pliny (*Nat. Hist.*, 30$_2$) we find the merest mention of "another class (*factio*) of magic derived from Moses and Iannes and Lotapes and Jews, but many thousand years after Zoroaster." In Tacitus (*Hist.*, iv, 81) we find a cock-and-bull story of how Vespasian in Alexandria, after consultation with physicians who assured him it was worth trying, restored sight to a blind man by his own imperial spittle, *applied as salve to the eyes*, and a feeble (*aeger*) hand to strength by tramping on it with his Cæsarean foot. Tacitus adds contemptuously: "Persons who were present even tell both tales now after there is no reward for lying." Comment seems needless.

Finally, we are referred to Lucian (*Philopseudes*, 16). In this delicious piece of satire on credulity Lucian makes Ion, among others, tell lie after lie of Münchhausen proportions concerning the feats of magicians; one of these is about "the Syrian from Palestine," who, for a suitable consideration, under impressive circumstances at full moon, will draw forth from an epileptic a demon speaking Greek or barbarian, as the case may be. Ion himself had seen such a demon come forth, black and sooty of complexion. Tychiades takes the history with grains of salt, remembering that, according to Plato, the senses are deceptive. As already said, this lie is drawn out of a web of lies, the absurdest that Lucian could invent. It seems to attest that Lucian regarded tales of demoniacal possession and exorcism as atrocious falsehoods. But still, you say, there were such tales. Certainly; that has already been admitted. But the tales are always told as rare prodigies, and are ridiculed by the intelligent. In all this there is no evidence that the first Christians meant any such charlatanry by their expulsion of demons, which all the indications show was a symbolic expression for the overthrow of paganism, for conversion to the Jesus-cult. Though it may be highly probable that some of a magic turn did use the name of Jesus to exorcise demons in the material and medical sense, yet such was not the main or prevailing sense among early Christians, who must have been thinking principally of spiritual and not of physical ailments and impotence. To be sure, as already said, the descriptive imagery and the dramatic colouring may have been borrowed from such clinical cases of epilepsy and lunacy; but it remains none the less certain that the Evangelists, in representing Galilee of the Gentiles as thronged with demons, whereas in Judæa there were none, were thinking, not of the Galilean conditions as insanitary compared with Judæan, but of the multiform heathen worship that prevailed there as opposed to the monotheism of Judæa.

Thus far it has been tacitly assumed, as universally admitted, that Galilee was, at least in large part, pagan. Nor does it now seem to call for any argument. Says Rabbi Hirsch, in the *Jewish Encyclopædia*, v, 554: "As early as Old Testament times the population of this region was greatly mixed; and it became more so after the downfall of the Ephraimitic kingdom.......Undoubtedly many Jews subsequently emigrated to that blessed land, so that the population became predominantly Jewish, as is described in the New Testament and by Josephus." The word "predominantly" might possibly give pause, but we may let it stand; ratios are here not exactly determinable. It is enough to quote one other sentence from the learned Rabbi: "The inhabitants, partly pagan, partly Jewish, are said to have been quarrelsome and of a disobliging disposition (*Ned.*, 48*a*; *Tosef.*, *Git.* vi)." In the Talmud (*Shab.*, 14*b*, 15*a*) it is declared that the "Land of the Nations" (Erez ha-Ammim), which can hardly be aught else than the Biblical "Circuit of the Nations" (Gelil ha-Goyim), is unclean. This point may, then, be regarded as settled.

But it must not be supposed that the Gospels, in describing the victorious march of the Jesus(-cult) from town to town, from city to city, were thinking solely of the region around the Sea of Galilee. By no means! They had in mind the triumphant progress of the new religion throughout the whole circumMediterranean empire; but with true dramatic instinct for the unity of place they symbolised this heathen world by that region best known to them, where all faiths and bloods had from time immemorial been seething together, by "Galilee of the Gentiles."

ADDENDUM III.

"*Blessed is he who is not offended in me*" (*i.e.*, in my unpretentious simplicity).—SCHMIEDEL.

PROFESSOR SCHMIEDEL himself mentions two great facts as explaining the impression made by the Jesus—that he "had compassion for the multitude and that he preached with power (more strictly, "as having authority"), not as the scribes." It seems hard to detect "unpretentious simplicity" in one that speaks "as having authority"; plainly, he is represented as *more* pretentious than the scribes, who have no great repute for over-modesty. The multitudes were astounded at his teaching—why? Because he was so simple and unpretentious? Far from it! It was the assumption, the pretension, the exercise of supreme power that confounded them and made them ask: "What is this? New doctrine authoritative! Even the spirits, the unclean, he enjoins, and they obey him" (Mark i, 22, 27). This, too, at the very beginning of his ministry—no simple, unpretentious, unobtrusive preliminaries, no gradual unfolding, no cautious, tentative preparation, no insensible dawn and development of the prophetic or Messianic consciousness. The voice falls direct from heaven. The divine doctrine leaps down from the throne of the Most High, panoplied in celestial armour, and hurls into instant flight the whole legion of pagan demons, of heathen gods. The notions of simplicity and unpretentiousness are absolutely excluded, and even reversed, in the Marcan representation.

But did he not "compassionate the multitudes"? Was not that simple and unpretentious? These, indeed, seem to be queer epithets to apply to compassion, nor are they anywhere hinted in the texts. Much more important, however, is the question, Why this compassion? The answer is instructive: "Because they were mangled and abandoned—as sheep having no shepherd." Hereto Mark adds most luminously: "And he began to teach them much"; Matthew and Luke, even more distinctly, make the Jesus comment on the situation thus: "The harvest is great, but the labourers few; pray, therefore, the Lord of the harvest that he send out labourers into his harvest." It seems almost superfluous to explain such language. Can anyone be so naive as to suppose that the writers are here speaking of literal multitudes literally following the Jesus round the rocky shores of Galilee? The author of 1 Peter ii, 25, knows much better; for, writing to the "elect strangers of dispersion," he tells them: "Ye were as sheep wandering, but are restored now unto the Shepherd and Bishop of your souls." Compare Clement, cited on p. 51.

The case, indeed, seems clear as day. The multitudes are the wanderers away from the true worship of God, whether Jew or pagan; these it is the mission of the Jesus-cult to restore. They are likened to a flock of unsheltered sheep dispersed and mangled by dogs and wolves. How are they to be gathered and healed? Only by instruction, by the "new doctrine." Mark represents the Jesus himself as teaching;

Matthew and Luke refine upon this, and introduce a prayer for the help of workers in the great harvest. It is quite ridiculous to suppose that this great harvest consisted of throngs from city and village that were feebly following up the peregrinations of the Jesus. Elsewhere this "harvest" is used to include all humanity, but in a sterner sense. Here the term refers clearly to the great mass of men who had strayed from the true worship, to which they were to be restored by the new propaganda, by the vigorous proclamation everywhere of the Jesus-cult. The prevailing imagination of the Jesus sitting on some mountain-side, discoursing with his disciples grouped around him, while far and near are strewn hundreds and thousands of fainting Galilean peasants, may indeed be pictorial, and may well enough employ the pencil of the artist or amuse the fancy of children; but it is quite impossible as an historic situation, and is wholly unworthy of the critical sense of grown-up men.

The verb "compassionate,"[1] used some eight times of the Jesus, is very significant, being the principal one of the extremely few terms anywhere used to attribute human feeling to the God. Its comparatively frequent use has gone far to shape the popular idea that the Gospels represent him as of a peculiarly gentle, tender, merciful, and sympathetic nature—a notion that modern sentimentalism embraces with great eagerness and with little demand for careful grounding. Now, it is true that the Gospels do thus ascribe to their hero "compassion"; but it is the compassion of God, *not* of man, just as the Mohammedan prays continually to God as "Allah, the Merciful, the Compassionate." The Greek verb, practically peculiar to the New Testament, is simply a Hebraism translating the Old Testament *r-ḥ-m*, which (in the sense of *pity*) is appropriated *almost exclusively to Jehovah*. So, too, in the New Testament it is practically confined to the Jesus. Its application to him by no means, therefore, can stamp him as conceived by the Evangelists as a man, but rather characterises him as a God, the vicegerent of Jehovah himself. On this point I have discoursed elsewhere (p. 96 *f.*) at length, and need not dwell longer at present.

---

[1] σπλαγχνίζομαι.

PART IV.

THE SILENCE OF JOSEPHUS AND TACITUS

⟡

IN the fierce attacks upon *Der vorchristliche Jesus* precipitated by the adoption, accentuation, and popularisation of its theses in the epoch-marking writings of Professor Arthur Drews, conservative theologians have very properly declined to take part, thereby combining (as Bacon would say) serpentine wisdom with columbine innocence. They have clearly perceived that the movement was not directed against their position, but against the citadel of their century-old foe, who would reduce their Divinity to the ranks of men; and at least one of the very greatest of them (in a letter to the present writer) rejoiced sincerely at beholding the sudden fall of that adversary. No! It is the liberal critic, so long enthroned in the seats of learning, who has been amazed to see his central concept of the purely human Jesus put on trial for its life and more than half convicted, and who, *ingemiscens tamquam reus*, has now for nearly full two years plied an unavailing pen in passionate protest against the audacity of this "assault upon the liberal theology."

In the sallies of the besieged much weight had been laid upon profane testimonies, particularly of Josephus and Tacitus. It is Chwolson in St. Petersburg who has bared his arm of might over the Josephine section;[1] it is Von Soden in Berlin who has stressed so strongly the Tacitean chapter.[2] However much we may reverence these scholars in their cooler moments, it is not easy to take their impassioned utterances seriously. They do not, indeed, take each other seriously. The very section that Chwolson so eagerly defends Von Soden declares (p. 11) to be "undoubtedly

---
[1] *Ueber die Frage ob Jesus gelebt hat.*
[2] *Hat Jesus gelebt?*, and in *Berliner Religionsgespräch*, p. 39.

interpolation" by Christian hands. Involuntarily one recalls the famous appeal "from Philip drunk to Philip sober," and wonders how the contending critics will write to-morrow. To track down the endless inaccuracies and fallacies of such hasty superficialities would be a weary and bootless task, like chasing field-mice in autumn: stamp them out here, and lo they stir the soil yonder! In this case to be just would be cruel; one can afford to be generous, and to pass over these *Flugschriften* as too flighty for detailed notice, and as not representing their authors properly.

However, the passages in question do really call for a calm and careful and thoroughgoing treatment, such certainly as they have not yet received in this furious Battle of the Booklets; and to such an examination we now invite the patient attention of the reader.

THE SILENCE OF JOSEPHUS

When the liberal critic is called on to justify his dogma of the mere humanity of the Jesus, his only recourse must be to some form of historical record. A merely human life is a matter merely of human history, to which accordingly appeal must be made. The history is either sacred or profane. The testimony of the former is not here in debate, and besides has been examined closely elsewhere by the present writer. Of profane history the witness is "brief but endless," if, indeed, there be any such witness at all. The first, and by all odds the most important, is found in the *Antiquities* of the Jewish historian Josephus—precisely the work in which one would search for it with the liveliest interest and the greatest confidence. The attestation, as we read it now, is clear, decisive, and unequivocal. Accepted at its face value, it settles for ever the question that now so agitates the head and heart of Germany. It deserves, then, the most conscientious and open-minded scrutiny.

Such a scrutiny discloses in the first place that the chapter in which the deposition is found is *concerned exclusively with calamities that overtook the Jews*. It is sandwiched between two other sections that tell of heavy disasters that befell God's people at Rome and Jerusalem. Now, unless this passage itself tells of some signal misfortune to his countrymen—and in spite of Chwolson it is hopelessly absurd and ridiculous to attempt any such construction—it seems impossible that Josephus should have introduced it in this connection. We make this preliminary observation in the hope that the reader will bear it constantly in mind from the very start, and because it is of itself absolutely decisive against the whole section and against every *emendation* thereof that apologetic ingenuity can suggest. There is not one word of the entire passage that can stand against this single consideration—namely, that all the rest of the chapter, both before and after, is devoted to the afflictions that scourged the countrymen of the historian.

Here, then, is this famous section reproduced in its (condensed) context: *Archeology,* Book XVIII, chap. iii.

§ 1. Pilate, procurator of Judea, removes the army from Cæsarea to Jerusalem for winter quarters, and, against all precedent, brings Cæsar's effigies by night into the Holy City. The Jews flock to Cæsarea protesting for five days, but in vain; the sixth day Pilate forms a plan to massacre them, but, struck with their heroic devotion in laying down their bared necks, he relents and orders back the images from Jerusalem to Cæsarea.

§ 2. Pilate undertakes to supply Jerusalem with water, using sacred money. The Jews protest clamorously and abusively. So he distributes among the populace soldiers in citizens' dress; at a signal (when the Jews refused to disperse) the soldiers draw their concealed daggers and slaughter: "And they bore themselves no way mildly, so that, the people being caught unarmed by the soldiers attacking fully prepared, many of them perished thus and some ran away wounded. And so the sedition was stopped.

§ 3. "And there appeared at this time Jesus, a wise man, if man indeed it be lawful to call him. For he was a doer of marvellous works, (a) teacher of men that receive the truth with pleasure. And many Jews and many, too, of the Hellenic (race) he brought over to himself. This was the Christ. And when on the evidence of the first men among us Pilate had condemned him to the cross, they did not cease who had loved him at first, for he appeared to them on the third day again alive, the divine prophets having spoken both these and myriad other wondrous things about him. And (even) until now the tribe of the Christians, named from him, is not extinct."

§ 4. "And about the same time another terrible misfortune[1] confounded the Jews."......Then follows the story of the dishonouring of Paulina in the temple of Isis by Mundus personating Anubis, and of the punishment of this sacrilege by Tiberius, who demolished the temple and crucified the offenders all but the principal, Mundus, himself.

§ 5. The misfortune of the Jews: 4,000 are banished from Rome for the wickedness of four, a Rabbi and three confederates, who procured gifts from Fulvia, wife of Saturninus, under false pretences.

We can hardly covet the critical insight that sees in this § 3 the hand of Josephus. *The chapter deals solely with the misfortunes of the Jews at Cæsarea, at Jerusalem, at Rome. § 3 is entirely out of relation to its context.*

Moreover, that § 4 follows immediately upon § 2 is plain to see in the words "*another calamity.*" The obvious reference is to the preceding massacre in Jerusalem. *There is no possible reference to* § 3.

Furthermore, the style is not that of the historian. It is plain, straightforward, uninvolved, in contrast with the tangled meshes of the Josephine sentence.

Still more, however, and decisively, *the writer of § 3 is a Christian*. He declares positively, "This was the Christ."[2] Posing as Josephus, he says of Jesus, "wise man," but instantly corrects himself, "if man indeed it is lawful to call him"; he describes Jesus as a doer of prodigies, as a teacher of the truth; he affirms distinctly the resurrection—"he appeared the third day again alive"; he accepts the whole body of ten thousand wonders told of him as Messiah and foretold of him by the divine prophets. Such faith as this, and such an open avowal, might satisfy even the Holy Office of the Inquisition.

Once again, the phraseology smacks strongly of the New Testament. Thus γίνεται in the sense of *comes* (Mark i, 4;

---

[1] ἕτερόν τι δεινόν.   [2] ὁ Χριστὸς οὗτος ἦν.

John i, 6 ; 2 Peter ii, 1 ; 1 John ii, 18) and the change from past to present tense ;[1] "that receive the truth with pleasure";[2] compare "the principal men" with "the head men"[3] of the Gospels, Acts, Epistles ; also " they that loved him at first " with John xiii, 1, " having loved his own which were in the world, he loved them unto the end"; also the "myriad wonders" with John xxi, 25, " The world itself could not contain the books that should be written."

Finally, the phrase "until now" recalls the New Testament "unto this day " (Matthew xxviii, 15), and indicates similarly a late date for the paragraph, surely later than 80 A.D., when Josephus wrote his *Archeology*. Schürer observes (§ 17, footnote 24) that "Josephus has certainly been interpolated by a Christian hand"; and in view of all the foregoing there should be no hesitancy in bracketing this section, with the great editor Bekker, as spurious.

To this internal evidence comes the decisive external fact that the section was unknown to Origen. This most learned of the Fathers, in his polemic against Celsus, had frequent and pressing occasion to use every scrap of outlying testimony to the Christian thesis assailed. As we shall immediately see, he quotes copiously and repeatedly from Josephus witnessing concerning James the Just ; he had every occasion and every motive to quote this incomparably far more relevant and far more important witness concerning the Christ. That he never calls it in evidence is morally conclusive proof that he did not know of its existence, which can only mean that it was not in Origen's copy of Josephus. No attempt yet made to evade this conclusion seems worthy of any notice. The fact that the passage is not mentioned by still earlier writers, as Irenæus, Tertullian, Clement of Alexandria, and others, affords corroboration, if any be needed, of the fact that *neither this nor any other available witness concerning Jesus* was to be found in the copies of Josephus in the hands of the Christian Fathers.

It seems, then, that the non-Josephine origin of this

---

[1] So also παραδόξων, as in Luke v, 26, εἴδαμεν παράδοξα σήμερον.
[2] *Cf.* Luke viii, 13, "receive the word with joy"; Acts xvii, 11, "received the word with all zeal"; James i, 21, "receive with meekness the engrafted word."
[3] ἄρχοντες.

section is indicated unambiguously by almost every kind of evidence that can be demanded in such matters. Its testimony would appear to be not for, but distinctly against, the position it was invented to support; for men do not fabricate documents to corroborate the true, but to recommend the false. Let us not insist on this, however, but remain content with the obvious fact that, on the most favourable reckoning possible, the section labours under the gravest suspicion, and can attest nothing save that itself is in the direst need of attestation.

Here at the outset it may be well to observe that the general hypothesis of Christian interpolation needs no vindication and involves no improbability. For that it is a fact in countless cases is admitted on all hands. Leaving aside the New Testament for the present, the list of outright pseudonymous Christian compositions, universally so recognised, is long and formidable. It is not necessary to burden these pages with any such list, since such lists are easily accessible and the general fact is nowhere in dispute. Moreover, of works probably genuine, it is the rare exception that has escaped interpolation. Jewish works were regularly adapted to Christian use by this approved process of intercalating Christian sentiments, dogmas, or allusions. Witness the Sibylline Oracles, the Testaments of the Patriarchs, and the Jewish Apocrypha in general. So far, then, from being antecedently improbable, such interpolation is very probable antecedently; it is more likely than not. Nevertheless, to leave a wider margin of safety, we shall employ this form of argument sparingly, not wherever its use is possible, but only where it is recommended by independent considerations.

A second reference of Josephus to Jesus might be imagined in the following paragraph (*Arch.*, XX, ix, 1) treating of the death of James, "the brother of the Lord":—

"Ananus, then, being such (as I have said), fancying he had now a fitting opportunity, since Festus was dead and Albinus was still on the road, assembles a Sanhedrin of judges, and having brought thither *the brother of Jesus, him called Christ (James was his name), and* some certain *others*, and having made accusations (against them as) lawbreakers, he delivered them to be stoned."

The words in italics[1] have been regarded as spurious—we think, correctly. Neander and others defend them, and McGiffert says (*The Church History of Eus.*, p. 127, n. 39): "It is very difficult to suppose that a Christian, in interpolating the passage, would have referred to James as the brother of the '*so-called* Christ.'"[2] Indeed! On the contrary, it is just because this phrase is the most approved Christian, evangelic, and canonic that we suspect it in Josephus. It meets us in Matthew i, 16; xxvii, 17, 22; John iv, 25. The depreciatory "so" is not in the Greek. Thus we read of "Simon the so-called Peter" (Matthew iv, 18; x, 2), "the high-priest the so-called Caiaphas" (Matthew xxvi, 3), "the feast the so-called Passover" (Luke xxii, 1), "the man the so-called Jesus" (John ix, 11), "Thomas the so-called Didymus" (John xi, 16; xx, 24; xxi, 2), "gate the so-called Beautiful" (Acts iii, 2), "tent the so-called Holy of Holies" (Heb. ix, 3), where depreciation is out of the question. The indication is merely that of a surname or nickname, or name in some way peculiar or extraordinary.

It seems incredible that Josephus should throw in such an observation at this stage without any preparation or explanation or occasion. Moreover, it is certain that Josephus has been interpolated elsewhere by Christian hands, and with precisely this same phrase; for Origen thrice quotes as from Josephus the statement that the Jewish sufferings at the hands of Titus were a divine retribution for the slaying of James: "Josephus says in his *Archeology*: 'According to wrath of God these things came upon them, for the things dared by them against James, the brother of Jesus the so-called Christ.' ......And he says that 'the people, too, thought they suffered these things on account of James'" (463) in Matt. xiii, 55. "The same [Josephus] seeking the cause of the fall of Jerusalem and of the demolition of the Temple......says: 'These [calamities] befell the Jews in vengeance for James the Just, who was brother of Jesus, the so-called Christ, since, indeed, they slew him, though being most just.'"—*Contra C.*, I, 47.

---

[1] τὸν ἀδελφὸν Ἰησοῦ τοῦ λεγομένου Χριστοῦ (Ἰάκωβος ὄνομα αὐτῷ) and καὶ ἑτέρους.
[2] τοῦ λεγομένου Χριστοῦ.

"Titus demolished Jerusalem, as Josephus writes, on account of James the Just, the brother of Jesus, the so-called Christ." —*Contra C.*, II, 13 *fin*. The passage is still found in some Josephus manuscripts; but as it is wanting in others it is, and must be, regarded as a Christian interpolation older than Origen (against Hilgenfeld, *Einleitung*, p. 526, who thinks the passage has been expunged from Christian manuscripts of Josephus!). Now, since this phrase is certainly interpolated in the one place, the only reasonable conclusion is that it is interpolated in the other. This notion that the death of James was avenged in the siege of Jerusalem is found in the bud in Hegesippus, who says: "And so he suffered martyrdom. And they buried him on the spot beside the temple.......This man became a true witness both to Jews and to Greeks that Jesus is the Christ. And straightway Vespasian besieges them" (Eus., *H. E.*, II, 23, 18).

But does not the phrase itself attest the mere humanity of the Jesus? Now, it is plain that if James or any one else was really the flesh-and-blood brother of the Lord or of Jesus, then this latter was assuredly not purely human. But is flesh-and-blood kinship meant by the term "brother"? It is not certain; it is not even probable. Winckler (in *Arabisch-Semitisch-Orientalisch*) and others have shown us how broad is the notion of brother in the East. In the New Testament itself the term is used continually, regularly, to denote religious relation, without the remotest hint of blood kinship. In the West and to-day it is similarly used of all members of an organisation, secular as well as religious. In the Gospels[1] Jesus himself is made to ask: "Who are my brothers?" And he answers: "They that do the will of my Father in heaven." Here, then, in the most ancient Church, we find distinct declaration that to be "brother of Jesus" was to keep the law, to do the will of the Father in heaven. Now, it was precisely this punctilious fulfilment of the law for which this James the Just was famous. This fact is well known and universally admitted, so that it stands in no need of formal proof.

---

[1] Matt. xii, 46–50; Mark iii, 31–35; Luke viii, 21. See also Matt. xxv, 40, xxviii, 10; 1 Cor. ix, 5; Gal. i, 19.

In Acts we hear a good deal of this James, but only in this character as the leader of the law-abiding disciples. No less an authority than Jerome (A.D. 387) has expressed the correct idea on this point. In commenting on Gal. i, 19, he says (in sum): "James was called the Lord's brother on account of his high character, his incomparable faith, and his extraordinary wisdom; the other Apostles are also called brothers (John xx, 17), but he pre-eminently so to whom the Lord at his departure had committed the sons of his mother" (*i.e.*, the members of the Church at Jerusalem). Similarly Origen, in immediate continuation of the passage cited (*C. Cels.*, i, 47). From 1 Cor. ix, 5, we see with distinctness that there was a class of Messianists, nearly co-ordinate with the Apostles, bearing the honoured name of "brothers of the Jesus," or "of the Lord"; also a class called "Those of Kephas." Hence in Corinth some said, "I am of Kephas"; others, "I am of Christ."

Indeed, it is never hinted that James was really consanguineous with Jesus. We hold, then, that this term "brother of the Lord," does by no means imply any family kinship—that it most probably designates a class of earnest Messianists, zealots of obedience; and we venture to set them in close relation with the Corinthian "Those of the Christ."[1] Surely, if a sect of early Messianists were known as particularly "They of the Christ," it is highly likely that they or some similar group should be known as "brothers of the Lord" or of "Jesus." Especially does this seem intrinsically probable when we remember that there is no evidence that this name was employed before the notion of the earthly human life of Jesus was already established, or at least establishing itself. That zealots should then call themselves and their earlier leader "brothers of Jesus" is no stranger than that Loyola should found the "Society of Jesus." Besides, we must never forget that names of the Christians did greatly abound, such as Saints, Disciples, Called, Elect, "of Paul," "of Peter," "of Christ," Nazorees, Gnostics, the Perfect, Pneumatics, and others. From all of which we conclude that the phrase in question, no matter

---

[1] οἱ τοῦ Χριστοῦ.

when first used, nor by whom, nor of whom, by no means implies any kinship, or furnishes any proof of the purely human character of Jesus.

THE SILENCE OF TACITUS

The next reference to Christ by a profane writer is found in Tacitus[1]:—

> Sed non ope humana, non largitionibus principis aut deum placamentis decedebat infamia, quin iussum incendium crederetur. Ergo abolendo rumori Nero subdidit reos et quaesitissimis poenis adfecit, quos per flagitia invisos vulgus Christianos appellabat. Auctor nominis eius Christus Tiberio imperitante per procuratorem Pontium Pilatum supplicio adfectus erat; repressaque in praesens exitiabilis superstitio rursus erumpebat, non modo per Iudaeam, originem eius mali, sed per urbem etiam, quo cuncta undique atrocia aut pudenda confluunt celebranturque. Igitur primum correpti qui fatebantur, deinde indicio eorum multitudo ingens haud proinde in crimine incendii quam odio humani generis convicti sunt. Et pereuntibus addita ludibria, ut ferarum tergis contecti laniatu canum interirent, aut crucibus adfixi aut flammandi, atque, ubi defecisset dies, in usum nocturni luminis urerentur. Hortos suos ei spectaculo Nero obtulerat et circense ludicrum edebat, habitu aurigae permixtus plebi vel curriculo insistens. Unde quamquam adversus sontes et novissima exempla meritos miseratio oriebatur, tamquam non utilitate publica sed in saevitiam unius absumerentur (*Annals*, xv, 44).

With respect to this famous passage we must observe first that, *if it be genuine*, it was written in the first quarter of the second century, near the close of the last work of the great historian, most probably after the death of Trajan (A.D. 117). At the most, then, it records only a report accepted at that time among Christians. Now it is not at all strange that the fiction (if it be a fiction) of the death under Pilate should be current at that date, nearly three generations after the feigned event. If such a report originated at all, it originated (gradually to be sure) at some time most probably in the first century; it may easily then have obtained currency and reached the ears of Tacitus before A.D. 110. Its reproduction at his hands, then, merely attests its existence at that date, but in no degree attests its correctness.

[1] For the translation and the context see *infra*, p. 246.

THE SILENCE OF TACITUS

Thus far on the supposition that the passage proceeds from Tacitus; we need make no other supposition for the purposes of our argument. Let it be genuine, if you will; it proves nothing that is worth debate. Since he has never attached any argumentative importance to the passage, the mind of the writer may be fairly supposed to be in a measure unprejudiced, and as a mere matter of critical candour he must not disguise from the reader that he most gravely doubts its genuineness. It has indeed been speciously contended of late that Poggio Bracciolini was the author of the *Annals*,[1] but there are very cogent reasons against this contention. This whole section, however, reads very much like fabrication, or at least emendation, of a Christian hand. Among other suspicious circumstances may be noted the following :—

(*a*) Such a remarkable persecution as here described, and such a passage from such an author, would have deeply impressed the early Christian mind. There is nothing else nearly equal to either in pagan history and literature of that century. We should expect them to stand out conspicuous in the memories and memorials of the following generations. We know how zealously the data of martyrdom were cherished and even invented at an early period. It is inconceivable, then, that an event so supremely memorable should have escaped all record and all reference. Yet what is the state of the case? *Early tradition is absolutely silent about both the Neronian persecution and the Tacitean testimony.* Paul would seem to have been in Rome about that time (A.D. 64). Surely he would have been involved someway in the proceedings. Yet there is no allusion to any part he played in the tragedy. True, in 2 Tim. iv, 6–8, we read : "For already I pour myself out as offering, and the time of my dissolution is come ; I have fought the good fight, have finished the course, have kept the faith ; henceforth is laid up for me the crown of righteousness which the Lord shall give me in that day, the Just Judge, and not only to me but to all who have loved his appearing." But in verses 16 and 17 the scene

---

[1] *Tacitus and Bracciolini. The Annals Forged in the Fifteenth Century.* London, 1878.

shifts suddenly: "At my first defence none was for me, but all forsook me—let it not be reckoned against them—but the Lord stood by me and strengthened me, that through me the preaching might be fulfilled and all the nations hear: and I was delivered from (the) lion's mouth. The Lord will deliver me from every evil work, and will save me unto his kingdom the heavenly."

Again, in verse 11 all have deserted him but one: "Only Luke is with me." But in verses 19-21 he is surrounded by a numerous company—"Eubulus and Pudens, and Linus and Claudia, and all the brethren." Out of such contradictions nothing can be made, save only that there is no hint at anything like the Neronian persecution. The writer or writers seem not to have known any tradition concerning it which they could work into these pastorals.

The first Epistle of Peter, addressed to the elect of the dispersion in Northern Asia Minor, is much concerned with the persecution and "fiery trial" that has overtaken them; but, though apparently written from Rome ("Babylon," v, 13), it contains not the remotest reference to the "fiery trial" through which it is supposed the church there had passed. Some reference, however, under such circumstances, would seem to be so natural as to be almost inevitable.

Not even in the Apocalypse do we find any clear or even probable allusion to an event that would have bulked so hugely in the early Christian consciousness. On this point we need not enlarge; enough to refer to the works of Mommsen and Neumann; even Furneaux admits that "the supposed references......are certainly in great part to be otherwise explained," though he still thinks there "are points in which such allusions can hardly be excluded"—an opinion that seems to be the last remnant of departing prejudice. Why, then, did the Apocalyptist not refer to this tremendous persecution distinctly, or at least unequivocally, if he had ever heard thereof?

Turning now to Clement of Rome, we find him (chap. v) very naturally setting before the eyes of his correspondents "the noble examples that belong to our generation." The fierce persecution detailed by Tacitus would have been perfectly known to him, yet he seems never to have heard

THE SILENCE OF TACITUS

of it. The sufferings of Peter he attributes to "unrighteous jealousy." "Not one, nor two, but more trials he underwent, and so, having borne witness, he fared to the appointed place of glory. By reason of jealousy and strife Paul exemplified the prize of patience. Seven times cast into bonds, exiled, stoned, made preacher both in east and west, he received the noble renown of his faith, having taught the whole world righteousness and come to the bounds of the west, and having borne witness before the rulers, so he departed from the world and fared unto the holy place, having become a chiefest pattern of patience." We do not pretend to know the exact meaning of such words; it seems doubtful whether Clement himself knew. But it seems certain that they convey no hint of the Neronic persecution as described in the *Annals*; nay, more, they seem to imply unmistakably that their author had never heard of any such "fiery trial."

Passing to the "Ignatians," we find the letter to the Romans written in a style and mood of extreme exaltation. "Ignatius" yearns passionately for the arena; he longs to be ground as wheat by the teeth of wild beasts. Surely, if he had ever heard of the terrible experience of the Romans themselves, such a rhetorician would have let some hint escape him. But he does not, and his silence appears to admit of but the one and the same explanation.

It is superfluous to pass in review the other Christian writers of this era. They are consistently dumb on the subject under discussion, and their collective stillness makes the argument from silence as convincing as in the nature of the case it ever can be.

Far down the stream of history, over one hundred years from the date of the conflagration, we find at last, in a fragment quoted by Eusebius (*H. E.*, iv, 26) from a *Libellus* addressed to Antoninus (Aurelius) by Melito, Bishop of Sardis (near 170 A.D.), the first Christian allusion to Nero as an enemy of Christians. It declares: "For *what has never before happened*, the race of the pious is now suffering persecution, being driven about in Asia by new decrees...... for our philosophy formerly flourished among the barbarians, but, having sprung up among the nations under thy rule during the great reign of thy ancestor Augustus, it became to

R

thy empire especially a blessing of auspicious omen. And a most convincing proof that our doctrine flourished for the good of an empire happily begun is this: that there has no evil happened since Augustus' reign......only Nero and Domitian, persuaded by certain calumnious men, wished to slander our doctrine, from whom also it has come to pass that the falsehood has been handed down by unreasonable custom of information ('sycophancy') against such (Christians)." One moment we may pause to note that the good bishop goes back to the reign of Augustus for the origin of "our philosophy," which had already existed among the "barbarians" (*i.e.*, the Jews—Tatian calls the Jewish Scriptures "barbaric"),[1] and which must then have been essentially monotheism—and then we observe that he has apparently *no knowledge and no idea* of the Neronian persecution as now set forth in Tacitus, and that he is arguing that good emperors have tolerated, while only the wicked have discountenanced Christianity. Here he adds: "But thy pious fathers corrected their ignorance, having frequently rebuked in writing many who dared to attempt new measures against them"—in evidence whereof he refers to Adrian's Epistle to Fundanus and to many others.

No new furrow need be driven through the field so well ploughed by Keim, Overbeck, Mommsen, Schiller, Lightfoot, Ramsay, and others. It is enough that Melito, who seems ot have been so exceedingly well versed in the relation of Christianity to the State, still gives no hint of anything resembling the Tacitean persecution. And yet to do so would have suited the purposes of his argument admirably. With great force he could have said: "Nero the matricide, the worst of men, Nero did indeed persecute us atrociously, to hide his own iniquity, as your own historian Tacitus bears witness; and behold what swift and just and terrible vengeance overtook him!" How could Melito have failed to make such a telling and obvious point?

Another descent brings us to Tertullian, who admittedly knew and made use of Melito's booklet in his own *Apologeticum*. His argument is the same, that good government

---

[1] In describing his own conversion (*Address to the Greeks*, chap. xxix).

favoured and bad government disfavoured the Christians, but he is far more reckless in assertion. He declares (c. 5) that "Tiberius, when intelligence reached him from Syria Palestine of what had there revealed truth of Divinity itself, reported to the Senate with the weight (*prærogativa*) of his own vote. The Senate, because it had not itself tested, rejected (his proposal); Cæsar maintained his judgment, threatening peril to accusers of Christians." Let the reader not be surprised at such history made to order. "Consult your records (*commentarios*); there you will find Nero the first that raged with Cæsarean sword against this sect when rising most at Rome. But in such a founder of our condemnation we glory even, for whoso knows him can understand that only something signally good was condemned by Nero. Domitian, too, made trial, a portion of Nero in cruelty; but, being also man, readily he checked his own beginning, restoring even whom he had banished. Such always our persecutors, unjust, impious, base, whom you yourselves are wont to condemn, those condemned by whom you are wont to restore."

Here one begins to suspect that Nero is made to play the *rôle* of persecutor only because he was so perfectly suited to the part. But even Tertullian reveals no notion of such a Neronian persecution as we read of in Tacitus. Yet he was acquainted with this historian, whose *Historiæ* he cites at length (c. 16), on whose name he puns, whom he cordially hates for defaming the Jews. Had he read of Nero's burning the Christians alive, would he have used such vague and commonplace imagery as "raged with Cæsarean sword" and "through Nero's cruelty they sowed Christian blood"? Remember that Tertullian was a rhetorician to his fingertips. Would he have neglected such an exceptional opportunity for the display of his thrice-favourite art?

It seems needless to discuss still later testimony, as that of Lactantius (*De mort. persec.*, 2), of Origen (Eus., *H. E.*, III, 1), of Eusebius (*H. E.*, II, 25), and of Jerome. These late writers have at last learned, after two centuries or more of ignorance, that Peter and Paul fell victims to Neronian fury; but they still have no idea that Nero falsely accused the Christians of setting the city on fire, nor do they hint that a "vast multitude" lit up the Roman night with the flames of their burning bodies. Not until the fourth century, in Ep. 12 of the forged correspondence of Paul and Seneca, do we read that "Christians and Jews, as if contrivers of (a) conflagration, when put to death are wont to be burned." But even here the allusion, if there be any, to the Neronian persecution is extremely vague.

It must be added that the Jews are here associated with the Christians; that they could hardly have been sharply separated in Rome A.D. 64; that they, far more than Christians, were open to the charge of hatred of the human race ("Against all others, hostile hate")—Tacitus, *H*. 5, 2; that they had already felt twice in Rome (under Tiberius and under Claudius) the weight of the imperial hand; that Lucan, Pliny, Persius, Seneca—all writers of that era—speak of the Jews with sharpness, never of the Christians—and it will appear practically impossible that they could have escaped in any such persecution as the Tacitean. But if they did not escape, if they suffered, this must have been known to their great historian and champion, Josephus, who was a young man at the time.

Now, this writer, in his *Archeology* (XX, 8, 3), protests against the gross inaccuracies and falsehoods of the biographers of Nero, both favourable and unfavourable, while disclaiming any intention to correct or supplement them in general. "But what things befell us Jews we shall exhibit with great accuracy,[1] shrinking to show plainly neither our calamities nor our sins." If, then, even a few Jews had fallen victims in the capital to Neronian calumny and savagery, there seems to be no doubt that Josephus would have known and noted it. Yet he gives not the slightest hint that any such rumour had ever reached his ears.

Here, then, we stand in presence of the unbroken and universal silence of over two hundred years concerning an alleged event of capital importance, transacted in the very centre of knowledge and information and rumour, yet never once mentioned by any one among many whose especial

---

[1] οὐ παρέργως.

interest it was to tell of it often and to dwell on it at length. Nor can any one suggest the slightest reason for this silence, for this studied suppression of a highly momentous and dramatic incident in a reign that was a favourite subject of historic delineation, and that lent itself especially to high colouring and picturesque exaggeration. Such considerations seem ample to weight the scale heavily against the genuineness of the passage in question.

(*b*) On looking more narrowly at the whole Tacitean context, we find that it suggests quite independently many doubts kindred and hardly less grave. The account of the great fire extends through six chapters, beginning with the thirty-eighth: "Follows a disaster; whether by chance or by guile of the prince is uncertain." A vivid description is given. Chap. xxxix tells how Nero did not return from Antium till the flames approached (as they ultimately devoured) his house. He took instant and popular measures to relieve the homeless and destitute, but "without avail, since rumour had gone abroad that at the very moment of the city in flames he had gone upon a private stage and sung the Fall of Troy, likening present ills to ancient calamities." Chap. xl tells of the end put to the conflagration at the foot of the Esquiline, and of its second outburst, involving fewer deaths but more widespread destruction. Chap. xli enumerates some of the elements of the fearful loss. Chap. xlii tells how "Nero made use of his country's ruins, and erected a house" in which the genius and audacity of Severus and Celer would defiantly outvie the prodigality of Nature herself. It seems plain that the immense achievements and immenser conceptions of these architects and landscape gardeners must have required years for their elaboration and even partial execution. Chap. xliii tells of the rebuilding of Rome itself, not in the old irregular fashion, but "with rows of streets measured out, with wide-wayed spaces, with limited height of buildings, and areas laid open and colonnades added to protect the frontage of the tenements (*insularum*)." This description is elaborated, and what part Nero took in the rebuilding is emphasised. These changes pleased in general both by their utility and by their beauty, though some there were that said the old was better.

A city cannot be rebuilt in such substantial fashion ("with stone from Gabii or Alba, impervious to fire") in a day or month or year, nor without enormous outlay of money; and the imperial treasury seems to have borne the weight of the expense. It is not strange, then, but nearly inevitable, that the *next* chapter should continue thus : "Meanwhile, by contributing funds, Italy was laid waste throughout, provinces subverted, and allied peoples and whatever States are called free. Even the gods fell a prey to this plunder," their temples being robbed of gold and votive offerings, and even the images of the gods themselves.

And so precisely does chap. xlv open, as the natural and almost inevitable continuation of chap. xliii, stating the necessary consequences of the methods and aims of Nero as therein set forth. Between these two chapters, thus so closely united in thought, we now read chap. xliv, *which has no intimate connection with either*.

"And these things (the gradual Neronian rebuilding) were provided by human counsels. Next *(mox)* were sought propitiations to the gods, and recourse was had to the Sibyl's books, whence followed supplication to Volcan and Ceres and Proserpine; and Juno was propitiated by matrons, first in the Capitol, then at the nearest point of the sea, with water drawn whence the temple and image of the goddess were sprinkled; and sacred banquets and night-long vigils did the women celebrate who had husbands. But not through human effort, not through largesses of the prince nor appeasements of the gods, did the ill report subside; but still the fire was believed (to have been) ordered. Therefore, to get rid of the rumour, Nero substituted as guilty and subjected to most exquisite tortures (those) whom, hated for their abominations, the populace used to call Christians. The author of this name, Christus, had been executed in the reign of Tiberius by procurator Pontius Pilate; and though repressed for the moment (this) pernicious superstition was breaking forth again, not only through Judæa, source of this evil, but even through the capital where all things hideous or shameful pour together from everywhere and catch the crowd. Accordingly, first were hurried away (to trial those) who confessed (the charge); then by information of these an immense multitude, not so much for the crime of incendiarism as hatred of the human race, were convicted (or conjoined, *convicti* or *conjuncti*). And to them perishing were added mockeries, (as) that clothed with hides of wild beasts they should die by mangling of dogs, or affixed to crosses, or doomed to flames, and, when day had departed, should be burned for purpose of nocturnal illumination. Nero had offered his gardens for that spectacle, and was exhibiting a circus show, mixing with the crowd in the garb of a charioteer or standing on a car. Whence, although towards persons guilty and deserving the most exemplary punishment, there arose pity, as if not for public good but unto the savagery of one man they were being sacrificed."

Let the reader of this chapter thus literally translated judge whether it fits in with either chap. xliii or xlv, which fall so naturally together. Let him note that the whole story is intrinsically improbable; that it implies a very old and long-established and numerous church in Rome, and a hatred on the part of the people that seems at that time quite incredible; that no proper meaning can be attached to "were confessing"—confessing what? Arnold naturally replies: the charge of "firing the city." But that seems wholly incredible. Surely they had not fired it, and would not lie against themselves. Ramsay thinks they confessed they were Christians; Von Soden even so translates it! Doubtless. But Christianity was not then a capital offence; it was only the crime of burning Rome that could bring down on them such condign punishment. Moreover, these "first seized" not only confess but implicate an "immense multitude." In what? In firing the city? Impossible! They were not guilty. In being Christians? Equally impossible. There was not an immense multitude of Christians in Rome; and even if we understand only a few score by this *multitudo ingens*, it seems impossible that the few first seized would betray the whole Christian community to such a monster as Nero. That would have been neither wise as serpent nor harmless as dove. Here, then, the story is unbelievable. Note, again, that the spectacle must have endured for a long time, else surely the Roman mob, used to such sights, would not have felt pity for a class of hated criminals who had burned two-thirds of Rome and caused unspeakable ruin and woe. And why do Suetonius (*Ner.*, 38) and Dio Cassius (62, 16, 1) and Pliny (*N. H.*, xvii, 1, 1, 5), who all have no doubt that Nero himself ordered the conflagration, and who must have known of such a long-continued slaughter of innocents, why do they never even remotely allude to such a tremendous matter? Lastly, when did this persecution take place? Naturally, one would suppose that the report started at once, while men's minds were wild with excitement, as did the rumour of Nero's fiddling mid the flames of Rome. But no one can gain such an idea from chap. xliv, which mentions the report after the account of Nero's architectural reconstruction, and indicates that he took severe measures not, as would be natural, in the heated state of public feeling, but only long after, and because the report refused to abate. This is not, indeed, incredible, but it is certainly perplexing.

And what can be the force or reference of "meanwhile" (*interea*), with which the next chapter (xlv) opens? If we omit chap. xliv, the reference is obvious, the term is so appropriate as to be almost unavoidable: Nero was rebuilding Rome on a scale of unexampled grandeur at incalculable outlay of imperial treasures. "What an abyss of expense! Whence came the necessary funds?" involuntarily exclaims the reader. The author answers: *Meanwhile* Italy, the provinces, the allies, the free states, the very sanctuaries of the gods were devastated to meet the prodigious cost. Now insert chap. xliv. At once the connection is broken, the thought is left hung in the air, extraneous and remotely related matters distract the attention, and when the subject is resumed in chap. xlv there is found nothing in chap. xliv to which the "meanwhile" can refer—for it is unreasoning to say "Nero was burning Christians and the people were moved to compassion, meanwhile the empire was plundered." We must go back to chap. xliii to find the natural attachment for chap. xlv—a clear indication that the intervening chapter has been interpolated.

(*c*) Does someone (as Von Soden) object that the style is too Tacitean not to be genuine? We reply that quite as good imitations are frequent enough. In his *Letters to Dead Authors* Mr. Andrew Lang has reproduced admirably a dozen widely diverse styles, none of them at all like his own. Such a *tour de force* is exceptional, but it shows that the limits of possibility in such matters are very wide. Besides, are we sure that the style is really so much like that of Tacitus? Careful scrutiny has perhaps not yet been made, but there are certainly counter indications. We pass over the well-known facts that the text is here particularly wavering; that it is strange that Tacitus should speak of Pontius Pilate merely as procurator, without specifying of what, whereas such a form of speech was most natural for the interpolator; that the extremely harsh judgment of the Christians is puzzling in the intimate friend of Pliny, from whom he would almost surely have learned better; that the "vast multitude" is an exaggeration more than Tacitean, and not at all paralleled by the *iacuit immensa strages* of *An.*, vi, 19,[1] and we would fix attention solely on one purely stylistic consideration, the expression *humani generis*. The whole sentence has sorely vexed the wits of commentators, but especially these words. Muretus (following Faernus?) boldly strikes out the word *humani*, and understands by *generis* the Christian race! Acidalius sees that this cannot be, and accordingly alters *humani* into *Romani*: they were condemned for hatred of the Roman race! Indeed, it seems almost impossible that Tacitus should have written *humani generis*. Everywhere else he writes *generis humani*.[2] It is in the last degree improbable that such a consummate stylist as Tacitus would here just this once deviate from his life-long habit, especially as the inverse order produces with the foregoing word a disagreeable hiatus: *odio humani*. No very delicate ear is needed to perceive that *odio generis* is a much pleasanter collocation. Besides, the whole weight of Tacitean related usage falls against the inversion. It is the fixed custom of the historian to modify *genus* by following and not preceding words. Thus *genus hominum* (three

---

[1] The slaughter is called immense because it struck "all" (*cunctos*) the implicated friends of Sejanus, without regard for age or sex or other conditions; but a multitude is huge only by its mere number.
[2] As *An.*, iii, 59; xii, 14; *Hist.*, i, 30; iii, 68; v, 25; *Ag.*, ii. Editors in general make no note of this fact. After this study was complete, the writer observed the remark of Nipperdey: "*humani generis*, Sonst sagt Tac. stets in der gewöhnlichen Ordnung *genus humanum*."

times, almost the same as *genus humanum*), *genus animalium*, *belli*, *militum*, *mortalium*, *mortis*, *questus pensi*, *orandi*, *maiorum*, *telorum*, *spectaculorum*, *studiorum*, *pugnæ*, *Arsacis*, *vitæ*, and *generis regii*. Apparent exceptions to this rule are readily seen to be due to rhetorical considerations, especially to the desire to maintain the favourite order: adjective, genitive (modified), noun, as in *omne mortalium genus* (*An.*, xvi, 13), *novum officii genus* (*Hist.*, i, 20), and to make emphatic, as in *oppidanum genus* (*An.*, vi, 15), *pernix genus* (*Hist.*, ii, 13). We may affirm, then, with much confidence that the inversion in question of itself stamps the passage as not probably from the hand of Tacitus.

. . . . .

By three entirely independent lines of inquiry we are led to precisely the same result. Look at it as you will, the chapter wears the appearance of being interpolated. Indeed, it must be, not unless one of these signs fail, but unless they all fail, unless all are simultaneously and in the same sense misleading. Even if the doubt raised by each one of these separate inquiries were not very strong, even if it still left the chances two to one in favour of the genuineness, yet the chance that all three would thus simultaneously deceive would be only eight in twenty-seven; the chances would be nineteen to eight in favour of interpolation. We have no choice then. Coerced by this consilience of results, we *must* regard the passage as probably interpolated, unless there be some strong antecedent reason in favour of genuineness and against interpolation.

Is there any such reason? Certainly not. The whole history of post-Apostolic and patristic literature shows that interpolation was a most familiar favourite. In fact, it would rather seem strange if such an opportunity had been neglected. We conclude, then, that this famous chapter, as it now stands, is with compelling probability to be ascribed to another hand than that of Cornelius Tacitus. But even if entirely genuine and uncorrupted, it would still be worthless in evidence, for it merely states a rumour about an alleged occurrence of nearly a hundred years agone. Accordingly, the passage is in all likelihood inadmissible in court; but even if admitted, it could prove nothing to the point.

OTHER PAGANS: FINAL REMARKS

The allusions of Suetonius to the Christians are the following: "Judæos impulsore Chresto assidue tumultuantes Roma expulit" (*Claudius*, xxv). "Afflicti suppliciis Christiani, genus hominum superstitionis novæ et maleficæ" (*Nero*, xvi). Both of these appear too slight for the basis of any judgment.

It will be noticed that there is no reference to the Founder of Christianity. The force of the *impulsore Chresto* is uncertain. It may refer to some Roman Jew named Chrestus, who stirred up his compatriots to riot, or it may refer to Messianic agitation among the Jewish populace, to their disputes among themselves about the Messiah, the Chrestus. Be this as it may, there is here no implication of the life and death in Galilee and Judea. Dio Cassius, however, says (ix, 6) he "did not expel" them, but forbade their assembling, and dissolved their clubs authorised by Gaius. On the other hand, Acts xviii, 2, refers the presence in Corinth of Aquila and Priscilla to this decree of Claudius expelling "all the Jews from Rome"—a statement almost certainly exaggerated.

The second mention occurs in a list of severe regulations made in Nero's time. If genuine, it would show merely that "Christians" were known as early as Nero, which would add nothing to our knowledge, and that they were on some occasions condignly punished. Possibly the notice in Tacitus is merely an expansion of the brief deliverance by Suetonius. A much more probable cause of the "punishments" would be some such disturbances as occurred under Claudius *impulsore Chresto*, or provoked Tiberius to expel the Jews from Rome (Suet., *Tib.*, xxxvi). Among the latter were included *similia sectantes*, whom also Tiberius *Urbe submovit sub pœna perpetuæ servitutis, nisi obtemperassent*. The *sectantes* are thought to be converts to Judaism; possibly they were incipient Christians. The words *nisi obtemperassent* seem to indicate great turbulence or unrest among the Jews under Tiberius near the supposed date of the crucifixion. This seems intrinsically highly probable, at least to us who regard the whole Christian movement as the outcome of generations, even centuries, of agitation among Jews and their proselytes. Sharp separation between Jews and Christians does not seem possible till the second century, especially the era of Bar Cochab.

The letter of Pliny to Trajan may also be quoted in this connection. It says nothing of the origin or Founder of Christianity; at most it tells only of the practices of the Christians in Bithynia about 110 A.D. There is no implication, not even the slightest, touching the purely human reality of the Christ or Jesus. Whether this correspondence of Trajan and Pliny be genuine or not is accordingly quite indifferent for the purpose of this discussion. Any investigation of the matter would be superfluous at this stage of the argument. Lucian (120–200 A.D.), in his *De Morte Peregrini*, xi, 41, in *Alexander*, xxv, 31, and in the spurious[1] *Philopatris*, 12, makes mention of "Christians" and the "man impaled in Palestine," but only under the Antonines; Dio Cassius also, but 220 A.D.

Herewith the references to Christianity in pagan literature before 150 A.D. are exhausted. After that date the Gospel story had certainly taken definite form; it is widespread among Christians, who are themselves numerous throughout the empire; it has certainly reached the ears of the heathen, and any number of allusions in profane writers would merely attest the currency of the Gospel story, but would supply no testimony whatever to its authenticity. It seems useless, then, to quote this literature any further. We close this scrutiny, therefore, with this result, already announced: *Profane history supplies no testimony whatever to the purely human character of Jesus.*

In order to estimate properly the value of this *argument from silence*, we must remember that apparently the profane writers could have had no motive in suppressing information

---

[1] In his "Le Christianisme à Byzance" (*Rev. Arché*, 1902, I, pp. 79–110), republished in *Cultes, Mythes, et Religions*, I, pp. 363–394, S. Reinach summarises the work of many learned predecessors, and shows clearly that *Philopatris* is the production of "a Christian anti-humanistic Greek" towards the close of the tenth century.

if they possessed it. Christianity was for them merely a pernicious and despicable superstition;[1] they would have been rather pleased to trace it back to a criminal crucified at Jerusalem. On the other hand, it is unlikely that any reference by the pagans would have been allowed by the Christians to perish. These latter were very jealous of all such material of argumentation, and cherished it, as is shown vividly by the admitted fact that they even invented it diligently.

Possibly the heathen may have felt little interest in the crucifixion, its antecedents, and its consequents; but the same cannot be said of Josephus. As a Palestinian Jew, a professional historian and a chronicler, it seems altogether impossible that he should not have known or have heard of the life and death of Jesus. He tells us minutely enough, if somewhat obscurely, of John the Baptist (*Arch.*, xviii, 5, 2), but John was in no way comparable with Jesus. In fact, he fills his pages with events altogether trivial by the side of the words and deeds of the Nazarene. It is not only to us, at this 1,900 years' remove, in the perspective of history, that the events appear in such relative significance. There was nothing in the career of John to match the execution on Calvary; nothing to pair with the works of Jesus, minimise them as you may. If Jesus was purely human, then he was an astounding personality; in name and fame the Baptist must have been comparatively insignificant. Consider, too, how closely the twain were related, the Forerunner and the Messiah. For the gossipy annalist to know of John, but not of Jesus, would be as if the contemporary historian of the Reformation should know of Zwingli, but not of Luther.

We dismiss, then, the hypothesis that Josephus was ignorant of the Christ, if the latter was purely human, as altogether impossible. But, knowing of him, could he have passed him by in silence intentionally? It seems hardly possible. If Josephus was a Christian (in secret), surely he would let pass no such opportunity to do his faith inestimable

---

[1] The terms used by Tacitus, Pliny, and Suetonius are strikingly alike, and suggest, but do not prove, some kind of interdependence or common dependence: *Exitiabilis superstitio, superstitionem pravam et immodicam, superstitionis novæ et maleficæ.*

service. If he was sincerely an orthodox Jew (as almost certainly he was, so the Christian writers themselves attest), he must have believed that his countrymen did right in rejecting the pretender; he must have rejoiced in their action. Why, then, suppress it? Or even if he was uncertain in mind, then he must have pondered the matter, must have deemed it of high importance; and, as it occupied his thoughts, why did he forbear all expression? No! we cannot understand the silence of the historian, except on the supposition that Jesus was unknown to him historically. It was precisely this circumstance that puzzled the Christians themselves of the early centuries, and induced one of them to cut the Gordian knot by interpolating Section 3. In fact, the marvel would be if some one had not made just such an interpolation. As already observed, such insertion of apt material at proper places was a favourite form of that early logic.

Bishop Lightfoot admits, with apparent irritation, that Josephus has preserved a "stolid silence about Christianity," but thinks this "cannot be owing to ignorance; for a sect which had been singled out for years before he wrote, as a mark for imperial vengeance at Rome, must have been only too well known in Judea." Of course, the allusion is to the Neronic persecution, and the reasoning sounds plausible. But we have just seen that this persecution is a matter for the very gravest doubt. Moreover, we see no reason why the Messianic agitators in Rome should take their cue from Palestine, or why the name "Christian" might not have been known in Rome even earlier than in Palestine. In fact, the name was not Palestinian, if we may believe Acts xi, 26;[1] it was applied to the disciples at Antioch, and was for an uncertain period only on the lips of enemies (not, however, *Christians,* but *Chrestians*).[2] We see, indeed, no reason why such a movement might not have started independently in various places and nearly simultaneously. That there was originally any unity or central dependence in the propaganda is decisively negatived by Acts in more than one place, as already set forth in *Der vorchristliche Jesus.* It seems unquestionable that the greatest variety of

---

[1] *Cf.* xxvi, 28; 1 Peter iv, 16.
[2] From Χρηστός=Χριστός, Blass, *Gram. N. T. Grk.*, pp. 8, 63.

OTHER PAGANS: FINAL REMARKS

faith prevailed in the early communities;[1] from Rome to Jerusalem no inference is allowable.

Moreover, be it said, not only does the fact that the Gentile called groups of the new faith by that contemptuous name of "Chrestians" by no means imply that these recognised the name, and thought of themselves as distinct from Jews and proselytes, but the opposite seems attested by Acts xxi, 20, where it is said to Paul: "Thou seest, brother, how many myriads there are among the Jews of them that have believed, and all are zealots for the law." These, then, had by no means separated themselves from the faith of their fathers; they were still one with the people.

If, then, Josephus knew of Christianity in Palestine, as is likely, he knew of it as one among many shades of religious enthusiasm or conviction, which had not detached itself from the general mass, which had not yet taken definite shape and outline. As thus inchoate and nebulous, or confounded with the Essenes, it may have appeared to him of little significance, and easily have been passed over when he treated of the principal sects of Jewish philosophy (*B. J.*, II, 8; *Arch.*, xviii, 1). *It is only when we assume the current hypothesis concerning the origin of Christianity* that the silence of Josephus appears strange and "stolid." But if it came "not by observation," so that one could say, "Lo here!"; if its coming was like the gentle play of summer lightning, illuming the whole circuit of the Mediterranean, shining all round nearly simultaneously, it may very well have long escaped recognition as a distinct phenomenon. Especially if, as seems now to be proved decisively,[2] it was in large measure a *mystery*-religion propagated in great secrecy, if it was first heard in the ear and only much later proclaimed on the house-top,[3] if the "beautiful deposit"[4] of doctrine was committed to the novitiate under solemn and awful circumstances, and only after "the beautiful confession" had been made under imposition of hands "before many witnesses,"[5] then such a secret cult, carefully "guarded,"

---

[1] "*Les sectes, si nombreuses dès les premiers temps du Christianisme.*" (Reinach, *Cultes, Mythes, et Religions*, i, 397.)
[2] In the present volume.
[3] Matt. x, 27; Luke xii, 3.
[4] παραθήκη, 1 Tim. vi, 20; 2 Tim. i, 12, 14.
[5] 1 Tim. vi, 12, 13.

might long escape the notice, or at least the interested attention, of a Josephus. Such reflections seem to break completely the force of the great Bishop's argument, of which the sinew lies in the tacit assumption of all that theory of the beginnings of Christianity which we set out to disprove.

How, then, shall we sum up the situation? Thus:—

(*a*) It is morally certain that the Josephine passage (*Arch.*, xviii, 3, 3) is a Christian interpolation.

(*b*) The Josephine passage concerning James (*Arch.*, xx, 9, 1) has certainly been tampered with by Christian hands, and, as it now reads, is almost surely an interpolation.

(*c*) The chapter in Tacitus lies under the very gravest suspicions.

(*d*) The sentences in Suetonius *may be* genuine, but they attest nothing strictly relevant. Like may be said of the Pliny-Trajan correspondence.

(*e*) Even if the utmost should be conceded to these pagan authorities, they would still bear witness to two things only: (1) That so early as Nero there were so-called Christians or Chrestians in Rome, and that they fell under the extreme displeasure of that emperor. (2) That so early as perhaps A.D. 117 the origin of the Christian cult was referred to a Christ that was said to have been crucified in Judea by Pontius Pilate (say A.D. 30) eighty or ninety years, nearly three generations, before.

Further than this these profane depositions do not go. It is seen at once that they do not touch the real point at issue, and we may now re-state as fully proved our first thesis: *Extant profane literature is silent concerning the life, career, and death of a purely human Founder of Christianity.*

But may there not be non-extant profane testimony, over which the oblivion of centuries has settled? Impossible! For remember that the Christians were keen-witted and numerous; that they were nurtured in age-long controversy; that they had every reason, incentive, and opportunity to preserve any and every profane witness to the traditional origin of their system, which would have been invaluable in their debate with unbelievers. Men like Justin, who peered into every cranny and crevice of Scripture for confirmation of their story, like Clement and the apologists who ransacked every corner of pagan literature for materials of argument, like Melito and Tertullian and the whole industrious hive of interpolators and pseudonymists who invented history and scriptures wholesale as needed—not six generations of these, one and all, would have neglected or overlooked any and every profane testimony in their own behalf, when even a single one would have been the end of controversy.

No! The fact that no Christian writer cites any such testimony is decisive proof that there was no such testimony to cite; and we may now finally affirm that the negative external witness, of contemporaneous history and literature, is as clear, as strong, as complete, as conclusive, as in the nature of the case it is possible for such witness to be. The negative internal witness of the New Testament itself has already been found to be eloquent and unequivocal. Positive counter-proofs in great number and variety all converge like meridians upon the same thesis. In a word, the purely human Jesus of the critics is denied and the Divine Jesus of Proto-Christianity is affirmed by every form of consideration that has yet been adduced. What else is needed to shape the judgment of unbiassed reason?

ADDENDUM I.

THE reader may not unnaturally ask, "But what has the illustrious Guglielmo Ferrero to say on this subject?" His notable work on the *Greatness and Decline of Rome* comes down to 14 A.D., just half-a-century short of the Conflagration; but elsewhere, as in his Lecture on Nero (*Characters and Events of Roman History*, pp. 103–141), he glances at the flames, though scarcely with a severely critical eye. "The history of Cæsar's family, as it has been told by Tacitus and Suetonius," he expressly rates as a mere "sensational novel, a legend containing not much more truth than the legend of [the] Atrides" (p. 138); and yet, strange to say, precisely where this novel is least credible, where it ceases to be intelligible

s

even, and where the apparent attestation is reduced one-half, being that of Tacitus alone, unsupported by Suetonius, precisely there he accepts it eagerly, not merely at par, but rather at a premium, and without the smallest grain of critical salt to save it. Witness the following quotations :—

"An inquiry into the causes of the conflagration was ordered. The inquest came to a strange conclusion. The fire had been started by a small religious sect......whose name most people then learned for the first time : the Christians.

"How did the Roman authorities come to such a conclusion? That is one of the greatest mysteries of universal history, and no one will ever be able to clear it. If the explanation of the disaster as accepted by the people was absurd, the official explanation was still more so" (p. 131).

And again : "......but it certainly was not philosophical considerations of this kind that led the Roman authorities to rage against the Christians. The problem, I repeat, is insoluble. However this may be, the Christians were declared responsible for the fire ; a great number were taken into custody, sentenced to death, executed in different ways, during the festivals that Nero offered to the people to appease them. Possibly Paul himself was one of the victims of this persecution" (p. 133).

"Behold how small a fire how great a wood enkindles!" How much more about this "inquiry" and "inquest" does Ferrero know than did Tacitus, and yet Tacitus is Ferrero's only authority, and that, too, an authority already emphatically discredited as "a sensational novel"! The plant of history would seem to be a hardy annual, and at times might be likened to a grain of mustard-seed. It is interesting to surprise it now and then as it grows.

But the important point is that the brilliant Italian distinctly and repeatedly declares "the problem is insoluble." And well he may. For while no one will question the keenness of his analytic faculty or the vigour of his reconstructive imagination, yet even these and more can hardly avail to make clear the general detestation of the few "pious idealists" whom "the people used to call Christians," while the same name had never yet been heard "by the most of the people"; or how to explain how "a great number" (strictly "an immense multitude"—as Church and Brodrib render it) could be sentenced and executed out of "a small and peaceful congregation."

Gibbon, and more especially Schiller, have argued that it was the Jews who were slaughtered in such numbers and amid such torments. Impossible, as we have seen; for in that case Josephus would have known and made mention of such a calamity to his countrymen. And why should Tacitus commit the blunder of substituting the nearly unknown Christians for the familiar Jews? Others have guessed that the Jews under the patronage of Poppæa incited Nero against the Christians—their own kinsmen! But not only is this conjecture a wholly gratuitous calumny on the Jews, but it presupposes a bitter hatred and an ancient grudge of Jews against their Christian brothers, such as was unreal and impossible at that time even in Jerusalem, much more among the liberal Jews of the Dispersion (compare Acts xxi, 20; xxviii, 17-25). Moreover, if the Jews had slandered the Christians in such infamous and ruinous fashion, why does not at least one among so many Christian authors, all of whom would have eagerly exploited any such fact or any such rumour, make some mention or give some hint of such a prodigious iniquity? No! Ferrero is right, and his admission is significant: it is quite impossible to understand the "mystery" of the Tacitean passage regarded as genuine; "no one will ever be able to clear it." What, then, is the obvious suggestion? Is it not that the incomprehensible chapter is spurious, or at least altered beyond recognition from some unknown original?

The temptation is great to hazard some speculation as to the genesis of this chapter (44), and to connect it with the strange fortunes of the *Annals*, as preserved in the two unique Medicean manuscripts; however, we will not put forth upon any such sea of conjecture, but will hug close the safe shore of Ferrero's avowal that the assumed "genuineness of the passage in Tacitus"—so far from being "not open to reasonable doubt"—confronts us with an insoluble riddle, "one of the greatest mysteries of universal history."

ADDENDUM II.

I.

THE foregoing article having very naturally provoked hostile criticism, it may be well to note some of the more important, and at the same time to introduce some additional evidence.

It has been urged, as by Kampmeier (*The Monist*, January, 1911, p. 112), that "the Tacitus passage is copied by Sulpicius Severus" (Neque ulla re Nero efficiebat, *quin ab eo jussum incendium* putaretur. Igitur vertit invidiam in *Christianos*, actæque in innoxios crudelissimæ *quæstiones;* quin et novæ mortes excogitatæ ut *ferarum tergis contecti laniatu canum interirent*. Multi *crucibus affixi* aut *flamma* usti, plerique in id reservati, ut cum *defecisset dies, in usum nocturni luminis urerentur.—Chron.*, ii, 29). It is seen that, although neither author has copied "almost verbally," yet the agreements in phrase (here in italics) are in at least two places so marked as to exclude the notion of independent origin. But what is the dependence? There is no reason to suppose that Sulpicius has taken from Tacitus (except that his date is near 400 A.D.). Indeed, it seems far likelier that the author of the Tacitean passage has simply worked up the Sulpician passage, or perhaps still likelier that each is drawing from some unknown common source. Nothing can be proved decisively at this point.

It is vain to urge that Sulpicius has apparently drawn upon Tacitus in describing the unnatural nuptials of Nero. Says Tacitus in *Ann.* xv, 37 : " Ipse per licita atque inlicita fœdatus nihil flagitii reliquerat quo corruptior ageret, nisi paucos post dies uni ex illo contaminatorum grege (nomen *Pythagoræ* fuit) *in modum solemnium conjugiorum denupsisset*. *Inditum imperatori flammeum*, visi auspices, *dos et genialis torus et faces nuptiales, cuncta denique spectata, quæ* etiam *in femina* nox operit." And Sulpicius (*Chron.*, ii, 28, 2) : " Adnotasse contentus sum hunc eo processisse ut *Pythagoræ* cuidam *in modum solemniorum conjugiorum*

ADDENDUM II.

nuberet; inditumque imperatori flammeum, dos et genialis torus et faces nuptiales, cuncta denique quæ vel *in femina* non sine verecundia conspiciuntur *spectata.*"

The coincidences are italicised, and it is seen even more clearly that the passages are not independent. Yet it by no means follows that Sulpicius was quoting from Tacitus. For Tacitus himself had his sources (since he wrote at nearly two generations' remove from Nero), which are quite unknown to us, but must almost certainly have contained some such specifications as appear now in the two historians. There is, then, no good reason why the two may not be quoting from a common source. Precisely such phenomena meet us at every turn in historico-literary investigations.

But even if it were granted that Sulpicius is here quoting from Tacitus, we could not conclude that he was quoting in the other case likewise. That would be such an out-and-out inference from particular to particular as even Mill would not allow. *If*, indeed, we *knew* that Sulpicius had quoted from Tacitus in the one case, and if we *knew* that the Tacitean passage existed at the time of Sulpicius in the other case, then we might with probability conclude that Sulpicius was quoting the passage *as* from Tacitus in the other case. Even then we could still not conclude (in the presence of the considerations already adduced) that the passage was actually written by Tacitus, *if* we were not sure that Tacitus had not been interpolated—and sure we can never be. In view, then, of all these facts, especially of these three *ifs*, it appears impossible to find in Sulpicius any valuable evidence against the view here maintained. Indeed, it seems strange to call into court such witnesses as Sulpicius Severus and the fabricators of the Paul-Seneca correspondence. When all the elder witnesses are dumb, will you break silence with words not uttered till nearly 300 years after the event in question? Will you establish by an obscure chronicler of to-day some all-important feature of the London fire of 1666, some supreme dramatic moment unattested by Pepys or any other authority? Such is not the method of historical criticism.

Some persons in desperation have referred to certain lines in Juvenal, Seneca, Martial; but these do not seem worth any notice whatever. At best and at most they can merely attest what is not in dispute—namely, that such cruel and unusual punishments were not so unusual as we might desire or suppose. But this makes not against but *for* the supposition that the Tacitean passage is supposititious. For the inventor would naturally invent along the lines of common knowledge, and would not needlessly fly in the face of probability.

Some years ago attention was emphatically called to the supposed testimony of that notable mosaic, the "Ascension of Isaiah," to the supposed martyrdom of Peter under Nero, and it is now recalled thereto, as by Kampmeier and others. Without discussing the "Beliar" of this "Ascension," it may suffice to cite the very recent judgment of Weinel, who displays notoriously little sympathy with the new criticism (Hennecke's *Neutestamentliche Apokryphen*, p. 205): "It were indeed most highly interesting, if we had here an older witness of the martyrdom of Peter in Rome; but that cannot be made certain."

It is a grave mistake to suppose that early Christian writers had no temptation to cite profane witness to the historicity of the Jesus, because "that was a settled fact" with "their Christian readers." It was not "a settled fact" even with all "Christian readers." The existence of the Docetists and other still more enlightened Gnostics, as well as the fierce polemic of Tertullian, Irenæus, and others, shows clearly that this so-called "fact" was questioned, and even rejected, in many Christian quarters. Besides, these Christian writers did by no means write merely for "Christian readers." Often they had a pagan audience in mind. Their frequent "Apologies" and "Exhortations" were addressed exclusively to the "Gentiles" or "Greeks." Moreover, their bitter need of historical attestation is unequivocally witnessed by their *repeated invention* of just such attestations, as in Josephus and Tertullian (already cited, p. 243), in Justin and others.

The all-important—indeed, the decisive—moment in the whole matter, which was perhaps not sufficiently stressed in the original article and cannot be stressed too strongly, is this: It is *not* now, and has *never* been, denied that Nero

ADDENDUM II.

may have persecuted Christians, *may* even have executed some, possibly Paul or Peter, or both. On this point we have no decisive evidence. The writer has no interest of any kind in questioning over-strictly the supposed testimonies to a Neronian persecution. It is the *Tacitean* persecution, described in the famous forty-fourth chapter, that is called in question, as admittedly inexplicable, and not only unsupported by testimony, but virtually excluded by unbroken silence in every quarter, even where its fame would have resounded loudest and longest. *Here is the heart of the matter.* It is vain to pile up hints of a mere Neronian persecution, even were they wholly unambiguous and not so hopelessly equivocal; all such are irrelevant. It is the Tacitean persecution that calls for verification, and *none is forthcoming*. When the skull of a man is broken, it is idle to fix attention on a fracture of his arm. Now, since it is not pretended that Tacitus invented the story in question, in discrediting the authenticity we also discredit the genuineness, *as it stands*. What *may* have lain at its base it is needless to conjecture.—That this Tacitean account can hardly be accepted at its face-value seems to be growing clearer even to the liberal critical consciousness. Witness the recent work of Geffcken, *Aus der Werdezeit des Christentums*.

Since one apocryphal document ("Ascension of Isaiah") has been called to the stand, it may be well to admit some others. In the "Martyrdom of Paul" (Lipsius, *Acta Apocrypha*, I, 102–107), referred by Zahn to A.D. 150–180, we find the Apostle executed by Nero in the midst of a fierce persecution at Rome, which, however, is wholly unrelated to the conflagration; the Tacitean passage and motive are not only not mentioned, they are plainly excluded. Of course, the whole story is fiction; but if the forty-fourth chapter, or any tradition consistent with that chapter, had been known to the apocryphist, it is hardly possible that he would have unnecessarily contradicted it by necessary implication. Again, in the Acts of Peter (Lipsius, *A. A.*, I, 45–103), according to Schmidt dating from A.D. 200–210, we find this pillar Apostle also executed under Nero, *but by the prefect Agrippa* and for personal reasons, his preaching having alienated many wives and concubines from their husbands and lords.[1] Thereupon Nero is angry, having wished to punish Peter still more severely, refuses to speak with Agrippa, and meditates the extermination of all the brethren discipled by Peter, but is dissuaded by a vision, and remains satisfied with the sole sacrifice of the Apostle. Here, again, the Tacitean account, along with any similar tradition, is positively excluded. To be sure, this martyrdom is imaginary, at least in its details; but the mere imagination shows convincingly that the great Neronian persecution in connection with the conflagration, as detailed in the forty-fourth chapter, *had no place in the Christian consciousness* of that author, and hence of that era. When we turn to the Acts of John, we see how eager these romancers were to attach their fancies to historical facts. Had any such attachment been possible in the case of the martyrdoms of Paul and Peter, it would have been zealously effected. The complete absence of this Tacitean persecution from attested Christian consciousness, in which it would have rooted itself ineradicably, cannot be understood without impugning the actuality of the persecution itself.

Finally, the whole story presents all the hall-marks of a fiction, of a gradual growth in the Christian mind. The nearer we approach the event in question, the vaguer and dimmer it becomes. As we touch it, lo! it dissolves into air. For one hundred years after its supposed occurrence the mighty persecution is not mentioned. The earliest Christian writers, those who would certainly have had a personal or next to personal knowledge of the alleged execution (of the Christians as incendiaries), betray no consciousness that anything of the kind had ever taken place. They speak fluently about the sufferings and martyrdoms of their brethren. Some allusions to the alleged Neronian holocaust lay directly across their path. *Why do they all avoid it?* In the second century the notion of Nero as persecutor begins to present itself more and more frequently, and details of his cruelty multiply more and more. Still there is no hint of any Tacitean persecution, of any connection with the great conflagration; on the contrary, such

---

[1] Is this an echo of the words of Clemens Romanus: "Zeal hath alienated wives from husbands" (vi)?

ADDENDUM II.

a connection is by implication emphatically excluded. At length, in the fourth century, it is suggested, in a fabricated correspondence, that Christians and Jews had been punished as incendiaries. At last, in the fifth century, we read the details in the terse Sulpicius, "the Christian Sallust." In the famous forty-fourth chapter of the *Annals* of Tacitus we find still greater elaboration. The suggestion seems irresistible that the chapter represents an advanced stage of a process that had been slowly at work for hundreds of years. Are not such evolutions familiar to the student of history? Does he hesitate to recognise them when much less clearly revealed in profane records? Do not precedents for such interpolations abound? Was there not the strongest motive and even temptation to give historic colour to the whole Christian doctrine, especially to its central concept, the Jesus? Does not even Tertullian (in the passage quoted) dare to represent Tiberius as convinced by "intelligence from Syria Palestine"? Does not Justin (*A.*, i, 35, 48) still earlier appeal to a fictive official report of the trial of Jesus?[1] In fact, unless I widely err, this strain towards historisation, especially in the Western Church, has been the main determinant of old Christian literature and dogma.

It is both interesting and important to note that Windisch (*Theol. Rundschau*, April, 1912, p. 117), though unsympathetically reviewing *Ecce Deus*, seems to concede the contentions of this Part IV practically *in full*, saying: "The ungenuineness of the Christ-passages in Josephus is strikingly demonstrated; fully as worthy of attention appear to me his deductions (*Ausfuchrungen*) concerning Tacitus."

---

[1] ἐκ τῶν ἐπὶ Ποντίου Πιλάτου γενομένων ἄκτων.

PART V.

THE KINGDOM AND THE CALL TO REPENTANCE

STATISTICS

THE census of the use in the New Testament of the term "Kingdom" is at first sight rather formidable. Its appearances number fifty-four in Matthew, nineteen in Mark, forty-four in Luke; but only four in John, eight in Acts, one in Romans, four in 1 Cor., one in Galatians, one in Ephesians, two in Colossians, one each in 1 and 2 Thessalonians, two in 2 Timothy, three in Hebrews, one in James, one in 2 Peter, six in Revelation. Let the Millian logicians depreciate perfect induction as they may, such a complete enumeration as the foregoing can hardly fail to be instructive, whether or no it involve any sure inference. Some things, at least, appear to lie on its very face. It is plain that as a ruling idea the Kingdom is present in the Synoptics in a sense in which it is not present in any of the other New Testament writings. But even in these it is by no means present in equal measure. Deducting five references in Matthew, as many in Mark, and six in Luke, as not to the Kingdom of God, we have for the Synoptics in order forty-nine, fourteen, thirty-eight. It is seen that the use in Mark is not of the same order of magnitude as in Matthew and Luke. This may be due in a measure to the prevailing narrative form of Mark, whereas Matthew and Luke are more concerned with sayings, parables, and discourses.

We notice further that "Kingdom of the heavens" is almost the exclusive form in Matthew, occurring thirty-three times; only four times we find "the Kingdom of God" (xii, 28; xix, 24; xxi, 31, 43), and three times there is a reference to "Thy Kingdom," or "The Father's Kingdom" (vi, 10, ; xiii, 43 ; xxvi, 29), once to the "Kingdom of the Son of Man" (xvi, 28) ; other sporadic cases do not call for notice. In Mark, however, the "Kingdom of God" appears fourteen times, the other uses being sporadic. In Luke the "Kingdom of God" appears thirty-two times ; the other uses are scattered, and from both Mark and Luke the Matthæan form, "Kingdom of the heavens," is entirely absent. Elsewhere "Kingdom of God" appears thirteen times ; "Kingdom of the heavens" never. This latter phrase, then, is strictly Matthæan. It might seem to characterise the author himself (or his school) rather than his source, for in the parallel passages in the Gospels we find the one form in the first, the other in the second and third—*e.g.*, "Nigh is come the Kingdom of the heavens" (Matthew iii, 2 ; x, 7), but "Nigh is come the Kingdom of God" (Mark i, 15 ; Luke x, 11). It seems strange, then, that the "Kingdom of God" should appear at all in Matthew. In one case (xix, 24) "Kingdom of the heavens" is preferred by Tischendorf ; in another (xii, 28) the whole verse is unrepresented in Mark, but agrees almost exactly with Luke (xi, 20), whence it would seem to be a later insertion—a conjecture greatly strengthened by the use of $\phi\theta\acute{a}\nu\omega$ in the late (Alexandrine) sense of *come*, a word not elsewhere found in the Gospels. The other two examples in Matthew are found in xxi, 31, 43—in a chapter whose text makes us often pause. Clearly it has been subject to much alteration. In the parable of the two sons, in the answer of the Jews, it was with the Christian Fathers a question whether should be read "the first" or "the last." The Sinaitic Syriac confirms the reading "the first," against the judgment of Tischendorf ; some primitive corruption is certainly present. The verse 31 can lay no claim to originality ; it seems to be a late addition. Similarly verse 43 is in a region of proved interpolation ; verse 44 is no longer adopted in critical texts. The late character of verse 43 is plain on its face, for the writer speaks of *taking away* the Kingdom of God from the Jews and giving it to another people, an idea utterly discordant with the notion of the Kingdom that prevails in the Gospel—namely, of something coming, but not then possessed by the Jews ; yea, in fact, never possessed by them. Hence we may with confidence mark all these passages as late accretions to the earlier form of the Gospel, which then appears never to have used the phrase "Kingdom of God."

Hereby the first Gospel is distinctly marked as Hebraic, as in large measure thought out, if not, indeed, more or less completely composed originally, in Aramaic. In later Old Testament writings Deity is spoken of as God of heaven (2 Chr. xxxvi, 23 ; Ez. i, 2, *et passim*; Neh. i, 4, 5; ii, 4, 20 ; Jon. i, 9 ; Dan. ii, 18, *et passim* ; once, indeed, Dan. iv, 23, "Until thou have known that rulers are heavens," heaven seems to be identified with God). In 1 Maccabees the name of God is avoided, heaven and other circumlocutions taking its place. The Rabbis also shunned the awful name, often using "Place" (*Maqôm; cp*. the Gnostic *Topos*) instead. Wetstein (on Matthew xxi, 25) illustrates the frequent Talmudic use of heaven instead of God. It is indeed plain and undisputed that the Matthæan form breathes a genuine Hebraic spirit. But when Wellhausen says that the people, especially in Galilee, were in Jesus's day not so far advanced, and that he spake as the people and not as the scribes, we recognise the opinion of a great critic ; yet we cannot quite recognise "he spake as the people" as the equivalent of "he taught as one having authority." When Wellhausen further says that Jesus calls God regularly God, and not the Father in heaven, one would hardly suppose that in Matthew, where this latter term so abounds, he names God thirty times, and in Mark only twenty. There is, then, no avoidance of the word "God" by the Jesus of Matthew ; and Wellhausen's reason for regarding "Kingdom of God" as the original expression seems imaginary.

The statistics of this word "Father" as applied to God are, indeed, not without interest. In Matthew we find it so used forty-five times ; in Mark, five ; in Luke, seventeen ; in John, 118 ; in Acts, three (all at the beginning—i, 4, 7 ; ii, 33) ; in Romans and 1 Cor., each four ; in 2 Cor., five ; in Gal., four ; in Eph., eight ; in Phil., three ; in Col., four ; in 1 Thes., four ; in 2 Thes., three ; in 1 Tim., two ; in 2 Tim, one ; in Titus, one ; in Philm., one ; in Heb., three ; in James, three ; in 1 Peter, three ; in 2 Peter, one ; in 1 John, twelve ; in 2 John, four ; in Jude, one ; in Rev., five.

The term is seen to be familiar to nearly every page of the New Testament, but an especial favourite with John, and in less degree with Matthew and the author of Ephesians. This fact is interesting as characterising the *circles of thought* from which these compositions emanated, but it has no significance as indicating aught about the Jesus.

The conception of this Kingdom, whether of God or of the heavens, seems to be unmistakably and very distinctly Hebraic. In the book of Daniel we find (ii, 44) that "the God of heaven shall set up a kingdom that shall never be destroyed." In iv, 3, "His Kingdom (is) an everlasting Kingdom," "from æon to æon" (34). In vii, 13, 14, this everlasting and indestructible Kingdom is given (seemingly by the Ancient of Days, primeval deity) to "One like the Son of Man," apparently to a man-like Being, in contradistinction from the beasts to which transient dominion had been given, which can signify nothing but the people Israel. In vii, 18, 22, 25, 27, it is specified that this everlasting, imperishable Kingdom belonged of right and of fact to the "saints of the Most High," who are therefore symbolised by the manlike figure. In the first seven chapters of Daniel the preferential term for Kingdom is *Malku*, which, being the Chaldee form, is almost peculiar to Daniel, who uses it fifty-five times (used also in Ezra four times); in the next chapters, viii, x, xi, the term uniformly used (thirteen times) is *Malkuth* (used also in i, 1, 20; ii, 1), which, however, occurs in eleven other books of the Old Testament, but is yet a later form rare in earlier Hebrew. This fact seems interesting as indicating certain otherwise well-known lines of cleavage in *Daniel*. Other familiar Hebrew terms for Kingdom, as *Melukah, Mamlakah,* and *Mamlakuth,* do not occur in Daniel (except *Melukah* in i, 3, in the sense of King). In the Talmud use varies between *Malku* and *Malkutha* (Syriac).

NATURE OF THE KINGDOM

It thus appears that the earliest form of the conception was Kingdom of God (as early as Psalm cxlv, 11, 13, though the phrase itself does not yet occur)—that is, Kingdom

NATURE OF THE KINGDOM

established by God and possessed by the Saints (Israel), in which, therefore, God, the One God, was worshipped. As the term "God" came to be used less and less, being supplanted by such paraphrases as "Heaven," "Place," "the Holy Blessed He," "Lord of Ages," "Who spake, and all became," "Alone of the Ages," etc., the original Kingdom of God became regularly Kingdom of the Heavens (*Malkuth Hash-Shamayyim*). When this latter phrase is found exclusively in Matthew, the former exclusively in Mark and Luke, the indication is clear that the two phrases (the former more Judaically coloured) have proceeded from different spheres of influence; but no inference as to the Jesus having used the latter, having spoken as did the people, appears to be allowed or suggested.

Weber has shown clearly that in rabbinic circles the Kingdom of God or the Heavens was equivalent to the Kingdom of the Law; to take on the latter was to take on the former; where reigned the Law, there reigned God—and conversely. But even here the idea of an organisation was not absent. The Kingdom did not consist in the mind or temper or obedience of the individual, but in the organised totality of all the subjects of the law, of the worshippers of the One God. The individuals are members of the Kingdom, as the native or naturalised American is a citizen of the United States. Of course, such cannot be the New Testament sense, in so far as the *Law* is concerned; and yet this latter sense must be closely related to the rabbinic, and is, in fact, derivable therefrom, on changing Law into Gospel.

Into the wilderness of discussion concerning the Messianic expectation and related notions—as of the Son of Man—it is not our purpose to enter *at present*.[1] The one point to be

---

[1] The question concerning the "Son of Man" and the flock of cognate ideas and problems is one of the most obscure and intricate hieroglyphs that have ever puzzled the investigator. It seems hardly proper to broach such a deep-rooted and wide-branching theme unless in its own especial volume. It is enough at this point to state the fact, of which the proof is reserved, that all the meridians of evidence converge on the propositions that both the systematic application of the term to Jesus in the Gospels and the equally systematic non-application in the other New Testament Scriptures, as well as the extra-canonic witness, Jewish, pagan, apocryphal, show that the term, however derived, denoted not a mere man, a magnetic rabbi, but a heavenly and divine Being, who might, indeed, *appear*, like Zeus or even Jehovah, clothed in the garment of humanity, but is entirely misunderstood when conceived as a man,

made clear is that throughout the New Testament, particularly in the Gospels, the Kingdom is some kind of organisation. In most cases this is so plain that any attempt at proof the reader might resent as superfluous and almost insulting. In a few, however, the sense is not so near the surface, and there might possibly be—indeed, there has been—some diversity of opinion. It will be necessary, then, to examine New Testament usage, especially in the Gospels, with some care, particularly the very rare cases in which there might seem to be some reason for doubt. In Mark the Kingdom is uniformly represented as an organisation, or even as an organism, especially as growing gradually in secret (iv, 11, 26–32), and as something that one enters (ix, 47; x, 23, 24, 25), even as one is admitted into a society. Only one expression might at first sound strange: "Whoever shall not receive the Kingdom of God as a little child, he shall in nowise enter therein. And having called them,[1] he blessed them, laying his hands upon them" (x, 15, 16). But the rabbis spoke of taking on the Kingdom in taking on the law, and Mark's phrase appears aimed at the Jewish party, who were unwilling to receive the Kingdom of God composed mainly of such little children—that is, of Gentile converts.

In Matthew the same representation is found. In xiii, 41 ("they shall gather out of his Kingdom all that cause stumblings," etc.) the reference to organisation is particularly clear. In Luke only we find two verses (xvii, 20, 21) that might possibly indicate that the Kingdom is something internal, a state of mind. "The Kingdom of God cometh not with observation;[2] nor will they say, lo! here it is, or there it is; for lo! the Kingdom of God is among you."[3]

---

the son of Joseph and Mary. See Schmidt's exhaustive treatment in the *Encyclopædia Biblica* ("Son of Man"), Reitzenstein's *Poimandres*, Hertlein's close-reasoned monograph, *Die Menschensohnfrage im letzten Stadium*, and Badham's article on "The Title 'Son of Man'" in the *Theol. Tijdschr.* (1911), pp. 395–448, which finds that "'Second Adam' or 'Saviour' was the meaning which attached to the term when the Gospels were written."

[1] So reads *D*, also the Sinaitic Syriac; the "taking them in his arms" is a later sentimental variation. It seems clear that "laying his hands upon them" indicates them as standing before him, *not* as already in his arms. Note also Burkitt's rendering of verse 13: "And they brought near to him children, that he should lay his hand upon them." Embrace is not contemplated, and almost excluded.

[2] μετὰ παρατηρήσεως. [3] ἐντὸς ὑμῶν.

This text is the Gibraltar of liberal critics, who translate it "within you," "in your hearts," not "among you," and maintain strenuously that their Jesus herewith formally rejects the current notion of the Kingdom as something external or political or social-organic, and sublimes the concept into that of a great internal all-regulative and transvaluating spiritual Idea. Let us hear one of the very greatest, who has brought so much light from the Old Testament to the New. Wellhausen translates ἐντὸς ὑμῶν by "Innerhalb von euch," and adds, "es ist inwendig von euch." "It is, therefore, something quite other than the future kingdom of the Jews"— which may be readily granted. "But it is also not the Christian community [which can by no means be granted] which in Matthew is ordinarily understood thereby"—where *ordinarily* (gewöhnlich) will bear a great deal of emphasis. "The ἐντός signifies more than ἐν μέσῳ (in the midst)." Where is the proof? "Rather is the Kingdom of God here, just as in the parable of the leaven, conceived as a principle that works invisibly in the hearts of individuals." A beautiful modern thought, which Chamberlain has exploited fully, but entirely foreign to the New Testament. Observe that Wellhausen gives no proof whatever. He adopts this interpretation in the teeth of all precedent and evidence, solely because it conforms to the liberal "Jesusbild," itself a mere imagination. He himself declares, in the next sentence, speaking of the correct view, which he declares "altogether impossible": "To be sure, in the following address to the disciples it is nevertheless treated as possible." In fact, he admits an inherent inconsistency (innere Differenz) between his own interpretation and the notion of the Kingdom elsewhere present in the Gospels. The truth is, his exegesis is quite without any support in the Gospels, or even in the whole New Testament. The illustrious critic adduces, and can adduce, only one even apparent parallel— the parable of the leaven. But is this a real parallel? Read the two parables (Matthew xiii, 31–33; Luke xiii, 18–21). The first likens the Kingdom to a grain of mustard-seed, smaller than all the seeds, but growing up to be a veritable tree, in whose branches birds may dwell. What is the meaning? Is the Kingdom here a principle in the heart of the individual? Impossible! It is manifestly an organisation, at first inconspicuous, gradually assuming colossal proportions—which consists perfectly with the idea elsewhere presented in the Gospels. But the second parable? Since the two are given in immediate connection by both Evangelists, the presumption is that they present the same or similar ideas under varying imagery. "Another parable. Like is the Kingdom of the heavens to leaven, which a woman took and hid in three measures of meal till all was leavened." That is, the Kingdom is an organisation hid now in the great mass of society, but gradually extending itself till it includes the whole. What truer or clearer picture of the Kingdom, of the Jesus-cult, of Christianity, could be desired? Why seek for some other meaning when a perfectly satisfactory meaning lies on the open hand? Wellhausen himself cannot deny that the meal typifies "a foreign substance (the world or the Jewish people?)," but he thinks the Kingdom is "ein durchdringendes Prinzip." The Kingdom a permeative principle! Do permeative principles grow like mustard-plants? He himself perceives that this is mere fancy; for he says in the next sentence: "It is, however, notwithstanding the Christian community." There! the cat has escaped from the bag! Call it a penetrative principle if you will; but the leaven, the Kingdom, remains the Christian community, the secret organisation of the primitive disciples, who are themselves called "the salt of the earth," salting and saving the whole social body.

It seems, then, that this, Wellhausen's only parallel passage, runs directly counter to his own interpretation. It must now be added that the translation of ἐντὸς ὑμῶν by "within you" is quite impossible, for it is the Pharisees that are addressed, who are certainly not here conceived as having the Kingdom in their hearts. Wellhausen perceives the difficulty, at least partially, and speaks of this address as "auffallend" (surprising), but offers no explanation. Still more, however, the *Sinaitic Syriac relieves all doubt* on the subject by declaring unambiguously "among you" ("unter euch," as Merx renders it), and *not* "within you"; so Burkitt translates: "For lo, the Kingdom of God among you!"

Only a word is necessary concerning the "observation."

Since the organisation was secret, since the cult was carefully guarded in mysteries and parables, of course the Kingdom came not with observation, with any open show or manifestation, and men could not say of it, "Lo, it is here, or lo, it is there." Nothing, then, remains unexplained in this celebrated passage, which turns out to be in complete accord with the general New Testament doctrine of the Kingdom. To dwell on such verses as John xviii, 36, Romans xiv, 17, 1 Cor. iv, 20, would not be complimentary to the intelligence of the reader; but he may be asked to reflect on Matthew xiii, 47, in which the Kingdom is likened unto a net cast into the sea and catching both good fish and bad. What organisation but has unworthy as well as worthy members? How impossible any other interpretation! And how characteristically John has dramatised the parable into history (xxi, 1–14)!

PREACHING OF THE KINGDOM

Holding fast the results thus far attained, that the Kingdom of God is the organisation or society in which God, the One God, is recognised and properly worshipped (that is, the community of the monotheistic Jesus-cult), we must now broach the interesting and important but difficult question of the preaching of the Kingdom and the call to repentance. At this point, unfortunately, the testimony is neither quite so clear nor so unanimous as might be desired. In Mark i, 15, we hear as the keynote of the Jesus-preaching: "The time is fulfilled and the Kingdom of God is at hand; repent ye, and believe in his Gospel." Mark does not say that the Baptist preached the approaching Kingdom, but only the baptism of repentance, and the remission of sins, and the mightier Coming One who would baptise with the Holy Spirit. Similarly Luke, with many additional details, but with no mention of the Kingdom of God, which first appears in iv, 43, as preached by the Jesus. In the same sense the Fourth Evangelist is silent. Turning to Josephus (*Ant.*, xviii, v. 2), we read of "John surnamed the Baptist; for Herod slays him, a good man who bade such Jews as cultivate virtue and practise justice towards one another and piety towards God to join in baptism; for so indeed also the baptism would appear acceptable to him, they using it not for apology for certain sins, but for purification of the body, supposing indeed the soul also thoroughly purified beforehand by righteousness." This seems to be a queer explanation of the "baptism unto remission of sins," but there is no hint of the Kingdom. Josephus goes on to say that the people thronged this preacher and were willing to do whatever he advised; so that Herod, fearing a rebellion, seized him and sent him to the castle Macherus, where he was put to death. As we can detect no motive here for falsification, this account would seem to be about as credible as anything else in Josephus; in any case, we are not able to control it. It might perhaps consist with John's preaching the imminent arrival of the Kingdom, but certainly does not imply the same.

In Matthew iii, 2, alone we read that the Baptist came preaching in the Wilderness of Judæa, and saying: "Repent ye, for nigh is come the Kingdom of the Heavens." Now exactly these words are put into the mouth of the Jesus (iv, 17) as the keynote of his preaching, sounded only after John was cast into prison. We may suspect that here there is something unhistorical. It could hardly be, after John had preached for some considerable time, after he had been cast into prison and his movement had spent its force, that the Jesus would resume precisely his formula and slogan in preaching in Galilee. The effect of such preaching had already been discounted. People would have said: "Oh! that is an old story. John told us all that some months ago. Now he's in prison." We may say, then, with much confidence that this repetition is very improbable.

Nevertheless, the statements may shadow forth an historical situation. The preaching of the Baptist seems to present a Jewish side of the great Christian movement. Its main content (according to the Gospels) appears to have been the Coming One, which was nearly related to the Messianic expectation, but may have referred either to Jehovah himself or to his plenipotentiary representative. With this Coming One seems also to have been associated the notion of a judgment. The object of this latter was in the main the condemnation of the heathen world and the glorification of Israel, about which the Apocrypha and the expounders of the Apocrypha discourse interminably, and which might easily and naturally pass over into an overthrow of polytheism and establishment of the monotheistic Jesus-cult. Concerning the real intent, content, and extent of this Johannine movement we know very little, and conjecture seems idle. At present we must resign ourselves to ignorance. The representations in the Synoptics and in Josephus appear too meagre to warrant any significant positive inference.

But what does this preaching tell us about the Kingdom? Wellhausen (Matthew iii, 2) says: "That the Kingdom of God—*i.e.*, the judgment or the wrath to come—is nigh at hand." Surely he cannot mean to identify the Kingdom with the Judgment or Wrath; he means merely that the coming of the Kingdom involves the coming of the Judgment and Wrath. The Kingdom would seem to mean only the divine government, the rule of the earth by God mediately or immediately. In Jewish minds this might very naturally fuse with the Messianic Kingship and the exaltation of Israel. But in Gentile minds it would hardly do so. They would most probably have found such a Kingdom little to their taste. As preached to the Gentiles of Galilee the establishment of the Kingdom of God could hardly mean aught else than the conversion of Pagandom to the worship of the One true God. This notion was very closely related to the pure Judaic notion of the Kingdom of the Heavens as the Reign of the Law, since the heart of this latter was the *Shema*, "Hear, Israel, Yahveh Our God Yahveh is One" (Deut. vi, 4). But the two were not quite the same. Inevitably the Kingdom itself would then consist of converts to this faith. As a body these would form the Kingdom, whose essence would be Theoseby—the worship of the One God.

REPENTANCE IN THE OLD TESTAMENT

So understood, the force of the preaching becomes clear. "Repent" is more properly "Change your minds." The repentance[1] is nothing but conversion, the Hebrew *shûb*, the

[1] μετάνοια.

Aramaic *tûb*, which is *turning*. *Shûbû* (turn ye) was the cry of the prophets. Turn from what to what? It is a great mistake to suppose that a moral reformation is primarily meant, though of course it was involved as a consequent. The turning was always religious; it was from idolatry to Yahveh-worship, from false religion to true. "For they served idols......turn ye from your evil ways" (2 Kings xvii, 12, 13). "Ye children of Israel, turn again unto Yahveh" (2 Chron. xxx, 6). "Turn ye unto him from whom the children of Israel have deeply revolted" (Isaiah xxxi, 6). "Return unto me, for I have redeemed thee" (Isaiah xliv, 22). "Return, thou backsliding Israel," "Turn, O backsliding children," "Return, ye backsliding children; I will heal your backslidings" (Jer. iii, 12, 14, 22). "Return now everyone from his evil way......Because my people hath forgotten me, they have burned incense to vanity" (Jer. xviii, 11, 15). Also Jer. xxv, 5, 6, and xxxv, 15: "Return ye now every man from his evil way,......and go not after other gods." "Repent and turn from your idols" (Ez. xiv, 6). "Turn, turn ye from your evil ways......ye lift up your eyes toward your idols" (Ez. xxxiii, 11, 25). "O Israel, return unto Yahveh" (Hos. xiv, 1-4). "Turn ye to me" (Joel ii, 12, 13). "Turn ye unto me......turn ye now from your evil ways......Turn you to the stronghold" (Zec. i, 3, 4; ix, 12). "Return unto me" (Mal. iii, 7). Similar are nearly one hundred others. *Uniformly*, then, the turning is to Yahveh, from false gods. To be sure, the prophet conceives this conversion as bringing all good in its train, just as idolatry drags all evil (*cp.* Rom. i, 18-32); but in every case this turning is from false to true worship. We may indeed say that the conception of *morality as morality* is scarcely present at all in the Old Testament. Surely this does not mean that the Hebrew did not value morality. He valued it most highly and practised it diligently—not, however, as primary, but as secondary; not as original and independent, but as dependent and derivative. For him the source of moral obligation was not found in the nature of things (as for the Greek), not even in his own nature, but in the expressed will of God. The seat of authority was nowhere on earth, but in heaven. The basis of ethics was not subjective, but objective.

Morality was a vigorous growth, but rooted nowhere in earth; it was an offshoot from the giant stem of religion. "If any one worship God (θεοσεβὴς ᾖ) and do his will, him he hears" (John ix, 31). Worship comes first, then obedience, and therewith all is said. This but echoes the dictum of Qoheleth, "Hear the sum of all [speech]: Fear God and keep his commandments; for this is [the duty of] every man." It is clear, to ethics is conceded no independent existence. The prophets are unwearied and vehement in their exhortations to repentance and to righteousness. Turn, turn, they cry unceasing—from what? "From your evil way." What evil way? The context shows in every case that the evil way is idolatry or some form of unfaithfulness to Yahveh-worship. Turn to whom, to what? The same context shows in every case that it is to Yahveh and his service.

Of all the prophets the one in whom the purely ethical comes clearest to the light is Amos. Yet, though for rhetorical purposes he sets forth the injustice and oppression of the priestly and official class with terrible vigour, yet even in him the prime motive is religious. His indignation is against the false worship at Bethel and Dan and Gilgal. It is the iniquity of the ministers of a false religion that he denounces. After fierce predictions against the surrounding heathens he turns to Judah: "Because they have despised the laws of Yahveh and have not kept his commandments, and *their lies caused them to err*, after which their fathers walked." These "lies" are nought but idols ("Götzenbilder," Buhl), as so frequently in the Old Testament. Next he denounces Israel, and, though scourging avarice and vice, he lets us know that it is these as connected with the State religion of Jeroboam that provoke him, for they "profane my holy name"......"in the house of their god." The luxury he inveighs against is the luxury of the priests, the pomp of the false religion; hence "I will also visit the altars of Beth-el." It is this same half-heathen service that is so emphatically rejected in the famous passage v, 21–26. It is their idolatry, their worship of Moloch and Kêwan (Saturn) (v, 26, 27), that will land them in captivity. The righteousness and judgment of verse 24 are only the strict fulfilment of the Torah of Jehovah. Similarly in vi, 13, "ye rejoice in

Lo-debar," whether this be "nought thing"—*i.e.*, idol—or Mahanaim (2 Sam. ix, 4; xvii, 27), a place of idol-worship. Also in viii, 14, the "sin of Samaria" is the false god or false worship.

Even in the most spiritual of the Psalms the case is not otherwise. In 51 the poet (who seems to be nothing else than the people Israel in captivity) bewails his apparent rejection by God; he can understand it only as a punishment for his (the people's) sins. But all the sin was against God and God only; "against thee, thee only, have I sinned and done evil in thy sight"; that is, it was not ethical, but religious. He prays earnestly for restoration to favour, in which case he will convert sinners and "teach transgressors thy ways"; that is, he will propagate monotheism and the Law. True, it is said, verses 16, 17: "For thou desirest not sacrifice; else would I give; thou delightest not in burnt offering. The sacrifices of God are a broken spirit: a broken and a contrite heart, O God, thou wilt not despise."[1] And naturally, for in captivity such forms of worship were impracticable; the will had to be taken for the deed; but as soon as "the walls of Jerusalem" were rebuilt, "then shalt thou be pleased with the sacrifices of righteousness, with burnt offering and whole burnt offering; then shall they offer bullocks upon thine altar." We all know that the reference of this Psalm to David is quite impossible. The apex of poetic and philosophic merit is attained in Psalm 139; yet the closing verses (19–24) show that the philosophy and ethics of the writer are still strictly religious, that he even hates with perfect hatred all that do not worship with him the One God of the universe.

Like holds for Isaiah, even Deutero-Isaiah. Large-hearted and spiritual-minded as he is, nevertheless before all else he is a religionist, a Yahveh-worshipper, only derivatively and in second line a moralist. This thesis may be tested and proved by countless verses. Consider the *Great Arraignment* (chap. i).

---

[1] Even if certain critics should be right in holding that the Psalmist has here attained a strictly "evangelic" standpoint, the foregoing results would not really suffer; for it would be only a noteworthy individual exception, such as might readily arise without altering the general state of the case—and the closing verses would then be understood as a consciously corrective addition (Kautzsch).

In spite of such verses as 17, the sin of the people is apostasy (5), is defection from Yahveh (4), is idolatry (21, 29). In ii, 9, 18, 20, 22, the land is full of "not-gods," against which the prophet inveighs with passion. In v, 24, the sin is the same. In x, 10, 11, the "not-gods" confront us again, and so on to the end. The whole book is intensely religious, the prophet champions the Yahveh-cult unweariedly, and his truly lofty ethics is a deduction from his religion. We need say little of Micah and the rest. From i, 6*f*, iii, 5, iv, 5, v, 13*f*, vi, 16, and similar passages, it is clear that this prophet was of the same spirit, that for him also morality was a corollary from the worship of Yahveh. Even in the Gospels the case is not really different. The *first* commandment is still the *Shema*, with the requisition of intense and exclusive worship of the One Jehovah-God. Love for neighbour is the *second* and far less emphatic commandment (Mark xii, 28–34).

We repeat, then, the prophetic cry *Šûbû* means always one, and only one, thing—"Turn ye" from idols unto God; its content is primarily always religious, never ethical. The Aramaic prefers the later *tûb*, "return," but the content remains the same. Several times the *Šûb* of the Old Testament is rendered by ἐπιστρέφω (convert) in the New Testament, and is then generally rendered in Syriac by *tûb*. Repentance and conversion were then essentially the same in the apostolic consciousness; they referred primarily to the turning away from idols unto the one living God. This is clearly expressed in Acts xx, 21—"Repentance unto God"—where turning unto God must be meant. Of course, it is not affirmed that repentance does not and can never mean anything else but this conversion, but only that as the slogan of the primitive preaching it meant, and could mean, nothing else.

REPENTANCE IN THE NEW TESTAMENT

Let us examine New Testament usage still more carefully. In Rev. ii and iii the verb is used seven times: Ephesus is praised, but is bid "repent and do the first works," "because thou hast left thy first love" (ii, 5). Plainly some religious error, some defect of faith is meant, some falling away from true worship; there is no hint of moral dereliction. Pergamos, too, is commended, but is also reproved for compromise with idolatry in the matter of eating things sacrificed to idols, and is bid repent solely on this score. The repentance is purely religious and non-ethical. Similarly Thyatira, only more explicitly; her sole sin is this same compromise with paganism in the person of that woman Jezebel, and from this alone she had failed to repent. Sardis meets with sharp reproof, and is summoned sternly to repentance. It is not said specifically for what; still, the inference is sure that it was religious defilement, some infection of false worship; for it is said, "Thou hast a few names in Sardis which did not defile their garments" (iii, 4). Laodicea is fiercely rebuked—why? Plainly and solely for want of zeal in the crusade against polytheism. The Church had become secularised; in the sharp issue between the many and the one it did not take sides uncompromisingly—it was neither cold nor hot. Hence it, too, is exhorted to be "zealous, therefore, and repent." There is no reason to doubt that the reference of the term in question is purely religious, as elsewhere.

Once more, in ix, 20, 21, we find "the rest repented not of the works of their hands, that they should not worship devils, and idols of gold......neither repented they of their murders, nor of their sorceries, nor of their fornication, nor of their thefts." Here the repentance is again in first line purely religious, a turning from false worship. Of the four additional specifications in verse 21, the second and third are also religious, the reference being to heathen service; while the first and fourth are either such veiled allusions or else allude to offences in some wise thought as connected with idolatry. The sufferers were only idolaters, "only such men as have not the seal of God on their foreheads" (ix, 4). Finally, in xvi, 9, 11, the case is particularly clear: "They blasphemed the name of the God......and repented not to give him glory......and blasphemed the God of heaven......and they repented not of their works." The latter phrase is the same as in ix, 20, where the works are defined as works of idolatry, and the object of repentance is implied to be giving God glory; hence the repentance can be nothing else than turning from heathenism. The testimony of Revelation is direct, unequivocal, decisive.

In 2 Cor. xii, 21, the Apostle speaks of many that "repented not of the uncleanness and fornication and lasciviousness which they committed." It seems plain that these severe terms here designate, as so often in the Scriptures, religious impurity — that is, some form of idolatrous deeds, some unfaithfulness to God. In Acts ii, 38; iii, 19, we have the ostensible first preaching, addressed apparently to Jews, with the exhortation, "Repent and be baptised," "Repent and turn"; but it has been shown in *Der vorchristliche Jesus* that all this is only part of Luke's scheme to make the Christian movement issue solely from Jerusalem, against the facts in the case. The author has taken the exhortation to Gentiles and applied it to Jews. Notice also that they were to receive the *Holy Spirit*—naturally, when they renounced the *unclean spirits* (demon-gods) they had been serving. There is here, then, no real violation of the rule. In viii, 22, Simon is urged to "repent of this thy wickedness"; but this addendum to the earlier story cannot be received as historic, as already shown in *Der vorchristliche Jesus*. It is the beginning of that misrepresentation of Simon which extends throughout the Fathers, and particularly the Clementines.

In xvii, 30, Paul declares: "The times of ignorance therefore God overlooked; but now he commandeth men that they should all everywhere repent." The ignorance was ignorance concerning God, true religion, monotheism, as is plain from verse 29: "We ought not to think the Godhead is like unto gold," etc.; hence the repentance is certainly a turning away from idolatry. In Acts xxvi, 20, we find "that they should repent and turn to God, doing works worthy of repentance." This mandate can hardly mean aught else than to forsake idolatry and then worship God properly. We need not be surprised that the writer makes this call go forth to the Jews also, since we have repeatedly shown that the early Christians insisted that the Jews themselves were not true worshippers of God; indeed, the whole speech of Stephen is but an elaboration and historical illustration of this position, as comes clearly to light in vii, 51, 52, 53. Only from this standpoint is the speech intelligible.

In Luke the word "repent" occurs ten times. In x, 13, and xi, 32, the reference is clearly to the abandonment of idolatry; also it may well be the same in xiii, 3, 5, and also in xv, 7, 10. The sinner here is opposed to the just. This latter is none other than the Old Testament Ṣaddîq, he who fulfils the law, who worships God aright—" for the most part with reference to the divine law given to the Israelites; hence of the faithful pious Israelites in opposition to the backsliders " (Buhl)—transgressors, the wicked, etc., who, though not heathen, deported themselves as heathen in their irreligion. There is no reference to the inner moral life. In xvi, 30, in the Lazarus parable, it is again a question of religion, of accepting the Kingdom, the Jesus-cult; no question of ethics is involved. The remaining passage—xvii, 3, 4—is noteworthy. At first sight it seems merely a question of private neighbourly relations. But careful consideration shows this to be impossible. The preceding verses, 1, 2, show that the matter in hand is the stumblings of the "little ones"—*i.e.*, the Gentile converts. Such stumblings were, of course, very frequent, and the verses teach patience therewith. It was very hard for such a convert to give up at once all his pagan ways; often he would stumble and sin, fall back into heathenry; but as often, if he repented, he was to be forgiven and restored. The repentance is religious; it is the same return to true worship from false. And who is to forgive? Who is the "thou"? The individual Christian? Certainly not. It is the Christian community, the Christian consciousness. Wellhausen sees here, indeed, only the individual Christian, thus reducing the passage to unreason; but he recognises that in the parallel in Matthew (xviii, 6*f*, 15, 21 *f*) there is distinct reference to the congregation (*Gemeinde*).

The sycamine tree is hard to understand. The following suggestion is hazarded: In presence of the immense fact of polytheism and the weakness of human nature, involving the necessity of infinite patience and forbearance, the task of converting the world, of really establishing true worship, seemed almost hopeless. The faith even of the Apostles might waver. Nevertheless, the task would yet be accomplished. The sycamine tree of idolatry would yet be removed from earth, and cast into the sea along with the legion of demon-gods. It is not strange that the system of polytheism should be thus symbolised, since the Kingdom of God has elsewhere the mustard seed and plant for its emblem.[1]

But why a mulberry-tree rather than some other? The question is difficult, at present perhaps impossible, to answer. Unless we take this tree as a vague general symbol of firm wide-rootedness, like the live-oak of the Gulf Coast, we must have recourse to philology. The Syriac form is *Thûtha,* and the Mishnic name for mulberry is *Tûth.* One might think of the like-sounding but unlike-spelled *Taut* (Phœnician principle of the universe) and of the related Egyptian *Thoth;* possibly there might be a reference to the whole scheme of things to be revolutionised by the new faith. Also we find in Levy's *Wörterbuch,* II, 534) a queer citation under *Tothavah* (sojourner) : " Woe, woe, Tothavah expels the house-lord—*i.e.,* the idol is worshipped instead of God." The word might then conceal an allusion to the system of idolatry which the new faith, small now as a mustard seed, would yet uproot and destroy. The Evangelists were by no means incapable of such far-sought allusions ; but nothing more is suggested here than that some such, if far better, explanation will sooner or later make the matter clear.

It must not be forgotten that Luke makes mention (xix, 4) of another related tree, the sycomore, the Hebrew *shiqmah,* Aramæan (pl.) *shiqmin.* Hence the Greek συκάμινος (sycamine) seems to have come. The botanists assure us that the two trees are quite distinct, and the Syriac terms are not identical ; still, it seems not altogether certain that the Evangelist thought of the difference. In any case, it appears impossible not to recognise in Zacchæus—Zakkai = pure, innocent (Jah ?)—a symbol of the Jewish element that accepted the Jesus-cult.[2] Even Keim (*J. v. N.*, III, 47–50) recognises "the easy explicability of the later origin of the whole story, which Luke evidently took from his Ebionite Gospel." Whether now the sycomore be only an enlivening detail is

---

[1] *D*, agreeing with Syriac (Curetonian ; see Burkitt's version), inserts also the reference to mountain-moving (as in Matt. xvii, 20). Can it be that the mountain symbolises Mosaism (from Sinai), and the mulberry-tree polytheism, both to be removed by the new faith ?

[1] The case is not essentially altered if Cheyne be right, and Zakkai = Zacharjah (=Jah remembers) ; nay, even if the primitive Zikhri be a tribal name, for the question is about the popular understanding of the name, and not about a scientific etymology.

not easy, nor of much moment, to determine; but it might not seem too far-fetched to understand by this tree also the same pagan system, through which Zacchæus had indeed elevated himself, out from which, however, he comes by accepting the Jesus-cult (receiving the Jesus into his house).

Returning from this long digression, we observe that in six out of the seven uses of "repent" in Matthew and Mark the sense is that of turning from idols unto God; in the seventh only, the words of the Jesus are also ascribed to John. In view, then, of all the foregoing, we seem fully justified in questioning the propriety of this ascription. John seems, indeed, to have been an ascetic, and to have introduced a baptism symbolic of thorough purity; he may undoubtedly have called for a more rigorous religious and even moral life, to fit the people for the coming of the One, since it was a common idea that the Kingdom was delayed by the imperfect service of Israel. But it was still not the moral, but the religious, faultiness of Israel that postponed the advent. It was the "general view that Messiah cannot come until the people repent and perfectly fulfil the law. 'If all Israel would together repent for a whole day, the redemption by Messiah would ensue.' If Israel would only keep two Sabbaths properly, we should be immediately redeemed" (Schürer, *G. d. j. V.*, II, 11, § 29). Plainly, the sole question was one of perfect obedience, of religious service. One should here recall the words of Weber (*Jüdische Theologie*, 243): "From this point of view we perceive that sins were not regarded primarily, but only secondarily, as ethical actions." Even if the Baptist, reviving the methods of the old prophets, had cried out "Repent," he would have meant it in the old prophetic sense of "Turn ye" unto God and his pure service, away from the corruptions introduced by contact with paganism.

A few words seem necessary concerning the noun "repentance." A glance at any and all of the eight uses of the word in the Gospels (Matthew iii, 8, 11; Mark i, 4; Luke iii, 3, 8; v, 32; xv, 7; xxiv, 47) shows that they are all perfectly consistent with the meaning—conversion to true worship from false, to monotheism from polytheism. In Acts xi, 18, xx, 21, the sense here championed is strongly recommended as the only sense satisfactory; the use in xxvi, 20, consists thoroughly therewith; in xiii, 24, xix, 4, the reference is to John's baptism, of which enough has been said; in v, 31, the author speaks of God's giving "repentance to Israel and remission of sins," where the term seems to be used in the sense it bears in the old prophetic exhortations to Israel. In Romans ii, 4; 2 Timothy ii, 25; 2 Peter iii, 9, the sense here advocated is demanded. In 2 Cor. vii, 9 and 10, "Ye sorrowed unto repentance," and "Sorrow, according to God,[1] worketh repentance unto salvation." We know little or nothing of this incident; but it seems hard to believe that it did not involve some religious error on the part of the Church. We note, further, that their repentance was caused by their sorrow, and was by no means the sorrow itself, which seems to be marked by the phrase "according to God" as having distinct reference to religion. The natural conjecture would appear to be that part of the congregation had fallen back into some heathenish practices, for which they heartily grieved, from which they turned again to God.

In Heb. vi, 1, we meet with the marvellous exhortation: "Wherefore having put aside the word of the beginning of the Christ, let us be borne on to the completion, not laying down again foundation of repentance from dead works and of faith toward God." We are not concerned to unravel this enigma, but only to find out the sense of repentance. We notice that it stands in immediate connection with "faith toward God" ($\dot{\epsilon}\pi\dot{\iota}$ $\theta\epsilon\dot{o}\nu$). The instant suggestion is that the "dead works" are either heathen or semi-heathen forms of worship, such as Christians conceived even the Jewish rites and ceremonies, festivals, new moons, and the like, to be. Certain it is that there is no suggestion of anything ethical. In the sixth verse it is declared impossible to renew certain apostates[2] "unto repentance." Here there is no doubt whatever. Clearly the apostasy is from the true faith, from God, and the repentance is the return thereto. Unequivocal also is the next passage (xii, 17), where it is declared of Esau that "he found no place of repentance, though he sought it (the blessing) diligently with tears." Evidently

---

[1] κατὰ θεόν. [2] παραπεσόντας.

what he sought was restoration to divine favour, to the prerogatives of the chosen servant and worshipper of Jehovah, which he had surrendered to his younger brother. Whatever moral quality could possibly go with Esau's act belonged to his diligent search (for the blessing) with tears, which, however, was entirely unavailing. That it is relapse to some form of idolatry or false worship that the author has in mind is also made clear in verses 15, 16, by the terms "defiled," "polluted," "fornicator," all of which refer to heathenism, and by the quotation concerning the "root of bitterness," which refers to an idolatrous person corrupting the faithful by his presence and example, as is plain from Deut. xxix, 16–18, to which the writer plainly alludes.

CONCLUSION

This analysis has been tedious, but it was necessary, and apparently leaves no doubt that the prevailing and almost exclusive reference of repent and repentance is to conversion from some form of imperfect or idolatrous worship to the pure worship of the one "God in person of Christ." It seems probable that the primitive reference of sin, especially in the "putting or sending away of sins," was in New Testament usage always to the renunciation of idolatry, of errors of faith or practice. These were indeed conceived to draw along in their train all forms of vice, as is very clearly stated in Rom. i, 18–32, where the whole acrostic of iniquities is deduced from polytheism, from refusal to have God in knowledge (i, 28). This passage is highly instructive, and states the New Testament doctrine with more distinctness and emphasis than does any other. It seems impossible, after pondering it carefully, to question in any important feature the outcome of the foregoing investigation.

Such unexpected results derive great importance from the fact that they confirm in a striking and decisive manner the conclusion already reached (p. 46 *ff*) concerning the essence and sovereign virtue of the proto-Christian proclamation. If, as maintained, the primitive propaganda was directed primarily and consciously against the prevailing idolatry, if it was an organised revolt against polytheism, then, indeed,

CONCLUSION

its battle-cry must have been, or at least must have signified, "Change your minds," "Turn ye from gods to God"; then, indeed, "repentance from dead works and faith unto God" must have been "the word of the beginning of the Christ," the very basis of the new religion universal. The consequent here is indeed true, but does not in this reasoning formally imply the antecedent. On the other hand, if such actually was the battle-cry of the missionaries, and if such was its sense, if their call to repentance really meant "Abandon your idols and worship only the one living God" (the Jesus, who would thus save them from their *sins*, their *idolatries*), then, indeed, the vital content of their preaching could have been nothing else than the great truth of monotheism, and the aim of their crusade could have been naught but the redemption of mankind from "the polytheistic error," from "the bitter bondage of the tyrannising demons." Now, however, by entirely unrelated processes from entirely unrelated premises we have shown that here the antecedent is actually true; and from it the consequent follows of necessity. In other words, the necessary consequent of an antecedent already established (p. 46 *ff*) has itself been shown wholly independently to be an historic-literary fact; and this fact has been shown to carry with it the former antecedent as its own necessary consequence. It would be hard to supply, and unjust to require, a more stringent demonstration.

It should not pass unnoticed, since it supplements and confirms the foregoing, that the Hebrew word for *repent*, in the familiar and now almost exclusive sense of *regret* or *rue*, is the onomatopoetic *nāḥam,* to sigh, to groan. In the Old Testament it is used especially with Jehovah, now affirmatively, now negatively. Its New Testament equivalent, and indeed translation, is *metamélomai*, used five times (Matthew xxi, 30, 32; xxvii, 3; 2 Cor. vii, 8; Heb. vii, 21), quite distinct from *metánoia*.

PART VI.

"A CITY CALLED NAZARET"

PRELIMINARY

SINCE the appearance of the memoir on the *Meaning of the Epithet Nazorean,* the matter has been treated by many critics from many points of view. It is not the purpose of this work to review these treatments, though one or two observations thereon may be allowed.

It seems strange that Kampmeier should feel it necessary to call my attention to the elegy of Kalir (A.D. 900?), since my language as quoted, "for nearly a thousand years after Christ," shows clearly enough that the elegy was present in my mind at the time of writing—else why the round number, "nearly one thousand"? Samuel Klein (*Beiträge zur Geographie und Geschichte Galiläas*—1909) seeks to date the original of the catalogue between the years 135 and 300 of our era, with what success it is needless to discuss. That some "city called Nazaret" may have been known in Galilee some centuries after A.D. 1 would be hardly worth controverting.

In the *Protestantische Monatshefte* (xiv, 6, 208–213) Schwen argues at length over the "Epiphaniusstelle," declaring "the theological critics have here capitulated in part." His main thesis is that "Nazoree and Nazaree are in Epiphanius clearly distinguished." Few are likely to find his proofs satisfactory. The mere fact that the spelling varies from MS. to MS. at nearly every appearance of the word, that Mark x, 47, presents seven, and Luke xxiv, 19, even eight forms, among them ναζωραιος, ναζοραιος, ναζαραιος, combined with the fact that the Semitic sibilant Sadhe (in Naṣarja, Noṣri, Naṣrat) is commonly rendered by σ and not by ζ, shows clearly both that the forms are all equivalent, and that νασαραιος is the more primitive and more nearly correct. Even, then, if we should (though we do not) admit Schwen's "Hauptaufstellung," nothing would be gained for the cause he would rescue. It would only be Epiphanius who sought to make a distinction where there was no difference. It was natural that he should strive hard to do so; but it would be very unwise for us to mistake his efforts for success. In spite of all the adverse learning that has been brought to bear upon the central positions of the original article—that the sect of the Nazarees was pre-Christian, and that their name is derived not from a city called Nazareth, but from the Semitic stem N-Ṣ-R (to guard)—these positions remain as yet unshaken, and indeed not seriously assailed.[1]

NEW TESTAMENT USE OF "CALLED"

Reserving, then, the right to enter into further details of criticism, if at any time it should seem worth while, we now strike into an entirely different path of research, and without any foreboding at the start as to whither it will lead us. The observation may possibly be not without importance that Matthew does not say (ii, 23) Nazareth or a city Nazaret, but a "city called Nazaret."[2] The phrase sounds innocent

---

[1] Such, indeed, is the recent judgment of Bousset (*Theol. Rundschau*, October, 1911): "The theological attempts to explain this remarkable state of case [in Epiph.] must thus far be accounted failures"—he mentions by name Wernle, Schwen, Schmiedel, Schmidtke. At the proper time and place it may not be hard to show that his own attempt is scarcely more successful, labouring under the grave burden of a superfetation of hypotheses. It is still more interesting to note further that in the same leading article Bousset seems to surrender Nazareth as the source of the names Nazaree, Nazoree, and, indeed, the "city" itself as a geographic reality (p. 381). One admires the candour of the critic, but wonders, after this "capitulation in part," what there remains for the historicist to defend? If Nazaree be not from Nazareth, if this latter be imaginary, then can anyone doubt that Nazaree is a religious designation, that it is in some wise, no matter how, related to the Hebrew stem N-S-R (to guard), and that Nazareth itself is most probably derived therefrom? These momentous and immediate consequences have been clearly foreseen by the Liberals in general, hence the exceeding fierceness with which they have defended the citadel that Bousset has now surrendered. They have rightly felt that the fall of Nazareth is the fall of historicism itself. It remains to add that Winckler entertains no doubt that "From the concept neçer is named the religion of those that believe on the 'Saviour'—Nazarene Christians and Nosairier"—precisely as I have contended. See my note in *Das freie Wort*, July, 1911, pp. 266-8.

[2] πόλιν λεγομένην Ναζαρέτ.

enough and accords perfectly with Greek usage, and yet may well give us pause. This participle "called"[1] is applied elsewhere in the New Testament four times to cities: "A city called Nain" (Luke vii, 11), "A city called Bethsaida" (Luke ix, 10), "A city of Samaria called Sychar" (John iv, 5), "Into Ephraim called city" (John xi, 54). The point is that all these names are suspicious or peculiar. Of Nain the best criticism feels very uncertain. The Nain of Josephus (*B. J.*, iv, 9, 4*f*) does not suit, being near Edom; whereas Luke's Nain should be near Shunem. Since the Lucan story is clearly a symbolism modelled on 1 Kings xvii, 8–24, the suggestion lies very nigh that Nain is for Naim, mentioned in the Midrash (*Ber. rabba*, 98, on Gen. xlix, 15), and this a mere disguise (of the Evangelist's) for Shunem. So Cheyne, *E. B.*, 3263. Nestle (*Phil. Sac.*, 20) most ingeniously suggests that "Nain" transliterated back into נחים might mean "the awakened," in which case it would clearly be merely a symbolic name made to fit the miracle.

Coming now to Bethsaida, we find that this was the old name for a city rebuilt, enlarged, and renamed *Julias*; so that Bethsaida was not the real name in use at the time of the composition of the Gospel.

Concerning the city called "Sychar" the wisest know nothing, and into the circle of eternal strife about it we need not enter. Critics incline to identify it with Sychem, thinking the Evangelist may have arbitrarily changed the name for some hidden reason; he may, so to speak, have given the place this name. Enough that Sychar is elsewhere unknown, and takes its place along with Ephraim, Ænon, Salim, and the rest, as a "somewhat improbable place-name" (Cheyne, *E. B.*, 4829) of the Fourth Gospel.

The case of Ephraim is not quite parallel; the form of words is not quite the same, as the reader has observed. However, in view of the general character of the Fourth Gospel, it seems highly probable even to Keim (following in the wake of Späth) that the name is here symbolic, not meant really to designate any special city: "In fact, it is a near-lying idea to regard it as representative of the rejected, but

---

[1] λεγομεν—; in Luke, καλουμεν—.

finally redeemed (Hos. i, 11), land of the Ten Tribes and the Samaritans. *Cf.* i, 590: Messias filius Ephraim (iii, 8n)." It seems, then, that in all these cases the word "said" (λεγομένη) most probably denotes an epithet applied, it may be, by the writer himself; so that it might without violence be rendered "so-called," or even "which we may call."

This probability seems greatly heightened when we consider other similar uses in the New Testament. Of these there are about twenty-seven, such as: "Jesus the so-called Christ" (Matthew i, 16; xxvii, 17, 22); "Simon the so-called Peter" (Matthew iv, 18; x, 2); "Matthew so-called" (Matthew ix, 9), supposed to be named Levi (Luke v, 27); "the so-called Judas Iscariot" (Matthew xxvi, 14); "prisoner famous called Barabbas" (Matthew xxvii, 16); "place called Golgotha, which is Skull's Place so-called" (Matthew xxvii, 33); "the so-called Barabbas" (Mark xv, 7); "the feast of unleavened bread the so-called passover" (Luke xxii, 1); "the so-called Judas" (Luke xxii, 47); "Messias comes, the so-called Christ" (John iv, 25); "a pool the so-called [in Hebrew] Bethzatha," or "the surnamed," ἐπιλεγομένη (John v, 2); "the man the so-called Jesus" (John ix, 11); "Thomas the so-called Didymus" (John xi, 16; xx, 24; xxi, 2); "at a place called Lithostroton, but in Hebrew Gabbatha" (John xix, 13); "the so-called Skull's Place, which is called in Hebrew Golgotha" (John xix, 17); "A gate of the temple, the so-called Beautiful" (Acts iii, 2); "Synagogue so-called of the Libertines," or "of the so-called Libertines" (Acts vi, 9); "for even if there are so-called gods" (1 Cor. viii, 5); "Those called uncircumcision by the so-called circumcision" (Eph. ii, 11); "Exalting himself against every so-called god or object worshipped" (2 Thess. ii, 4); "tent the so-called Holy of Holies" (Heb. ix, 3). Add "the high-priest the so-called Caiaphas" (Matthew xxvi, 3) and "place called Gethsemane" (Matthew xxvi, 36), where the parallel in Mark xiv, 32, is peculiar—"place of which the name is Gethsemane,"—and "Jesus, the so-called Justus" (Col. iv, 11). There remain only five or six cases in which a similar phrase is used, as "which is called"; but these need not detain us.

We note that in all these cases the word "called" is used to introduce a name either additional or in some way peculiar, so that it might be rendered "surnamed." The enumeration is exhaustive for New Testament usage[1]; and if there be any such thing as reasoning from complete induction, we must admit that Matthew, in writing "city called Nazaret," seems to betray a consciousness that he is using this name epithetically, or at least in some way peculiarly. He seems to be saying, "a city that for the purposes of my representation may be called Nazaret." Why? In order to explain the term Nazoræus!

Some of these cases will well repay further examination. As to the place called Gethsemane—*i.e.*, "Wine-press of Olives"—no one knows anything whatever about it, and its topographic reality appears highly problematic. The conjecture seems to lie close at hand that the name is purely symbolical, suggested by the famous passage in Isaiah: "Thy garments like him that treadeth in the wine-fat" (*Gath*). This latter term means wine-press, and apparently never anything but wine-press.[2] The combination Gath-shemani (wine-press of oil or olives) is singular, and seems very unlikely as the name of a place. But why may it not mean simply "wine-press of Olivet"? As Wellhausen well remarks, the word is not Aramaic, but Hebrew. Such a name must have descended through centuries, if it was a name at all. This it would hardly have done had it not designated some place of importance; and in that case we should probably have heard of it. It is very unlikely, then, that there was any place named *Wine-press of Olives*. The symbolism seems perfectly obvious. The wine-press is that of Isaiah (lxiii, 2)—the wine-press of divine suffering. This explanation seems so perfectly satisfying in every way that it appears gratuitous to look further. That the Evangelist was thinking of Isaiah seems clear from his separating the Jesus at this point from his disciples: "I have trodden the wine-trough *alone*, and of the peoples there was *no man with me*";

---

[1] It has not seemed necessary to consider in general the kindred use of καλουμεν—.

[2] To be sure, a wine-press might be used for various purposes (as in Judges vi, 11); and the word *gath* may sometime have been used inaccurately for the word *bad(â)*, which regularly means *olive-press*, as in *Pea.* vii, 1, where *gath* "certainly means an olive-press." Elsewhere, however, the difference between the two words, as between the two things, seems to be observed consistently.

and (the later?) Luke adds: "There appeared to him an angel from heaven, strengthening him"—not human, but divine, help was needed. Herewith is explained also the "impremonition" of the disciples, which Wellhausen finds so puzzling and inconsistent (*Ev. Matth.*, p. 139). The whole scene is designed to *pathetise* the idea of a suffering God, and at the same time to fulfil the words of the prophet in a far higher than the prophet's sense. There was need thus to import pathos, for the notion of suffering was naturally so foreign to the idea of God, though native to the idea of man, that the representation ran the risk of appearing unreal, a transparent make-believe. Hence the increasing care with which each succeeding evangelist elaborates the details of the wondrous picture—with sublime success.

Of course, some one will say that the Isaian divine warrior is triumphing over his enemies, that his garments are red with *their* blood; whereas in the Gospels it is the Jesus that is suffering, and his garments are stained with his own blood (Luke xxii, 44). Very true, indeed. The idea of the wine-press has been taken over, but not merely taken over; it has been Christianised in transit. Vengeance has been turned into self-sacrifice. There is nothing strange in this. It is the habit of the New Testament writer to seize upon an idea or phrase of the Old Testament, and transform it to suit his own purpose. In this case the transformation is precisely what we might expect. Can any one fail to perceive the delicate and beautiful suggestion in the combination, "wine-press of olives"? In Isaiah it was the wine of wrath and vengeance that gushed out from under the press; not so in the Gospels. There it is still the wine-press (Gath) of the prophet; but it is the oil of healing and salvation that flows gently forth for all the nations.

In regard to the "pool the so-called (in Hebrew) Bethzatha" (John v, 2), the case appears clear as day. That the whole story is a transparent symbolism seems too plain for argument. Our modern editors have cut out verse 4, following venerable manuscripts, but forsaking common sense. For manifestly some such verse is absolutely necessary to give semblance to the whole story, and is indispensably implied in verse 7. But the early copyists of ℵ, B, C, D, and others, as well as many translators, seem to have had no relish for the angel of verse 4, and accordingly left it out, though Tertullian (*De Bapt.*, 5) declares the "intervening angel used to disturb the pool Bethsaida," which carries the attestation of the idea of the verse back to the second century, far behind any Gospel manuscript.

That this pool symbolises (Jewish) baptism or outward purification is clearly seen in the Sinaitic Syriac palimpsest, which renders it in verse 7 by (a word meaning) *baptism*. Verse 2 is lost from this ancient manuscript, but the Curetonian has *place of baptism*. The cripple of thirty-eight years is evidently Humanity, that had been waiting just thirty-eight centuries for the coming of the Jesus-cult to heal it. The symbol sets forth vividly the impotence of the ethnic Jewish religion of rites, ceremonies, purifications, and the omnipotence of the spiritual religion, the new doctrine of the Jesus. On the details of interpretation we do not insist. But either the whole account must be accepted as fact, as history, or else it must be interpreted symbolically. Now, if any man really interprets it as historic fact, we have no quarrel with him, but neither have we any discussion; he is beyond the pale of our argument. On the other hand, if we understand it as symbolism, then there was no such topographic pool and no such name therefor; the name "Bethesda" becomes a part of the symbolism, and the word λεγόμενον has the sense we have found to be uniform in the Gospel. Besides, it is a matter of common knowledge that no such pool is elsewhere mentioned, or is anywhere discoverable in Jerusalem. Says Godet, who, naturally, accepts the story literally, rejecting verse 4 : " Comme il est impossible d'identifier la piscine de Béthésda avec l'une des sources thermales dont nous venons de parler, elle doit avoir été recouverte par les décombres, etc."!

Let us now pass to the "place called Lithostroton, but in Hebrew Gabbatha" (John xix, 13). However, we need not tarry there long. It is well known that all attempts in all ages, even by the most ingenious and erudite and sympathetic scholars, to locate this "stone-strewn" spot have failed utterly. Now at last it has become clear that they have all the while been seeking in the wrong region, in Jerusalem, whereas the "pavement" glittered only in the fancy of the Evangelist. It may suffice to refer to the "conclusion" of Canney in the *Encyclopædia Biblica*, 3640 : " It seems not unlikely, therefore, that the place Lithostroton-Gabbatha existed, as a definite locality, only in the mind of the author." The Greek and Hebrew words were hardly mere conceits. The author had some reason for preferring them to others— reasons that we may or may not be able to discover. That he gave the place any name at all was merely a part of his general scheme of vivid dramatic representation, by means of well-imagined details.

Only a few steps further on we come to "the so-called Skull's Place, which is called in Hebrew Golgotha" (John xix, 17). Surely these two "places" are nearly related. Why should one be taken and the other left? The search for Golgotha has been quite as futile as for Gabbatha. But the surrender of the latter did not seem to involve such serious consequences ; hence it has been more readily made. However, the reasons are the same. There is not the slightest ground for retaining either as a chorographic entity. Matthew, in fact, hints distinctly that the name "Golgotha" is a creation, by translating it into Greek (xxvii, 33).

On the other examples it seems needless to dwell. The "so-called" names seem to be all secondary or surnames or nicknames given for this reason or for that. Thus, "the high-priest the so-called Caiaphas" was really named Joseph, as we learn from Josephus (*Ant.*, 18, 2, 2,[1] and *Ant.*, 18, 4, 3[2]). "The so-called Judas" was merely Judæus, the Jewish people.

It appears, then, that the epithet "so-called" (λεγομεν-) prefixed to a name in Gospel usage uniformly implies that such is *not* the proper name, but is a surname or nickname, or it may be merely a fictive name for a mere imagination. In no case does it appear to be the real name of a real thing. Such at least is the induction made with all care up to the "city so-called Nazaret." In every one of thirty-one cases such is the result. What, then, shall we say of the thirty-

---

[1] Ἰώσηπος ὁ καὶ Καϊάφας διάδοχος ἦν αὐτῷ.
[2] Ἰώσηπον τὸν καὶ Καϊάφαν ἐπικαλούμενον—Joseph him also surnamed Caiaphas.

second case, the case of Nazaret? We need not invoke the calculus of probabilities.[1] Common-sense demands imperiously that the one and only authenticated sense be given to the term here, *unless* some positive and decisive counter reason can be given for the other sense. Everyone knows that no such opposing reason has ever been either discovered or invented; on the contrary, very strong and wholly independent reasons have been assigned (in *Der vorchristliche Jesus*) for regarding the name as invented to explain the much older appellative Nazaræus, and not one of these has yet been invalidated.[2] If, then, there is any virtue whatever in complete induction, the case seems closed against Nazaret as a proper name of a "city so-called."

Let no one cite the fact that Nazareth occurs eleven times without the qualifying "so-called." A hundred negative instances would weigh naught against the one positive instance. So, too, the high-priest is eight times simply "Caiaphas," and only once the "so-called Caiaphas." The surname may very well be used without the participle, as the officer may appear without his badge; but the presence of the participle in a single case defines the surname, as the badge once worn defines the officer. It is superfluous, then, to examine the eleven cases any further, though such examination would strongly corroborate our contention.

CONCLUSION

Now at last we are prepared to answer the objection brought forward so exultantly by Weinel and Weiss, to

---

[1] This is indeed a special case of a very important general problem: There are n balls in a bag, all known to be either white or black. There are drawn out at random w white balls and b black ones, and none is replaced. What is the chance that the next ball drawn out at random will be white? The answer is $\frac{w+1}{w+b+2}$. If, in the special case in hand, w equals 31 and b equals zero, the answer will be 32/33. Hence there would be only one chance in 33 that Nazaret is used in Matt. ii, 23, as the ordinary name; there would be 32 chances in 33 that it was used as some kind of a surname, nickname, or fictive name, as in the other cases examined. The probability might, indeed, seem far higher than this calculation would show it to be; for it has not been considered that the 31 cases out of 32 indicate strongly that such is the uniform usage of the writer; that there can really be no black balls at all. But the result given is sufficient for the purposes of this argument. We do not grudge our opponents their three per cent. of probability.

[2] See note, p. 292.

mention no others, that no one would have written Matthew ii, 23, "He settled in a city so-called Nazareth," when any Galilean could at once have objected, "There is no such city." So, too, the Judæan might have protested that there was no such place as Gabbatha or Golgotha or Gethsemane, and no such pool as Bethzatha. But Matthew and John would have cared for none of these objections, no more than any poet or novelist would care for a charge of nominal inaccuracy brought against his imaginations. Why might not imaginary parents of an imaginary child settle in an imaginary town? Neither would Matthew or Luke have been moved greatly by the easy demonstration that there was no slaughter of babes in Bethlehem, and no transmigration of peoples at census-taking; on the contrary, that they were commanded to *stay at home*, each at his own hearth-stone;[1] and still more that there was no "darkness over the whole earth until the ninth hour" "from the sixth hour." This latter statement, in all the Synoptics, was the directest possible slap in the face of all experience, if accepted literally; how, then, could the Evangelists have exposed themselves to such a stunning rejoinder as Weinel and Weiss would have given them? What could they have replied to such keen-witted critics? They would have smiled wearily, and said: "Gentlemen, alas! that you do not understand. The letter killeth, the spirit maketh alive. We are not writing history; we are writing Gospel. We are very sorry you do not see our meaning; but if our Gospel be hid, it is hid to them that are lost" (2 Cor. iv, 3).

No! we must never forget that the Scriptures were written for believers, and *not* for unbelievers; for those within, and not for "those without." Such readers, "discipled for the Kingdom of the heavens," might be trusted to "understand all parables." They would not balk at eclipses at impossible seasons, whether they lasted three minutes or three hours; they would not stumble over any number of imaginary topographic and other details, nor over patent anachronisms and absurdities, nor over miraculous narratives galore. For

---

[1] ἐπανελθεῖν εἰς τὰ ἑαυτῶν ἐφέστια—edict of Gaius Vibius Maximus, on occasion of census-taking in Egypt, A.D. 104.

their well-informed sense, even over-instructed to take nothing literally, would in every case pierce through the thin shell of speech down to the inner kernel of meaning ; the god of this world had not blinded their thoughts so that the light of the Gospel should not shine through into their hearts. A thousand such objections as this of Weinel and Weiss might, indeed, have been urged, and actually have been urged repeatedly, by the blinded unbelievers, who see the sign and mistake it for the signified ; but they are senseless and impossible for us after He " has shined in our hearts unto illumination of the glorious Gnosis of God."

PART VII.

(I)SCARIOT(H)=SURRENDERER

FORM AND MEANING OF THE WORD

THAT there is a weird fascination in evil would seem to be illustrated in the perennial interest that blooms around the name of Judas Iscariot. With the ancients it is the synonym of sin; with Dante "that soul up there that suffers heavier sentence" is the eponym of the lowest circlet of Cocytus, at the apex of the funnel of hell, champed by the central jaws of Satan, at the absolute zero of the divine warmth of the world. Each new commentary, each new "Life (?) of Jesus," has its fine-spun theory of the motives that actuated the great sinner, just as the ancients regaled themselves each with his own fancy concerning the sinner's death. These fancies and theories seem one and all to have about equal worth—namely, none at all. Illustrious scholars, whom it is mercy not to name, have strained the powers of rhetoric in description and denunciation of the appalling iniquity of the Treasurer of the Twelve Apostles, lashing themselves into foam over the utterly passionless and indifferent words of the Synoptics. None of this sound and fury should detain the sober-minded critic a moment; but the questions remain perplexing and important: Who was Judas? What means (I)Skariot(h)? It is the last of these that must be treated first. After all that has been written on the subject, it seems surprising how little appears sure or even highly probable. The form of the name, occurring ten or eleven times, is itself most uncertain. In Matthew x, 4, it is "Judas the Iskariotes," but in xxvi, 14, the article is omitted. In Mark iii, 19; xiv, 10, it is "Judas Iskarioth"; but in xiv, 43, "Judas (the Iskariotes)," where the authorities for and against the parenthesis seem nearly balanced. In

Luke vi, 16, we read "Judas Iskarioth"; but in xxii, 3, "Judas the (so-) called Iskariotes." In John vi, 71, and xiii, 26, we read "Judas, (son) of Simon Iskariotes"; but in xii, 4, "Judas the Iskariotes," and in xiii, 2, "Judas, Simon's (son) Iskariotes." Six times we find the suffix "who delivered him up" (*never* "who betrayed him"), once along with "the Iskariotes," Matthew x, 4. Seven times we read "one of the twelve," once "one of His disciples." Altogether this "Judas" meets us twenty-two times, besides John xiv, 22, where we find "Judas, *not* the Iskariotes." The textual variants are countless. Among the more important is the reading "from Karyotes" (απο καρυωτου) in א, and others at John vi, 71; also the same in *D* at John xii, 4; xiii, 2, 26, and (with the article ὁ prefixed) in xiv, 22; also the form "Skarioth" in *D* at Mark iii, 19; Luke vi, 16; John vi, 71; also "Scariotes" in *D* at Matthew x, 4; xxvi, 14; Mark xiv, 10. This *D* is so highly esteemed by great text critics, such as Volkmar, Zahn, Nestle, that they consider its strange reading απο καρυωτου as the original and even the only original reading in John (which Tischendorf also admits as possible), and as confirming the translation of Iskarioth as "Man of Kerioth," as if from the Hebrew '*ish q'riyyôth*, and this derivation may be called the accepted one. Holtzmann, *e.g.*, says in *Hand-Commentar*, i, p. 97: "Iskarioth=the man from Kariot in Juda, Josh. xv, 25." This interpretation, however, is encountered by every kind of improbability. Dalman rejects it (*Die Worte Jesu*, pp. 41, 42), recognising *Iskarioth* as the "original" form "unintelligible to the Gospel writer himself." His subtle philological reasons may be passed over. The more significant facts seem to be that the *q'riyyôth* of Josh. xv, 25, is not a city or town at all, but is the plural of the dialectic form *qiryath* (city), and refers to a "group of places" (Cheyne) in a district Hezron not really belonging to Judah, the Revised Version reading correctly Qerioth-Hesron; while the Qerioth of Jer. xlviii, 24, 41, Am. ii, 2, belonged to Moab. Keim (*Jesus von Nazara*, ii, 225, *n.* 2), though regarding the meaning "Man of Karioth" as certain, saw the improbability of these Qerioths, and accordingly discovered in Josephus a third, now called Kuriut—namely, Koreæ (*B. J.*, i, 6, 5; *A.*, xiv, 3, 4), or

FORM AND MEANING OF THE WORD

Korea (*B. J.*, iv, 8, 1), in the north of Judah; but few or none seem to have followed him in this identification. Wellhausen (*Ev. Marci*, p. 25) clearly sees the impossibility "of thinking of the Hebrew *'îsh* and translating 'Man of Karioth,'" and, rejecting the notion that it is a gentilitial, wisely inclines to regard it as "a name of reproach like Bandit (*Sicarius*)." Moreover, it must be remembered that the Syriac form (*Skariota*) militates strongly against the identification with the Hebrew איש קריות. For this Syriac form written in Hebrew letters is סכר (יו) טא in both Sinaitic and Peshita, with occasional variants in other less important MS. It is seen that the Syriac has ס, not ש, and כ, not ק—divergences by no means inconsiderable. Of course, it may be plausibly said that the Syriac has merely transliterated the Greek, as in many other cases—*e.g.*, *estratiota* from *stratiotes* (soldier). But the Syriac form presupposes the absence of the initial *I* from the Greek. True, the Syriac cannot let the word begin with a vowel; however, it would not drop the *I*, but would prefix an Alaf א, as in the transliteration of Akylas, Euodia, Iconium, Olympas, Italia, Hymenius, and countless others, or else a Yod (י), as in Italica (Acts x, 1).[1] For every reason, then, we must reject the accepted interpretation "man of Karioth" as impossible, and at the same time the notion that the term is a gentilitial at all. Moreover, it seems quite impossible to bring the name Iskariot into any connection with the venerable and wide-spread stem שכר, meaning *drink*, or with any place-name whatever.

At this point, then, the idea of the Hon. Willis Brewer (*The Open Court*, August, 1909) that the name is connected with the Hebrew root S-K-R, and means *hired*, deserves serious consideration. This root occurs often in the Old Testament—about forty-seven times—always in the same sense of *hire*, *wages*, *reward*, *price*. In all these cases the Hebrew letters are שכר, whence the common Aramæan terms for *wage* (*sekhîroth*) and *wage-earner* (*sakhîr*); but in one case (Ezra iv, 5) the later form סכר is used, agreeing exactly with the Syriac *skar-iota*. That Judas should be called the

---

[1] Of course, Arimathæa is no exception, since the A seems to represent the Ha in the Hebraic Ha-Ramathaim.

x

hired sounds very plausible, especially in view of the use made by Matthew (xxvii, 9, 10) of the passage Zech. xi, 12, where *my price* (שכרי, *sekharî*) is twice mentioned. However, while admiring this suggestion, we must not adopt it hastily. For the older narrative (in Mark) makes no mention of this Old Testament passage. The name would seem, then, to have originated independently. Besides, the termination remains unexplained, though this is not so important, and one feels that an active rather than a passive sense is demanded.

But there is another root S-K-R (סכר) appearing in the Old Testament, and *once* in the exact sense which the New Testament seems to require. In Isaiah xix, 4, we read: "And *I will give over* Egypt into the hands of a cruel lord." It is true this stem regularly means "shut up," in Hebrew, Aramæan, and Syriac, and so may be rendered even here (Cheyne); it is also true that Ezek. xxx, 12—"I will *sell* the land into the hand of the wicked"—suggests that the ס may be a mistake for מ, *sikkarti* for *makharti*. But neither of these facts can affect the case, for the text was certainly read and understood in that day precisely as it is now. This is proved by the Septuagint, which renders the *sikkarti* by παραδώσω = *I will deliver up*. It is well known that this Greek verb παραδιδόναι does not mean to *betray*, but to *give up*, to *hand over*, to *deliver*, to *surrender*—like *forgive* in its absolute sense, as in Ben Jonson's line: "It shall, if you will; I *forgive* my right" (*Cynthia's Revels*, v, 2); and so it is rendered countless times everywhere in the New Testament, save in connection with Judas, where it is universally rendered *betray*. But *if the Evangelist had meant betray, he would have said it;* the Greek *prodidónai* was familiar and at hand, and is constantly used by ecclesiastical writers instead of the New Testament *paradidónai*. That *betray* was not meant, but *deliver*, is plain from the apparent avoidance of the notion *betray*. There were many occasions to speak of Judas as the *Traitor* (*prodotes*); but only in Luke vi, 16, is he so called, since there is no word *paradótes*, deliverer-up, *Ueberlieferer;* elsewhere a circumlocution is used, as "who delivered him up," etc. Furthermore, the Sinaitic Syriac version (*teste* Adalbert Merx) definitely terms him always the *Deliverer-up*, never the Betrayer, not even in Luke vi, 16, where alone the Greek does read *prodótes* (traitor).

At this point someone may take down Liddell and Scott, and read under παραδίδωμι : " Also with collat. notion of treachery, like προδιδόναι ; Lat. *prodere*, Xen., *Cyr.*, v, 4, 51 ; *Paus*., i, 2, 1." Now, undoubtedly, a man might surrender traitorously, even as he might kiss, or embrace, or write, or speak, or do many other things traitorously. But all this by no means implies that to kiss, to embrace, to write, to speak, ever means to betray. Accordingly, in none of the instances cited is it proper to render the word by *betray*. Whatever "collateral notion" of treachery may be present is to be found in the circumstances of the case, not in the word used, which still means simply "deliver up." In Xen., *Cyr*., it is stated that two strongholds under fear of Cyrus and persuasions of Gadatas were induced to give up their garrison (ἔπεισε παραδοῦναι τοὺς φυλάττοντας). Perhaps Gadatas did corrupt the authorities, but Xenophon has no interest in that fact; it would do no honour to Cyrus, and accordingly he is content to say they gave up the guards, with no further specification. He did not wish to say they betrayed the guards, else he would have said so; and Dindorf has correctly translated "perfectum est ut custodes dederent." In Pausanias's *Attika* we read that "at the entrance into the city there is a monument to the Amazon Antiope......that when Herakles laid siege to Themiskyra on the Thermodon, but was unable to take it, Antiope, enamoured of Theseus (who was warfaring with Herakles), delivered up the stronghold." Such was the story of the Troezenian Hegias; the Athenians told another. Doubtless the surrender in this case was traitorous enough. But there is nothing in the language to show it. Monuments are rarely erected to traitors; the story-teller was too gallant to blacken the memory of the Amazon, and hence he preferred to say she delivered up the stronghold. Now if someone says that the deed of Judas, however described, was quite as treacherous, the answer is that we have no interest in denying this assertion. We are not concerned with the moral quality of Iscariot's act, but only with the Evangelist's representation of the act; and without any palliation of his offence we must reaffirm that the Gospel everywhere represents it not as a betrayal, but merely as a surrender. It seems curious that the same word (he was delivered up) should be used of John the Baptist where there is no question of treachery, and yet no visible propriety in the term *deliver up*. Who surrendered him?—and why? It seems useless to conjecture. But however such questions may be answered, we may still say with perfect confidence that the Gospels everywhere represent Judas as the *Deliverer-up*, never as *Traitor*.

Now compare the words (I)Scariot(h) and *sikkarti* in their Hebrew and Syriac forms, one under the other:—

סכרתי
סכריוטא

Surely the resemblance is altogether too great to be accidental. It is still further increased almost to practical identity when we reflect that the form "Iskarioth," apparently the oldest, requires ת, instead of ט, and that the Syriac Alaf (א) is regularly used to vocalise, representing both ā and ē, and this long ē confounds with ī. However, on vocalisations, whether initial, medial, or final, one can lay no stress. The important point is that the epithet (I)Skariot and the Hebrew *sikkarti* (deliver up) are *nearly identical* in form. The immediate and unescapable inference is that (I)scariot(h) is only a very thinly disguised[1] form of the Hebrew, and simply means the *surrenderer;* so that the recurrent suffixes of the Greek text, "Who-also-delivered-him-up," "the deliverer-up," etc., are merely translations of the epithet (I)skariot(h), where the *kai* (also) in the Greek seems to re-echo the initial ו in the Hebrew. This seems to be as natural as possible—almost inevitable, for it can hardly be casual coincidence that the Greek suffixes yield the apparent meaning of the Semitic name. (I)skariot(h) is, then, precisely what Wellhausen felt it must be, a "Schimpfname," a sobriquet, an opprobrious nick-name—the most appropriate, and even unavoidable. We recall, finally, that in Isaiah

---

[1] Absolute identity is, of course, *not* to be sought for. The artist who first devised the name knew that the word in Isaiah (xix, 4) was a *verb*, and he designed to reproduce it in a *noun*-form not exactly but near enough to make the name a kind of riddle "vocal to the wise." One may suspect that he modelled the form Skariotes on Stratiotes, though there are other possibilities.

(xix, 4) the surrender is into the hands of a cruel lord, and in Ez. xxx, 12, the sale is into the hands of wicked men, echoes of which we seem to hear in the Gospel phrases, "into the hands of sinners" or "sinful men."—The possible claims of שקר (deception) in this connection, in spite of the phrase ממוג דשקר, need not be canvassed.

JUDAS=JUDÆUS

The second problem, of (I)scariot(h), would seem, then, to be solved, and, in fact, in a surprisingly satisfactory manner. But the question remains, "Who was Judas?" Against the view that he was a mere man, like Arnold or Burr, there lie the weightiest considerations. In the first place, the motive to surrender seems utterly lacking. The conceit that he wished to provoke Jesus to a display of miraculous power and an immediate establishment of the Kingdom is quite inadmissible, though championed by De Quincey and, *mirabile dictu*, by the *later* Volkmar (*Jesus Nazarenus*, p. 121). Suppose the plan had succeeded, what good would it have done Judas? Would Jesus have kept him in his place as treasurer after such treason? That Judas was a veritable devil from the start seems to be the most plausible explanation, and extreme orthodoxy might indeed maintain that he was chosen by Jesus because of his devilry, as an instrument towards the divinely appointed end. This would seem to be consistent enough, and orthodoxy shows itself here, as at so many other points, far superior in dialectic alertness to Liberalism, which is deplorably illogical, limping on both legs. But can any one seriously entertain such a notion? There is not the slightest hint of it in the Synoptics. These know nothing of Judas as a bad man. They say he "surrendered" Jesus to the authorities, nothing more. Even the money (a contemptible four-months' wages, according to Matthew) appears as a perfectly voluntary bonus in Mark's account, promised him after his proposal to the high-priests. But on this circumstance we lay no stress. It seems strange, however, that the Synoptics should have no word of condemnation for the surrenderer; still stranger that they should never assign any motive for the surrender, especially as they are very free with motives in general. Apparently they were no wiser than the moderns, and could find no explanation. Otherwise Luke would hardly have ascribed Iscarioth's conduct to the devil that had entered into him, which would seem to be a *dernier ressort*. John, according to his wont, goes much further, declaring that Judas was a thief, that the devil prompted him to the surrender, that Satan entered into him, who himself was a devil. All this we recognise at once as part of John's manner in working over the Synoptists. It seems even plainer from these imaginary reasons than from the discreeter silence of Matthew, and especially of Mark, that the Evangelists could imagine no plausible reason for the surrender. And yet the reason, had there been any, could scarcely have been kept so profound a secret. Moreover, even if it had not been discoverable, why were Matthew, and particularly Mark, so utterly indifferent thereto? Their fancies were lively; why did they not invent a reason? The only answer would seem to be that Mark at least felt that the matter was not one for the assignment of human motives; that it could not be understood in any such childish way.

If the surrender be contemplated from the side of the authorities, it is equally incomprehensible. What need had they of Judas and his kiss? None whatever. Undoubtedly they could have arrested Jesus at any time anywhere in broad daylight, in perfect safety. His disciples seem to have been unarmed or indisposed to much resistance, even if one did cut off an "earlet." He himself sits apparently alone and unnoticed, quietly watching the throng cast in contributions to the temple treasury. And what need to fear the people, who cried "Crucify him, crucify him"? Look at it, then, which way you will, the surrender appears unmotived, unnecessary, unintelligible. Moreover, it seems to have formed no part of the earliest tradition. In the Apocalypse (xxi, 14) the Twelve appear unbroken in array, as immovable foundations of the celestial city-wall; there is no hint of defection. "The Apostle," too, speaks of the Jesus as appearing to the Twelve, though it is possible that twelve might be used here technically, even if only eleven had been present. To be sure, he does refer to a surrender in the words, "the same night in which he was surrendered," but makes no allusion to the surrenderer. Some one may say such allusion was unnecessary. Perhaps; but on closer scrutiny we are astounded at the nature of the Apostle's statement: "For it is from the Lord that I received what I also delivered to you, that the Lord Jesus, etc." (ἐγὼ γὰρ παρέλαβον ἀπὸ τοῦ κυρίου, ὃ καὶ παρέδωκα ὑμῖν). Notice the emphatic position of the ἐγώ : Whatever others may say, "I received from the Lord," etc. Critics in despair may say that "from the Lord" means from the Jerusalem Church, the *Urgemeinde* of German imagination. But such a consummate Grecian as Georg Heinrici knows better, and plainly tells us (in Meyer's *Kommentar*, pp. 325 *f*) that there is no such reference. It is, indeed, plain that none of the Apostle's readers would think of understanding "I received from the Lord" as "I received from Peter or John"; it is only the bewildered modern commentator that could stumble on such an idea. The reference must be to some form of supernatural revelation. Hence it can at most testify to a subjective experience of the Apostle's, not to any tradition of the Twelve. Besides, the present writer seems to have proved decisively that *this passage is an interpolation in the Corinthian Epistle* (pp. 146 *ff*). As to the account (in Acts i) of the election of Matthias (of whom we never hear again) to the vacancy caused by the lapse of Judas, its late origin lies open to view in the statements about the field Akel-damach = field of sleeping = cemetery. The consciousness revealed is clearly impossible for one speaking of an event that could have occurred at the earliest less than two months before. The speech, then, has been composed by the historian ("for the Scriptures must needs be fulfilled") and placed in the mouth of Peter. We notice that Judas is here spoken of as a "guide."

We are unable, then, to find the notion of a man Judas as surrenderer in the earliest extra-evangelic forms of the Christian story; outside of the Gospels there is no real support of the statements that the Gospels themselves fail to make comprehensible. Now consider for a moment what it is that one can properly be said to surrender or deliver up. Surely nothing but what one has; surrender and delivery seem to imply previous possession. But in what possible sense could Judas be said ever to have possessed the Jesus? As a man, in none at all. Moreover, as the conduct of a man his surrender has been seen to be in every way unintelligible. But are we sure that he was a man? To my mind, he was surely not. Is it mere accident that *Judas* is so nearly *Judæus*? Or does he stand for Jewry, for the Jewish people? This seems to become a necessary hypothesis as soon as we perceive the impossibility of understanding Judas as a man. On this hypothesis everything becomes clear. The delivery was really to the Gentiles; the phrase, "They [the Jewish authorities] shall deliver him to the Gentiles," seems to belong to the earliest Gospel narrative (Matthew xx, 19; Mark x, 33; Luke xviii, 32), and to lay bare the heart of the whole matter. It is noteworthy that while in Matthew and Mark the surrender to the Jewish authorities is mentioned first, and afterwards the surrender to the Gentiles, in Luke this latter alone is mentioned. Luke certainly presents generally a younger form than Mark, but occasionally, it would seem, an older, which need not surprise us. I suspect that the oldest thought was of the surrender of the great Idea of the Jesus, of the Jesus-cult, by the Jews to the heathen. This, in fact, was *the supreme, the astounding, fact of early Christian history, and engaged intensely the minds of men.* It is not strange that it should find such manifold expression by parable and by symbol in the Gospels. The wonder would be if it had not. The story of Judas and his surrender seems to be the most dramatic treatment the great fact has anywhere received. Other less elaborate sketches are found in the parables of Dives and Lazarus, of the Prodigal Son, and of the Rich One who "with lowering look went away (from Jesus) sorrowful, for he had many possessions" (the Law, the Prophets, the Promises, the Oracles of God). That Israel is here meant becomes evident, if not already so, when we compare Mark x, 22, "But he with lowering look, at the word, went away grieving,"[1] with Isaiah lvii, 17, "And he was grieved, and went on with lowering look in his ways."[2]

---

[1] ὁ δὲ στυγνάσας ἐπὶ τῷ λόγῳ ἀπῆλθεν λυπούμενος.

[2] καὶ ἐλυπήθη καὶ ἐπορεύθη στυγνὸς ἐν ταῖς ὁδοῖς αὐτοῦ. In Kautzsch's *Text Bibel* (1904) we find the Hebrew translated (by Victor Ryssel) thus: "Then went he backsliding thence on self-chosen way." In the latest edition Budde

JUDAS = JUDÆUS

The prophet is describing God's dealing with Jacob, who is still his Beloved, though grieved for a brief season (βραχύ τι). The very rare Septuagint verb στυγνάζω shows that Mark is merely re-echoing Isaiah, although Dittmar does not note the parallel. There are enough other considerations that confirm this interpretation; but there is space to mention only one—namely, that the Jesus "loved" this Rich One. Now, this ascription of such a feeling to the Jesus is quite without parallel in Mark, whose picture of the Jesus is singularly devoid of human attributes—σπλαγχνίζομαι (used thrice of the Jesus) is an exception that strongly confirms the rule; it merely renders the Old Testament רחם, *constantly* and practically *exclusively* used of or in connection with *Jehovah*, exceptions being really confirmatory. The explanation is simple and near-lying. Says Jehovah (Hosea xi, 1): "When Israel was young, then I loved him." That Matthew (xix, 16-26) felt such to be the reference is hinted with exquisite art in the word νεανίσκος, which he applies to the Rich One, who, according to Mark, had kept all commands "from his youth," which must then have been behind him. But Matthew, as every one knows, was a literalist, setting great store by the exact words of the Scripture; and, observing that Israel was young when loved, he boldly turned Mark's One (εἷς) into a Youth (νεανίσκος). What other explanation can be offered for this "correction of Mark"?

Of course, it is easy to say that the symbolism of Judas (=Judæus) has not been carried out consistently. The surrender is made to the Jews themselves (high-priest and other dignitaries), who then deliver to the heathen. We answer that the symbol has come down to us only in a highly elaborated and historicised form; such elaboration must always do violence to the original idea. A symbol, no more than a metaphor, will bear pressing, though often pressed. A single point of even remote resemblance will suffice for any simile.

> Beholding whom, men think how fairer far
> Than all the steadfast stars the wandering star!

In a cool hour Mr. Lang would doubtless confess and deny

---

translates it thus: "And he went apostate, whither his heart drove him (*strictly*, on the way of his heart)."

not, and that, too, without prejudice to the great beauty of his verses, that the likeness of Lord Byron to any known member of our planetary system is extremely faint and elusive. The ways of the overworker are past finding out; it would be idle to attempt to trace the steps that have conducted to such a composite result as now lies before us in the Gospels. Yet even there the evidences of gradual evolution from Mark to John are open and manifest. Let us remember that even the former transports us not to the source, but only half-way up the stream. When we consider other parts of the evangelic narrative and note the rich harvests — thirty, sixty, a hundred-fold — that have been garnered from single seminal ideas, the development assumed in the present case seems scarcely excessive. But the interpretation of Judas here suggested is not presented as a finality nor as proved by the considerations advanced. It is part of a general system of New Testament exegesis; it stands or falls with the present writer's total conception of the genesis of Christianity, to which it lends, but from which in far greater measure it borrows, strength.

Not so, however, the decipherment of (I)scariot(h). This is a philologic matter, not by any means sharing the fate of any theory of Christian origins, but apparently solitary as Kant's Thing-in-Itself. But even it may nevertheless enter into relations. For the well-attested *D*-form, $απο καρυωτου$, must now appear as an early attempt to interpret the epithet Iskariot, the force of which was no longer felt. Hereby a strong sidelight is thrown on a seemingly similar attempt to interpret the far more important epithet, *Nazaraios*. It seems to be proved that this appellative was a very old one, antedating our era (see *Der vorchristliche Jesus*, ii); in fact, we find the name *Naṣiru* embedded in a list of tribes or classes on the clay tablet inscription of Tiglath-Pileser III. We may be sure that the name is not derived from Nazareth, but is a development from the familiar stem N-Ṣ-R, meaning *guard*, *protect*. However, in Matthew ii, 23, the term is deduced from Nazareth, which city, under various forms of the name, is thoroughly naturalised in our Gospels. Even in Mark i, 9, we read that "Jesus came from ($απὸ$) Nazareth of Galilee." This seems like a later addition to the narrative,

JUDAS = JUDÆUS 315

as indicated by the title Ἰησοῦς, used here without the article, but elsewhere regularly with it, in this Gospel.[1] Moreover, the text is uncertain; the reading εἰς for ἀπό may be older. In Matthew (xxi, 11) we find "the prophet Jesus ὁ ἀπὸ Ναζαρέθ," and the same Greek phrase also in John i, 45; Acts x, 38. We may now understand this phrase. It seems to be nothing but an attempt to explain *Nazoraios*, precisely as απο καρυωτου is an attempt to explain (*I*)*skariot*. As to Nazareth itself, of course it is there now, plain to see;[2] but in olden times it seems to have borne another name, Hinnaton, according to the testimony of the El-Amarna tablets and the Annals of Tiglath-Pileser III. Both words mean the same—namely, defence, protection; and we may now see how the "city called Nazareth" may have come into being. The new name Nazareth, meaning defence, was applied to the old town Hinnaton, meaning protection. Some perceived that this name would not yet yield the desired gentilitial Nazaree, and accordingly wrote it Nazara, the form preferred by Keim, but too weakly attested. It would seem, then, that the mystery surrounding these names is clearing up.

The passages in the tablets are, according to Winckler: In 11 (13-17), letter of Burraburiaš, King of Karduniaš, to Naphururia, King of Egypt: "Now my merchants, who journeyed with Aḫi-ṭâbu, and tarried in Kinaḫḫi on business: after Aḫi-ṭâbu went on his way to my brother, in city Ḫi-in-na-tu-ni of land Kinaḫḫi [i-na (âlu) Ḫi-in-na-tu-ni ša (mâtu) Ki-na-aḫ-ḫi, etc.]." Ki-na-aḫ-ḫi = Canaan. Further, 196 (24-32), in the continuation of a letter we find: "But Surata took Lapaja out of Magidda, and said to me, 'Upon a ship I will bring him to the king.' But Surata took him and sent him from (city) Ḫinatuni home [u ji-tar-šir-šu iš-tu (âlu) Ḫi-na-tu-na a-na bîti-šu]."

The inscription in the *Annals* (as edited by Paul Rost, 1893) reads: "1. 232 — — — [šal-lat] (âlu) Ḫi-na-tu-na, 650 šal-lat (âlu) Ḳa-na — — — — (captives) (city) Ḫi-na-tu-na, 650 captives (city) Ḳa-na — —." As the record is lost after Ḳa-na, we cannot be sure that Cana of Galilee is meant. If

---

[1] Vocatives and i, 1, x, 47, xvi, 6, naturally excepted.
[2] Yet Burkitt seems to think the modern has naught to do with the ancient village, which latter he would rather identify with Chorazin.

one should find a scrap of paper torn immediately after the letters *Adria*, one would not be sure that the reference was to Adria in Italy; it might be to Adrianople. But since Ḥinatuni was certainly in Canaan, the suggestion of Cana, six miles north of our Nazareth (= Ḥinatuni), appears to lie near at hand.

That Judas Iscariot typifies the Jewish people in its rejection of the Jesus-cult seems so obvious, it seems to meet us so close to the threshold of the inner sense of the New Testament, that it may move our wonder that any one should overlook it. However, the ablest, and even the boldest, the most lynx-eyed, critics have passed it by. In Cramer's *Catena* we find only inanities on the theme of Judas; he is no longer the Surrenderer, but the Traitor (*prodotes*)—*pro* has, indeed, quite displaced *para*—and his covetousness and general vileness wax page after page. At John xiii, 30, it is asked: "Why does the Evangelist say that it was night when Judas went out? To teach us how reckless he was, for not even the time (of day) could restrain his impulse." From such there is naught to hope. Bruno Bauer, of course, "resolved" the whole thing into a caustic curve, formed by reflections from the Old Testament. In this case he found the main surface of reflection in Psalm xli, 9: "Yea, mine familiar friend, in whom I trusted, which did eat of my bread, hath lifted up heel against me" (*Kritik der evangelischen Geschichte*, xiii, 85, 4). "Out of that Psalm-word the whole scene has arisen." But he does not seem to connect Judas with Jewry. Strauss discusses Judas at length (*Leben Jesu kritisch bearbeitet*, §§ 118, 119), but without throwing any light on the matter. Volkmar, who fixed his gaze so intently on the Gospels, and who saw deeper than any of his contemporaries (with the possible exception of Loman), in his great work *Marcus* (p. 555) declared that "for Mark, Judas, one of the Twelve, is the *symbol of the Judaism that slew the Christ, which in the first disciples was most closely united with Him till the end.*" Iskariot, however, he still regarded as historical and as "actually notorious as apostate." Upon him Mark seized as a fitting vehicle for his own idea of Judaism, and the fusion of the symbolic and historic yielded us Judas-Iskariot. Volkmar has no doubt that this last word means

"Man of Kerioth," and is rightly explained by *D*'s form, απο καρυωτου, in John. The great Züricher had wonderful insight. His *Marcus* (1875) is, indeed, a volume of visions; but it is almost unreadable, and was long since sealed with the seven seals of oblivion, which even Wrede could not loose. He himself shrank back half affrighted at what he saw, and in his swan song (*Jesus Nazarenus*, 1882) we seem to hear a palinode. Meantime his central critical thesis of the priority of Mark has become a commonplace of criticism, though the Logia-source, so diligently exploited by Matthew, might seem to boast justly still higher antiquity. Volkmar's notion that the Pauline Mark, by insistence on the phrase "One of the Twelve," means to hint that a certain element of the old Judaism clung to the last to "the primitive group of disciples," has, indeed, a certain plausibility; but it seems to assume a primitive group that never existed, to make this Gospel unnecessarily controversial, and to magnify a relatively insignificant matter, as did Baur's criticism in general, even in its later and most severely critical presentments.

ADDENDUM I.

In the *Hibbert Journal*, July (1911), p. 891, Professor Cheyne thinks the derivation of Skariot from *sikkarti* " might perhaps pass if *sikkarti* occurred in a passage like Psalm xli, 9, one of the stock-passages on which a pre-Christian scheme of the life of the God-man would be based. Otherwise not, etc."

The syllogism seems to be that no unfamiliar passage would be used by the artist in constructing "the scheme of the life, etc."; this (Isaiah xix, 4) is an unfamiliar passage, therefore it would not be so used—a very pretty Celarent, but for a limp in both legs. We have no right to suppose that passages unfamiliar to us were also unfamiliar to the men of one book, the intense religionists of the border centuries. The number of direct citations from the Old Testament in the New and in related works is very great, but the number of hints and oblique allusions to the Old Testament is far greater still. Dittmar's extremely compacted *Catalogue of Parallels*, containing only the numbers of chapters and verses, but no word of citation, covers sixty-four large pages, and yet makes no pretension to completeness. It would appear that the *whole* of the Old Testament was embraced in the collective religious consciousness of that era. While some passages might be called stock-passages, yet almost any passage, even in Nehemiah or Canticles or Esther, might at any moment be called into play. So much against the major premiss *de jure,* as Arnauld would say. But the minor is equally faulty *de facto*. For it happens that the immediately preceding verse (xix, 2) is actually exploited in the Gospels—Matthew xxiv, 7 ; Mark xiii, 8 ; Luke xxi, 10 ("Nation against nation, and kingdom against kingdom"); at least, so think Dittmar and others. There seem to be still other echoes in the New Testament, but on these we need not insist. It seems plain that the "Utterance of Egypt," whether Isaianic or not, is no unimportant part of the book of the Prophet, nor is there any reason for depreciating it or supposing it unfamiliar to the pre- and Proto-Christians.

Professor Cheyne wisely recognises that "Jesus of Nazareth was not betrayed or surrendered to the Jewish authorities, whether by 'Judas' or by any one else." Still further he declares : "The 'Twelve Apostles,' too, are to me as unhistorical as the seventy disciples." These things are nobly and bravely said.[1] But the illustrious critic still clings, not, indeed, it would seem, to any real, living, breathing, pulsing Jesus the man, but to the merest simulacrum, as empty of any value as the exuviæ of animals. The Jesus of orthodoxy is, indeed, a glorious being, although without scriptural or other warrant. The Jesus of Renan is also not inglorious, though no more historically and far less logically warranted. The Jesus of Cheyne and Loisy and Wellhausen

---

[1] It seems strange to add that "the surrender......cannot be separated from the end of the surrenderer; if the one is symbolical, so also ought to be the other." For the separation is actual in Mark, who says nothing of the "end" of Judas. Plainly the contradictory stories of his end (Matthew xxvii, 3–10, Acts i, 15–26) are much later fancies. That the Jews took no offence at the symbolism of which they "do not appear to have had any inkling," need move no one's wonder. Surely there was enough else "offensive" in the New Testament which they passed by in silence.

ADDENDUM I.

is not only precisely as unwarranted, but is also weak, miserable, and functionless, entirely superfluous on the stage of history, explaining absolutely nothing, but blocking every otherwise satisfactory explanation, an utterly unmanageable fifth wheel to the car of critico-historical theory. Why such scholars should insist on retaining such a factor after reducing its potency absolutely to zero is truly bewildering. The motive, whatever it may be, seems entirely illogical, and yet it can hardly be sentimental, for the simulacrum in question satisfies no emotional need; it is not especially lovable, not beautiful, not attractive, not impressive, not even particularly, much less uniquely, admirable.[1] Verily such a critic may exclaim: "Me miserable! Who shall deliver me from this body of death?"

Professor Cheyne thinks there is need for some general theory that shall "explain whole groups of similar names in the Old and New Testaments"—a consummation devoutly to be wished; and no man has ever lived more competent to frame one. He holds "that all the surnames of the Apostles in the Gospels come from *old* names of regions or districts with which the families of the bearers had been connected, and the true meaning of which had generally been long forgotten"—a most ingenious hypothesis; but in the nature of the case it would require a huge amount of well-sifted evidence to give it standing. Accordingly, "Iscariot, then, is a corruption of an old name, the full form of which was Ashhart, or, with the gentilic suffix, Ashhartai." One awaits with lively interest the production of the proofs which Professor Cheyne must have in reserve. Meantime, if the "Twelve Apostles" were unhistorical, were not the "bearers" of the surnames of the Apostles as well as their families equally unhistorical? And what, then, shall we think of the "regions or districts with which the families of the (imaginary) bearers had been connected"? One can hardly be sure in

---

[1] Nay, alas! the case is even worse, far worse. According to the "eschatological theory," now in full feather and favour, the latest cloud-form of critical "dust that rises up and is lightly laid again," the Jesus was nothing but an "ignorant enthusiast"—but one of many!—whose foolish teaching has conquered the intelligence of the alien Aryan race and shaped the civilisation of thousands of years! Such criticism must be thrice welcome in Ultramontaine circles, for it constitutes the *reductio ad absurdum* of Rationalism, a demonstration that he who runs may read and understand and never forget.

such matters, yet it might appear that ungeographical regions or districts were quite good enough for unhistorical Apostles. And when every other obstacle is overcome, how shall we explain the central fact that Skariot is so often declared gratuitously to be "the surrenderer," unless this be what Skariot really means? This is the coincidence that can hardly be accidental, and is explained by no other etymology of the name. One need not insist on the obvious fact that, if Iscariot be a corruption of Ashḥarti, it is a corruption sufficiently corrupt.

Professor Cheyne asks: "Need I remark that, in Hebrew, 'the guardian' would be *ha-noṣer*, not *ha-noṣri*?" Inasmuch as three pages of *Der vorchristliche Jesus* (47-50) are given to the consideration of this point, the answer would seem to be that one need not. But when it is said that "surely neither Hannathon nor Nazareth means *defence*," it must be replied that authorities seem to differ. Professor Cheyne refers to *Hannathon* and *Nazareth* in the *Encyclopædia Biblica*. One may read the nine lines on "Hannathon" and the interesting article on "Nazareth" repeatedly, without finding any reason for the statement just quoted. Professor Haupt declares: "Both Hittalon and Ḥinnathon mean protection"—a judgment, so far as Ḥinnatuni is concerned, confirmed by other most eminent Assyriologists. As to Nazareth, the force of the termination may be uncertain, *even as the termination itself is*, but hardly the stem *Nazar*, which appears in the older form *Nasar-aioi;* and about the Hebrew *Naṣar* (to guard) there is no doubt.

The interpretation given to the name of "the city called Nazareth" as "the place of shooting plants" does not convince at once by its inherent plausibility.

In the statements that "the name underlying Nazareth is clearly Reṣin (or Rezon)," that "the people transposed the letters to produce a more pleasing or obvious sense, and Nazareth (place of shooting plants) and Nazorai (Nazarene) were the results," we recognise the conjectures of a supreme scholar; but we do not forget that just such a scholar (Bentley) similarly conjectured that "darkness visible" should be read "transpicuous gloom," as producing "a more pleasing or obvious sense." It may be that Paris is but such an inversion of Serap(h), the people having transposed the letters to disguise the allusion to the ancient worship there of Serapis; but the judgment does not approve itself on bare statement. It may not be out of place to remark that Bousset now surrenders Nazareth as the original of Nazaree, and apparently also as a geographic entity. He looks with favour on Wellhausen's *second* view, that "*Gen* is the garden," and that Gen-nesar means *Garden* of Nesar or Galilee (though Cheyne himself corrects—after Buhl—the notion that Halévy, to whom Wellhausen appeals, says Nesar=Galilee). *Gan* is certainly *garden;* but why think it present in Ge-nesar, especially as Wellhausen himself has said that the "*Ge* is certainly גיא" (valley), quite unrelated to *Gan?* In fact, it is hard to keep up with the recent conjectures of Orientalists concerning Nazareth, for "thick and fast they come at last, And more and more and more." But they all seem ephemeral, for they overlook the central and vital fact that Nasaree was a *religious* term or designation; it expressed some religious peculiarity of the sect that bore it; and when the multiplied conceits of linguistic ingenuity are all finally laid to rest the obvious reference will be seen to be to the perfectly familiar and apparent Hebrew stem *naṣar* (to guard). As Winckler has so well expressed it: "From the concept *neçer* is named the religion of those who believe on the 'Saviour': Nazarene-Christians and Nosairier. Nazareth as the home of Jesus forms only a confirmation of his Saviour-nature, in the symbolising play of words." (See my note in *Das freie Wort*, July, 1911, p. 266.) The notions of Guardian and Saviour are so closely akin that *Servator* and *Salvator* are used almost interchangeably as applied to the Jesus.

ADDENDUM II.

In view of the great importance attaching to a correct interpretation of the incident of the Rich One, it may be well to look at the recital more narrowly than has been done already

(p. 98 *ff*), even at the cost of a certain amount of repetition. It is found in Mark x, 17-31; Matthew xix, 16-30; Luke xviii, 18-30. Observe in the first place that the incident takes place just as Jesus enters Judæa. The One comes running, and falls down on his knees (worshipping), and asks: "Master, what good shall I do that I may have life everlasting?" This seems to imply at the very least that the One knew well of the Jesus, and recognised in him a superhuman knowledge, a personality that called for *worship*. Now, this seems nearly impossible on any probable theory of the human Jesus. For he had not been in Judæa, and we can hardly believe that the fame of his deeds had so excited the imaginations of the most pious Judæans as to prompt such worship and such a question. We observe further that this One is suffering from no ailment. He seems to be in perfect health, he *runs*, whereas the Galileans were practically all invalids: "And followed him many, and he healed them all" (Matthew xii, 15). Neither does the Jesus find any leper or demoniac or other sick person in Judæa, save only blind beggar Bartimaios (son of Timaios). Why was this? Was not the salubrity of Galilee quite equal, if not indeed superior, to that of Judæa? Why do all maladies and miseries vanish, leaving only health and wealth behind, as soon as we cross the border of Judæa? There seems to be but one answer. The one disease that, under a "legion" of names, afflicted Galilee of the Gentiles was false worship, irreligion. On that alone did the Evangelist have his eye fixed; that alone was destroyed by the introduction of the Jesus-cult. But in Judæa, where the true worship prevailed, it was quite impossible there should be wrought any miracles in healing pagan error. None the less, there was blindness in Jewry, whether among the Jews proper or among the proselytes, neither of whom recognised the Jesus-cult when it came. Some of the humbler were healed of this blindness, and became his followers. Such seems to be, in general, the meaning of the miracle of Jericho, though as to details opinions may go wide asunder.

It seems hard to reason with any one who, as the learned Keim (*Jesus von Nazara*, iii, 53), thinks that "the reasons preponderate in favour of the historicity of this incident,"

ADDENDUM II.

and tries to rationalise it by piling up lofty phrases about the "*Wogen* and *Wallen* of the religious spirit," and "a trust which, with its tempestuous onset, could directly enhance the vital and neural energies of the body and restore the diseased or destroyed power of vision for a time or for ever." Such pages as 51–53 form very melancholy reading. That Blind Bartimaios is an emblem seems sure beyond all doubt. Witness the fact that Matthew does not hesitate to make two of the one, probably glancing at both worlds, the Gentile and the Jewish.[1] But what does he symbolise? That is not so clear. The obvious suggestion is the Jewish world, as indicated by the circumstances of time and place, by the "Rabbouni," and by the repeated cry, "Son of David." It seems strange, however, that the Jew should be typified by a beggar, sitting by the wayside. More likely, the *Gentile proselyte* to Judaism was in the writer's mind. He was, indeed, a beggar, sitting by the road that led to the true worship, to Jerusalem, on the outskirts, at the gateway of the Holy Land. Strabo (16, 2) speaks of the Egyptian-Arabic-Phenician amalgamation in Jericho. Herewith the only plausible interpretation of the name, as "Son of the Unclean" (Bar-timai), corresponds perfectly; but against such exposition the fact seems to weigh that "blind" and "unclean," though each highly appropriate to the Gentile, are nevertheless not germane and do not naturally combine. Putting aside the notion of certain lexicographers, upheld by Hitzig and adopted by Keim, that *timai=samia=*blind, like the Arabic *'amiya*, we have left only the supposition that Timaios is Greek, meaning *highly prized*—a name peculiarly fit for Israel. The Syriac text reads *Timai Bar Timai*, and we may justly suspect some text corruption. An Aramaic-Greek hybrid, Bar-timaios, is much more improbable as an historic than as an allegoric name. Origen seems to have felt that Timaios must be Greek, not Semitic, for he calls Bartimæus "the eponym of honour." Wellhausen, though inclined to regard the name as "a patronym," nevertheless subjoins: "Timai may be an abbreviation of Timotheus, as Tholmai of Ptolemæus." In

---

[1] Precisely as, with a similar side-glance at Jewry, he presents *two* demoniacs on the coast of the Gadarenes—unwilling to admit the God of the Jews as quite the true God?

that case it would be pure Greek, and mean *honouring God*, clearly designating Israel. When Wellhausen adds that "*save* has here the simple sense of *make whole*," and that "*follow* is not used in the sublime religious meaning," one may be allowed to reserve one's judgment, or even to ask, "Quare, commilito?"

Whether, then, blind Timæus Bartimæus typifies the Jew or the proselyte may be left undecided, though it seems sure that he is the emblem of the one or the other; but no such uncertainty seems to hang over the Rich One of the earlier verses.[1] Unless we err totally in understanding the health of Judæa and the diseases of Galilee—and error seems most unlikely—we *must* interpret the Rich One as the faithful Israel. With this the answer of the Jesus agrees perfectly: "The commandments thou knowest." True of the Jew, and of him alone. Similarly his response: "All these I have kept from my youth." So could speak faithful Israel alone. We have already seen how the love of the Jesus is Jehovah's love for "Israel when a child." Now comes the famous answer: "One thing thou lackest. Go, whatever thou hast, sell and give to the poor; and thou shalt have treasure in Heaven; and hither, follow me." We know and have discussed the rest. Observe the article before *possessions* (τὰ χρήματα). Hard, impossibly hard, for "those that have *the possessions* to enter into the Kingdom of God." No reason for this difficulty is hinted. The disciples are amazed, and rightly. If the Rich (the Jew) cannot enter, who then can? All attempts (from the ordinary standpoint) to rationalise this teaching have failed. We of to-day are quite as much puzzled as the disciples. Failing utterly to understand it, we reject it or misinterpret the explanation of the ancient copyist, "them that have relied upon (the) possessions." Yet the case is simple enough. The Rich One is Israel—rich in promises, privileges, prerogatives, in the Law, the Prophets, the Oracles, in possessions many. The poor are the Gentiles, the despised Lazarus. The all-conquering peculiarity of the Jesus-cult was its universalism.

---

[1] It seems almost, and yet perhaps not quite, superfluous to observe that there can be raised here no question of chronologic or topographic order, since we are dealing, not with events, but with ideas.

It admitted Jew and Gentile on equal terms into the Kingdom. The former was called on to renounce his high prerogatives, to share his divine privileges with the latter. Not unnaturally, he hesitated, he refused; with lowering look he went away from the Jesus, deeply grieved, for his *possessions* were precious. It was in these that he placed his hope; and the reviser of the text had a just insight, and by no means "spoiled everything," as Wellhausen thinks (*Ev. Marci*, p. 87), when he added (to verse 24) "for them that have trusted in (the) possessions"—a phrase plainly describing the Jews. The stupefaction of the disciples now appears perfectly natural: if the Jews could not enter the Kingdom, they for whom the Kingdom was primarily intended, the case seemed desperate. Who could enter? The answer of the Jesus expresses the abiding faith of the early Christians that in spite of the almost unanimous turning away of Israel, of his temporary "hardening," he would yet enter into the Kingdom in full triumph and glory. To men his salvation might seem impossible, but not to God, with whom all was possible, who would work some miracle in his behalf. The honour of the Almighty was pledged for the exaltation and glorification of his Chosen People. In precisely the same spirit has the "Apostle" (Romans ix–xi) poured upon this supreme paradox of Christianity the full flood of his rabbinical dialectic. Surely the antinomy presented a problem worthy of his utmost powers. His solution agrees precisely with that of the Marcan text. Apparently impossible, the salvation of the Jew is none the less a divinely logical necessity, "for the gifts and the calling of God are without repentance" (xi, 29). For a time, indeed, he may be partially hardened; but only "until the fullness of the Gentiles be come in." Then he, too, shall enter in the meridian splendour of redemption: "and so all Israel shall be saved," cries the Apostle (xi, 26); and, wonder-struck at the marvellous inversion of salvation, he bursts into the noble apostrophe: "O depth of riches and wisdom and knowledge of God! How unsearchable his judgments and inexplorable his ways!" The mental attitude of the Evangelist is exactly the same, but, of course, expressed in his own subtle and esoteric manner. He beholds the amazing inversion—Gentiles thronging into the Kingdom, while "the sons of the Kingdom are cast forth into the outer darkness" (Matthew viii, 12); but he cannot doubt of the ultimate salvation even of the most recalcitrant, and he frames his faith in the aphorism, "But many shall be—first last and last first," wherein the allusion to Jew and Gentile seems too obvious for discussion.

This interpretation of the famous Gospel incident seems, then, to be thoroughly satisfying in every detail; moreover, these details are so many that it appears in the last degree improbable that a radically wrong interpretation should fit so perfectly at every point. It would be well-nigh miraculous if a mere historical incident, artlessly narrated, should lend itself in so many and all particulars unforcedly to a symbolic interpretation. The marks of design are too many and too obvious. On the other hand, to understand this account historically is very difficult, if not downright impossible. Who can believe that a Rich One would meet the stranger Jesus as he started towards Jerusalem, would run forward, fall upon his knees and worship, and ask, "What shall I do to inherit everlasting life?" Or that the Jesus would require that he should sell all his possessions and give them to the poor? What good could such folly accomplish? Or that the Jesus would pronounce it impossible for any rich man to enter the Kingdom save by a miracle? History has not verified, but has flatly and repeatedly and continually contradicted, such a dictum in every age and in every clime. And what worthy or adequate meaning can be given to First and Last, inverted into Last and First, save that of Jew and Gentile? Surely not that of Loisy (*Les Évan. Syn.*, ii, 20).

We must, then, regard the symbolic exposition of this incident as possessing a degree of probability as high as the nature of such matters admits; in other words, as virtually certain. This result is not only important and luminous in itself, but its light is reflected over the whole body of the Gospel. It shows by a striking example how the Evangelist thought as he wrote, how he wished his readers to understand him. Once we have looked steadily into the depths of the mind of Mark, the enigma of the New Testament becomes an open secret.

POSTSCRIPT

During the passage of this work into print, a passage made slow by the tedium of correcting proofs across an ocean and a continent, there have appeared a number of publications treating directly or indirectly of *Ecce Deus* (the original German edition of this book, published, with eye single to the interests of freedom and culture, by Herr Eugen Diederichs, of Jena), some of which, in order that the reader may be put *au courant* with the discussion, should be noticed in this volume. Here is not the place to enter into elaborate consideration of replies to *Der vorchristliche Jesus*, such as Schwen's recent "Replik an W. B. Smith" (in Hilgenfeld's *Zeitschrift für wissenschaftliche Theologie*),[1] since the special matters therein set forth are in the main untouched in the present work. It seems proper, however, to call attention to *The Historicity of Jesus*, by Professor Shirley Jackson Case, of the University of Chicago. Elsewhere[2] I review the book at some length, having studied it with much satisfaction. What concerns us here is that its author, though knowing *Ecce Deus* and citing it repeatedly, has made no attempt whatever to answer it, to rebut the evidence it brings forward against the "historicity" in question. The reader may find his own explanation of such an omission in a work professing to be a "complete and unprejudiced statement," wherein "no phase of any consequence in the history or in the present status of the problem is ignored." The only logical conclusion would be that Professor Case regards the present work as of no "consequence"—an opinion that might interest

---

[1] However, one amendment is needed in Schwen's estimate of the general situation: "It is the question of a completely new interpretation of religious history in the time of the Roman Emperors, of the overthrow both of liberal and of conservative Christianity." Plainly Schwen means theology, or interpretation of "Christianity." Christianity itself, true, proper, primitive, and militant, suffers no violence in these volumes.

[2] In a forthcoming number of the *Open Court*.

by its uniqueness and by reminding one of the prediction of Noah's neighbours, that it would be only a passing shower. Meanwhile the gravity of considerations ignored by the Chicagoan is attested not only in numerous reviews, but still more in the ominous appearance of such articles as Macintosh's in the *American Journal of Theology* (1911, pp. 362-372), " Is Belief in the Historicity of Jesus Indispensable to Christian Faith ? " and of similar discussions by such as Bousset, Troeltsch, Hermann. In spite of all protestations, the meaning of such scriptures seems quite unmistakable. Critics are inquiring if it be "indispensable" only because they begin to suspect it may prove indefensible. They are preparing cautiously, not indeed to surrender—oh, no ! perish the thought, never for an instant could that be dreamed of—but merely to evacuate overnight the citadel hitherto deemed impregnable. How long before some forget in their new surroundings that imperial palace whence they came, and even that they were ever there?

The elaborate article by Meyboom in the *Theologisch Tijdschrift* breathes such a spirit of generous appreciation that it might very properly be commended to the reader without comment. It may be well, however, to observe that its chief complaint, that against the broad generality and even vagueness of certain contentions, seems to strike a failing that leans to virtue's side. Avowedly the book sketches only the outlines ; it declares explicitly that many details must yet wait long to be filled in. This lies in the nature of the case. Where strictly historic evidence is so scanty, where the oldest documents were hidden "sayings," where the facts were so early and so studiously concealed, where they were systematically transmuted often beyond recognition in the utterly interested representations of *ex parte* reporters, it were miraculous if at first much more than general indications were possible. It is only the drift of the stars in their courses that we may hope to recognise. In a movement that stretched itself through nearly three centuries, that spread itself over well-nigh the whole circum-Mediterranean region, we must often be content with a "somewhere" and a "somewhen," and any present attempt at higher precision may be deprecated. Nor is such precision a real desideratum. The one important "question of the day" is that of the "historicity," the pure humanity, of the Jesus. The details though not indeed absolutely, are yet relatively, unimportant. Once the pure divinity, the non-humanity, of the Jesus clearly made out, all the other things in their time and their turn will be added. With the new theory of Christian origins it fares quite as with other new theories in historical and even in physical science. In grounding the general doctrine of descent with modification, it is only the very broad and vague propositions that are at first recommended: as that in *some* way all living organisms are directly derived from ancestors, and these from pre-ancestors, and so on in unbroken order back indefinitely. But in *what* way derived—that is another question. To say "By Natural Selection" was, and still is, premature. As over against the elder hypothesis of special creations, it is indifferent *how* they may have been derived, how the modifications may have been brought about, though in other regards it may be extremely important.

Exactly similar is the present case of New Testament theory. The general outlines are already clear: there is no longer any good reason to maintain the liberal dogma of the purely human Jesus; there is the amplest reason to fold it up and lay it aside for ever, to adopt the formula of Origen, "The God Jesus" (*C. Cels.* vi, 66). But a score of questions remain yet, and may long remain, unsettled. Gradually, reluctantly, they will yield up their answers; in no case will they shake the fundamental results now attained. Said Lincoln at the famous conference with Davis: "Let me write the first sentence, 'The Union shall be maintained,' and you may write all the rest." The sense in which these subsidiary questions may be answered cannot disturb the movement of our thought on these matters, nor greatly modify the significance of the results now attained—for the problems that confront us in the religion, the worship, the church, the society, the civilisation of to-day.

It is not uncommon to find in the writings of historicists obscure allusions to convincing arguments for the historicity, which, however, they yet hold in reserve. It seems a pity that anyone should thus hide his light under a bushel. In the *Theologische Revue,* in adjudging *Ecce Deus,* the temperate Catholic Kiefl generously admits, "The book is, without doubt, *geistvoll geschrieben*"; but he holds that, "however pointed the author's critique and manifoldly correct (*treffend*), yet the proof of his counter-hypothesis is just as defective." He protests against "shoreless allegorising," but assigns no reasons, and finds the main fault to lie in giving so much attention to Schmiedel's Pillars while "rather ignoring other proofs." This sounds strange in view of the detailed treatment of the arguments from personality, and the Pauline Witness, and some others. The facts in the case may be understood easily. Schmiedel himself has openly declared (p. 17, quoted *supra*, p. 33) there are no other really cogent arguments than those derived from these same or similar passages. Besides, these "pillars" are tangible, palpable, whereas the supposed "other proofs" yet wait for distinct formulation.

Thus Wendland would rest his case on the "Aramaic foundation of the Synoptics and the existence of a mission independent of Paul." Now, here are two arguments declared to be "sufficient." But how so? Each of them stands on one leg only—an unsteady posture for a syllogism. To make out any semblance of reasoning we must supply each with a helpmeet, a major premise. What shall it be? Wendland gives no hint. The like holds of much ostensible argumentation for the historicity. When the major is supplied, it will be found to be either false or unrelated to the conclusion. Similar examples might be cited. It is hardly fair to expect your opponent to frame your premises as well as to expose your fallacies. When these mysterious "other proofs"[1] are formulated as clearly and logically as the "pillar-proofs," then will they receive quite as careful consideration—and, it may be predicted, with quite similar results.

Such being the general reticence of the spokesmen of Historicism, it is gratifying to find in Case's book (p. 269) a summary of pro-historical arguments, more complete than is elsewhere found in the same compass. He says:—

---

[1] Hereby we are reminded of the barrister who declared : " And now, Your Honour, if this argument be rejected as invalid, I have another that is equally conclusive."

[1] The New Testament data are perfectly clear in their testimony to the reality of Jesus's earthly career, [2] and they come from a time when the possibility that the early framers of tradition should have been deceived upon this point is out of the question. [3] Not only does Paul make the historical personality of Jesus a necessary preliminary to his gospel, [4] but the whole situation in which Paul moves shows a historical background in which memory of this individual is central. [5] The earliest phases of Gospel tradition have their roots in Palestinian soil, [6] and reach back to the period when personal associates of Jesus were still living; [7] while primitive Christology shows distinct traces of Jesus, the man of Galilee, behind its faith in the heavenly Christ. [8] The disciples' personal memory of this Jesus of real life is also the fountain from which the peculiarly forceful type of the new community's vitality takes its start.

By this statement of long-desiderated " other proofs," which we have taken the liberty to separate and numerate for easy reference, Professor Case has made the public greatly his debtor. A few observations may be permitted.

A. It seems noteworthy that the Pillars shine by their absence only. Professor Case would seem to regard them almost as lightly as Schmiedel regards all Case's " other evidences." This seems very remarkable, for Schmiedel is by no means alone in pinning his faith to the Pillars.

B. The favourite inference from the unique, incomparable, and wholly uninventible personality is likewise slurred, if not, indeed, entirely omitted. This seems even more remarkable still, for this has undoubtedly hitherto been the trump argument of many historicists.

(1) The assertion that "the New Testament data are perfectly clear, etc.," ignores both the facts in the case and the whole symbolic interpretation set forth in *Ecce Deus*. If this interpretation be measurably correct, then these "data" would seem to be " perfectly clear in their testimony " *against* the historicity in question. Unless this interpretation be shown to be erroneous, this leading argument in the list must fall to the ground; and what is said in (2) about the " framers of tradition " would appear to lose all its meaning.

(3) The statement concerning Paul is scarcely correct; it is rather the very reverse of the truth. See *supra*, 146 *ff.*, and Schläger's article already cited.

(4) Professor Case would seem to be Hegelian, and to uphold the identity of opposites.

(5) Like Wendland's, the argument that tradition "roots in Palestinian soil" tries to stand on one leg, most awkwardly. As a matter of fact, we have no reason to suppose this Christian movement originated in Palestine or in any other one place. The pictorial representation in the Gospels is *staged* as in Palestine, and for the reason stated in Matthew iv, 15, 16—to fulfil the prophecy about the dawn of a great light on "Galilee of the Gentiles." Nearly all the topical references of the Gospels are derivable directly or indirectly from this *motif*, and it is noteworthy how much of the evangelic picture remains in the air without a local habitation, and sometimes without a name. The Judæan ministry is an afterthought—not present in the Logoi-source (Q), as Harnack now concedes—and is a highly elaborate reflection from the mirror of prophecy, sacred and profane.

(6) "When personal associates of Jesus were still living" assumes everything in dispute, as indeed is elsewhere done in Professor Case's book.

(7) Herein may lie a modest allusion to the Pillars; in any case, their downfall carries Case's assertion along with it.

(8) The closing sentence about "personal memory" may be a rather grudging concession to the old personality argument, and is quite too vague to form any basis of discussion. That the *absence* of any such "personal memory" is a distinctive mark of the early preaching has been clearly set forth in this volume. It is enough for the reader to remember that Paul's was the most "peculiarly forceful type," that he "laboured more abundantly than they all," and that he admittedly had no such "personal memory." Nor will the reader fail to note the vagueness that marks all the considerations advanced in the passage quoted.

In view of all the foregoing, it seems doubtful whether historicists in general will thank the Chicagoan for his statement of the case.

A single observation touching the favourite mode of refutation in vogue with historicists, the argument by silence. It is, perhaps, not strange that it has suggested to able German reviewers a counter-conclusion *from* silence. Fullest hearts may indeed be slow to speak, but not always fullest heads. The man who had not a wedding garment on seems to have maintained a most dignified and impressive silence; nevertheless——.

Having already made ample answer (in *Auseinandersetzung mit Weinel* and in the Preface to the second edition of *Der vorchristliche Jesus*) to the full blast of German bugles, one feels under little obligation to reply to "the horns of elfland, faintly blowing" in Bacon's contribution to the *Hibbert Journal* (July, 1911). They may, however, serve one useful purpose—to point a needed remark upon the type of reasoning to be employed in such discussions. It would seem that even a babe in logic might grasp the distinction between a chain and a warp, between a serial and a parallel arrangement of proofs. In mathematics the first order prevails; the conclusion hangs by a single thread. If this break, it falls to the ground. Enough to expose a single error in the sorites; the whole deduction is thereby invalidated—the chain is no stronger than its weakest link. Far otherwise in history, in life, where it is the second order that holds. The evidences are arranged side by side, like threads in a loom. It is their combined strength that supports the conclusion. The warp is far stronger than even its strongest strand. We speak of the evidence as "cumulative," of the "consilience of results," of the convergence of indications. Manifestly, to refute such argumentation it were not nearly enough to detect weak threads in the warp and grave uncertainty in various indicia. Nay, it must be shown that none of the filaments hold, that they all snap both severally and collectively, that all the concurrent indications both singly and together mislead.

The just critic of this book or of its predecessor not only will but must appraise it where it is most, and not merely where it is least, strong. Even if the evidence were inconclusive at a dozen points, it might still be conclusive at some others, and that would be enough; yea, it might be indecisive at every point considered singly, and yet decisive (with very high probability) when all were considered together. It is the whole body of facts and arguments adduced that must finally sway the mind. When, therefore, critics rest content with essaying to show some want of stringency in the proofs here and there, but make no attempt to invalidate the whole mutually independent but mutually corroborative array of indications,[1] they would appear to betray a peculiar conception of the nature of evidence, and to suggest the query whether Hilbert's, Peano's, and Russell's be the only New Logics.

The foregoing is certainly an old story; and yet it must be kept ever new, for it is persistently forgotten, *e.g.* even by Windisch (*Theol. Rundschau,* 1912, pp. 114 *ff.*), who, while discreetly generous in judging *Ecce Deus*, yet finds it "fragmentary, and therefore unsatisfying," "a series of unconnected essays," and urgently calls for "no more fragmentary sketches, but connected, rounded-off presentations." All this, on which Windisch lays such especial stress, seems indeed only half-bad. It might be worse. Some books are very smoothly "rounded-off," and yet do not satisfy. All books, in fact, have the defects of their qualities; and this lack of artistic unity has been openly declared by the author. The reader must see that "a completely new orientation" (Schwen) cannot be presented in the "rounded-off" form desired. If the author should wait until such a "presentation" became possible, his friends the enemy would exultingly insist on passing to the order of the day. New evidence is offering itself daily, new aspects are disclosing themselves constantly, new perspectives opening up on every hand. Doubtless many years must elapse before the readjustment and realignment can be complete.[2]

Meantime the evidences, though avowedly "fragmentary," are not "therefore unsatisfying." The evidence for scientific doctrines does often satisfy in spite of being very fragmentary, for it attests with a sufficiently high degree of probability. In fact, it is well known that our knowledge is patchwork. But when Windisch speaks of "unconnected essays" he goes

---

[1] Herewith it is far from hinted that even in minute details such critics have prevailed thus far at any single point of attack. On the contrary, their signal and universal failure seems to be variously admitted in their own ranks, as already indicated at several points in this volume; nay more, to judge by the temper displayed too often, it must be an open secret to these critics themselves; for it is a sound ethical maxim in law, and surely much more so in theology, to revile only the opponent whom you cannot refute.

[2] If Windisch thinks the publication of such essays premature, then he is at variance with Pfleiderer and with other such masters, at whose urgence it was begun.

far astray. As well describe the meridians of longitude as "unconnected"—they hang together tightly at the poles. So the numerous lines of proof in this book are, indeed, *independent*—herein lies their logical worth: an error in one does not involve an error in any other—they must all be refuted simultaneously, for even if all failed but one, and that did not fail, the *one* conclusion would still be reached and established; but they are *not* unconnected, for they all converge upon the same conclusion, which holds them all together in unity. The complaint of Windisch lies, then, against an æsthetic fault—the condition of a logical merit. However, as the days glide by, the independent arguments will become each for itself a more "rounded-off" whole, and some subsequent volume may appeal more powerfully to Windisch's artistic sense. Meanwhile, this mutual independence by no means absolves opponents from the obligation of answer; on the contrary, it piles up such obligation higher.

A reviewer must be allowed to decide *ex cathedrâ* and without argument. Sometimes, however, Windisch does assign reasons, as when he is horrified at the statement that Hebrews does not make the faintest allusion to the Gospel delineation, and cites Hebrews v, 7, in refutation. The passage was in the mind of the author, as appears from the language used (p. 92), but it does not contain the allusion imagined. Of course, most commentators refer it to Gethsemane; but even the conservative Köstlin, who was certainly guiltless of any foreboding of recent criticism, could find no such reference. The representation does certainly *agree* in some measure with the Gospel account—an account, by the way, that would do grave dishonour to any courageous *man*, who would certainly not "for his godly fear of death" "pray and plead with tears and mighty cry for deliverance from death," which millions of ordinary mortals have met without a blush. The passage is an attempt, perhaps not quite happy according to our standards, to poetise, or rather to *pathetise* (most naturally[1]), the self-sacrifice of the great High Priest, the Dying God, a many-coloured thread that ran all through the web of ancient consciousness. There is no evidence at all

---

[1] See p. 296 *supra*.

that it is based on Luke or on any other Gospel. In fact, the indications point the other way. It would be far more likely for the Gospels to dramatise the verse in Hebrews, or still more probably its original. It is needless to elaborate, nor do we raise here any critical question about these four verses (7–10), though such a one as Windisch must perceive that a serious question may be raised; but it seems strange that anyone can read the whole of this Epistle at a single sitting without being struck by its wide remove from the modern liberal, and even from the ancient evangelic, conception.

The surprise of Windisch that so little note is made of Justin Martyr's witness to the Gospel story is scarcely warranted; for the explanation lay before him in *Ecce Deus*. The witness need not be denied; it is merely worthless, being vitiated by the Martyr's bizarre conception of (Gospel) history as a fulfilment and reflection of Old Testament prophecy and scripture. Such a theorist would not hesitate to declare that so-and-so had happened, and had been recorded in *Memoirs of the Apostles*, if only he thought he had found its type in the Old Testament. Does not even Chrysostom teach explicitly that prophecy must over-ride even the historic facts themselves? And did not Tertullian write: "And buried, he rose again; it is certain, because it is impossible"?[1] The modern critical mind is no measuring rod for the early Christian.

Windisch thinks that to "propagate monotheism in the form of a Jesus-cult is to cast out the devil through Beelzebub." Exactly so the Scribes and Pharisees seem to have thought (Mark iii, 22), but not so the proto-Christians. He imagines a contradiction between the worship of the pre-Christian Jesus and the doctrine that proto-Christianity was an aggressive monotheism. But wherein does it lie? He neglects to state. Meanwhile, does not even Deissmann delight in the phrase, "the monotheistic cult of Jesus"? Windisch's sense of contrast might appear to be pathologically acute.

---

[1] "Et sepultus resurrexit; certum est, quia impossibile est" (*De Carne Christi*, v).

The argument from "The Didactic Element" he condenses thus : "Jesus said something else than Cicero and Aristotle, etc.; therefore Jesus is no historic personality." This summary, he admits, is "grob gesagt"; verily! so inept, indeed, that one suspects there may be some misprint, some mistake not of Windisch, but of the devil. The real argument is that the "Sayings" bear no witness to a unique, definable, and uninventible personality, because even the most distinctive are not original, but are adaptations of the wingèd words of ancient wisdom ; since one might naturally look for some individual impress on the real sayings of a marvellous human teacher, its absence bears witness against the historicity in question. This reasoning is not hard to understand ; why does Windisch prefer to caricature rather than to answer it?

Another pupil of Schmiedel's has come bravely to the rescue of the Pillars, which, it is admitted, "are powerfully assailed," by adding, like Neumann, to their number (Meltzer, "Zum Ausbau von Schmiedels Grundsäulen"—*Prot. Monatsh.*, 1911, H.12, 461–476). His additions outnumber the first array, being about a dozen ; and some of them, which had long ago occurred to the present writer, deserve notice, though neither singly nor collectively can they sustain the burden laid upon them. Windisch admits that Meltzer's collection "must be sifted," nor will the very finest sieve retain aught worth saying. Still this second vintage of Zürich, only in less degree than the first (for "the old is better"), calls for attention, as being of all "so-called" evidences the least intangible. At the start, however, it is keenly interesting to note that Windisch himself now surrenders five of the original nine passages (Mark xiii, 32 ; xv, 34; Matthew xi, 5 ; xii, 32 ; xvi, 5–12) as "not convincing"; only Mark iii, 21 ; x, 18; viii, 12 ; vi, 5, would he still "let count." When such a pillar as the cry on the cross (Mark xv, 34) is abandoned reluctantly as "not able to bear" (*nicht tragfähig*), one's interest and confidence in pillars is "nigh unto vanishing away."

Meltzer's second row of columns stands thus :—Mark x, 40=Matthew xx, 23 ; Mark xiv, 33=Matthew xxvi, 37 ; Matthew xvi, 28 ; xxiv, 30, 34 ; xi, 20–24=Luke x, 12–18 ;

Matthew xv, 22-28 ; xi, 19 ; Mark iii, 22 ; ii, 7 ; xii, 35-37 ; v, 39 ; Matthew v, 9, 45 ; Mark viii, 33 ; Luke ix, 54 *ff.* Add the betrayal of Judas, denial of Peter, stupidity of disciples, depreciation of disciples, flight of disciples. Our first observation is that only half are found in Mark. Now, of the original nine, the four that still maintain themselves (even in the judgment of Windisch) are all in Mark ; all not in Mark are now rejected. It is doubly unlikely, then, that any of this new colonnade not found in Mark will support themselves even in the minds of liberal critics.

These six that are in Mark, since it is not possible to examine all minutely now and here, we may judge not by the foot, but by the head, for the chief is this : Of the seats at right and at left hand in the kingdom Jesus says : " This is not mine to give, but for others it is made ready " (Mark x, 40, Burkitt's translation). On its face the whole story seems to be a comparatively late invention, with what motive it is not easy to say—possibly as a setting for the great saying about humility (Mark x, 43-45) ? We have no reason to believe that even the obscure Sinaitic form—given above—is the original, nor can anyone say what the original was ; considerable change took place even in passing to Matthew. But, even as it now stands, it is far from clear that a worshipper of "the god Jesus " might not have written it. For such a one might, and did, distinguish his Saviour-God from the God Most High, as is done in Hebrews and elsewhere. Thus the Apostle explicitly affirms that the Son must reign as God for a certain time, and then become himself subject to the Father (1 Corinthians xv, 24-28). It is idle to ask, How can these things be ? Few or none of us can understand them ; but how many can understand the higher spaces or the relativity of space and time ? It is enough that the worshippers of " the God Jesus " did actually preach and teach a host of such un-unified and semi-contradictory doctrines " concerning the Jesus." Such inconsistencies have, indeed, infected theology in all ages, the present not excepted. Homer did not hesitate to represent even the Father of the gods as yielding to Fate, and bound by oath " not to be loosed by any god." Says the oracle (*Herod.*, i, 91) : " The foredoomed Fate it is impossible to escape, even for a god." Compare also Hebrews vi, 17, 18. It seems strange that Meltzer should lean on such a pillar. How easy it was for the ancient, even the Judaic, mind to distinguish between God very high and God Most High, is clearly seen in the strange doctrine of *Meṭaṭron* so conspicuous in Hebrew writings, who is purely divine, who discharges the divinest functions, who even bears the ineffable name of God, and yet must not be worshipped being not quite God Himself.[1]

Surely nothing more need be said about the "Betrayal," and the reader may safely be left with the other mentioned misdoings of the disciples. Even if unable to comprehend a certain incident fully, we should be irrational to adopt the hypothesis of Meltzer; on this point Windisch is in at least partial accord with the present writer, of whom he says (in reviewing *Ecce Deus*) : " With acumen he shows, first of all, that Schmiedel in his propositions proves the impossible; what is for us a contradiction need by no means have been felt as such by the Evangelists." Only on the Denial need we pause to say that it seems to be one of the most profoundly significant stories in the Gospels; it must be taken and understood as part and parcel of the whole picture of Simon Peter, both canonical and extra-canonical, especially in relation to Simon Magus, of whom he appears to be an orthodox transfiguration. This difficult matter requires special treatment not possible in this connection. But to accept the episode as simple history, without suspecting any deeper meaning, and to find therein a proof invincible of historicity, is to push naïveté to the wall.

Only one other of these new nurselings need we mention, which Windisch also recognises as most "important of all" —the reproach of being "gluttonous and a winebibber" (Matthew xi, 19); the other passages (Mark iii, 22; ii, 7) surely call for no notice. It has long seemed to the present writer that the Matthean verse (*cf.* Luke vii, 34) is by far the most plausible that the historicists can produce; for surely gluttony and winebibbing are not divine, but human—all too human. Observe, however, that the passage is not in Mark,

---

[1] See my article in the *Open Court* of July, 1912.

and that it is transparently merely ascribed to Jesus. Moreover—and here is the core of the matter—it is a late reflection of the Christian community, how late none can say. At this point we are glad to be able to prop ourselves on the penetrating study of Dibelius (*Die urchristliche Ueberlieferung über Johannes den Täufer*, 1911), who recognises these verses (xi, 18, 19) as "the interpretation by the congregation of a parable of Jesus." Enough that they are not historical, nor primitive, nor refer to anything historical in the naïve sense. The concluding statement, that "Wisdom was justified of her works (her children all)," indicates that we are here in a difficult region of Gnostic thought, and far away from the pleasant paths of history.

At length we come to the latest publication of the honoured Professor Rudolf Steck, on "The Genuine Witness of Josephus to Christ" (*Prot. Monatsh.*, 1912, 1-11). Written in the author's clear, scholarly, excellent style, it is mainly devoted to stating and re-arguing the criticism of Credner on the passage in the *Antiquities* (xx, 9, 1) concerning "James, the brother of Jesus, the so-called Christ." It is not necessary to rekindle the discussion. Since even Zahn now recognises the passage as interpolated (*Forschungen z. G. d. nt. K.*, vi, 305), the matter may be allowed to rest. But Steck, while unwilling to admit the interpolation, perceives that such a single mention of Jesus without any explanation is intolerably lonesome and highly improbable (p. 8). Hence he very justly finds himself constrained to consult once more the far more famous interpolation (*Ant.*, xviii, 3, 3), and, if possible, extract from it some information. All other hypotheses failing, he falls back on that of the Dutch critic Mensinga (*Theol. Tijdschrift*, 1883, 145-152), who, rightly feeling how hard it is to believe that Josephus could have kept silence concerning the man Jesus, found himself conducted to the hypothesis that Josephus had said something—namely, not only that the Christians believe in the divine nature and origin of Jesus, but that the idea originated in a certain material incident not very creditable to the new faith (hence expunged by Christians and supplanted by the extant section 3!). Then would follow the Paulina incident in Rome as a parallel. It seems hardly necessary to discuss this notion of the Hollander. Steck himself states it as a bare hypothesis, upon which he shrinks from laying stress. In fact, it wrecks on one patent fact—that the *slaughter* of the Jews (described in § 2) is followed in § 4 by the statement that "at the same time a second terrible thing confounded the Jews." Now, this *second* (ἕτερον) is intelligible only if § 4 follows upon § 2, for ἕτερος (as Steck correctly observes) is "the other of two." But Steck avers that δεινόν (terrible) cannot refer to the *slaughter* in § 2, but must refer "properly to something mighty, strange, extraordinary"—as he with Mensinga thinks, to some scandal about Joseph and Mary! This is a mere question of fact, and, with all due deference to the Bernese Professor, we must insist that the primary and regular meaning of δεινός is *dire, dread, frightful, terrible*, being from δέος, *alarm, affright, pale fear, terror*. Says Homer of the archer-god: "Terrible arose the clangour of his silver bow."[1] Such must be the meaning here, for only something terrible (and not a piece of scandalous gossip about two peasants) would have "confounded (ἐθορύβει) the Jews." The hypothesis of Mensinga has really appealed to no one, and is simply a last resort of Steck's to save the passage about the "brother," which he sees must be saved if the historicity is to be plausibly defended. The article of this distinguished critic is valuable as setting forth in clear relief the exigencies of the liberal situation.

Let us, then, sum up the matter. In spite of the frequent references to "his brethren" in the Gospels (and Acts i, 14), no serious argument for the historicity is based thereon, save the Schmiedelian pillar-proof already sufficiently treated. There remain only the two Pauline passages. In the first of these (1 Cor. ix, 5) the phraseology, "The other Apostles and the brethren of the Lord and Kephas," combined with the party-cries given in 1 Cor. i, 12, "I am of Paul, I of Apollos, I of Kephas, I of Christ," very strongly suggests, wholly apart from all questions of "historicity," that we here have to deal with a class of the new religionists, that "the brethren of the Lord" are either identical or in line with those who said, "I am of Christ." While it may not be

---

[1] "And there was heard a dread clanging of the silver bow."—Walter Leaf.

possible to demonstrate this strictly, it seems a thoroughly satisfactory view of the matter, in every way probable, and impossible to disprove. In the second passage (Gal. i, 19) the phrase is, "James the brother of the Lord." Now, if what has just been said be correct, there is nothing here to give us any pause. James was simply one of a circle, perhaps very select and interior, who for their fervour and strict devotion were known as "brethren of the Lord," or perhaps "of Christ." Herewith everything seems adequately explained in entire accord with the Gospel use of the phrase "my brethren." Moreover, we must note that the words, "brother of the Lord," sound very strange as designating at that early day a flesh-and-blood brother of a man Jesus. "The Lord" was the very highest name for the enthroned world-ruling Saviour-God; it denoted specifically the Jehovah of the Old Testament. It seems extremely unlikely that in any case such a kinsman should be called "brother of the Lord." Surely it would have been just as easy and far more natural to call him "brother of Jesus." The fact that he is never thus called seems to point directly to the spiritual and directly away from the carnal sense of brotherhood. Strongly confirmatory is the further fact that in the much later interpolation in Josephus we no longer read the "brother of the Lord," but "the brother of Jesus, him called the Christ." This interpolator of "the falsified Josephus" (Zahn) undoubtedly meant fleshly brotherhood, and accordingly he says, as he should say, "brother of Jesus"; so, too, would the Apostle have written had he meant the same thing.

It seems, then, that the New Testament contains no clear token of any such carnal kinship, and yet, if any such really existed, it seems strange that no trace of it should be detected; strange that neither father, nor mother, nor brother, nor sister, nor any other kinsman of such a man Jesus should ever be heard of in authentic or probable historical connection. Wonderfully apt are the words of Hebrews (vii, 3): "Without father, without mother, without genealogy, having neither beginning of days nor end of life." Such is the Jesus of primitive Christianity.

It has hardly seemed worth while to notice the vigorous contention of Berendts *Die Zeugnisse vom Christentum im slavischen "De Bello Judaico"* des Josephus, 1906; also *Analecta zum slav. Josephus,* in Preuschen's *Zeitschrift,* 1908; pp. 47-70), that Josephus inserted in the first edition of his "Jewish War" an elaborate notice of "Christ and the Christians," which he afterwards expunged as "the course of the spiritual development of his people led away from Christianity" (p. 75), since even the most sympathetic critics (as Schürer, *Theol. Literaturzeitung,* 1906, 262 *ff.*; and Case, p. 260) clearly perceive and declare that his zeal and erudition have miscarried.

What then, finally, is the witness of Josephus? The famous § 3 is certainly a Christian interpolation. All efforts, even the most ingenious, to find therein any traces of an original (now Christianised) testimony have conspicuously failed; and they will continue to fail, for the opening words of § 4, a "second terrible thing," point clearly and unambiguously back to the first "terrible thing," the slaughter described in § 2. Hereby these sections are shut down upon each other, and any intervening third section is excluded.

But when this section is surrendered, so is the other phrase in question, "brother of Jesus," etc., for other reasons and because Josephus would hardly have introduced such an isolated notice. So, then, it appears that this Jewish historian of that time and country makes no mention of Jesus—a fact inexplicable even to *Historiker* themselves on their own hypothesis. Hence their strenuous defence of the indefensible. We thank Professor Steck for his able and honest article. It seems that each renewed investigation confirms more and more securely the conception herein set forth of the Origins of Christianity.

INDEX OF PASSAGES

OLD TESTAMENT

Genesis:
i, 1, 2 ... ... 157, 159
ix, 4 152
xlix, 15 293

Leviticus:
xvii, 11, 14 152

Deuteronomy:
vi, 4 277
xii, 23 152
xxix, 16–18 288

Joshua:
xv, 25 304

Judges:
vi, 11 ... ... 295, n. 2

2 Samuel:
ix, 4 280
xvii, 27 280

1 Kings:
xvii, 8–24 293
xxii, 11 115

2 Kings:
xvii, 12, 13 278
xvii, 24–33 68
xvii, 24–41 102

2 Chronicles:
ii, 16 30
xxx, 6 278
xxxvi, 23 269

Ezra:
i, 2 269
iv, 5 305

Nehemiah:
i, 4, 5 269
ii, 4, 20 269

Psalms:
xxii, 1 201
xxii, 17 142
xxiv, 3, 4 128
xxxvii, 2 128
xli, 9 317
xli, 10 316
li, 16–19 280
xcvi, 5 54
cix, 28 128
cxxvi, 5, 6 128
cxxix, 19–24 ... 280
cxlv, 11, 13 270

Proverbs:
viii, 1 166
viii, 12 ff. ... ...158 f.

Isaiah:
i, ... 280
i, 4, 5, 17, 21, 29 ... 281
ii, 9, 18, 20, 22 ... 281
v, 1–7 ... ... 122 n.
v, 24 281
x, 10, 11 281
xix, 4 ... 104, 306, 308, 317
xix, 41 309
xxxi, 6 278
xxxv, 5 f. 203
xliv, 6 17
xliv, 22 278
lii, 13–liii, 12 ... 65
lv, 1 128
lvii, 17 ... ... 99, 312
lxi, 1 203
lxi, 2 128
lxiii, 2 295

Jeremiah:
iii 107
iii, 12, 14, 22 ... 278
xviii, 11, 15 278
xxv, 5, 6 278
xxxi, 24 128

xxxv, 15 278
xlviii, 24, 41 ... 304

Ezekiel:
iii, 1 124
ix, 2, 3, 11 112
x, 2, 6, 7 112
xiv, 6 278
xxiii 107
xxx, 12 ... 306, 309
xxxiii, 11, 25 ... 278

Daniel:
i, 1, 20 270
ii, 1 270
ii, 18 269
ii, 44 270
iv, 3 270
iv, 23 269
vii, 13, 14, 18, 22,
  25, 27 270
viii, x, xi 270
x, 5 270
xii, 6, 7 112

Hosea:
i, 11 294
viii, 1 102
ix, 3–6, 15 102
xi, 1 ... ... 195, 313
xiv, 1–4 278

Joel:
ii, 12, 13 278
ii, 32 221

Amos:
ii, 2 304
ii, 16 111
v, 21–24, 26, 27 ... 279
vi, 13 279

Jonah:
i, 9 269
i, 17 30

INDEX OF PASSAGES

Micah:
i, 6 *f.* ... 281
iii, 5 ... 281
iv, 5 ... 281
v, 13 *f.* ... 281
vi, 16 ... 281

Zechariah:
i, 3, 4 ... 278
ix, 12 ... 278
xi, 12 ... 306

Malachi:
iii, 7 ... 278

1 Maccabees:
v, 19 ... 125

NEW TESTAMENT

Matthew:
i, 16 ... 235, 294
i, 21 ... 17
ii, 23 ... 292, 299, 300, 314
iii, 2 ... 129, 276 *f.*
iii, 3 ... 136
iii, 7, 12 ... 129
iii, 8, 11 ... 286
iii, 9 ... 73
iv, 15 *f.* ... 332
iv, 17 ... 129, 276
iv, 18 ... 235, 294
iv, 19 ... 29
v, 9, 45 ... 338
v, 25 ... 125
v, 28 ... 126
v, 45 ... 127
vi, 7 ... 144
vi, 10 ... 268
vii, 2 ... 130
vii, 12 ... 127
vii, 13, 14 ... 130
vii, 16–21 ... 127
vii, 19 ... 129
vii, 22 ... 214
vii, 24–27 ... 128
vii, 29 ... 179
viii, 11, 12 ... 102
viii, 12 ... 326
viii, 31 ... 211
ix, 9 ... 294
ix, 30 ... 97
ix, 34 ... 23
ix, 36 ... 38, 51, 179
x ... 60
x, 1 ... 57
x, 2 ... 235, 294
x, 4 ... 304
x, 7 ... 268
x, 14, 15 ... 144
x, 21 ... 130
x, 26, 27 ... 43
x, 27 ... 255
x, 34, 35 ... 144
x, 42 ... 118
xi, 5 ... 180
xi, 5 ... 337
xi, 5, 6 ... 202 *f.*
xi, 7–15 ... 114
xi, 12 ... 43
xi, 17 ... 130
xi, 18 *f.* ... 340
xi, 19 ... 338 *f.*
xi, 20–24 ... 144
xi, 20–24 ... 337
xi, 25–30 ... xviii, 118
xi, 27–29 ... 165
xii, 15 ... 38, 322
xii, 24, 27 ... 213
xii, 27, 32 ... 192 *ff.*
xii, 28 ... 268
xii, 30 ... 125
xii, 31 ... 180
xii, 32 ... 337
xii, 39 ... 202
xii, 46–50 ... 236
xiii, 11 ... 34
xiii, 41 ... 272
xiii, 43 ... 268
xiii, 47 ... 29, 275
xiii, 52 ... 36
xiii, 55 ... 235
xiii, 58 ... 201
xiv, 17–21 ... 123
xv, 22–28 ... 338
xv, 32–38 ... 123
xvi, 4 ... 202
xvi, 5–12 ... 204
xvi, 5–12 ... 337
xvi, 28 ... 268
xvi, 28 ... 337
xvii, 18 ... 211
xviii, 1–6 ... 118
xviii, 6 *f.* ... 118, 284
xviii, 10 ... 113, 118
xviii, 14 ... 118
xviii, 15 ... 284
xviii, 17 ... 144
xviii, 21 *f.* ... 284
xviii, 27 ... 97
xix, 13–15 ... 117
xix, 16 *f.* ... 322
xix, 16–26 ... 313
xix, 17 ... 126, 195
xix, 24 ... 267 *f.*
xx, 19 ... 312
xx, 23 ... 337
xxi, 3 ... 136
xxi, 5, 7 ... 155
xxi, 11 ... 315
xxi, 17–22 ... 114
xxi, 25 ... 269
xxi, 31, 43 ... 267 *f.*
xxiii ... 144
xxiii, 11, 12 ... 127
xxiii, 33 ... 129
xxiii, 34 ... 166
xxiv, 7 ... 318
xxiv, 30, 34 ... 337
xxiv, 36 ... 197
xxv, 40 ... 236
xxvi, 3 ... 235, 294
xxvi, 6–13 ... 106
xxvi, 14 ... 294, 303
xxvi, 26–29 ... 146
xxvi, 29 ... 268
xxvi, 36 ... 294
xxvi, 37 ... 337
xxvi, 69 ... 187
xxvii, 3–10 ... 318
xxvii, 9, 10 ... 306
xxvii, 16 ... 294
xxvii, 17, 22 ... 235, 294
xxvii, 33 ... 294, 298
xxvii, 46 ... 197
xxviii, 6 ... 136
xxviii, 10 ... 236
xxviii, 19 ... 70

Mark:
i, 1 ... 96
i, 1–3 ... 209
i, 4 ... 232, 286
i, 9 ... 314
i, 13 ... 210
i, 15 ... 268, 275
i, 17 ... 29
i, 22 ... 227

INDEX OF PASSAGES

i, 24 ... 61	x, 18, 40 ... 337 f.	viii, 28 ... 196
i, 27 ... 227	x, 22 ... 312	ix, 10 ... 293
i, 41 ... 96	x, 23 ff. ... 272	ix, 12–17 ... 123
i, 43 ... 97	x, 33 ... 312	ix, 49 f. ... 125, 214
ii, 7 ... 338 f.	x, 43–45 ... 338	ix, 54 ff. ... 338
ii, 19, 20, 22 ... 121	x, 47 ... 291	x, 1 ... 136
ii, 27 ... 125	xi, 3 ... 136	x, 11 ... 268
iii, 14, 15 ... 57	xi, 12–14 ... 114	x, 12–18 ... 337
iii, 19 ... 303	xi, 20 f. ... 114	x, 13 ... 283
iii, 21 ... 180, 190	xii, 28–34 ... 281	x, 17–20 ... 57
iii, 21 ... 337	xii, 29–30 ... 75	x, 33 ... 97
iii, 22 ... 213	xii, 35–37 ... 338	x, 38–40 ... 106
iii, 22 ... 336, 338 f.	xii, 36 ... 193	x, 38–42 ... 104, 136
iii, 28 ... 194	xiii, 8 ... 318	xi, 15 ... 213
iii, 29 ... 193	xiii, 11 ... 193	xi, 19 ... 192, 213
iii, 31–33 ... 193	xiii, 12 f. ... 130	xi, 20 ... 268
iii, 31–35 ... 122	xiii, 32 ... 180, 197	xi, 23 ... 125
iv, 11 ... 33, 272	xiii, 32 ... 337	xi, 29 ... 202
iv, 11, 12, 34, 36 f., 40, 60	xiv, 2–9 ... 106	xi, 32 ... 283
iv, 21 f. ... 34 ff.	xiv, 5 ... 97	xi, 39 ... 136
iv, 21–23 ... 43	xiv, 10 ... 303	xi, 49 ... 166
iv, 24–34 ... 35 f.	xiv, 22–25 ... 146	xii, 1 ... 204
iv, 26–32 ... 272	xiv, 32 ... 294	xii, 3 ... 255
iv, 28 ... 75	xiv, 33 ... 337	xii, 10 ... 193 f.
iv, 33 f. ... 33 f., 37, 40, 60, 130	xiv, 43 ... 303	xii, 42 ... 136
	xiv, 51 f. ... 111, 183, 199	xii, 58 ... 125
iv, 36 ... 34	xv, 7 ... 294	xiii, 3, 5 ... 284
v, 1–13 ... 59	xv, 34 ... 180, 197	xiii, 6, 7 ... 115
v, 1–20 ... 117	xv, 34 ... 337	xiii, 15 ... 136
v, 39 ... 338	xvi, 5 ... 112	xiii, 32 ... 211
vi, 5 ... 337	xvi, 9, 12, 14 ... 154	xv, 7 ... 286
vi, 5 f. ...140, 180, 201 f., 213	xvi, 15 ... 70	xv, 7, 10 ... 284
		xv, 20 ... 97
vi, 34 ... 38, 96, 123	**Luke:**	xvi, 1–9 ... 144
vi, 34–44 ... 123	i, 77 ... 87	xvi, 19–31 ...28, 72, 102
vii, 28 ... 102	ii, 11, 26 ... 136	xvi, 20 ... 103
viii, 1–9 ... 123	ii, 52 ... 208	xvi, 23–25 ... 103
viii, 2 ... 96	iii, 3 ... 286	xvi, 30 ... 284
viii, 12 ... 180, 202	iii, 8 ... 73, 286	xvii, 1, 2, 3, 4 ... 284
viii, 12 ... 337	iv, 43 ... 275	xvii, 2 ... 118
viii, 14–21 ... 180, 204	v, 4–10 ... 29	xvii, 5, 6 ... 136
viii, 33 ... 338	v, 26 ... 233	xvii, 11–19 ... 103
ix, 22 ... 96	v, 27 ... 294	xvii, 20 f. ... 272
ix, 23 ... 140	v, 32 ... 286	xviii, 1–6 ... 144
ix, 38 ... 211	vi, 16 ... 304, 306 f.	xviii, 6 ... 136
ix, 38–40 ... 214	vi, 43–49 ... 127 f.	xviii, 15–17 ... 117
ix, 40 ... 125	vii, 11 ... 293	xviii, 18 ... 322
ix, 42 ... 118	vii, 13, 19 ... 136	xviii, 19 ... 126, 195
ix, 47 ... 272	vii, 22 ... 180, 202	xviii, 32 ... 312
x, 1 ... 98	vii, 23 ... 203	xix, 4 ... 285
x, 13–16 ... 117	vii, 24–28 ... 114	xix, 8 ... 136
x, 15 f. ... 272	vii, 32 ... 130	xix, 31, 34 ... 136
x, 17 f. ... 180, 194, 322	vii, 34 ... 339	xix, 40 ... 73
x, 17–31 ... 72	vii, 36–50 ... 106	xxi, 10 ... 318
x, 18 ... 126	viii, 10 ... 34	xxii, 1 ... 235, 294
x, 17, 21, 22 ... 98 f.	viii, 13 ... 233	xxii, 3 ... 304

xxii, 17–20	146	*Acts:*		vii, 24	131
xxii, 44	296	i	172	viii, 19–21	70
xxii, 47	294	i, 14	341	ix–xi	101, 325
xxii, 55 *f.*	187	i, 15–25	318	xiv, 17	275
xxii, 61	136	i, 21	136	xv, 3, 4	154, 199
xxiii, 34	xiv, 144	ii	172	xv, 19	214
xxiv, 3	136	ii, 38	283		
xxiv, 19	291	iii, 2	235, 294	*1 Corinthians:*	
xxiv, 34	136	iii, 19	283	i, 12	341
xxiv, 47	286	iii, 21	183	i, 24, 30	166
		iv, 33	136	ii, 6 *f.*	41
John:		v, 14	136	ii, 9	42, 130
i, 6	233	v, 16	211 *f.*	iv, 20	275
i, 45	315	v, 31	287	viii, 5	294
iv, 18	102	vi, 9	294	ix, 5	236 *f.*
iv, 25	235, 294	vii, 51–53	283	ix, 5	341
v, 2	294	viii, 4	85	x, 14–22	151
v, 2–9	296 *f.*	viii, 5–13	11	x, 16 *f.*	150, 152
vi, 5–71	123	viii, 7	211 *f.*	x, 20	192
vi, 71	304	viii, 9–11	159	x, 20 *f.*	211
vii, 20	211	viii, 13	103	xi, 23	150
vii, 53	108	viii, 16	136	xi, 23 *ff.*	133, 146
viii, 12	108	viii, 22	283	xi, 23–26	152
viii, 32 *f.*	73	viii, 27–40	65	xii, 2, 3	217
viii, 39 *ff.*	73	viii, 40	86	xii, 3	192
viii, 48 *f.*	211	ix, 1	136	xii, 8–11	214
viii, 52	211	ix, 3–7	155	xii, 27	152
ix, 11	294	x, 1	305	xii, 28	214
ix, 31	75, 279	x, 38	58, 88, 212, 315	xv	200
x, 20 *f.*	211	xi, 18	286	xv, 1–11	153
xi, 16	235, 294	xi, 26	254	xv, 8	133, 159
xi, 33, 38	97	xiii, 14	86	xv, 24–28	338
xi, 46, 53	102	xiii, 24	287	xv, 28	130
xi, 54	293	xiv, 15	71		
xii, 2	106	xvi, 16	211	*2 Corinthians:*	
xii, 4	304	xvi, 17	196	iii, 6	196
xii, 31	200	xvii, 11	233	iv, 3	300
xiii, 1	233	xvii, 29, 30	283	iv, 10	132
xiii, 2	304	xviii, 2	251	v, 1–4	200
xiii, 26	304	xviii, 11, 18	149	v, 3	113
xiii, 30	316	xviii, 24, 25	125	vii, 9, 10	287
xiv, 12	222	xix, 4	287	viii, 9	199
xiv, 22	304	xix, 12	211 *f.*	xii, 12	214
xiv, 30	200	xix, 12, 13, 15, 16	211	xii, 21	283
xvi, 11	200	xx, 21	281, 286		
xviii, 16, 18, 25	187	xxi, 20	255, 259	*Galatians:*	
xviii, 36	275	xxii, 6–9	155	i, 15–17	134
xix, 13	294, 297	xxvi, 12–15	155	i, 16 *f.*	155
xix, 17	294, 298	xxvi, 20	283, 287	i, 19	121, 237, 342
xix, 38	45	xxvi, 28	254	ii, 20	132
xx, 17	237	xxviii, 17–25	254	iii, 1	132
xx, 24	235, 294			iv, 8 *f.*	71
xxi	29, 172	*Romans:*		iv, 24	145
xxi, 2	235, 294	i, 18–32	278, 288	vi, 17	132
xxi, 1–14	30, 154, 275	ii, 4	287		
xxi, 25	233	vi, 4, 6	132		

INDEX OF PASSAGES

Ephesians:
i, 23 152
ii, 2 200
ii, 11 294
iii, 18 131
iv, 4 152
iv, 12 152
iv, 17 71
v, 23 152
v, 30 152

Philippians:
ii, 5–11 198

Colossians:
i, 19 152
ii, 2 52
ii, 8–15 88
ii, 14 f. 200
ii, 17, 19 152
iv, 11 294

2 Thessalonians:
ii, 4 295

1 Timothy:
iii, 16 ... 22, 55, 65, 133
vi, 12, 13 255
vi, 20 ... ... 42, 255

2 Timothy:
i, 12, 14 ... ... 42 f., 255

ii, 25 287
iv, 6–8 239
iv, 16 f. 239
iv, 19, 21 240

Titus:
ii, 13 52

Hebrews:
ii, 18 167
iv, 14 86
iv, 15 167
v, 7 ... ... 335 f.
vi, 1 287
vi, 6 142
vi, 17 f. 339
vii, 1 196
vii, 3 ... ... 93, 183
vii, 3 342
ix, 3 ... ... 235, 294
xii, 17 287

James:
i, 17 10
i, 21 233
iii, 6 10

1 Peter:
ii, 2 ... ... 118, 186
ii, 25 227
iv, 16 254
v, 13 240

2 Peter:
ii, 1 233
iii, 4, 8 189
iii, 9 287
iii, 10 183

1 John:
ii, 18 233
iv, 2 187

2 John:
7 137

Jude:
25 52

Revelation:
i, 8 17
ii, 5 ... ... 281 f.
iii, 4 ... ... 281 f.
v, 6 91
ix, 20 f. 282
x, 10 124
xiii, 8 91
xiv, 6 f. ... 75, 145, 156
xvi, 9, 11 282
xvi, 13 211
xviii, 2 211
xix, 14 112
xxi, 6 17
xxii, 13 17

INDEX OF NAMES

Abbott, 100
Acidalius, 249
Ælianus, 126
Ælius Adrian, 223, 242
Æschylus, 13, 72, 99
Agrippa, 263 f.
Ambrosius, 168
Anaxagoras, 131
Antiochus, 127, 162
Antoninus, 131, 163, 241
Apollonius, 47
Aristides, 48 f., 50, 72
Aristotle, xiv, 13, 70, 111, 127, 157, 337
Arnold, 81, 247
Asklepios, 72
Athenagoras, 46
Augustine, 29, 30, 118
Augustus, 241

Bacon, B. W., 111, 212, 333
Bacon, Francis, 229
Badham, 271
Barzellotti, 127 f.
Basilides, 12, 86, 88, 206
Bauer, B., 20, 316 f.
Baumann, 190
Bechtel, 29
Bekker, 233
Bentley, 320
Berendts, 342
Binet-Sanglé, xviii, 81, 190
Bishop, 114
Blass, 155, 254
Bolland, 210
Botten, 194
Bousset, xix, 81, 87, 292, 321, 329
Bracciolini, 239
Brandt, 141
Brewer, 305
Bruno, 12
Brutus, M., 163
Budde, 312

Buhl, 279, 284, 321
Burkitt, xiii, 146, 272, 274, 285, 315, 338
Butler, 142
Byron, 314

Calvin, 12, 59
Canney, 298
Carneades, 70, 162
Case, 330 ff., 327, 343
Cato, 163
Celsus, 168
Chamberlain, 81
Cheyne, 285, 293, 304, 306, 317, 318, 321
Chrysippus, 162
Chrysostom, 336
Chwolson, 229-231
Cicero, 163, 337
Clemens Alex., 51 f., 72, 222, 227, 233
Clemens Rom., 240, 264
Cohen, 116
Colton, 128
Conybeare, 32, 70
Cramer, 316
Cumont, 69, 132
Cyrus, 130

Dalman, 304
Dante, 303
Davis, 329
Deissmann, 336
Delitzsch, 68, 92
Democritus, 70
De Quincey, 309
Didache, 150
Diederichs, 327
Dindorf, 307
Dio Cassius, 248, 251 f.
Diogenes Laertius, 196
Dittmar, 313, 318
Domitian, 242
Drews, 119, 229

Eddy, Mrs., 59, 183
Egli, 30
Eisler, 30, 130
Eleazar, 224
Empedocles, 42, 130
Epicharmus, 156
Epicurus, 70
Epictetus, 131
Epiphanius, 45, 159
Eucken, 79
Euripides, 13
Eusebius, 70, 223, 241, 243
Ewald, 20

Ferrero, 257 ff.
Fox, 59
Fundanus, 242
Furneaux, 240

Gautama, 81
Geffcken, 49, 263
Génébrand, 194
Gibbon, 259
Gladstone, 142
Godet, 297
Grotius, 194

Halévy, 321
Harnack, xiii–xvi, xviii–xxi, 9, 11–13, 48, 64, 81, 86, 92, 131, 143, 206, 332
Harris, xxi, 50
Harvey, 221
Haupt, 13, 107, 123, 320
Hegel, 119
Hegesippus, 236
Heinrici, 133 f., 311
Heitmueller, 150, 157, 217
Hengstenberg, 30, 108
Hennecke, 262
Heraclitus, 118
Hermann, 328
Herodotus, 130, 338

INDEX OF NAMES

Hertlein, 271
Hilbert, 333
Hilgenfeld, 86, 236, 327
Hippolytus, 86, 88, 118, 159, 199
Hirsch, 225
Hitzig, 323
Holsten, 20, 133, 148
Holtzmann, 43 *f.*, 57, 111, 190, 194, 304
Homer, 162, 338, 341
Horace, 162
Hort, xiv
Hoyer, 17
Huss, 12
Huxley, 117

IGNATIUS, 206
Irenæus, 26, 159, 206, 221 *ff.*, 233, 262

JENSEN, 8
Jerome, 30 *f.*, 115, 121, 237, 243
Jonson, Ben, 306
Josephus, 83, 223, 226, 229 *f.*, 234–238, 253, 256, 259, 262, 277, 293, 298, 304, 340, 342 *f.*
Jülicher, xx, 37, 39, 40, 61
Justin, 51, 53, 56, 150, 206, 214, 218 *f.*, 256, 262, 265, 336
Justus, 83
Juvenal, 261

KALTHOFF, 8
Kampmeier, 260, 262, 291
Kant, 76
Kautzsch, 280, 312
Keim, 30, 81, 111, 177, 212, 242, 285, 293, 304, 315, 322 *f.*
Kiefl, 330
Klein, 291
Knox, 12, 59
Köstlin, 335
Kreyenbühl, 123

LACTANTIUS, 38, 50, 243
Lang, 248, 313
Lazzaretti, 173
Leaf, 341
Leibniz, 112

Leonardo, 14
Levy, 285
Liddell, 307
Lietzmann, 17, 131
Lightfoot, 242, 254
Lincoln, 14, 329
Linnæus, 6
Lipsius, 263
Loisy, xi, xiii, xvi, xviii, xix, 78, 95, 106, 111, 318, 326
Loman, 316
de Loosten, 190
Lucan, 75
Lucian, 224 *f.*, 252
Lucretius, 70, 162
Luther, 12, 14, 59, 253

MACINTOSH, 328
Mallock, 70
Manetho, 224
Mann, 78
Marcion, 12, 194, 206
Margoliouth, xxii
Margolis, xxiii
Martial, 261
McGiffert, 235
Melanchthon, 12
Melito, 241 *f.*
Meltzer, 337, 339
Mensinga, 340 *f.*
Merx, 102, 126, 274, 306
Metatron, 339
Meyboom, 328
Meyer, 133, 134, 194
Milton, 8
Minucius Felix, 52
Mohammed, 15
Mommsen, 240, 242
Moses, 224
Mueller, 95, 187
Muretus, 249

NAPOLEON, 78
Neander, 235
Nero, 238, 251, 256 *f.*, 262 *ff.*
Nestle, E., 293, 304
Nestle, W., 126
Neumann, 181, 208 *f.*, 240
Nicolardot, 95
Nipperdey, 249
Novalis, 67
Numa, 219

ŒHLER, 220
Olshausen, 111
Oppian, 30
Origen, x, 29, 37, 45, 50, 54, 103, 166, 168, 204, 217, 233, 237, 243, 323, 329
Overbeck, 242
Ovid, 127

PARKER, 59
Paulsen, 119, 184
Paulus (Sergius), 163
Pausanias, 307
Peano, 333
Pepys, 261
Pérès, 78
Pericles, 127
Persius, 244
Pfleiderer, 194, 334 *f.*
Philo, 52, 83, 142
Phocylides, 128
Photius, 83
Pindar, 125, 198, 208
Plato, 13, 46, 48, 65, 70, 75, 142, 161
Pliny, 224, 248, 252 *f.*
Plutarch, 42, 127
Porphyry, 219
Posidonius, 162
Preuschen, 70, 86, 343
Protagoras, 70
Ptolemy, 6
Pythagoras, 126

QUADRATUS, 223

RAMSAY, 59, 242, 247
Rassmussen, 172, 190
Reinach, S., 111, 142, 252, 255
Reitzenstein, 160, 271
Renan, xvi, 20, 81, 172, 177, 318
Reuss, 108
Réville, 177
Robertson, 8, 181
Robinson, 50
Rochefoucauld, 128
Rost, 315
Russell, 6, 334
Ryssel, 312

SCHÆFER, 190
Schechter, xxii, xxiii
Schiller, 242, 259

INDEX OF NAMES

Schläger, 331
Schleiermacher, 67
Schmidt, 194, 222, 263, 272
Schmidtke, 292
Schmiedel, xi–xiii, 9, 20, 25 f., 31, 33, 41, 81, 97, 110, 142, 177, 208, 213, 221, 223, 226, 292, 330, 337, 339, 341
Schürer, 233, 286, 343
Schweitzer, xviii, 124
Schwen, 291 f., 327, 334
Scott, 307
Seneca, 245, 261
Socrates, xiv, 13, 15, 72, 162
von Soden, 9, 81, 160, 229, 247
Sophocles, 13, 72, 127
Spinoza, 158
Steck, 340, 341, 343
Strabo, 323
Strauss, 111, 316
Suetonius, 248, 251, 253, 256 f.
Sulpicius Severus, 260 f., 265

Tacitus, 224, 229, 238, 251, 253, 256 f., 259 ff.
Tatian, 53, 113, 242
Tertullian, 26, 150, 158, 208, 219 f., 223, 233, 262, 265, 242, 297, 336
Thales, 46
Theognis, 128
Theophilus, 53
Thoma, 123
Thucydides, 41
Tiberius, 252, 265
Tischendorf, 268, 304
Trajan, 252
Troeltsch, 328

Usener, 70

Valentinus, 12, 206
Vespasian, 224
Volkmar, ix, x, 30, 32, 81, 177, 304, 309, 316 f.

Washington, 14
Weber, 271, 286
Weinel, 262, 299, 301, 333
Weiss, J., xviii, 95, 299, 301

Weizsäcker, 44
Wellhausen, xiii f., xvi, xix, 20, 34, 36, 37, 39, 60, 104, 111, 166, 193 f., 269, 273 f., 277, 284, 295, 304, 308, 318, 321, 323 ff.
Wendland, 330, 332
Wendling, 95
Wernle, 78, 292
Westcott, xiv
Wetstein, 44, 269
Whately, 78
Winckler, 236, 292, 315, 321
Windisch, 2, 334–339
Wohlenberg, 111
Wrede, xviii, 20, 143, 317

Xenocrates, 159
Xenophon, 307

Zahn, 43, 44, 73, 111, 114, 131, 155, 263, 304, 340, 342
Zimmern, 112
Zoroaster, 224
Zwingli, 121, 253